DEVIANT
BEHAVIOR

DEVIANT BEHAVIOR

John A. Humphrey

Saint Anselm College

PEARSON

Prentice Hall

Upper Saddle River, New Jersey 07458

Library of Congress Cataloging-in-Publication Data

Humphrey, John A.
    Deviant behavior / John A. Humphrey.—1st ed.
        p. cm.
    Includes bibliographical references and index.
    ISBN 0–13–089351–X
    1. Deviant behavior.   I. Title.
    HM811.H86 2006
    302.5'42—dc22

                                2005014010

Editorial Director: Leah Jewell
Executive Editor: Christopher DeJohn
Supplements Editor: LeeAnn Doherty
Editorial Assistant: Kristin Haegele
Senior Marketing Manager: Marissa Feliberty
Marketing Assistant: Anthony DeCosta
Prepress and Manufacturing Buyer: Mary Ann Gloriande
Cover Art Director: Jayne Conte
Cover Design: Bruce Kenselaar
Director, Image Resource Center: Melinda Reo
Manager, Rights and Permissions: Zina Arabia
Manager, Visual Research: Beth Brenzel
Image Permissions Coordinator: Debbie Latronica
Photo Researcher: Diana Gongora
Cover Image: "Road Puzzle" by Larry McEntire/Stock Illustration Source, Inc.
Composition/Full-Service Project Management: Bruce Hobart/Pine Tree Composition, Inc.
Printer/Binder: Hamilton Printing Company
Cover Printer: Lehigh Press
Text Typeface: 10/12 Palatino

Credits and acknowledgments borrowed from other sources and reproduced, with permission, in this textbook appear on appropriate pages within the text.

The Internet makes possible access to scientific papers, research reports, and government documents as they are issued across the world. This continual flow of information challenges us to question what we think we know, to extend the boundaries of our understanding, and to ask questions not posed before. *Deviant Behavior* takes advantage of the opportunities provided by global information sharing but recognizes that specific Web sites for each source of information may change over time. While the Web sites reported in this text were in use at the time of its publication, inevitably some of them will change, or no longer be available. Every effort was made to include the most current information in this edition of *Deviant Behavior*; subsequent editions promise to do the same.

Pearson Education LTD.
Pearson Education Singapore, Pte. Ltd
Pearson Education, Canada, Ltd
Pearson Education–Japan
Pearson Education Australia PTY, Limited

Pearson Education North Asia Ltd
Pearson Educación de Mexico, S.A. de C.V.
Pearson Education Malaysia, Pte. Ltd
Pearson Education, Upper Saddle River, New Jersey

10 9 8 7 6 5 4 3 2 1
ISBN 0-13-089351-X

To my family.

Contents

Preface

Deviant behaviors—bizarre, unexpected, predatory, or self-destructive acts—are inherently interesting. The paradox of deviance—the fascination with behaviors that are essentially abhorrent—is threaded through this text. An individual asking for the return of his personal property seems, on the surface, to be making a reasonable request, not one that would be of any particular interest. However, when federal inmate Ted Kaczynski, the infamous Unabomber, asks for the return of his unused bomb and related paraphernalia, the request becomes national news. Consider, for example, the events in Durham, New Hampshire, a small town of about 13,000 inhabitants and home of the University of New Hampshire. Seven female university students or recent graduates awoke in their apartments to find that their clothes had been cut off in the night. The assailant, dubbed "Jack the Snipper," could only be described in shadowy terms by his victims. Speculation abounds about the offender's motivation, his possible psychiatric disorder, and the danger of escalating harm to his victims.

"Jack the Snipper's" ability to seemingly strike at will captured national attention. ABC's *Good Morning America*, CNN, MSNBC, and Fox News, among others, interviewed the chief of police in Durham. None of the victims was physically or sexually assaulted, nothing was stolen, and no damage to property occurred. Yet, the atypical form of deviance is sufficient cause to mobilize the leading national news services in the United States. The case of "Jack the Snipper" did not remain a local issue in a small New England university town; rather, it drew worldwide attention.

Interest in deviant behavior is self-evident, not only within the United States but across the globe. *Deviant Behavior* is written not only to foster that interest but also to provide students with empirically verifiable information and a range of theoretical perspectives on deviant behaviors. The intent is to explore the social contexts of deviant behavior, its precipitants, and its consequences. This book is written for undergraduate students in courses on deviant behavior and related issues; we do not assume that the student will have taken other courses in the social or behavioral sciences. An introductory chapter considers various approaches to the definition of deviant behavior, the forms that deviant behavior may take, the utility of deviance in society, and the theme of the book.

The theme of the book is prompted by the September 11, 2001, terrorist attacks in the United States. The events of that day redefined the study of deviant behavior in the twenty-first century. Deviant behaviors would no longer be adequately understood by limiting their study to specific geopolitical areas. The processes of globalization and their consequences give rise to emerging forms of deviance around the world. The theme of the book is that the reciprocal relationship between the processes of globalization and the sociocultural milieu is essential to our understanding of deviance in the twenty-first century.

Two chapters on the theoretical understandings of deviant behavior follow the introductory chapter. Deviant behaviors are considered on two levels of analysis: the individual or micro-level and the societal/subcultural/group or macro-level. The micro-level of analysis considers why certain individuals engage in deviant behaviors, whereas the macro-level seeks to explain why rates of deviant behaviors vary across sociocultural groupings.

Each substantive chapter includes an "At a Glance" section that provides an overview of the form of deviance being considered. Portraits of deviants or their victims introduce each substantive chapter. The student is provided with the most current empirical information on a wide range of deviant behaviors, from criminal acts to extreme forms of otherwise typical behaviors. The major sociological and social-psychological perspectives on deviant behavior are integrated into each chapter. Theoretical formulations of individual engagement in deviant behavior are distinguished from those that account for variations in rates of its occurrence. A chart appears at the end of each substantive chapter that defines the key variables of each theory and provides hypotheses that may account for the specific form of deviant behavior being considered.

Substantive chapters include criminal homicide, domestic violence, sexual offending, property crime, white-collar and organized crime, cyberdeviance, alcohol abuse, illicit drug use, mental illness, and suicide. In addition, there are chapters on terrorism, extreme forms of everyday behaviors (workaholism, web surfing, and extreme sports), and positive deviance, which focuses on the processes involved in innovation and creativity.

This book is firmly grounded in traditional sociological and social-psychological understandings of deviant behavior. It nonetheless presents a challenge to students interested in exploring the emerging shape of deviance in the twenty-first century. The study of deviant behavior is undergoing a radical transformation. *Deviant Behavior* encourages students to become engaged in that process.

Acknowledgments

This book is the result of the unique contributions of highly valued colleagues/ friends, the trust and support of my family, and the thoughtful comments of several reviewers. My initial interest in deviant behavior was sparked by courses taught by William J. Farrell during my undergraduate days at St. Anselm College. His ability to inspire intellectual curiosity, the wonder of discovery, and the desire to contribute to the well-being of society, including its most deviant members, markedly influenced my academic career. From my first days in graduate school to the present, Stuart Palmer has been my mentor, colleague, and valued friend. His keen insight into the precipitants of deviant behavior and its consequences continues to prompt questions that merit exploration. Scientific inquiry, of course, is premised on framing meaningful questions.

Much of the theoretical material in this book is based on an earlier text, *Deviant Behavior: Patterns, Sources, and Control,* in which Stuart Palmer graciously included me as a co-author. Unquestionably, Stuart Palmer's innovative thought and lucid understanding of the human experience is threaded through this book.

The project began with a casual conversation with Frank Schmalleger at the American Society of Criminology meetings a few years ago. His willingness to assist in the development of a text on deviant behavior, his ability to frame questions that ultimately shaped this work, and his mastery of the process involved in writing a textbook set this project in motion. From its very inception, and at each stage in the development and writing of the book, the guidance of Frank Schmalleger was critically important.

This book would not have been possible without the invaluable collaboration of Meredith Huey, a former graduate research assistant and now sociology doctoral student at the University of Georgia. From the design of the book to its publication, Meredith's wide-reaching grasp of theoretical underpinnings and substance of deviant behavior and her insight into and proximity with the undergraduate experience were invaluable. She substantially contributed to each chapter of the book and was primarily responsible for drafting chapters on mental illness, sexual offending, and property crime. Her uncanny ability to identify sources of information, extract key research findings, and present them in an interesting and readily understandable way to undergraduate students contributed immeasurably to the completion of this book. Similarly, Julia Capone contributed significantly to the graphic presentations and other creative aspects of this book. Often, Julia took our rather vague thoughts about how to construct a chart or figure and converted them into imaginative and meaningful visual representations. Her enthusiastic support for this project, insightful suggestions for revision, and enduring tolerance and friendship are most appreciated.

In the end, this book depended on the editorial expertise and professional judgment of Christopher DeJohn, Executive Editor of Sociology at Prentice Hall, who guided us through the complex process of writing an undergraduate textbook. His patient willingness to discuss any aspect of the book, his remarkable problem-solving ability, and his sense of creative balance, while rare, are indeed unmistakable and profoundly important. The following reviewers provided invaluable insight: Robert F. Meier, University of Nebraska at Omaha; Gary Faulkner, University of North Carolina, Wilmington; Travis Langley, Henderson State University; B. Keith Crew, University of Northern Iowa; William J. Farrell, St. Anselm College; John Broderick, Stonehill College; Craig Hemmens, Boise State University; Phillip W. Davis, Georgia State University; Steven R. Burkett, Washington State University; and Giri Raj Gupta, St. John's University. Finally, most vital to the completion of this book was the trusting support of my family who no doubt wondered why, in the dark of night, I would still be writing about deviant behavior.

John Humphrey
Lee, New Hampshire

DEVIANT
BEHAVIOR

CHAPTER 1

Introduction to the Study of Deviant Behavior

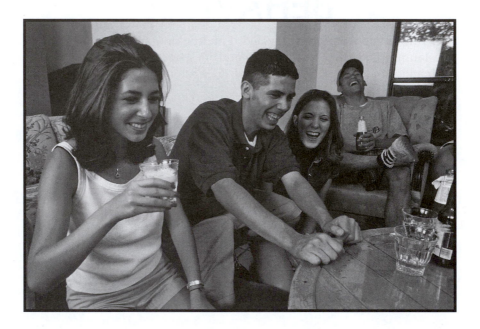

After reading this chapter you show know:

- ☐ How deviant behavior is defined.
- ☐ Processes by which social/legal norms are created and violated and the consequences of social/legal norm violation.
- ☐ Dimensions of deviant behavior.
- ☐ Functions of deviant behavior for society.

Deviant behaviors may be considered along a continuum from the mildly annoying to the widely condemned. Loud talking and uncontrolled laughter in a restaurant is certainly annoying, but does not reach the level of public condemnation that the bombing of an airliner killing all passengers aboard would. Yet the boisterous restaurant patron and the terrorist responsible for the deaths of innocent strangers typically do not think of their behaviors or themselves as deviant.

The Definition of Deviant Behavior

The definition of deviance is problematic, involving a complex interplay between the actor, the offended party, and the wider societal audience. Sociologists approach the problem of defining deviance in several ways. Each approach contributes to our overall understanding of the intricacies inherent in acts of deviance. Two sociological concepts—culture and social organization—are particularly useful in determining whether certain behaviors are deviant. **Culture** refers to "a body of widely shared customs and values which provide general orientations toward life and specific ways of achieving common goals" (Palmer and Humphrey 1990: 2). Culture is fundamental to the social order, relatively stable over time, yet it may provide a dynamic approach to the continually evolving challenges of everyday life. Changes in customs and values may originate among certain segments of the society—for example, adolescents and young adults who are involved in continual changes in style of dress, patterns of speech, and forms of entertainment. Another example would be special interest groups that seek to foster the acceptance of particular rights or protections, usually of vulnerable populations or the environment. These cultural changes may become institutionalized and persist through time, or they may be short-lived and disappear from the social landscape. The value of body piercing and tattooing may well dissipate over time, as do styles of dress and verbal expression. Culture provides meaning and stability to everyday life while allowing for innovation, creativity, and the reassessment of traditional customs and values. Culture, then, provides a backdrop for the establishment of acceptable behaviors. Behaviors that fall outside defined cultural parameters are considered, in varying degrees, deviant (see also Linton 1955).

Social organization provides the means for carrying out the complex network of social interactions between individuals, social groups, and institutions. A central purpose of social organization is to ensure that conflict and discord in social interactions do not impede the effective functioning of society. Everyday life is remarkable devoid of mass disruption. For the most part, the daily interactions of more than 6.3 billion persons worldwide are carried out in a reasonably predictable and orderly way (U.S. Bureau of the Census 2004). Millions of cars travel at high speeds in close proximity to one another, planes take off and land within minutes of each other, transnational business and commerce is conducted around the clock, and individuals communicate across time and cultures worldwide largely without incident.

Social interaction is organized by a complex set of social norms and roles. **Social norms** are those generally agreed upon guides for behavior that provide boundaries for interpersonal relations. **Social roles** are defined by a set of social norms for the behavior of individuals who occupy given statuses within society. For example, a college professor occupies a given status within the academy and in the larger society. Norms for the appropriate behavior of college professors serve as guides to carry out the role of a faculty member.

Social norms may be classified as *expectational* or *behavioral*. **Expectational norms** refer to behaviors that are ideal for individuals who are enacting a particular social role or who are in a given social situation. Expectational norms govern the behavior of persons in positions of high responsibility—e.g., surgeons, airline pilots, heads of state, and persons in extreme life-threatening situations. Acceptable error in the operating room, at the controls of an airliner, or in the Oval Office is extremely limited. Surgeons, for example, are expected to operate on the afflicted part of the patient's body—to always amputate the correct limb and to remove all surgical instruments from the patient's body following an operation. Yet, as we know, medical malpractice, pilot error, and political misjudgment does occur, often with dire consequences.

Behavioral norms refer to what persons typically do when occupying a particular social role or in a given social situation. Students are expected to attend class, yet most students miss class on occasion. A minority of students adhere to the expectational norm for class attendance, while most students follow more flexible "behavioral" norms. Behavioral norms are significantly influenced by social demographic and situational characteristics. Younger persons are given more flexibility in the ways they dress, speak, and interact in public than are older persons in positions of more responsibility. Behavioral norms establish a range of acceptable behaviors and, therefore, are far less rigid or exacting than are expectational norms.

Strict adherence to expectational norms—always telling the truth and answering questions in a completely honest way—is required when testifying in court or filing an income tax return. However, honest candor is deviant when your mother asks, "How do you like my new hairdo?" In short, expectational and

Expectational Norms

Surgeons are understandably held to an extremely high standard of care. Yet, gross surgical malpractice cases are on the rise across the United States. Undamaged limbs are amputated, healthy organs removed, and holes are drilled into the wrong side of a patient's head. Beginning on July 1, 2004, the Joint Commission on Accreditation of Healthcare Organizations may revoke the accreditation of hospitals and other surgical sites if they do not comply with new safety regulations. The entire surgical team—surgeons, anesthesiologists, nurses, and technicians—must now take a "time-out" before making an incision in a patient. They must all agree that they have the correct patient on the operating table and that they are actually going to perform the correct surgical procedure. It is mandatory that surgeons "literally sign the incision site, while the patient is awake and cooperating if possible, with a marker that won't wash off in the operating room."

Adapted from: http://www.comcast.net/news/print.jsp?fn=/apnes/XML/1500_Health_medical/e2a5d7. . .

behavioral norms appropriate guide social interactions differently for persons who occupy particular social roles and who are in well-defined social situations (Palmer and Humphrey 1990: 2-5).

Societal Reaction

Norms governing many behaviors may not be clearly defined, universally accepted, or consistently followed. The societal reaction approach to defining deviant behaviors is particularly useful when there is a lack of consensus about appropriate behavior. While some behaviors are considered inherently deviant—murder, rape, or burglary—the definition of other behaviors depends, in large part, on the social characteristics of the actor, the victim, the social context of the behavior, and the social audience that observes or becomes aware of what occurred. Racial or ethnic slurs, for example, may be viewed as simply the remarks of an ignorant person or cause for removal from public office. Graffiti has alternately been considered an eyesore, malicious damage to public property, or an art form worthy of civic recognition.

The societal reaction approach to the definition of deviant behavior contends that behaviors are essentially neutral and take on meaning only when defined by some social entity (Becker 1963). The societal reaction approach to the understanding of deviance involves a three-step process of defining behaviors, labeling the actors, and responding to the label attached to the actor. Social behavior may be defined as good or bad, moral or immoral, admired or condemned. Individuals who engage in such behaviors are then labeled as deviant or not depending on their social characteristics and the circumstances of the behavior. The intentional ending the life of another human being may be criminal homicide, an act of self-defense, or legally justifiable as in the case of the execution of a condemned prisoner or the shooting of a dangerous person by a police officer in the line of duty. The societal response to the behavior dictates the extent of its deviance. If both the behavior and the actor are labeled as deviant, then the societal reaction or degree of public condemnation of the behavior and the offender indicates the severity of the deviant act. Formal or informal controls may be used to resolve the situation. An enraged wife who runs over her adulterous husband with her Mercedes-Benz may be found as justified in her actions or sentenced to 20 years imprisonment for willful homicide. Underage drinking, recreational use of marijuana, or public decency offenses may be formally prosecuted or handled informally without the imposition of an official sanction.

In short, the process of defining behaviors as deviant or not, and the public response to the act and the actor established a boundary between acceptable and unacceptable behavior in a given society. Norms and values have been established; social organization and culture have been defined.

Issues in the Study of Deviant Behavior

Deviant behavior must be understood on several conceptual levels. Beyond the morality or ethics involved in the deviant act or the repugnance of the offenders lie several related conceptual issues: (1) how social and legal norms are created, by whom, and under which conditions; (2) who violates social norms and the etiology of their violation; (3) the possible societal reactions to norm violation; (4) the consequences of norm violation for the offender and for the larger society; (5) which methods of social control are used for which forms of social and legal norm violations and for which kinds of offenders; and (6) the impact of the use of formal or informal controls on subsequent social and legal norm violation. Figure 1.1 depicts the complex processes involved in the study of deviant behavior. Two fundamental issues are How do certain behaviors become defined as deviant? and What accounts for the development of social and legal norms? (see Weitzer 2002: 2–4).

Social and legal norms provide the framework for interpersonal relations within social groups. They are essential for their survival over time, ordering interaction and ensuring that important tasks are accomplished. William Graham Sumner (1906) classifies social norms by the severity of sanction for their violation. He identifies three forms of social norms: *folkways, mores,* and *laws.* Folkways refer to everyday practices commonly observed within a given culture, (e.g., observing holidays by sending cards and gifts at certain times of the year, courteous behavior in public, or responding in customary ways to the greetings of others). Certainly sending Christmas cards in July, pushing others aside to get to the head of the line at the movie theatre, or telling another person about all your problems when asked, "How are you?" would be a violation of widely accepted folkways. The violation of a folkway may result in the avoidance of the offender or simply considering him or her as strange. Mores refer to norms that govern more impor-

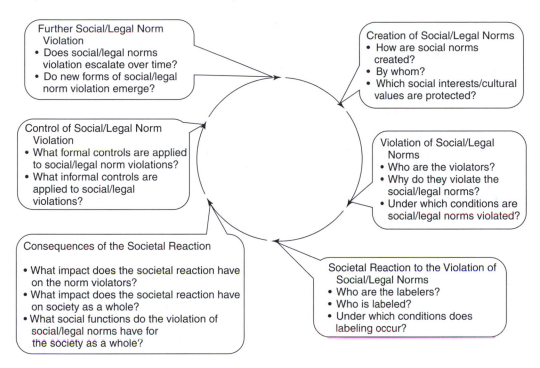

Figure 1.1 Issues in the Study of Deviant Behavior

tant sociocultural behaviors. Matters of morality and ethics, appropriate dress, and use of inoffensive language are guided by the mores of a society. When mores are violated, the offender is subject to more stringent social reprisals than are exacted against the violators of folkways. Ostracism, dismissal from a job, or irreparable damage to one's reputation may follow the violation of mores. Finally, laws are considered the most serious form of social norms. Laws provide a codification of the specific elements of crimes and civil torts and possible sanctions for their violation. Unlike the violation of folkways and mores that invoke informal sanctions, violation of laws may result in a formal, governmental response.

Typically, the central interests of a group are defined by the recognized leaders of the group or the members who have garnered the most power, influence, or resources. Social constructionists are primarily interested in the processes involved in the formulation of social and legal norms, the imposition of a deviant label on certain violators.

The violation of important social and legal norms is inevitable. A wide array of etiological factors that underlie involvement in deviant behavior have been advanced by theorists who take a positivistic approach to the study of deviant behavior. Positivistic theorists and researchers take an objective view of

A clash of cultures—a young Amish girl buying a soft drink from a vending machine.

deviance. That is, certain behaviors are deviant in themselves, and certain social, psychological, or biological factors explain why certain individuals engage in those behaviors. Possible precipitants of rates and individual involvement in deviant behaviors are considered throughout this book. The functional utility of deviant behavior for the survival of a society is also discussed later in this chapter.

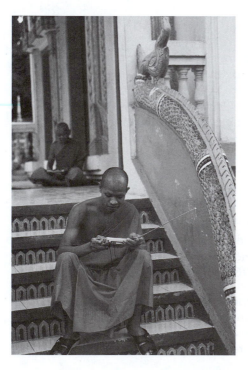

A Buddhist Monk outside his monastery in Phenom Penh, Cambodia is trying to find a radio station he likes.

The social reaction to the violation and the offenders varies by the severity of offense, the social characteristics of the victim and offender, and their social relationship (Black 1976). Societal reaction or labeling theorists and researchers focus on the consequences of labeling certain norm violators as deviant and the societal reaction to them (see Schur 1971 and Becker 1963).

Social control theorists and researchers are interested in the ways in which social groups and society as a whole impede the commission of deviant and criminal acts (see Hirschi 1969). Formal and informal control mechanisms are used to control criminal and other deviant behaviors. Formal controls refer to official sanctioning of certain norm violators, typically by agents of the criminal justice system. Offenders may be arrested, adjudicated by the courts, fined, placed under supervision in the community, or incarcerated. The involuntary hospitalization of persons considered to be psychiatrically ill is another means of formal control. Informal social controls typically involve unofficial means of sanctioning deviants within a group. Gossip, ridicule, exclusion from group activities, and ostracism are common forms of informal control. As we see in Figure 1.1, the attempts to control deviant members of a social group may well exacerbate their offensive behavior. Rather than changing their behavior, the deviants may, for example, escalate their offending, engaging in more severe forms of violence or theft or becoming engaged in newer forms of deviance. This results in the necessity for creating more stringent norms or increasing the penalties for existing social and legal norms. The processes of deviant behavior are thereby set in motion. Redefined norms lead to the inevitability of their violation, and renewed societal sanctioning of offenders.

As tolerance of deviant behaviors decreases, societies may evolve into an ever-tightening spiral of more stringent social and legal norms, the propensity to define increasingly more of its members as deviant, and the development of more punitive control strategies. If this downward spiraling process is not reversed, then a repressive system of social control emerges that may well lead to the demise of the society.

Dimensions of Deviance

Deviant behaviors may take on various social dimensions that serve to distinguish them from one another. Most forms of deviance involve behaviors that are carried out in patterned and predictable ways. For example, criminal homicide, armed robbery, and date rape involve offenders and victims and social contexts that transcend individual incidents. That is, typical patterns of interaction between offenders and victims and common social circumstances characterize many forms of deviant behavior. Other forms of deviant behavior are more idiosyncratic or unique to given individuals and, therefore, do not form repetitive patterns of interaction or are not characterized by common social contexts.

Other dimensions of deviant behaviors include whether they are positive or negative, innovative or routine, individual or group behaviors, and episodic or chronic. Many of these dimensions of deviance overlap one another, resulting in the complex, multidimensional nature of deviant behavior. However, to understand how each dimension characterizes the expression of deviance, we will consider them along separate continua (Palmer and Humphrey 1990: 5-10).

Patterned versus Idiosyncratic

Deviant behaviors, for the most part, form patterns of social interactions. That is, deviant behaviors are carried out in similar ways by individuals who have never met one another, across widely scattered geographically areas. Date rape, for example, involves offenders, victims, and social circumstances in Mississippi that closely resemble those in New York City. The precipitants of many forms of deviant behaviors transcend sociocultural space and individual actors. The sociocultural and subcultural influences on male–female interactions, the distortion of behavioral and verbal cues, and social circumstances marked by social isolation, excessive drinking, and other drug use combine to increase the likelihood aggressive behaviors. The need of young men to dominate and control their female acquaintances or dates leads to forced sexual behaviors.

Over time patterns of deviant behavior become institutionalized and are imbedded in the sociocultural fabric. Sociocultural influences shape the motivations for deviant behaviors, the ways they are carried out, and the social contexts in which they occur.

Far less common are the idiosyncratic forms of deviant behavior. Idiosyncratic deviance is unique to particular individuals, typically less socially visible, and may simply be regarded as "odd." Paying a contested property tax bill in pennies delivered to the tax office in 55-gallon drums or using a dead husband's handicapped parking permit are examples of idiosyncratic deviance. While undeniably deviant, these behaviors are not likely to be repeated or to form institutionalized patterns of behavior.

An Asian street merchant combines the time-honored means of transporting goods with the business advantages provided by a laptop computer.

Clara Harris, a Houston dentist, was sentenced to 20 years in prison and fined $10,000 for running over her adulterous husband with her Mercedes Benz.

Positive versus Negative

Deviant behaviors are commonly thought to involve acts that are legally, morally, or ethically prohibited, or at the very least to be annoying to others. Deviant behavior is thought to have negative consequences for particular individuals, and by extension to society at large. A person is the victim of a violent act, of property theft or destruction, of slander or false rumor, of loud noises and graffiti.

However, deviant behavior need not be thought of in exclusively negative terms. Acts that deviate from normative modes of thinking and acting are necessary for creative problem solving and to bring about social and political change. Scientific advances and creativity in the arts and literature are the consequence of persons deviating in positive ways from conventional practices. Positive deviants are willing to think differently about important problems, offer alternative solutions to them, and inspire others to think differently about the world around them. Mother Theresa provides an apt example of a positive deviant whose extraordinary works affected the lives of millions of persons unknown to her scattered around the world.

Civil rights activists in the South during the 1960s provided the opportunity to vote for a significant number of African Americans across the country, prompted the desegregation of schools and universities, and drew attention to the widespread denial of the Constitutional rights of criminal defendants adjudicated in state courts.

Innovative versus Routine

The innovative process is inherently deviant—a departure from an existing mode of thought, or view of the physical or social world. *Innovation* refers to the combining of two or more theoretical concepts or material objects in a new way. By reordering ideas or physical phenomena, discoveries are made and problems are solved. Innovation may come about by years of careful experimentation or in a flash of insight. Artistic and scientific breakthroughs occur in both ways. More typically, creative insights follow the arduous task of painstaking research and thought, but not always.

Innovative forms of deviance may be either positive or negative in their consequences. Scientific discoveries and breakthroughs in the ways we understand the physical world, uniquely perceptive literary and artistic contributions, and philosophical insights are examples of positive forms of innovative deviance. Innovative forms of deviance may also have negative consequences. Cybercrime and terrorism may involve innovative ways of accessing secured computer networks or disrupting the flow of information around the globe.

Routine forms of deviance are far more common than innovative deviance. Routine deviant behaviors typically do not require high levels of cognitive ability or involve concerted effort. Acts of violence, drug and alcohol addition, and most property offenses can be carried out with little effort or extensive planning.

Individual versus Group Deviance

Deviant behaviors may be committed by persons alone, in small groups, or in large crowds. Most forms of deviant behaviors are engaged in by lone offenders or in the company of a few, trusted companions. Acts of violence—murder, rape, armed robbery and so on—are typically committed by a lone offender. Cybercrime and terrorism, sex offenses, mental illness, suicide, and substance abuse are other examples of individual forms of deviance.

Group deviance may involve the unplanned, spontaneous acts of persons largely unknown to one another who are drawn together for a common purpose. The unruly and often violent outbursts of disappointed soccer fans provide an example of this form of group deviance. Similar kinds of group outrage and acts of destruction may be sparked by minority residents of an inner city following a police shooting of one of their members.

A second form of group deviance depends on an organizational structure and the complicity of a network of persons. Organized criminal activity, corporate malfeasance, and terrorism, both international and domestic, require intricate networks of participants and complex means of communication to be successful. Invisibility and secrecy are hallmarks of organized group deviance. To be able to operate in public view, without public attention, is essential to the persistence of group deviant activities.

Less organized and sophisticated are gang-related forms of group deviance—usually acts of violence directed toward rival gangs. Predatory and retaliatory activities of street gangs are highly visible and typically require little long-range planning. Gang violence is often a spontaneous response to a perceived threat from archrivals.

Episodic versus Chronic Deviance

Deviant behavior may be confined to certain situations and thereby take on an episodic expression. Or, it may be persistent and transcend the immediate social circumstance. Extreme situations may give rise to forms of behavior that individuals would not engage in otherwise. Cannibalism is abhorrent to most people; however, when facing certain starvation, an individual may well eat parts of a deceased occupant of their lifeboat lost at sea. Similarly, binge-drinking partygoers may engage in behaviors that are inconsistent with their sense of morality or ethical principles.

Persistent deviance, however, transcends any situational boundaries. The behavior of a person afflicted with alcoholism or addicted to another drug or gambling is not situation-bound. Rather, the chronic deviant persistently engages in aberrant behavior across a wide range of social situations.

Functions of Deviant Behavior

It is commonly thought that crime and deviant behavior are harmful elements in any society and must be prevented or, at the very least, strictly controlled. Yet, as we shall see later in the text, deviance is viewed as vital to the functioning of any social group.

Emile Durkhiem (1938), one of the founders of modern sociology, argued that crime and deviance are not pathological elements of society, but are vitally important to its survival. In short, deviant behaviors serve an essential function for societal well-being. Durkheim (1938: 67) notes that "crime is normal because a society exempt from it is utterly impossible." To Durkheim, the existence of a particular social entity—an entire society or a constituent community—depends on the formation of strong collective sentiments about the kinds of behaviors that are appropriate for its members. These collective sentiments define behaviors that are good or bad, moral or immoral, legal or illegal. In a sense the collective sentiments about behavior establish distinct boundaries that separate the social collectivity from others and acceptable and unacceptable behaviors among its members. Everyday life is ordered; the work of the community gets done.

The Amish community, for example, has well-defined boundaries between itself and the larger society. The rejection of the conveniences and technological advances of conventional society sets the Amish community apart from its neighbors. Within the Amish community consensually held norms, values, and beliefs clearly demarcate acceptable from unacceptable behavior. Daily interaction among the members of the Amish community is carried out in an orderly and predictable way. Durkheim (1938: 70) argues that, "Crime is, then, necessary; it is bound up in the fundamental conditions of all social life, and by that very fact it is useful, because these conditions of which it is a part are themselves indispensable to the normal evolution of morality and the law."

Following the lead of Emile Durkheim, sociologist Kai Erickson (2005) explains how certain behaviors are defined as deviant, the function that deviant behaviors serve in a given community, and the consequences of attempts to control

Rumspringa: An Amish Custom

The Amish live by a strict set of customs and moral principles. Yet, before an Amish youth commits to the Amish way of life, he or she will participate in the Amish ritual of *rumspringa* or period of "running around." *Rumspringa* begins when Amish youths turn 16 and continues until they are married, usually between 19 and 22 years of age. During *rumspringa* the young Amish young men and women have not been baptized into the Amish faith and, therefore, are not technically ruled by their parents or the church. *Rumspringa,* then is a time for experimenting with things outside the world of the Amish. Close friendships are formed that continue for a lifetime. A central feature of *rumspringa* is participation in a youth group known as a "gang."

Donald B. Kraybill writes: "About twenty-seven youth groups, called 'gangs,' ranging in size from 50 to 150 members, crisscross the Lancaster settlement. By the age of 10, an Amish child will be able to name some of the groups—Bluebirds, Canaries, Pine Cones, Drifters, Shotguns, Rocky, and Quakers—and even describe some of their activities. Youth are free to join the gang of their choice. Young people from the same church district or family may join different groups. The gangs become the primary social world for teens before they marry, but the groups vary considerably in their conformity to traditional Amish values.

"Some groups are fairly docile, but others engage in boisterous behavior that occasionally makes newspaper headlines. The reputation of the various groups signals how plain or rebellious a young person likely will be. . . . The more rowdy boys 'dress around,' that is, shed their sectarian garb. Hatless. Wearing styled hair and store-bought jackets, they may 'pass' as typical youth in a bar or movie theatre. Young men in some groups will have fancy reflective tape on their buggies and perhaps a hidden radio or CD player inside.

"Members of the more rambunctious groups drive cars and sponsor dances, called 'band-hops,' featuring Amish bands with electric guitars and kegs of beer. Wilder parties often involve the use and abuse of alcohol. And, 'youth are occasionally arrested for driving cars and buggies under the influence of alcohol.'"

Adapted from: Kraybill, D. B. 2001. *The Riddle of the Amish.* Baltimore: The Johns Hopkins Press, pp. 145–146.

deviant behavior. Erickson (2005: 6) argues that: "Deviance is not a property *inherent* in any particular kind of behavior; it is a property *conferred* upon that behavior by the people who come into direct or indirect contact with it." As such, "deviance refers to conduct which the people of a group consider so dangerous or embarrassing or irritating that they bring special sanctions to bear against the persons who exhibit it" (Erickson 2005: 6). Deviant behaviors mark the boundaries of a community. Each community occupies a particular "cultural space" and has a distinct "cultural identity." Boundaries emerge then from the "networks of social interactions" that link the daily lives of the members of a community (Erickson 2005: 9–10). The boundaries of a community tend to shift over time, behaviors that were previously considered deviant become commonplace. Yet, the effective functioning of a community depends on the establishment of boundaries that separate conformist from deviant behavior. Deviant behaviors in a sense define the community's identity. Erickson (2005: 19) writes: "Every human community has its own set of boundaries, its own unique identity, and so we may presume that every community also has its own characteristic styles of deviant behavior."

If deviant behavior is vital to the functioning of communities, is it then not likely, Erickson (2005: 13) asks, that "they are organized in such a way as to promote this resource"? The agents of social control—police, courts, correctional and psychiatric institutions—may actually perpetuate the very behaviors that they are intended to control. The process of labeling an individual as deviant, long-term segregation from the community, and marginally humane treatment at the hands of their custodians may significantly reduce the chances of a successful conventional life.

Other Functions of Deviant Behavior

Identity.　There are several other latent or unintended functions of deviant behavior. First, involvement in various forms of deviance provides a sense of identity, albeit a negative identity, to persons who are unable to gain status or recognition in legitimate ways. Often teenagers who are not successful in school, who are excluded from athletic competition, or who cannot excel in other areas will be attracted to delinquent gangs. The gang provides a sense of belonging, recognition, and identity. Thus, if conventional means for gaining an identity are not available, then deviant means may be sought.

Warning of the Need for Social Change.　Mass deviance—urban riots, commandeering public buildings, and other acts of civil disobedience—signal the need for social change. Public outrage sparked by unfair social policies, discrimination, or persistent inequality in access to social resources—health, education, and employment—may prompt governmental intervention.

Rapid increases in the use of illicit drugs, the emergence of newer "designer" drugs, or waves of teenage suicidal behavior may well signal the need for societal attention to discontent among the young. Deviant behavior may also provide a means for bringing about social change. Innovative forms of deviance—for example, the use of computer chat rooms as group support for troubled persons—can provide an alternative to more visible and costly psychological care.

Scapegoating and Tension Release.　The deviants in society provide an ongoing group of persons—some criminal, some eccentric, others simply annoying—who can be blamed for many of the ills experienced by persons who have escaped the deviant label. The deviants can be segregated from the mass of society, treated in aggressive and demeaning ways, and stigmatized, often for life, for their deviant behaviors. Once the label of felon, psychotic, or sex offender has been applied, it most often becomes the "master status" of that person (Becker, 1963: 33–34).

Individuals who are not publicly known as deviant can direct their feelings of frustration, anger, resentment, or simply low self-worth at the deviant. Deviant members of society, then, provide a target for others to vent their pent-up rage and general sense of discontent.

Employment.   Societies around the world invest a significant amount of their financial resources and social capital in attempting to control and treat their deviant members. The criminal justice system alone employs hundreds of thousands of persons in federal, state, and local law enforcement agencies, courts, and correctional institutions and community-based programs. In addition, psychiatric institutions, therapeutic communities, and public and private agencies employ a vast number of medical personnel, psychologists, social workers, counselors, and occupational and recreational therapists attempt to change the lives of deviant members of society. An unimaginable economic burden would be created if suddenly criminal and deviant behaviors were eliminated from society. In short, crime and deviance fuel the economy by providing a livelihood to a vast array of social control agents.

Theme of the Book

> *For globalization is not incidental to our lives today. It is a shift in our very life circumstances. It is the way we now live.*
>
> —Anthony Giddens (2000: 31)

This book considers the **processes of globalization**—which include immediate worldwide communication, transnational commerce and trade, and borderless opportunities for political and cultural exchange—as they impact the nature and extent of social deviance in U.S. society and throughout the world. The central theme consists of the reciprocal relationship between the processes of globalization and the sociocultural milieu is fundamental to our understanding of deviance in the twenty-first century.

> *Globalization lies at the heart of modern culture; cultural practices lie at the heart of globalization . . . this is (a) reciprocal relationship . . .*
>
> —John Tomlinson (1999:1)

This theme derives from the work of two-noted British social theorists—Anthony Giddens (2000) and John Tomlinson (1999)—who argue that a reciprocal relationship exits between globalization and culture. Giddens (2000: 28) observes that globalization is "political, technological and cultural, as well as economic." It has an uneven impact on local cultures around the world, strengthening the resolve of some, altering the fabric of others.

Tomlinson (1999: 2) views globalization as a "complex connectivity—the rapidly developing and ever-densening network of interconnections and interconnectivity that characterize social life." Tomlinson's

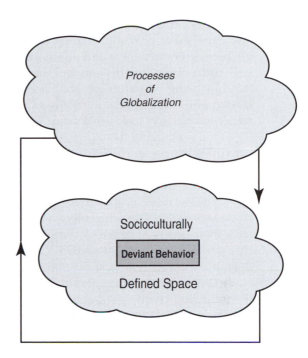

Figure 1.2   Theme of Book

conceptualization of globalization is consistent with that of McGrew (1992) and others (see Lash and Urry 1994; Castells 1996; 1997), who stress the reciprocity of global cultural and economic influences. Globalization then involves the reciprocal influences of economic influences and culture. Not only does the global flow of goods and monetary resources reshape culture, but culture, in turn modifies the impact of international trade.

Figure 1.2 shows the reciprocal relationships among the processes of globalization and socioculturally defined space—the immediate social context of everyday life. The processes of globalization, characterized by an intricate web of interrelationships and interdependences, impact the makeup of socioculturally defined space by altering cultural values and meanings attached to everyday behaviors. For example, the value and meaning of time, interpersonal relationships, and material possessions are largely affected by global transmission of Western culture and economic structures. A sense of time urgency, more egalitarian relations between men and women, and the need for material goods to provide pleasure, entertainment, and a sense of self-worth are by-products of globalization. As the needs and wants of persons in less developed areas of the world begin to parallel those common among persons in the West, a sense of relative deprivation may well follow. Dissatisfaction with one's life circumstances and feelings of frustration about the opportunities to change them may drive some individuals to engage in self- or other-destructive forms of deviant behavior.

Affected is the relative importance of cultural traditions with the symbols and rituals that provide meaning for life beyond mundane existence. The struggle between materialism and immediate gratification on the one hand, and adherence to traditions of altruism and the centrality of common purpose on the other hand, is being waged in remote places across the globe. The processes of globalization also influence the normative structure of everyday life. Gender inequality, structural barriers to education and economic opportunities, and the relative ability of the young and the old to influence their life circumstances are emerging issues even in less developed countries.

In brief, the processes of globalization alter the socioculturally defined space in which we live. Cultural and social change, in turn, influence individual behavior. Opportunities to engage in impersonal forms of deviant behaviors may become more attractive. The emergence of cyberdeviance and transglobal terrorism with their potential to wreak widespread havoc has created the need for innovative strategies for global security, a transnational justice system, and unprecedented cooperation among the nations of the world.

The major sociological and social psychological formulations considered in the following chapters show how culture, social structural arrangements, and interpersonal relationships explain and predict deviant behavior. There is, then, an increasing need for theoretical formulations to take into account the reciprocal relationships among the processes of globalization, socioculturally defined space, and deviant behavior.

Book Overview

Deviant Behavior explores deviance in the United States and around the world. A wide range of deviant and criminal activities is addressed throughout the book. Each chapter provides an overview of the prevalence and incidence of specific forms of deviant behavior. The substantive chapters follow a similar format: At the outset the issue of definition is addressed; next the prevalence, trends, and patterns of the behavior are presented; related special topics and particularly deviant subgroups are also discussed. Each chapter concludes with a consideration of the leading theoretical explanations for either the rates or incidence of deviant and criminal behaviors.

Special Features

Chapters include several special features. Each chapter begins with a section entitled At a Glance. The purpose is to provide the reader with a quick introduction to each form of crime or deviant behavior, offering interesting facts and relevant statistic. Key Concepts and Learning Objectives are presented at the front of each chapter in order to prompt readers on what to look for in the chapter and what they should know after reading the chapter. Portraits of Deviance are distributed throughout each chapter. Each portrait describes specific types of crime and deviance and provides a picture of deviance in real life and across the globe. A special box for theoretical explanations outlines the relevant theories that explain each type of deviance and offers sociological predictors and hypotheses that apply to each theory. Summary sections provide a concise conclusion for each chapter.

Organization

This book is divided into six major parts. Part One: An Overview of Deviant Behavior defines deviance and offers theoretical perspectives to explain deviance. Two chapters are devoted to the explanation of deviance. The first chapter examines individual behavior. Part Two is composed of three chapters and addresses violent forms of deviant behavior including criminal homicide, assault and battery (Chapter 4), domestic violence (Chapter 5), and suicide (Chapter 6). Parts Three and Four are organized around other categories of deviance including mental illness (Chapter 7), alcohol abuse (Chapter 8), illicit drug use (Chapter 9), sexual offending (Chapter 10), as well as property crime (Chapter 11), white-collar and organized crime (Chapter 12), and cyberdeviance (Chapter 13). Additional chapters on positive deviance (Chapter 14) and extreme forms of everyday behavior (Chapter 15) form Part Five. These specialized types of deviance are somewhat unique to the book as they are often overlooked in the study of deviance. This book concludes with Part Six: Terrorism (Chapter 16), which provides an overview of terrorism in the United States and around the world.

Chapter Summary

Deviant behavior may be considered along a continuum. Definitions of deviance involve a complex interplay between:

- The actor
- The offended party
- The wider societal audience

Cultural and social organization in a society help define what is deviant for that particular society. Social norms—expectional and behavioral—guide social interaction and provide boundaries for acceptable and unacceptable behavior.

Deviance must be understood on several conceptual levels:

- Creation of social norms, by whom, and which social interests/cultural values are protected.
- Violation of social/legal norms and under what conditions.
- Labeling of deviance, who is labeled deviant, and under what conditions does labeling occur.
- Societal reaction to norm violators.
- Formal and informal controls of social/legal norm violation.
- Escalation of social/legal norms violation over time and whether new forms of social/legal norm violation emerge.

Deviance may be distinguished along several social dimensions:

- Patterned versus idiosyncratic
- Episodic versus routine
- Individual versus group
- Positive versus negative

Although commonly thought of as harmful, deviance serves a number of functions for society:

- Defines boundaries and collective sentiments.
- Provides identities for persons unable to gain status or recognition in legitimate ways.
- Signals a need for change.
- Provides for scapegoating or tension release.
- Provides employment of persons to control deviant members of society.

Key Concepts

Culture: A body of widely shared customs and values that provide general orientations toward life and specific ways of achieving common goals.

Social organization: The means for carrying out the complex network of social interactions between individuals, social groups, and institutions.

Social norms: Generally agreed upon guides for behavior that provide boundaries for interpersonal relations.

Social roles: A set of social norms for the behavior of individuals who occupy given statuses within society.

Expectational norms: Behaviors that are "ideal" for individuals who are enacting a particular social role or who are in a given social situation.

Behavioral norms: What persons "typically" do when occupying a particular social role or in given social situation.

Processes of globalization: Complex set of processes that involve immediate worldwide communication, transnational commerce and trade, and borderless opportunities for political and cultural exchange.

Critical Thinking Questions

1. Imagine a society without deviant behavior—where everyone continually conforms to the prevailing social norms. Describe the daily lives of the inhabitants of such a society. What are the advantages and disadvantages of total conformity for the society as a whole and for its individual members? Is it possible that a society without deviant behavior would persist through time?

2. Devise a strategy for the definition of deviant behavior that differs from the normative and societal reaction approaches discussed in this chapter. What forms of deviant behavior might emerge from your definition of deviant be-

havior? What forms of deviant behavior defined by the normative or societal reaction approach might be omitted?

3. Why are the vast majority of deviant behaviors routine and institutionalized and so few are considered innovative or idiosyncratic?

4. Discuss examples of how the processes of globalization alter local cultural influences on everyday life. How do geographically defined cultures modify the effects of globalization? How does globalization affect forms of deviant behavior in urban areas, small towns, and rural places around the world?

CHAPTER 2

Theories of Individual Forms of Deviant Behavior

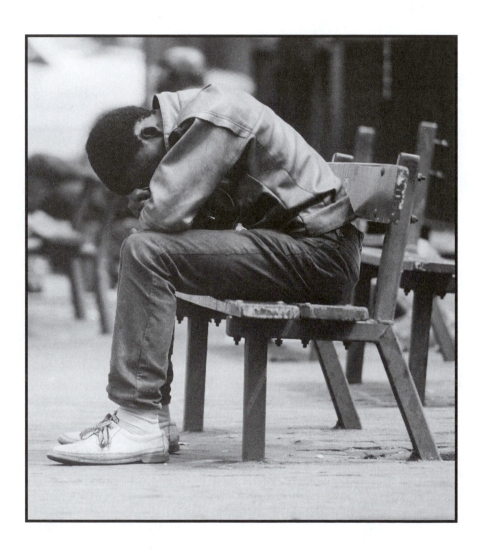

LEARNING OBJECTIVES

After reading this chapter you should know:

☐ The contributions of the Age of Enlightenment to the understanding of deviant behavior.

☐ The assumptions and formation of a scientific theory of deviant behavior.

☐ The criteria for evaluating a theory.

☐ The conceptual beginnings, early development, and more recent advances of the central theoretical formulations of individual forms of deviant behavior: the classical school, societal reaction or labeling, and control.

☐ The methodological and theoretical advances of the developmental or life course perspectives on the onset, persistence, and desistence of deviant behavior.

> *The deviant is one to whom the label has been successfully applied. . . .*
> —Howard Becker (1963: 9)

Attempts to understand socially deviant behavior using explanations derived from the empirical world are relatively recent phenomena. For most of recorded history, extra-terrestrial forces were viewed as causing aberrant human social behavior. More commonly, demonic possession was thought to precipitate deviant behaviors (Huff 1978). The devil controlled or strongly influenced the actions of persons, causing them to commit acts of violence, theft, and wanton destruction of property. Denial of sacred precepts and the failure to participate in religious ceremonies and observe their practices could also be the result of the influence of the devil. Social control of deviant behavior depended on rooting the devil out of the possessed person. Too often that meant the execution of the deviant person. By the middle of the eighteenth century, there were 350 crimes punishable by death in England (Radzinowicz 1948).

> *Offenders are but one element in a crime, and perhaps not even the most important.*
> —Marcus Felson (1998: 73)

The Age of Enlightenment, alternately known as the Age of Reason, swept Europe during the seventeenth and eighteenth centuries. Causes for the occurrence of phenomena in the world, whether physical or social, were being sought in the natural order, in the realm of empirical reality. Metaphysical and spiritual forces were being questioned as the primary and exclusive causes of physical events and human behaviors. Answers to the questions of "why" and "how" things happened, it was argued, are to be found within the phenomena themselves. The causes of physical events—the weather, the potential of the earth to produce edible vegetation, and the workings of the human body—were sought in the interplay of observable physical forces. Likewise, the precipitants of social behavior were to be found in the makeup of human beings and in the social milieu in which they live.[1]

The contributions of the Classical School during the time of the Enlightenment led to a rethinking about influences on human social behavior and the

[1]The Enlightenment posted at www.wsu.edu:8080/~brians/hum_303/enlightenment.htm

structure of social life. The search for Natural Laws to account for phenomena in the physical world led to a desire to discover the laws that governed the social forces that shaped behavior. Faith in the potential of reason and science marked the Enlightenment period. Theories that explained and predicted events in the physical world, such as Newton's discovery of gravity and Galileo's observation that the earth revolves around the sun, marked scientific breakthroughs in the seventeenth and eighteenth centuries. The **scientific method**—observation, hypothesis development, data collection and analysis, and hypothesis reformulation—drove the quest for knowledge. Scientific theories soon replaced other sources of knowledge—tradition, belief systems, and political and sacred authority. The Age of the Enlightenment was marked by a widespread rejection of State and Church as the sources of knowledge. Scientific explanations sought to supplant all other understanding of the world and the way it operated.[2]

This chapter provides an overview of theoretical formulations designed to explain and predict individual forms of deviant behavior. Three theoretical foci guide the discussion of theories of individual form of social deviance: the **Classical School,** the **societal reaction or labeling perspective,** and **social control theory.** Developments within each theoretical focus are traced from their conceptual beginnings, early development, and more recent advances.

What Is a Theory?

Fundamental assumptions of science are that phenomena in the world are knowable through our senses and that they are causally related to one another (Goode and Hatt 1952). To the extent that physical events or behaviors recur in a patterned way, they are viewed as causally related. A central objective of science is to discover the causal relationships among phenomena and, as a result, predict the probability of the occurrence of a given phenomenon by knowing the nature of its relationship to other phenomena. The tides, for example, are predictable with reasonable accuracy by knowing the variations in the gravitational forces of the Earth, the sun, and the moon.[3]

It is essential to understand what a scientific theory is and how best to assess it. Simply put, a **scientific theory** is a set of interrelated and interdependent propositions designed to predict a given phenomenon. A *proposition* is a statement of the relationship between at least two variables, or phenomena, in the empirical world that are subject to change. For example, age is a variable because it increases over time, a test score is a variable because it may vary among individuals or it may change for the same individual at different times. Fully developed theories are rarely found in the social sciences. Rather, conceptualizations or descriptions of the possible relationships among social variables are more common. The eminent social theorist, Robert K. Merton (1957: 9), observes:

> A large part of what is now called sociological theory consists of general orientations toward data, suggesting types of variables which need somehow to be taken into account, rather than clear, verifiable statements of relationships between specific variables.

[2]Ibid.

[3]Ocean Tides posted at: geog.oue.bc.ca/physgeog/contents/8r.htm

The theoretical formulations considered in this chapter fall into the category of what Merton (1957: 5) calls "theories of the middle range" or conceptualizations of social phenomena. To Merton (1957: 5–6), theories of the middle range are positioned somewhere between "minor working hypotheses" and a "master conceptual scheme," which accounts for a "very large number of empirically observed uniformities of social behavior."

Criteria for Evaluating a Theory

Sociological theorist, Ronald Akers (1994: 6–12) sets forth criteria essential for the evaluation of a scientific theory in general and theories of crime and deviance in particular. These criteria are logical consistency, scope, and parsimony, testability, empirical validity, and usefulness and policy implications. *Logical consistency* refers to the clarity of the concepts or variables that are used to form the propositions. A theory must also be constructed by logical and consistent ordering propositions. Internal inconsistency of propositions and definition of theoretical concepts are essential elements of a scientific theory.

Scope refers to "range of phenomena" accounted for by the theory. Theories of deviance or crime, for example, that are limited to one form of behavior, say shoplifting, are far less useful than a more encompassing theory of criminal behavior. Related to the scope of a theory is *parsimony*—the ideal in science to discover the simplest theoretical explanation for the broadest set of occurrences. Einstein's theory of relativity $E = MC^2$ is an example of a parsimonious theoretical formulation. Einstein discovered that energy and mass are equivalent and that energy is a function of mass times the velocity of light squared.

The *testability* of a theory is crucial to its usefulness to scientist around the world. Unless a theory lends itself to empirical scrutiny, evidence cannot be gathered to assess the validity of its propositions. A theory must be able to be falsified, before it can be accepted even provisionally. A theory may not be testable because the concepts or variables included in the propositions are so ill-defined that they cannot be empirically measured. Or, the propositions are not logically ordered. While it is not necessary to measure each concept in a theory, it is critical that the concepts are linked with the measurable concepts in a logical and consistent way.

The *empirical validity* of a theory is the most fundamental assessment criterion. Unless there is scientifically credible evidence that supports a theory, wholly or in part, it may well be abandoned for more promising theoretical formulations. The strength of the evidence in support of a theory and the consistency in the findings of support are key indicators of empirical validity. It is important to understand that causal relationships stated in scientific theories are cast in probabilistic terms. That is, the hypothesis that the greater the X, the greater the Y means that as X increases, the more likely Y is to follow, not that X will always follow from Y.

The *usefulness* and *policy implications* are also important criteria in evaluating a theoretical formulation. Empirically valid theories of criminal and deviant behavior are invaluable in designing and implementing prevention and intervention programs and policies. Key questions that legislators, law enforcers, and public policy makers continually ask are: What works, and for whom? Rather than approaching the control and prevention of criminal and deviant behavior in a haphazard way, public officials want to know the wisest expenditure of tax dollars. Sound theoretical formulations guide the formation of effective public policy, assist the deviant members of society, and reduce continued victimization (Akers 1994: 6-12).

The Classical School

Two social philosophers, **Cesare Beccaria** (1963) in Italy and **Jeremy Bentham** (1948) in England, are largely responsible for the development of the Classical School of thought during the time of the Enlightenment in the eighteenth century. Ceasare Beccaria, a shy Italian social philosopher, wrote a ground-breaking work— *On Crime and Punishment*—setting out the principles that underlie human social behavior. To Beccaria, individuals commonly hold three basic characteristics: *free will, rationality,* and *manipulability.* Beccaria viewed humans as rational beings who possess free will. Their decision to act or refrain from acting involves a conscious, voluntary, and deliberate process. Manipulability refers to the rational pursuit of self-interest. Underlying the decision to act is the principle of hedonism. The **hedonistic principle** holds that persons are motivated to maximize their pleasure and minimize their pain. When deciding to act a certain way, say to commit a deviant act, a person weighs the amount of anticipated pleasure from the action against the amount of pain that may result from committing the act. Simply put, if the pain that attends an act of deviance exceeds the pleasure derived from it, then its commission is less likely.[4]

The English social thinker, Jeremy Bentham (1948), pursued this utilitarian approach to deterrence of crime and deviance. He devised a **hedonistic calculus** that would link the appropriate penalty or pain to the each criminal offense. By knowing in advance the penalty for a particular crime, the would-be offender would be deterred. Both Beccaria and Bentham were opposed to the death penalty as a nonutilitarian form of punishment. Inflicting a sufficient amount of pain on the offender, they argued, may effectively deter criminal and deviant behaviors. Given their ability to freely decide to act (free will) and their innate sense of reason, potential offenders would rationally decide to forego acts of deviance.

Recent Advances in the Classical School

In the later part of the twentieth century, sociologists adopted the principles of human behavior outlined in the eighteenth century by Cesare Beccaria and Jeremy Bentham. The **deterrence doctrine** set forth by **Jack Gibbs** in the mid-1970s is based on the principle of hedonism. Gibbs translates hedonism into terms consistent with a cost-benefit analysis. The potential costs (or pain) involved in committing a deviant or criminal act must be less than the anticipated benefits (or pleasure) before an individual will decide to engage in the behavior. Humans are viewed as rational decision-making individuals who continually assess the relative cost and benefits before deciding to act. In short, a rational decision-making process precedes willful engagement in crime and deviance.

[4]www.criminology.fsu.edu/crimtheory/beccaria.htm

Medieval children striking back at the "devil" in their friends.

A logical derivative of the deterrence doctrine is British criminologists **Derek B. Cornish** and **Ronald V. Clarke's** (1986 and 1987) development of **Rational Choice Theory** and their development of *Situational Choice Theory.* Both theoretical perspectives focus on an individual's conscious, rational decision making. Again, the costs of acting are weighed against the benefits, and a decision is made. Situational choice theory, however, involves an assessment of the environment in which the criminal or deviant acts are to be played out. The structural features of the situation—lighting, surveillance equipment, police patrol and citizen watch organizations—influence the probability of deviant behavior. To Cornish and Clarke, *target hardening,* or making physical spaces more defensible and less attractive to perpetrators, deters deviant behaviors. Of course, this may simply lead to **crime displacement,** changing the location of criminal and deviant behavior to a more conducive environment (Cornish and Clarke 1987: 933–947).

A related conceptualization is **Lawrence Cohen** and **Marcus Felson's** (1979) **Routine Activities Theory.** Routine activities refer to an individual's lifestyle that influences the likelihood of becoming a victim of criminal activity. Walking alone late at night, being publicly intoxicated, and displaying large amounts of cash to strangers certainly increase one's vulnerability to crime. Cohen and Felson (1979: 590) argue that crime is most likely when three conditions are present: a suitable target, a motivated offender, and the lack of a capable guardian. A suitable target may be a vulnerable person on the street, an isolated convenience store in a rural area, or residence in a high crime neighborhood. Motivated offenders may be present in variety of settings but only choose to strike when a suitable target is present and a capable guardian is absent. It is the convergence of these three conditions that increases the probability of criminal victimization.

Sociologist **Jack Katz** (1988) provides an insightful analysis of the **seduction of crime**—the exhilaration that accompanies the commission of a criminal or deviant act. Katz observes that most sociologists focus on the sociocultural conditions and social processes that are associated with crime and deviance. The sociological precipitants of crime and deviance are considerably removed from the actual commission of the deviant act. To Katz the central question is: Why are people who are not inclined to commit a crime one moment determined to do so the next? The answer, Katz argues, lies in the sensual experiences that result from involvement in criminal or deviant behavior. Crime itself is seductive. The very act of committing a crime results in an intensely pleasurable emotional experience. A rush of adrenalin, a sense of euphoria, or a sensual feeling may wash over the offender. In short, the sensual dynamics inherent in criminal and deviant activity motive its participants and serve to perpetuate their involvement.

Societal Reaction/Labeling Perspective

The **Symbolic Interaction Theory** in sociology provides the foundation for the societal reaction or labeling perspective. **Charles Horton Cooley** (1902) and **George Herbert Mead** (1934) are largely responsible for the inception of symbolic interaction perspective within sociology. It was their observation that interpersonal interaction is primarily symbolic. Individuals attach meanings to the gestures, verbal communications, and behaviors of others. One's sense of self is also a product of symbolic social interaction. In Cooley's concept of a *looking-glass self*, he notes that the qualities that we assign to ourselves are those that we think others assign to us. We are, in a sense, a reflection of what we think others think of us. Our sense of self then is a social construction—the result of an interactional process through which the self acquires meaning and self-definition.

George Herbert Mead provides an understanding of the process by which a child develops a unique sense of self. To Mead, humans communicate by means of

Cesare Beccaria (1738–1794), Italian lawyer and social theorist, wrote *An Essay on Crimes and Punishments* (1764)—a foundation for modern deterrence theory.

gestures and symbols. A child begins to give meaning to the gestures and symbolic communications—usually words and pictures—used by others to converse with him or her. In time a child attributes to him- or herself certain characteristics and value to others. Messages of love or disgust, acceptance or rejection, joy or burden may be transmitted to a child. Mead terms this process as *taking the role of the other,* or the ability to view one's self from the perspective of another person. The process of defining and redefining one's self is a lifelong process. Yet the effects of negative labeling in early life may well have long-term adverse effects.

The early work of **Frank Tannenbaum** (1938) underscores the importance of the labeling in perpetuation and escalation of deviant behavior. In 1938, Frank Tannenbaum, a professor of history, recognized that delinquency is a result of a process of "tagging" or labeling first the offensive acts of a juvenile and second the juvenile him- or herself. The process begins with the community as a whole defining the troublesome behaviors as criminal or delinquent offenses. The perpetrators are then seen as violating the law and subject to being processed by the justice system. Tannenbaum viewed the process of arresting, adjudicating, and imposing a sentence by the court as the **dramatization of evil.** Once an individual is "tagged" or labeled as a delinquent, he or she tends to be ostracized by the community. The process of being isolated from conventional society leads to association with others who have also been labeled a delinquent. As a consequence, the likelihood of continued involvement in delinquent activities is markedly increased.

The societal reaction perspective was advanced in the 1950s and 1960s by the work of **Edwin Lemert** (1967) and **Howard Becker** (1963). Lemert provides an analysis of the process of becoming a deviant. He contends that the process involves two stages of development: *primary deviance* and *secondary deviance.* Primary deviance typically refers to minor norm violations—petty theft, use of graffiti, public drunkenness—that may well not evoke an official response by the criminal justice system. The offender usually does not define him- or herself as a criminal or deviant, but simply a prankster. However, if an act of primary deviance does result in a public response and an official action is taken—for example, an arrest for shoplifting—then the label of criminal is applied. The process of being arrested, booked, fingerprinted, and adjudicated in court serves to publicly label the offender. Secondary deviance then occurs when the individual's primary deviance becomes publicly known and the person is adjudicated a delinquent or criminal. In response to this negative label, the primary deviant may engage in further deviance "as a means of defense, attack, or adjustment to the overt and covert problems created by the consequent societal reaction to him"(Lemert 1967: 237). In the secondary deviance stage, offending becomes more frequent and typically more serious. The deviant defines himself as "bad"—a rejected person who will retaliate against the society that wronged her or him.

In a similar vein, Howard Becker points out that deviance is essentially a social creation. He writes: "*social groups create deviance by making the rules whose infractions constitute deviance,* and by applying those rules to particular people and labeling them as outsiders" [emphasis in original] (Becker 1963: 9). Becker contends that behavior is essentially neutral; in itself it is neither good nor bad. Others must define a person's behavior before it can take on a social value, a judgment of right or wrong, moral or immoral, harmful or benign. Simply put, the process of creating a deviant involves three stages. First, an act must be defined as a deviant act. Second, the actor must be defined as deviant person. The third stage, however, is critical in the process of becoming a deviant. In the third stage of the process, the actor must accept the label of deviant and define him- or herself as a deviant. Becker (1963: 9) observes: "The deviant is one to whom that label has been successfully applied."

More recently, sociologist **Howard Kaplan** (1980) has elaborated on the labeling/societal reaction perspective. Central to Kaplan's formulation is the assumption that behavior is motivated by the desire to achieve and maintain a sense of self-esteem. A person's self-esteem typically derives from his or her ability to recognize highly valued personal characteristics in him- or herself, accept positive evaluations from others, and the ability to avert negative responses from others. However, when a person's self-esteem is undermined, self-derogation—or negative attitudes toward one's self—may ensue.

To Kaplan, **self-derogation**—the process by which a person comes to accept the largely negative judgments of others—is the key concept in the etiology of deviant behavior. An individuals who is unable to establish a positive sense of him- or herself is less motivated to conform to the norms of conventional society. They may well seek alternate means to gain a sense of self-esteem. They may be attracted to deviant groups or lifestyles that provide opportunities for developing unconventional, yet in the view of their fellow deviants, self-enhancing attitudes.

Australian social theorist **John Braithwaite** (1989) adds another dimension to the labeling/societal reaction perspective. His highly innovative theory of **reintegrative shaming** challenges many of the current assumptions about crime deterrence and the rehabilitation of offenders. Reintegrative shaming occurs when the community conveys its disapproval of a deviant person's behavior, but maintains respect for the individual. The intention of reintegrative shaming is to send the message to the offender that deviant behavior will not be tolerated; nevertheless, the community values the offender as a person and wants him or her to be reintegrated into conventional society. Braithwaite draws the distinction between reintegrative shaming and stigmatization. **Stigmatization** involves "disintegrative shaming"—the person is labeled as criminal or deviant as well as his or her behavior (Braithwaite 1989: 101). Ostracized by the community, stigmatized persons are more likely to engage in further criminal or deviant activities. They may seek out deviant subcultures for support and personal recognition, further alienating them from the larger society.

A critical element in reintegrative shaming theory is the deliberate attempt to reassimilate the deviant into the community. By distinguishing between the inherent worth of a person from his or her misdeeds, the reintegrative shaming approach to crime deterrence and offender rehabilitation offers an alternative to the retributive response to deviant behavior.

Control Theory

Emile Durkheim's (1951) views on social integration and its effect on deviant behavior provide the backdrop for the development of social control theory. **Social integration** refers to the extent to which individuals accept common cultural

Actress Winona Ryder was found guilty of a $5,500 shoplifting rampage and felony vandalism at Saks Fifth Avenue.

values and societal norms to structure their behavior. **Travis Hirschi** (1969) conceptualized integration as a set of **social bonds** between individuals and conventional society. Rather than trying to discover why individuals engage in deviance, Hirschi posed the question: Why don't people commit delinquent acts?

Hirschi identifies four social bonds: *attachment, commitment, involvement,* and *belief.* Attachment refers to the intensity and variety of interests a person has in common with others in the community. Commitment is reflected in the amount of energy a person's expends on community-oriented activities. Involvement is indicated by the person's expenditure of time on projects of common interest. Belief means the acceptance of a common system of values and moral precepts. Hirschi concludes that the stronger the bonds between individuals and conventional social life, the less likely they would engage in deviant behavior.

In more recent years, **Michael Gottfredson** and Travis Hirschi (1990) have offered a reformulation of control theory. Their **General Theory of Crime** focuses on **self-control** rather than on bonds to conventional social life. Gottfredson and Hirschi (1990) contend that most crimes are not well planned, but are committed to satisfy an immediate need or desire. Low self-control is summarized by Tittle and Paternoster (1993: 482) as an:

- Orientation toward the present rather than the future (or short-sightedness)
- Attraction to physical rather than mental activities
- Insensitivity to the suffering of others (self-centeredness)
- Intolerance for frustration
- Inclination toward risk-taking and opportunism

Individuals who lack self-control, who are unable to resist the urge for immediate gratification are most prone to involvement in criminal and deviant behaviors. Criminal activity provides a person who has low-self control with several immediate benefits. Gottfredson and Hirschi (1990: 89–90) note that:

There is a long tradition of publicly shaming deviant persons to correct their faults and to deter others in the community.

- Criminal acts provide *easy or simple* gratification of desires.
- Criminal acts are *exciting, risky, or thrilling.*
- Crimes require *little skill or planning.*
- Crimes often result in *pain or discomfort for the victim.*

Sociologist **Charles Tittle** (1995) has set forth a control-balance formulation to explain deviant behavior. *Control-balance* refers to the relative amount of control a person has over others in a given situation. The key concept in control-balance theory is the person's control ratio. **Control ratio** refers to the amount of influence individuals have over forces that may control their behavior versus their ability to control those forces. Tittle assumes that individuals strive to maintain a sense of autonomy, a sense of self-determination. No one wants to be told what to do, as well as when and how to do it. Control imbalance often provokes feelings of humiliation, anger, and emotional distress. To correct this control imbalance and the resolve the negative emotions that accompany it, a person may resort to various forms of deviant behavior.

Tittle (1995) identifies five conditions that underlie the occurrence of deviant behavior:

- A predisposition toward being motivated for deviance
- A situational provocation that reminds a person of a control imbalance
- The transformation of predisposition into actual motivation for deviance
- The opportunity for deviant response
- The absence or relative weakness for constraint, so that the mental processes of "control balancing" will result in a perceived gain in control

In sum, persons who are motivated to engage in deviant acts need to establish a sense of autonomy, perceive an unbalanced control ratio, and experience a blockage in goal attainment. The immediate situation may trigger recognition of a control imbalance. If suitable opportunities for retaliatory acts are present and constraints against their commission are absent, then an individual may well respond in an antisocial way.

Theoretical Formulations Of Individual Forms Of Deviant Behavior

Theoretical Foundations

Classical School
	1. Beccaria (1764)	On Crimes and Punishment
	2. Bentham (1789)	An Introduction to the Principles of Moral and Legislation

Societal Reaction/Labeling Perspective
	1. Tannenbaum (1938)	The Dramatization of Evil

Control Theory
	1. Hirsch (1969)	The Causes of Delinquency

Early Developments

Societal Reaction
	1. Lemert (1951)	Primary and Secondary Deviation
	2. Becker (1964)	The Outsiders

Recent Advances

Classical School
	1. Cohen and Felson (1979)	Routine Activity Theory
	2. Cornish and Clarke (1986)	Crime as Rational Choice
	3. Katz (1988)	Seduction of Crime

Societal Reaction/Labeling
	1. Kaplan (1980)	Self-Derogation
	2. Braithwaite (1989)	Crime, Shame and Reintegration

Control Theory
	1. Gottfredson and Hirschi (1990)	A General Theory of Crime
	2. Tittle (1995)	Control Balance Theory

New Theoretical Approaches

Life-Course Formulations
	1. Wolfgang, Figlio, and Sellin (1972)	Delinquency in a Birth Cohort
	2. Wolfgang, Thronberry, and Figlio (1987)	From Delinquency to Crime
	3. Sampson and Laub (1993)	Life Course Analyses
	4. Farrington (1995)	Delinquent Development Theory

New Theoretical Approaches

The recognition that involvement in deviant behavior varies over time has led to the emergence of life-course perspectives. **Robert Sampson** and **John Laub** (1993) take a **developmental approach** to the understanding of the persistence and desistence of criminal activity across the life span. Their age-graded theory of informal social control proposes that changes in social bonds between an individual and conventional society across the life course account for variations in criminal and deviant behaviors. Two concepts are particularly important to their developmental formulation: trajectories and transitions. *Trajectories* refer to "pathways or lines of development throughout life. These long-term patterns of behavior may include work life, marriage, parenthood, or even criminal behavior" (Sampson and Laub 1993: 100). *Transitions,* however, are "short-term events embedded in trajectories which may include starting a new job, getting married, having a child, or being sentenced to prison" (Sampson and Laub 1993: 100). A related concept is a *turning point*—an abrupt event that redirects the course of a life trajectory.

A life-course trajectory that involves persistent involvement in criminal and deviant activities may be interrupted by transitions that change the nature of the social bonds between the offender and the larger society. Transitions tend to occur at particular ages across the life span. Marriage, stable employment, and becoming a parent tend to strengthen ties to the community. A turning point in the life of a chronic offender may be a graduation from high school, a significant job promotion, or a civic recognition for a heroic deed. To the extent that transitions and key turning points increase an individual's social bonds, they tend to decrease the probability of continued deviant behavior. Sampson and Laub (1993: 100) conclude that "age-graded changes in social bonds explain changes in crime."

As social bonds are strengthened so too is one's social capital. *Social capital* refers to the positive relationships between a person and other members of the community and its governmental and social institutions. Being a responsible individual who acts in the best interest of those around him or her results in the accumulation of social capital. Sampson and Laub (1993) point out that as social capital increases, involvement in crime and deviance decreases.

Issues related to the persistence and desistence of offending are considered in a Philadelphia birth-cohort study conducted by **Marvin Wolfgang** and his colleagues (1972) and British criminologist **David Farrington's** Cambridge Study in Delinquent Development (1986). In two birth cohort studies, Marvin Wolfgang and his colleagues at the University of Pennsylvania found that chronic juvenile offenders—those who commit five or more offenses—are developmentally different from single offenders and from nondelinquents. Compared to the nonchronic delinquents, the chronic offenders tend to have lower IQ scores, do less well in school, and are more likely to come from lower socioeconomic backgrounds. In addition, chronic offenders tend to commit their first offense at younger age. Wolfgang and his colleagues conclude that the earlier the age of onset, the greater the likelihood of chronic offending. A follow-up study showed that the seriousness of offending increased with age, but the actual number of crimes committed decreased over time (Wolfgang, Thornberry, and Figlio 1987).

The findings of David Farrington's developmental study of delinquents also show that antisocial behaviors—dishonesty and aggression—become evident as early as the age of 8 and given a certain social context may well persist into early adulthood. Young offenders from large families where discipline is particularly harsh and inconsistent, social and economic resources are meager, and siblings are also committing delinquent acts are more likely to be set on a trajectory of criminal involvement. Throughout their adolescent years and into adulthood, the persistent offenders tend to spend their time in all-male groups, drink excessively and use illicit drugs, and engage in aggressive and violent behaviors. In short, English delinquent youth are generally "less conforming and less socially restrained" (West and Farrington 1977).

Farrington (1986) also identified three key transitions that changed the life trajectory of a young offender. These transitions are: employment, marriage, and relocation. Steady employment with possibility of advancement provides an alternative to a relatively meaningless life on the street. Getting married to a person who is not involved in a deviant lifestyle is another important transition in the life of a delinquent. Moving to a low-crime area—the suburbs or a rural place—also tend to reduce the opportunities to continue a deviant career. These three transitions serve to restructure a person's everyday life and interrupt a crime-prone trajectory.

Chapter Summary

Scientific inquiry into human social behavior began to emerge during the time of the Enlightenment and has undergone a slow, uneven, often tumultuous development. The methods of scientific investigation are continually being refined, as are theoretical formulations of a wide range of social and behavioral phenomena. Advances in sociological and social psychological theories of behavior have largely occurred during the twentieth century.

- This chapter considers the:
  - foundations of scientific inquiry into deviant behavior, the
  - essential elements of a viable scientific theory, and
  - early development and recent theoretical advances designed to explain and predict deviant behavior.
- Sociological explanations of behavior discussed in this chapter include:
  - Classical School of Crime and Deviance
  - Societal Reaction or Labeling Perspective
  - Social Control Theory
- Each theory is designed to explain and predict the participation of individuals in various forms of deviant behavior.
- The Classical School of Crime and Deviance, rooted in the work of Cesare Beccaria and Jeremy Bentham, provide the foundation for:
  - Rational Choice Theory
  - Routine Activities Formulation
- Societal reaction or the labeling perspective derives from the early work of Charles Horton Cooley and George Herbert Mead. Among the most influential labeling theorists are:
  - Frank Tannenbaum
  - Edwin Lemert

- ○ Howard Becker
- ○ Howard Kaplan
- ○ John Braithwaite
- Emile Durkheim's concept of social integration and its consequences gave rise to the development of Travis Hirschi's social bonding theory and his later formulation of self-control theory with Michael Gottfredson.
- The developmental, or life-course approach takes into account the emergence, persistence, and possible desistence of engagement in deviant activities across the lifespan.

Key Names

Cesare Beccaria	Edwin Lemert
Jeremy Bentham	Howard Becker
Jack Gibbs	Howard Kaplan
Ronald V. Clarke	John Braithwaite
Derek B. Cornish	Travis Hirschi
Lawrence Cohen	Michael Gottfredson
Marcus Felson	Charles Tittle
Jack Katz	Robert Sampson
Charles Horton Cooley	John Laub
George Herbert Mead	Marvin Wolfgang
Frank Tannebaum	David Farrington

Key Concepts

Scientific method: Observation, hypothesis development, data collection and analysis, and hypothesis reformulation used in the quest for knowledge.

Classical School: School of thought developed during the time of the Enlightenment, based upon the idea that human beings possess free will and rationally decide to act or refrain from certain activities.

Societal reaction or labeling perspective: Theoretical perspective that focuses on how society reacts to and labeling deviance and deviant actors, and how these reactions and labels affect the deviant actor.

Scientific theory: A set of interrelated and interdependent propositions designed to predict a given phenomenon.

Hedonistic principle: Belief that persons are motivated to maximize their pleasure and minimize their pain.

Deterrence doctrine: The cost-benefit analysis of committing a deviant or criminal act.

Rational Choice Theory: An individual makes a conscious, rational decision before acting.

Routine Activities Theory: The likelihood of crime increases when there is a suitable target, a motivated offender, and the lack of a capable guardian.

Seduction of crime: The exhilaration that accompanies the commission of a criminal or deviant act.

Symbolic Interaction Theory: Theory that observes interpersonal interaction as primarily symbolic and meaningful.

Dramatization of evil: Process of labeling deviance and deviant actors to describe the arresting, adjudicating, and sentencing of offenders.

Self-derogation: The process by which a person comes to accept the largely negative judgments of others.

Reintegrative shaming: Process by which the community conveys its disapproval of a deviant person's behavior, but maintains respect for the individual.

Stigmatization: Disrespectful shaming; the person is labeled as criminal or deviant as well as his or her behavior.

Social integration: The extent to which individuals accept common cultural values and societal norms to structure their behavior.

Social bonds: The integration of an individual with conventional society.

General Theory of Crime: Focuses on self-control rather than bonds to conventional social life.

Self-control: Person's ability to alter responses and behavior in an effort to resist committing crime or deviance.

Control ratio: An individual's potential for control over circumstances relative to the potential those circumstances have to control her or him.

Developmental approach (life-course perspective): Attempts to understand the onset, persistence, and desistence of deviant activity across the life span.

Critical Thinking Questions

1. Devise an alternative to the scientific method for the explanation and prediction of deviant behavior. What are the advantages and disadvantage of your innovative method of investigating deviance?

2. What are the limitations of the scientific method of investigation? What kinds of questions are beyond the scope of the scientific method?

3. Are different theoretical formulations needed for different forms of deviant behavior? For example, can violent, property, and victimless deviant acts be explained by the same theoretical model?

4. Are different theoretical models needed to explain the onset of deviant behavior, the persistence, and desistence of that behavior? Which theoretical model (s) do you think best accounts for the onset, the persistence, and desistence of deviant behavior?

CHAPTER 3

Theories of the Variations in Rates of Deviant Behavior

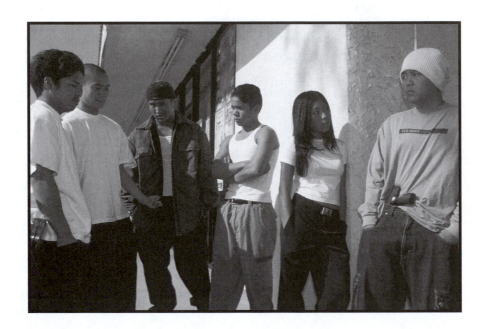

After reading this chapter you should know:

- ☐ The macrosociological approach to the study of rates of crime and deviance.
- ☐ The contributions of the conflict and functionalist perspectives for the study of crime and deviance.
- ☐ The conceptual beginnings, early development, and more recent advances in the theoretical foundations of the study of crime rates and social deviance, specifically those of the conflict approach, social integration/anomie, social disorganization, and differential association/social learning theories.

Scientific inquiry into the phenomena of deviance tends to focus either on the understanding of the incidence or prevalence of criminal or deviant behavior. The previous chapter focused on explanations of individual forms of deviance. The central question addressed in Chapter 2 was: Why do certain individuals engage in a given form of deviant behavior, while others do not? The present chapter considers a distinctly different sociological question: Why is deviance and criminality more prevalent in some subcultures or social groups than in others? Each question must be addressed at different levels of analysis. **Micro-level analysis** focuses on social processes and personal characteristics—labeling, social bonding, self-control or derogation—that may account for an individual's involvement in criminal or deviant behavior. **Macro-level analysis** considers the ways in which structural and cultural characteristics of social collectivities—societies, subcultures, social groupings—affect the *rates* of crime and acts of social deviance. The rate of crime or deviance typically refers to the number of offenses that occur for every 100,000 persons in a given population. Rates of crime and deviance vary widely around the world and within the United States. Subcultural groups and socioeconomic categories of persons are differentially involved in crime and deviance.

> *In the first place crime is normal because a society exempt from it is utterly impossible.*
>
> —Emile Durkheim (1938: 67)

> *The code of the street thus emerges where the influence of the police ends and where personal responsibility for one's safety is felt to begin.*
>
> —Elijah Anderson (1999: 34)

Attempts to explain variations in rates of crime and deviance rely on two macro-level theoretical perspectives: conflict and functionalism. Each of these perspectives and the development of theoretical formulations that derive from them are considered in this chapter.

The Conflict Perspective

Conflict can occur on several social levels: international, regional, cultural and subcultural, intergroup and interpersonal. Conflict may itself be deviant, or it may be a precursor to other forms of deviant behaviors. The *conflict perspective* focuses on the ways in which social conflicts affect the prevalence of criminal offending and deviant behavior.

Conflict Approach

The conflict approach to the understanding of crime and deviance is based in large part on **Karl Marx's** (1956) analysis of the structure of society. Marx argued that two conflicting classes—the *bourgeoisie* and the *proletariat*—serve to structure society. Because the bourgeoisie are the owners of the means of production in society, they control much of its wealth. The proletariat or working class sell their labor to the bourgeoisie but are compensated at a rate far less than its market value. In Marx's terms labor has a *surplus value*—the monetary gain of employers after paying the worker. *Structural inequality* is premised on the concentration of wealth and power in the hands of the bourgeoisie, their exploitation of the proletariat, and their ability to manipulate the legal system to their advantage. Marx argued that a class struggle would erupt, resulting in the overthrow of the bourgeoisie by the proletariat.

Several noted criminologists—**Thorsten Sellin** (1938), **Austin Turk** (1969), and **Richard Quinney** (1977)—have adopted a conflict perspective for their theoretical formulations of crime and deviance. To Thorsten Sellin, *conduct norms* define approved and disapproved behaviors within cultural groups. Deviance arises when the conduct norms of one cultural group or subculture clash with another. Conflicts in conduct norms may occur under three conditions: (1) when two cultural groups are in close proximity and the conduct norms of one group conflict with the neighboring group, (2) when the laws of a dominant cultural group govern the activities of a subordinate group, and (3) when members of one cultural group move into an area governed by another cultural group. In each instance, the norms that guide the conduct of a cultural group may be considered unacceptable by another and in the extreme may be defined as illegal. Persons who violate the conduct norms of another cultural group may elicit various forms of informal social control—gossip, ridicule, or ostracism—or may be criminally adjudicated (Sellin 1938).

Austin Turk's conflict model of criminality focuses on the balance of power between authorities in society and persons who are subjected to their control. Social order is maintained to the extent that the members of society accept and support the legitimacy of the authorities. Two sets of norms emerge to reduce the likelihood of conflict in society: norms of domination and norms of deference. The power of the dominant class is endangered when their authority is dependent on their ability to force its will on others, or when authority is premised on an egalitarian relationship with the less powerful in society (Turk 1969).

Turk specifies the two basic conditions under which social conflict is more likely to occur. First, there are marked differences in important cultural values between those with authority and less powerful members of society. Second, the less powerful members of society are well organized and committed to advancing their cause. As conflict increases so too does the likelihood that certain behaviors will be defined as criminal. Turk outlines two factors that increase the probability of official criminal sanctioning. First, behavior is more likely to be officially sanctioned when the agents of law enforcement consider it to be a significant criminal offense. Police officers may exercise their discretion not to make an arrest in matters involving minor transgressions, particularly victimless offenses. If the police and the agents of the court—the prosecutors and judges—agree that legal action is necessary to control the criminal behavior and to ensure public safety, then the offender is more likely to be arrested, prosecuted, and officially sanctioned by the courts. Second, the criminal transgressions of the less powerful in society are more likely to be criminalized than those of the more powerful. So-called "blue-collar" offenses—burglary, robbery, assault, and battery—result more often in official legal sanctioning than do "white-collar" crimes—embezzlement, insider trading, price-fixing (Turk 1969).

Richard Quinney points out that the understanding of crime involves two related processes: (1) legally defining certain behaviors as criminal and (2) imposing the label of criminal on those who engage in such behaviors. It is in the interest of the dominant class in a capitalistic system to control the behavior of the working class. Certain contradictions—poverty, inequality, and unemployment—are inherent in a capitalistic economy. These contradictions give rise to deviant and criminal behaviors among the working classes that justify the institution of repressive means of social control (Quinney 1977).

The legal order of the state is intended to further the interests of the corporate and business elite, the owners of the means of production. Criminal and deviant behaviors are social constructions fabricated by the dominant economic class to control the working masses. Richard Quinney's theory of the *social reality of crime* focuses on the processes involved in defining certain behaviors as criminal by the political and economic elite, the inevitability of involvement in criminal activities by the disadvantaged in society, and official sanctioning of offenders. In sum, the social construction of crime and deviance is essential to the perpetuation of interests of the dominant classes. By focusing the attention of the justice system on certain kinds of offenses, the criminal activities of the political and corporate elite are typically disregarded, or litigated in civil rather than criminal courts.

Alex Thio (1978) sets forth a power theory of deviance. He contends that deviance may be viewed along a range of lower to higher consensus acts. *Consensus* refers to the generally accepted judgment about the seriousness of a deviant act. Thio hypothesizes that the higher the consensus, the less the ambiguity about the potential or actual harm that results from the deviant behavior. Conversely, he argues the lower the consensus, the greater the ambiguity about the seriousness of the deviance.

Thio (1978: 81–86) summarizes his power formulation in three propositions:

1. The more power people have, the more likely they will engage in lower consensus deviance—the "less serious," more profitable, or the more sophisticated type of deviance—with lower probability of being labeled deviant.

   The more powerful members of society are able to influence the processes involved in criminalizing behaviors and in the enforcement of criminal statutes. As a consequence, the powerful focus political and media attention on certain forms of deviance and divert attention from others.

Quinney's Social Reality of Crime

- PROPOSITION 1 Crime is a definition of human conduct that is created by authorized agents in a politically organized society.
- PROPOSITION 2 Criminal definitions describe behaviors that conflict with the interests of the segments of society that have the power to shape political policy.
- PROPOSITION 3 Criminal definitions are applied by the segments of society that have the power to shape the enforcement and administration of criminal law.
- PROPOSITION 4 Behavior patterns are structured in segmentally organized society in relation to criminal definitions, and within this context persons engage in actions that have relative probabilities of being defined as criminal.
- PROPOSITION 5 Conceptions of crime are constructed and diffused in the segments of society by various means of communication.
- PROPOSITION 6 The social reality of crime is constructed by the formulation and application of criminal definitions, the development of behavior patterns related to criminal definitions, and the construction of criminal conceptions.

Source: Richard Quinney, 1970. *The Social Reality of Crime.* Boston: Little Brown, pp. 15–24.

2. It is more likely that the powerful will engage in lower consensus deviance and the powerless will commit higher consensus deviance.

   The powerful have opportunities to commit a wide range of economic and fraudulent crimes that are not available to the powerless. Because these offenses are largely "hidden" from public view, they are rarely included in official governmental report on criminal activity. Given vastly greater opportunities to engage in clandestine criminal activity, Thio contends that the powerful commit disproportionately more crime than the powerless.

3. Deviance by the powerful induces deviance by the powerless that, in turn, contributes to deviance by the powerful.

   The pervasiveness of the exploitive behavior of the powerful, their flagrant disregard for the welfare of the less fortunate, and their expedient sense of morality prompt acts of rage or low-profit property offenses (typically displaced on available targets). The offenses of the powerless routinely draw attention from the media and elicit a punitive response from the powerful. The wanton acts of the powerless provide the powerful with justification for their self-serving deviance.

More recently the conflict perspective has been extended to include consideration of family dynamics and issues related to gender. **John Hagan** (1989a) seeks to understand the link between social class and criminal behavior. More specifically, Hagan conceptualizes social class in terms of *power relations.* Social class distinctions imply varying degrees of social power. And power, Hagan argues, must be understood in relational terms. The concept of social class then is understood in the context of the social organization of work. Workers are organized along the lines of their relationship to ownership and authority. The social class of workers is defined by the extent to which they own a business, say, or can exercise authority over other workers. Hagan (1989a: 4) notes that "owners of businesses and persons of occupational authority are in a position to commit larger crimes than persons located in employee positions without authority."

Hagan (1989b) extends his power-relations concept of social class to an understanding of gender differences in the rates of juvenile offending. The power relations of the parents outside the home influence the balance of power within the family and impact the socialization experiences the children. When the power relations of the husband outside the home exceed those of his wife, the family tends to be structured along patriarchal lines. In families with a patriarchal family structure there is more concern with controlling the behavior of female children than that of their male siblings. The wider latitude granted boys within a patriarchal family provides greater opportunities for risk-taking and delinquent behaviors.

However, Hagan (1989b) notes that in more egalitarian families where the power relations of husband and wife outside the home are similar—relatively high or low—male and female children are more likely to be socialized in similar ways. That is, neither girls nor boys within the family are controlled more so than the other. Both genders, therefore, have a similar opportunity to engage in delinquent activities. In short, power-relations differentials outside the home affect the balance of power and control within the family. The balance of power control, in turn, serves to structure familial relations either in a patriarchal or egalitarian manner. The structure of the family influences the extent of power and control exerted over the children. Differential socialization experiences of male and female children explain gender differences in juvenile offending (Hagan 1989b).

Feminism

The **feminist perspective** on crime and deviance is rooted in the conflict view of the social order. While there is no single feminist theoretical formulation, there are common themes that contribute to the understanding of crime and deviance. Feminist theorists call attention to the gender-bias in theorizing and research on criminal and deviant behavior. Most studies of crime and deviance are limited to analyses of male offending. An *androcentric approach* to the study of deviant behavior has led to the emergence of the feminist perspective, an alternative theoretical understanding of crime and deviance. **Kathleen Daly** and **Meda Chesney-Lind** (1988), leading feminist theorists, note that two issues concern criminologists interested in gender and crime. The first issue is: Can theoretical formulations and research findings of studies that are limited to male offending be generalized to the participation of women in crime and deviance? The second issue is: What accounts for the disproportionate involvement of men in most forms of criminal and deviant activity?

Feminist theorists address these issues by focusing attention on an understanding of gender in society and its link to criminal and deviant behavior. The feminist view of gender is inextricably tied to gender stratification and its consequences for women in society. *Patriarchy* is seen as the prevailing social structure, in which men hold a dominant position over women and masculine attributes and behaviors are considered to be markedly preferable to feminine ones. A central theme of feminist theorizing is that male dominance permeates all aspects of social life, both conventional and deviant.

Feminist theorists argue that the influence of social class, race, and age on crime and deviance can only be understood in the context of a patriarchal social structure. Social inequities are inherent in social class positioning, ethnicity, and race, and issues related to age influence criminal and deviant behavior and shape the societal response to it. The disadvantages of social class, race, and age, however, exacerbate gender inequality. Gender inequality is then a central condition that runs through social life. Theories of crime and deviance, feminists argue, must be revamped to include consideration of the complex issues related to gender inequities and their consequences (see Danner 1989).

The Functionalist Perspective

The **functional perspective** focuses on the purpose, usefulness, or contribution that a given social phenomenon makes to the social order. Over time recurrent behaviors form patterns that persist, the functionalists argue, because they serve a useful purpose and contribute to the survival of the society. While **Emile Durkheim** (1938) provided the foundation for functionalism in the later part of the nineteenth century, **Robert K. Merton** (1968), the eminent Columbia University sociologist, most clearly articulated functional analysis of human social behavior. To Merton, functional analysis is limited to patterned and repetitive sociological phenomena—behavioral patterns, social roles, social norms and processes. Function refers to "observed consequences [of a given patterned and repetitive action] that make for the adaptation or adjustment of a given system" (Merton 1968: 51). Forms of deviant behavior are, then, patterned and repetitive actions that serve a function for society. Merton identifies two types of functions: manifest and latent. **Manifest functions** refer to "observed consequences [of a given patterned and repetitive action] that make for the adaptation or adjustment of a given system which are intended and recognized by participants in the system" (Merton 1968: 51). **Latent functions,** however, are "observed consequences [of a given patterned and repetitive action] that make for the adaptation or adjustment of a given system which are neither intended and nor recognized by participants in the system" (Merton 1968: 51). Conversely, **dysfunctions** refer to "observed consequences [of a given patterned and repetitive action] that lessen the adaptation or adjustment of a given system" (Merton 1968: 51).

Negative forms of deviance and criminal behavior are not typically thought to contribute to the survival of society. Rather, there is a deliberate effort to control deviant members of society and to prevent the occurrence of any form of prohibitive behavior. Emile Durkheim (1938) advances a radical different view of deviance. His functional approach rejects the notion that crime and deviance is simply pathological, but rather are normal occurrences in society. Crime, in one form or another, is a universal phenomenon. Forms of criminality have changed over time yet Durkheim (1938: 65–66) notes, "everywhere and always, there have been men who have behaved in such a way as to draw upon themselves, penal repression." Criminal behavior offends vital sentiments held in common by members of a society about the ways in which life should be lived. Violation of the basic norms of social life results in a collective response that reaffirms their importance.

Durkheim further contends that a society without crime is not possible. The establishment of social boundaries between what is considered to be "right and wrong" is vital to the functioning of a society. The *collective conscience* of a society is reaffirmed by the ways in which it responds to deviant acts. Collective sentiments form the basis for the normative structure of society. In the absence of generally agreed upon norms to guide behavior, social interaction would become unpredictable. The resulting chaos would make social life impossible. Durkheim (1938: 70) concludes that: "Crime is, then, necessary; it is bound up in the fundamental conditions of all social life, and by that very fact it is useful, because these conditions of which it is a part are themselves indispensable to the normal evolution of morality and the law."

Social Integration

Emile Durkheim sought to understand why rates of deviant behavior vary among social groups. In his seminal work, *Suicide* (1951), Durkheim argues that two social forces—integration and regulation—explain rates of suicide. By **social integration** Durkheim meant the extent to which persons were bound into social life, or alternatively isolated from it. A measure of social integration is the level of adherence to a set of common values. Durkheim hypothesizes that the greater the consensus about important beliefs, symbolic significance, and cultural goals, the greater the social integration of the group. *Social regulation* refers to the extent to which individuals are required to follow the guidelines for their behavior established by the group. The greater the social regulation, the clearer and more certain are the norms that govern social interaction. Social integration and regulation tend to complement one another. As social integration rises, so too does social regulation. Individuals hold common values that provide a foundation for the normative structure of society.

Both social integration and regulation can vary between exceedingly high levels in which the interests of the group supersede those of its individual members to exceedingly low levels in which interests of individuals take precedence over those of the group. Social integration and regulation can also change suddenly, leaving the group members without a sense of meaning and direction.

The extent of social integration and regulation, Durkheim argues, is linked with distinct forms of suicides. Durkheim sets forth three basic types of suicide: altruistic, egoistic, and anomic. *Altruistic suicide* is most common in societies characterized by particularly high levels of social integration. Individuals are enmeshed in the collectivity. If suicide is considered to advance the interests of the group, then its individual members are willing to sacrifice themselves. Conversely, *egoistic suicide* is more probable under conditions of exceptionally low social integration. Individuals tend to act to enhance their own ends; the effect of their behavior on the welfare of others is rarely considered. Few ties exist between individual members and the larger society. There is no sense of collective well-being. *Anomic suicide* is found when there is rapid change in social integration. Rapid social change creates chaos in the normative structure of society. A state of normlessness exists that leaves individuals without effective guidelines for their behavior. The consequence is often a marked increase in self-destructive behaviors. Conditions of extreme social regulation, Durkheim observed, may also lead to *fatalistic suicide*. Fatalistic suicide occurs when individual behavior is overly regulated by others, making personal autonomy unattainable. The loss of freedom of action, and the opportunity for self-actualization, may well lead to a sense of hopelessness and despair.

Robert K. Merton (1968) seeks to advance Durkheim's understanding of anomie and its consequences. In *Social Structure and Anomie* (1968: 132), Merton addresses the question of how "some social structures exert a definite pressure on certain persons in the society to engage in non-conforming rather than conforming conduct." Merton contents that most persons are socialized to want the same cultural goals—status, economic reward, social influence—but do not have the institutionalized means to attain them. As a consequence, **anomie**—a fundamental precursor of deviant behavior—may ensue. Merton's (1968: 134) "central hypothesis is that aberrant behavior may be regarded sociologically as a symptom of dissociation between culturally prescribed aspirations and socially structured avenues for realizing these aspirations." Anomie is then defined as the dissociation between cultural goals and available means for attaining them.

Anomie is experienced as **strain,** stress, or tension that requires some form of adaptation. Merton outlines a typology of individual adaptations to the condition of anomie in society. This typology offers a means/goals schema for the understanding of individual adaptations to the experience of anomie.

Conformity is the most typical adaptation to a state of anomie. Most persons in society accept the institutionalized means to culturally approved goals. Educational attainment, pursuit of advancement in one's occupation or profession, and community involvement are accepted means to social status and economic rewards. *Innovation* involves the acceptance of the culturally approved goals, but a rejection of the institutionalized means to achieving them. Innovators are persons who devise deviant means to acceptable goals. They may engage in negative forms of deviant behavior—theft, drug dealing, cybercrime—or innovate in a positive way by creating a work of art or by inventing a labor saving device. *Ritualism* refers to the process of lowering one's expectations for success to a level that is readily attainable. Ritualists do not aspire to increasing career advance-

A Typology of Modes of Individual Adaptation

Modes of Adaptation	Culture Goals	Institutionalized Means
I. Conformity	+	+
II. Innovation	+	−
III. Ritualism	−	+
IV. Retreatism	−	−
V. Rebellion	±	±

Source: Robert K. Merton, 1957. *Social Theory and Social Structure.* New York: Free Press, p. 140.

ment and economic gain. Rather, they seek stable employment that provides good benefits and an adequate retirement plan. They avoid risk-taking ventures, seeking only to live within a highly predictable comfort zone. *Retreatism* characterizes persons who reject both the culturally approved goals and the institutionalized means for achieving them. Retreatists choose to withdraw from conventional society and adopt an alternative lifestyle. Illicit drug use and excessive use of alcohol are common among retreatists. Involvement in cults that foster mentally aberrant and self-destructive behaviors is also characteristic of retreatist lifestyles. Finally, *rebellion* marks the rejection of both the institutionalized means and culturally approved goals and the adoption of new means and new goals. Rebels seek to overturn the existing social order and replace it with a new social structure. This may involve the wholesale repudiation of an entire system of government or the establishment of a rebellious subculture within the larger society (Merton 1968: 141–157).

Unlike Robert Merton, **Richard Cloward** and **Lloyd Ohlin** (1961) do not assume an equal access to the means for engaging in delinquent behaviors. Their formulation of differential illegitimate opportunities outlines three subcultures with markedly different patterns of deviance. Each of the three *subcultures*—criminal, conflict or violent, and retreatist—provides its members with different opportunities for criminal activity. *Criminal subcultures* are characterized by opportunities for engaging in crimes of theft, drug dealing, and other forms of profitable illicit activities. Fences are available to convert stolen goods in cash, drug suppliers furnish street dealers with a variety of illicit drugs, while pimps organize the activities of prostitutes. Cloward and Ohlin point out, however, that "would-be offenders" must be accepted into the subculture by proving their criminal skills and ability to work well within the existing organization. *Violent subcultures* develop in areas in which opportunities to profitable criminal activities are not available. Participants in a violent subculture rely on their physical prowess to gain respect and status within the neighborhood. *Retreatist subcultures* are composed of members who do not have opportunities for involvement in a criminal subculture and typically lack the physical ability to gain respect by the use of force or intimidation. Use of mind-altering drugs, involvement in cult rituals, and other forms of oppositional behaviors are characteristic of a retreatist subculture.

More recently **Robert Agnew** (1992) has set forth a strain theory of deviant behavior, based in part on previous conceptions of anomie. To Agnew **strain** is experienced when aspirations and expectations are not consistently linked with their fulfillment. Typically, the source of strain is negative social interaction, involving blockage by others to the attainment of important needs and goals. Sustained negative social interactions precipitate negative emotions—anger, rage, feelings of worthlessness, and anxiety or depression—may follow. Attempts to alleviate these negative emotions may involve engagement in negative behaviors—verbal or physical aggression or self-injurious behaviors. Strain may also lead to more creative problem-solving strategies. Innovative ways to deal with difficult people may be developed, or alternative paths to goal attainment may be followed (Agnew 1992: 47–88).

Chicago School: Social Disorganization

W. I. Thomas and **Florian Znaniecki** (1918) were instrumental in the early formulation of the social disorganization perspective on crime and deviance. Their work on the immigration of polish peasants to Chicago and the subsequent involvement of their children in delinquent behaviors contributed to the development of social disorganization theory. Thomas and Znaniecki observed that the norms for behavior in rural Poland no longer provided adequate guidelines for the everyday life in the city. Competing norms and values created a disorganized existence for Polish adolescents. To Thomas and Znaniecki, **social disorganization** simply meant that the norms for behavior tended to be disregarded by the individual group members. The bonds that existed between the individual and the community in rural Poland were undermined. The Polish community was shattered, no longer able to arrive at a collective solution to their problems.

Clifford Shaw and **Henry McKay** (1969) were instrumental in advancing the social disorganization perspective on crime and deviance. Two questions guided the development of their theoretical formulation. The first is: Why are rates of delinquency markedly higher in some neighborhoods than in others? The second and related question is: Why do rates of delinquency remain high in certain neighborhoods even when there is a fundamental change in its ethnic and racial make-up? In addressing the first question on the differential rates of delinquency, Shaw and McKay drew on Park, Burgess, and McKenzie's (1928) Concentric Zone Model. These authors observed that five concentric zones characterized Chicago: Zone 1, the Central Business District was at the center of the city; Zone 2, the Transitional Zone—which housed newly arrived immigrants in deteriorating living conditions, near factories, and unused buildings; Zone 3, the Working Class Area—mostly single family housing units; Zone 4, Residential Neighborhoods—in which the middle class lived in single family homes; and Zone 5, the Commuter Zone—suburban areas that housed the more affluent member of society. Crime and deviance were more commonly found near the center of the city, particularly in Zone 2.

Shaw and McKay (1969) found that the transitional zone was characterized by: heterogeneity, poverty, and mobility. Heterogeneity refers to a mixture of racial, ethnic, religious, and cultural groups living in the same neighborhood. A sense of community is noticeably absent; persons in the neighborhood are largely strangers; and values and social norms vary considerably across cultural groups. Poverty is pervasive; marginal employment and reliance on welfare is endemic to the area. Mobility of residents is a common occurrence. Individuals and families move from one location to another with the area, or move into another part of the city. The continual shifting of the population tends to disrupt everyday life, and contributes to the sense of community disorganization and instability. Shaw and McKay argue that it is the interaction of heterogeneity, poverty, and mobility that produces highly disorganized areas. It is within disorganized social environments that crime and deviance becomes thrive.

Shaw and McKay propose a cultural transmission theory to explain the persistence of criminal and deviant patterns of behavior in certain neighborhoods, despite widespread changes in the demographic composition of the residents. Social disorganization is a characteristic of an ecological area—a community or a neighborhood, not necessarily of individuals who reside there. A "differential system of values" within socially disorganized areas may encourage and reward legally prohibited behaviors. Adolescents who move into a socially disorganized neighborhood are exposed to cultural values and social norms that are at odds with conventional society. To Shaw and McKay, **Cultural Transmission Theory** refers to the process by which a differential system of values that support delinquent behaviors are culturally "passed on" from adolescents currently living in the neighborhood to the more recent arrivals (Shaw and McKay 1969).

Marvin Wolfgang and **Franco Ferracuti** (1967) sought to explain why violent behaviors tend to be concentrated in certain areas of cities. They observed that most violent behaviors are not well planned, but rather are spontaneous acts often prompted by relatively trivial disputes. They advance a subculture of violence thesis to account for disparities in rates of violence and typical forms of violent offending. To Wolfgang and Ferracuti a subculture of violence is characterized norms and values that support the use of violence to resolve interpersonal conflicts. The willingness to resort to violence is learned, largely unwittingly, by observing everyday interactions in the home or among persons on the street. A violent response in a conflictual situation becomes normative—an expectation for behavior. Significant value is place on the ability to act immediately and aggressively to resolve disputes. Failure to do so may well result in widespread ridicule and social isolation.

Walter Miller (1958), an anthropologist, provides insight into the everyday life in a lower class subculture. He observes that six *focal concerns*—trouble, toughness, smartness, excitement, fate, and autonomy—organize the daily life of residents within the inner city. *Trouble* refers to the ongoing difficulties confronted by members of the lower class. Economic insecurity, social rejection, and blockage to needed legal and medical resources compound the problems inherent in the everyday life of the lower class. *Toughness* refers to the emphasis placed on physical prowess and the ability to handle oneself on the street. *Smartness* is translated as means "street-smarts"—the ability to manipulate or to outwit others to one's advantage. *Excitement* in a lower class milieu often involves risk-taking and illicit behaviors. The deadening routine of life on the street is broken by illicit drug use, violence, and theft. *Fate* refers to the belief that most events in life occur randomly, beyond one's ability to influence them. Immediate gratification and a live-for-the-moment mentality guide most decision making. Last, *autonomy* or the desire to act independent from the dictates of others predominates. Freedom of action is highly prized and vigorously pursued. The combined effects of these focal concerns of lower class life markedly increase the likelihood of involvement in criminal and other forms of deviant behavior.

Albert Cohen (1955) provides another explanation of the effects of social class and subcultural participation on delinquent behavior. He argues that two related concepts—status frustration and reaction formation—account for delinquency among lower class boys. Cohen observes that lower class boys often are unable to succeed in traditional schools—largely middle-class institutions that expect students to observe definite rules for behavior and decorum. Unable or unwilling to comply with the middle-class values of punctuality, politeness, regard for others' property, and safety, lower class boys are considered troublemakers, more apt to be disciplined for their behaviors, and excluded from school activities and participation in athletic programs. Unable to gain approval and recognition, lower class boys experience status frustration. To cope with their status frustration, Cohen argues, they develop a reaction formation to their circumstances. That is, they adopt values that are radically different from those of the middle class. Rather than being on time for school, they are typically late or absent; politeness gives way to loud, unruly behavior; and the property of the school and

Groups of adolescents who hang out in high crime areas are "of interest" to the police and often subject to street "stops" and "frisks."

Sykes and Matza's Techniques of Neutralization

- *Denial of Responsibility:* Involves the contention that the blame for one's deviant behavior lies with others who have victimized the offender or adverse living conditions.

- *Denial of Injury:* Refers to the assertion that victim was not actually harmed or could well afford any monetary loss that was incurred by committing the offense.

- *Denial of the Victim:* Means that any wrong-doing is actually justified on the grounds that the "victim" had been involved in previous injurious acts. Justice has then been served by the act of retribution against the original offender.

- *Condemnation of the Condemners:* Is the view that those who would judge the person as deviant are themselves guilty of far worse offenses. Therefore, any attempt to negatively label the person is without merit and should be disregarded.

- *Appeal to Higher Loyalties:* Means that the deviant rejects the argument of conventional society that he or she is obliged to abide by its laws and moral code. Rather, the offender's loyalties lie with an oppositional subculture or group that often expect the person to engage in criminal or deviant acts.

Source: Gresham M. Sykes and David Matza. 1957. "Techniques of Neutralization: A Theory of Delinquency," *American Sociological Review,* 22: 664–670.

that of other students is common prey for theft and destruction. In addition, lower class boys band together in gangs or subcultural groups to provide them with a sense of belonging, approval, recognition, and status denied to them by schools and other middle-class-oriented institutions.

Gresham Sykes and **David Matza** (1957) are less concerned with the social forces that precipitate deviant behavior and more interested in the response of offenders to their own actions. They assume that persons who engage in deviant behaviors suffer a sense of guilt for their behavior. Sykes and Matza want to know how the deviants resolve their feelings of guilt and maintain a positive self-image. They identify five techniques that may be used to justify a deviant act and absolve the offender's guilt. The **techniques of neutralization** are denial of responsibility, denial of injury, denial of the victim, condemnation of the condemners, and appeal to higher loyalties (Sykes and Matza 1957: 667–669).

Elijah Anderson's *Code of the Street* (1999), an ethnographic account of life on the streets of Philadelphia, provides considerable insight into the dynamics of survival in the inner city. Residents of the inner city are typically not able to rely on the police for protection or the legal system for assistance with resolving

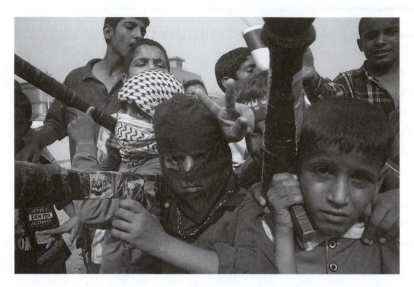

Middle Eastern children whose play anticipates their fighting to the death for the political causes of their homeland.

disputes. With little faith in law enforcement and the courts, they must rely on an alternative way to ensure their survival. A *Code of the Street* "emerges where the influence of the police ends and where personal responsibility for one's safety is felt to begin" (Anderson 1999: 34).

A key element of the *Code of the Street* is respect. Anderson (1999: 33) defines respect as "being treated 'right' or being granted one's 'props' (for proper due) or the deference one deserves." Survival depends on the ability to gain and maintain respect among other residents of the neighborhood. With respect comes protection from continually being challenged on the street, being provoked into proving one's worth. Those who have not gained respect from others in the neighborhood are subject to unprovoked attacks, both verbal and physical, by anyone who wants to gain personal respect. Respect is complex, often fragile commodity, difficult to establish and maintain, but once lost it is rarely regained.

Differential Association/Social Learning

The pioneering work of **Edwin Sutherland** (1947), widely regarded as the father of modern criminology, provides a foundation for theories of differential association and social learning. In addition, Sutherland's theory of **differential association** implies that the pre-existence of criminal subcultures is essential to the perpetuation of criminal and delinquent behaviors. The central hypothesis of differential association theory is that the greater the interaction with others who advocate the violation of the law, the greater the likelihood that the motives, rationalizations, and techniques for criminal offending will be learned and carried out.

Theoretical Formulations of Rates of Deviant Behavior

Theoretical Foundations

The Conflict Approach
    1. Marx (1844)   Class Conflict and the Law

Social Integration/Anomie
    1. Durkheim (1893)   The Normal and the Pathological
    2. Durkheim (1897)   Suicide

Chicago School: Social Disorganization   Cultural and Subcultural Understandings
    1. Thomas and Znaniecki (1918)   The Concept of Social Disorganization
    2. Shaw and McKay (1942)   Juvenile Delinquency in Urban Areas

Differential Association/Social Learning
    1. Sutherland (1947)   Differential Association

Early Developments

The Conflict Approach
    1. Sellin (1938)   Culture Conflict and Crime
    2. Turk (1969)   Crime and the Legal Order
    3. Quinney (1977)   Class, State, and Crime

Social Integration/Anomie
    1. Merton (1938)   Social Structure and Anomie
    2. Cloward and Ohlin (1961)   Delinquency and Opportunity

Chicago School: Social Disorganization   Cultural and Subcultural Understandings
    1. Cohen (1955)   Delinquent Boys
    2. Miller (1958)   Lower Class Culture
    3. Wolfgang and Farracuti (1967)   Subculture of Violence
    4. Sykes and Matza   Techniques of Neutralization

Differential Association/Social Learning
    1. Akers (1973)   Social Learning

Recent Advances

The Conflict Approach
    1. Hagan (1989)   Power-Control
    2. Daly and Chesney-Lind (1988)   Feminist Theory

Social Integration/Anomie
    1. Agnew (1992)   A General Strain Theory

Chicago School: Social Disorganization   Cultural and Subcultural Understandings
    1. Anderson (1999)   Oppositional Culture

Differential Association/Social Learning
    1. Akers (1998)   Social Learning and Social Structure

Elijah Anderson: On the Code of the Street

By the time they are teenagers, most young people have internalized the code of the street, or at least learned to comport themselves in accordance with its rules. . . . the code revolves around the presentation of self. Its basic requirement is the display of a certain predisposition to violence. A person's public bearing must send the unmistakable, if sometimes subtle, message that one is capable of violence, and possibly mayhem, when the situation requires it, that one can take care of oneself. The nature of this communication is determined largely by the demands of the circumstances but can involve facial expressions, gait, and direct talk—all geared mainly to deterring aggression. Physical appearance, including clothes, jewelry, and grooming, also plays an important part in how a person is viewed; to be respected it is vital to have the right look.

Even so, there are no guarantees against challenges, because there are always people around looking for a fight in order to increase their share of respect—or "juice," as it is sometimes called on the street. Moreover, if a person is assaulted, it is essential in the eyes of his "running buddies" as well as his opponents for him to avenge himself. Otherwise he risks being "tried" (challenged) or "rolled on" (physically assaulted) by any number of others. Indeed, if he is not careful, he can lose the respect of his running buddies or "homies" who can be depended on to watch his back in a "jam," the person is vulnerable to being rolled on by still others.

Source: Anderson, Elijah. 1999. *Code of the Street.* New York: W.W. Norton and Company, pp. 72–73.

Depiction of Charles Dickens' Oliver Twist and Fagin with other members of Fagin's band of pickpockets.

Sutherland's Nine Propositions of Differential Association

Edwin Sutherland (1947: 6–7) summarizes his theory of differential association in nine propositions:

1. Criminal behavior is learned.

2. Criminal behavior is learned in interaction with other persons in a process of communication.

3. The principal part of the learning of criminal behavior occurs within intimate personal groups.

4. When criminal behavior is learned, the learning includes (a) techniques of committing the crime, which are sometimes very complicated, sometimes very simple; and (b) the specific direction of motives, drives, rationalizations, and attitudes.

5. The specific direction of motives and drives is learned from definitions of the legal codes as favorable or unfavorable.

6. A person becomes delinquent because of an excess of definitions favorable to violation of law over definitions unfavorable to violation of law.

7. Differential associations may vary in frequency, duration, priority, and intensity.

8. The process of learning criminal behavior by association with criminal and anti-criminal patterns involves all of the mechanisms that are involved in any other learning.

9. While criminal behavior is an expression of general needs and values, it is not explained by those general needs and values since non-criminal behavior is an expression of the same needs and values.

To Sutherland (1947) criminal and deviant behaviors are learned in the same way as other forms of behavior are learned—from close personal association with others. The motive and rationalizations for committing the crime, along with the techniques for its successful execution, are learned from others who encourage criminal offending. The more individuals associate with others who advocate the violation of the law, and the more valued those associations become, the more likely they are to engage in criminal activities. Common need and values, Sutherland observes, do not explain criminal behaviors. The need for status, economic gain, or personal recognition and social influence may either lead to conventional behaviors or to illicit activities. Therefore, they do not provide an adequate explanation of the involvement in crime and delinquency.

Ronald Akers (1998) is largely responsible for the development of a social learning approach to the explanation of deviant behavior. His formulation of

Ronald Akers's Social Learning Approach to Deviance

Sociologist Ronald Akers (1998: 53–54) outlines the processes by which an individual is initiated into criminal or deviant behavior and either continues in or desists from that behavior. He argues that:

1. The balance of past and current associations, definitions, and imitation of deviant models, and the anticipated balance of reinforcement in particular situations, produces or inhibits the initial delinquent or deviant acts.

2. The effects of these variables continue in the repetition of the acts, although imitation becomes less important than it was in the first commission of the act.

3. After initiation, the actual social and nonsocial reinforcers and punishers affect the probability that the acts will be repeated and at what level of frequency.

4. Not only the overt behavior, but also the definitions favorable or unfavorable to it, are affected by the positive and negative consequences of the initial acts. To the extent that they are more rewarded than alternative behavior, the favorable definitions will be strengthened and the unfavorable definitions will be weakened, and it becomes more likely that the deviant behavior will be repeated under similar circumstances.

5. Progression into more frequent or sustained patterns, rather than cessation or reduction, of criminal and deviant behavior is promoted to the extent that reinforcement, exposure to deviant models, and norm-violating definitions are not offset by negative formal and informal sanctions and norm abiding definitions.

social learning considers both the motivation for engaging in deviant acts or conventional behaviors. To Akers, learning deviant or conforming behaviors involves four related processes: *differential association, definitions, differential reinforcement, and imitation.* Differential association means interaction with advocates of illicit activities more than with persons who encourage conformist behavior. Definitions refer to the meaning and value given to certain behaviors. Behaviors are not only delimited, but are judged to be good or bad, acceptable or unacceptable. Differential reinforcement means that behaviors for which a reward is granted or anticipated will be repeated. The greater the ratio of positive rewards to negative or neutral responses for engagement in a behavior, the more likely will the behavior continue. Imitation is the process by which individuals model admired behavior of others. These processes facilitate the learning process that accounts for both deviant and conventional behavior.

Chapter Summary

- This chapter considers macro-level theories from the conflict and functionalist perspectives.
  - Conflict theories are premised on the concept of structural inequality. Wealth and power are concentrated in the hands of the bourgeoise, who use their power to control and exploit the proletariat while manipulating the legal system and other social institutions to their advantage.
  - Functionalist theories focus on the purpose, usefulness, or contribution that a given social phenomenon makes to the social order.
- Sociological explanation of behavior discussed in this chapter include:
  - Conflict approach
  - Social integration
  - Chicago School of Thought: Social Disorganization, Culture, and Subcultural Understandings
  - Differential Association/Social Learning
- Karl Marx provided the foundations for the conflict approach. Other conflict theorists include:
  - Thorsten Sellin
  - Richard Quinney
  - Austin Turk
  - Alex Thio
- Advances in the conflict perspective include the power-control theory of John Hagan and the contributions of Kathleen Daly and Meda Chesney-Lind to the feminist understanding to the conflict approach.
- Emile Durkheim provides a foundation for the functionalist perspective and the theoretical development of the social integration/anomie approach. Notable theorists in the Durkheimian tradition are:
  - Robert K. Merton
  - Richard Cloward and Lloyd Ohlin
  - Robert Agnew
- The early work of W.I. Thomas and Florian Znaniecki, Clifford Shaw and Henry McKay, and others provide the basis for the perspective, sometimes referred to as the Chicago School of Thought. The development and more recent advances in the social disorganization theory are indebted to the contributions of:
  - Albert Cohen
  - Walter Miller
  - Marvin Wolfgang and Franco Ferracuti
  - Gresham Sykes and David Matza
  - Elijah Anderson
- Edwin Sutherland's differential association theory significantly influenced the formulation of social learning theory and the subcultural perspective. Ronald Akers is largely responsible for advancing a social learning approach to the understanding of crime and deviance. The recognition of

subcultural variations in the motivation to engage in deviant behaviors and the opportunities to do so run through the theoretical formulations of Albert Cohen, Richard Cloward and Lloyd Ohlin, Marvin Wolfgang and Franco Ferracuti, and more recently the ethnographic work of Elijah Anderson.

Key Names

Karl Marx	W. I. Thomas
Thorsten Sellin	Florian Znaniecki
Austin Turk	Clifford Shaw
Richard Quinney	Henry McKay
Alex Thio	Marvin Wolfgang
John Hagan	Franco Ferracuti
Kathleen Daly	Walter Miller
Meda Chesney-Lind	Albert Cohen
Emile Durkheim	Gresham Sykes
Robert K. Merton	David Matza
Richard Cloward	Elijah Anderson
Lloyd Ohlin	Edwin Sutherland
Robert Agnew	Ronald Akers

Key Concepts

Micro-level analysis: Focuses on social processes and personal characteristics that may account for an individual's involvement in criminal or deviant behavior.

Macro-level analysis: Considers the ways in which structural and cultural characteristics of social collectivities—societies, subcultures, social groupings—affect crime rates and acts of social deviance.

Feminist perspective: Theoretical perspective on crime and deviance that calls attention to the gender-bias in theorizing and research.

Functional perspective: Sociological perspective that focuses on the purpose, usefulness, or contribution that a given social phenomenon makes to the social order.

Manifest functions: Intended consequences of a social action that are recognized by participants in the social system and that benefit a given system.

Latent functions: Consequences of a social action neither intended nor recognized by the participants in the social system, but that benefit the system.

Dysfunctions: Consequences of a social action that lessen the adaptation or adjustment of a given social system.

Social integration: The extent to which persons are bound into social life or alternatively isolated from it.

Anomie: Normlessness; the dissociation between cultural goals and available means for attaining goals.

Strain: Stress experiences when aspirations and expectations are not consistently linked with fulfillment.

Social disorganization: Decrease of the influence of existing social rules of behavior upon individual members of the group, or the inability of local communities to realize the common values of their residents or solve commonly experienced problems.

Cultural Transmission Theory: Process by which traditions of delinquency are transmitted through successive generations.

Techniques of neutralization: Techniques used to justify a deviant act and absolve the offender's guilt.

Differential association: Term proposed by Edwin Sutherland to describe how individuals socially learn to commit criminal and deviant behavior. Also used by Ronald Akers.

Critical Thinking Questions

1. Rates of deviant behaviors in any given population or subgroup tend to be relatively low. For example, approximately 4 in 100 persons in the general population are involved in a major criminal incident in the United States in a given year. How do theories that explain rates of behavior account for the vast majority of persons who are not involved in criminal or other deviant behaviors?

2. How do social structural arrangements affect social processes that, in turn, account for variations in rates of deviant behaviors?

3. What social and political influences affect the development of theories that explain rates of deviant behaviors? How does the sociopolitical climate shape scientific inquiry into deviant behaviors?

4. What assumptions about society underlie the conflict, functionalist, social disorganization, differential association, and social learning theoretical perspectives?

CHAPTER 4

Homicide

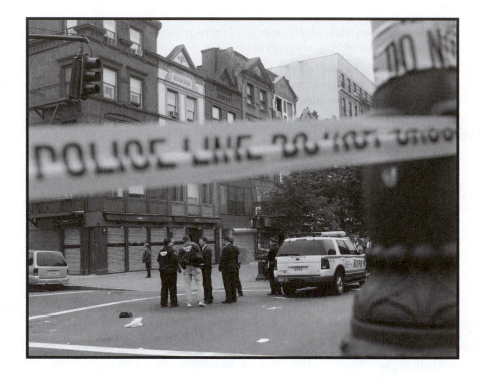

PORTRAITS

of Homicide

- Dr. Harold Shipman, a highly respected 54-year-old general practitioner, shocked his neighbors when he was convicted of murdering fifteen elderly women patients. Shipman injected his patients with lethal doses of morphine, then altered medical records and fabricated diseases that could have caused the suspicious deaths. To insure his cover-up of the deaths, he signed cremation orders for many of his deceased patients. Shipman's past was uncovered by investigators after the daughter of his last victim became suspicious that he was named the sole beneficiary of her mother's $620,000 estate. Because most of his victims were cremated, investigators are unsure of the extent of his murders, but suspect that the number could be as high as 150 victims. (*Source: Fox, J. A. and J. Levin. The Will to Kill: Making Sense of Senseless Murder.* Boston: Allyn and Bacon, 2001, p. 12.)

- A national audience watched as Susan Smith told of the alleged car theft and kidnapping of her two sons, Michael and Alex. Susan reported to police that while stopped at a traffic light a black man ordered her out of her car and drove away with her children in the back seat. Susan took a polygraph test and within days confessed to police that she rolled her car in a nearby lake with Michael and Alex strapped in their car seats. According to Susan, she killed her children because her new boyfriend would not stay with her because he did not want children. (*Source: Fox, J. A. and J. Levin. The Will to Kill: Making Sense of Senseless Murder.* Boston: Allyn and Bacon, 2001, p. 69.)

- David and Diane, high school sweethearts, were popular students and athletes with aspirations of becoming military academy cadets. When David confessed to Diane about his sexual relationship with another female student, Diane became jealous and insisted that David kill the other girl. The two conspired to beat and shoot her and vowed to keep their actions secret. After going to the military academy, Diane admitted her involvement to her roommates. Both Diane and David were arrested for the murder. (*Source: James Alan Fox and Jack Levin, The Will to Kill: Making Sense of Senseless Murder.* Boston: Allyn and Bacon, 2001, p. 59.)

LEARNING OBJECTIVES

After reading this chapter you should know:

- ☐ The types and definitions of homicide, assault and battery.
- ☐ Trends and patterns of homicide in the United States.
- ☐ Age, gender, and race patterns of homicide in the United States.
- ☐ Patterns of homicide among special populations.
- ☐ Risk factors for workplace violence.
- ☐ The stages of Luckenbill's homicide as a situated transaction.
- ☐ The definition of victim-precipitated homicide.

Introduction

In this chapter we will consider two forms of interpersonal violence: criminal homicide, and assault and battery. These two acts of violence are known legally as crimes against the person, ranging from the intentional killing of another human being to the intent to do bodily harm.

Definition of Criminal Homicide

In general, **criminal homicide** is the intentional killing of one human being by another without justification or excuse. **Justifiable homicides** include a court-ordered execution of a convicted offender or the killing of an enemy by a member of the military in the line of duty. **Excusable homicides** typically involve the accidental or non-negligent killing of another human being. There is no intention to kill, nor is there evidence of wrongful or flagrant carelessness on the part of the person who caused the death (Schmalleger 2002).

Those homicides that are not justifiable or excusable involve the intention of the perpetrator to place another human being in danger of bodily harm or death. Criminal homicide is legally separated into two forms: **murder** and **manslaughter.** Both murder and manslaughter are further divided into first and second degrees of seriousness. Two considerations serve to distinguish the levels of seriousness: premeditation and provocation. **Premeditation** refers to the "act of deliberating or meditating upon, or planning, a course of action" (Schmalleger 2002: 262). Two closely related legal concepts are malice and malice aforethought. **Malice** legally means the "intentional doing of a wrongful act without just cause or legal excuse" (Schmalleger 2002: 262). **Malice aforethought** means "an unjustifiable, inexcusable, and unmitigated person-endangering-state-of-mind" (Schmalleger 2002: 263). Both premeditation and malice aforethought imply a time lapse between the formation of the idea to kill in the mind of the offender and the actual carrying out of the murder. During the time lapse the perpetrator is able to make plans, to secure a weapon or strategy for killing the intended victim, and to deliberate on the final decision to carry out the killing. Typically, homicides that involve poisoning, lying in wait, and torture are considered first-degree cases.

The provocation of the victim is an important consideration when determining the degree of criminal liability in a murder case. **Provocation** of the victim may either be verbal, physical, or both and implies the active involvement of the victim in the lethal encounter. The victim may well have been the first one to use physical force against his or her killer (See Wolfgang's Victim-Precipitated Homicide

> *Is it hard for the reader to believe that suicides are sometimes committed to forestall the committing of murder? There is no doubt of it. Nor is there any doubt that murder is sometimes committed to avert suicide.*
>
> —Karl Menninger (posted at www.bartleby.com/63/14/2014.html)

> *A key element in the "Code of the Street" is respect— "being treated 'right' or being granted one's 'props' (or proper due) or the deference one deserves."*
>
> —Elijah Anderson (1995: 33)

considered later in this chapter). Or the victim may have verbally taunted the offender, thereby contributing to the fatal attack. Murder in the second degree is, in part, distinguished from murder in the first degree by the extent of the victim's provocation.

Similarly, manslaughter involves less premeditation or malice aforethought on the part of the offender and greater victim provocation than either murder in the first or second degree. Again, manslaughter is divided into first and second degree. In some jurisdictions, the degrees of manslaughter are known as voluntary or involuntary manslaughter or non-negligent or negligent manslaughter. The most serious form of manslaughter involves some degree of intention on the part of the offender to harm the victim. The assault, however, is typically carried out in a spontaneous act of violence, with little time for deliberation. Street fights or barroom brawls are typical examples of first-degree manslaughter. In many instances the eventual offender could easily have been the victim. Fatal encounters that erupt in the passion of the moment and involve considerable provocation—by the victim and/or offender—are legally processed as first-degree manslaughter cases.

Second-degree manslaughters, however, do not involve the intention to kill or to harm the victim, but result from the negligent actions of the offender. A person who is intoxicated or who is operating a motor vehicle illegally (e.g., speeding, carelessly or recklessly) and who causes the death of another may be held liable for second-degree manslaughter. Intentionality and provocation are not at issue in cases of second-degree manslaughter. Rather, the central consideration is the negligent or illicit behavior of the offender.

Definitions of Assault and Battery

Much confusion exists with regard to the meanings of the crimes of assault and battery. While the two crimes are related, each must be understood as distinct offenses. **Assault** may take either of two forms: (1) an attempt to commit bodily injury to another human being or (2) putting another in fear of imminent bodily injury. The crime of assault implies the present ability to carry out the assault—that is, the assailant must be in the presence of the intended victim. For example, an assault cannot be committed on the telephone or by threatening someone by email. In addition, the assailant must be physically able to carry out the intended injury. The harm to the victim, however, need not involve a serious injury. The crime of assault may occur simply by attempting to touch someone in an offensive way (Schmalleger 2002: 291).

Battery refers to the actual offensive touching or unwanted physical contact between the assailant and victim. The contact need not result in a physical injury to be considered a battery, simply the lack of consent of the victim to be touched is sufficient. Often the crimes of assault and battery are linked to refer to an offense that involves the actual physical injury of the victim. The most serious form of assault and battery is aggravated assault. **Aggravated assault** refers to "an assault which is committed with the intention of committing an additional crime, such as assault with intent to commit a felony; assault with intent to commit murder; assault with intent to commit rape, sodomy, mayhem, robbery, or grand larceny; and assault with intent to commit any other felony" (Schmalleger 1999: 293). Dangerous weapons, (e.g., firearms, knives, clubs) or objects that can be used as dangerous weapons, (e.g., rocks or bricks, ropes, belts, or clothing apparel) are typically involved in an aggravated assault. An abbreviation commonly used by law enforcement officers when booking an alleged offender for aggravated assault is: **ABWDWWITKRSBI**—**A**ssault and **B**attery **W**ith a **D**eadly **W**eapon **W**ith **I**ntent to **K**ill **R**esulting in **S**erious **B**odily **I**njury. This reflects the essential elements of the crime of aggravated assault and serves to distinguish it from the lesser forms of assault and battery.

Homicide around the World

Given the publicity that surrounds violence in U.S. society, it is often thought that the United States has the highest murder rate in the world. However, most recent data on homicide rates around the world show that homicide rates in seven nations exceed that of the United States. South Africa's homicide rate (75.3) is the highest in the world, followed by Colombia (64.6), Estonia (28.2), Brazil (19.0), Mexico (17.6), Philippines (16.2), and Taiwan (8.1). The U.S. rate (6.8) is similar to North Ireland's rate of (6.2), but approximately one-tenth that of South Africa and Colombia. The lowest rates of homicide across the globe are found in Ireland and Japan both with a rate of (0.62), Spain (0.95), Norway (0.97), Kuwait (1.01), and the Netherlands (1.11) (United Nations, Demographic Yearbook 2001).

The United States, however, does have the highest rate of gun-related homicides in the world. In a recent study of gun-related deaths, suicides, and accidents, the Centers for Disease Control and Prevention reports that of the thirty-six richest nations, the gun-related homicide rate in the United States (14.24) is five to six times higher than in Europe or Australia and New Zealand and 95 times higher than in Asia (Carter 1998). Put another way, in a recent year 45 percent of the gun-related deaths in the thirty-six richest nations in the world occurred in the United States. Other nations with high firearm homicides are Brazil (12.9), Mexico (12.7), and Estonia (12.3). Nations in the Far East and British Isles with the lowest rates include Japan (.05), South Korea (.12), Hong Kong (.14), Mauritius (.19), Singapore (.21), England and Wales (.41), and Scotland (.54) (Krug et al. 1998).

Patterns and Trends in Criminal Homicide

Over the past half century the homicide rate in the United States has varied widely, from rates below 5 per 100,000 persons in the general population in the 1950s to rates of about 10 in the beginning of the 1980s and at the end of that decade, and again in the early 1990s. More recently, there has been a decline in the homicide rate in the United States. The homicide rates at the turn of the century are similar to homicide rates in the 1960s. The sharp fall in homicide rates that began in the mid-1990s extended through the end of the twentieth century. However, at the beginning of the new millennium an increase in the homicide rate, particularly in urban areas, was evident (Fox and Zawitz 2004).

Homicide Rates by Size of Place

Homicide rates vary widely among urban, suburban, small cities, and rural areas. Homicide is disproportionately committed in large urban areas. Rural areas, small cities, and suburban areas have rates well below half of those found in urban places. Cities of 100,000 residents or more account for one-half of all the homicides committed in the United States; one-quarter of the homicides occurred in cities with a million residents or more. Therefore, when homicide rates decline in larger urban places, the rate for the country as a whole falls sharply (Fox and Zawitz 2004).

Structural Characteristics
of Criminal Homicide

Homicide is structured by the age, gender, and race of the offender and the victim. That is, the probability of killing someone or being killed is influenced by these basic structural characteristics of the individual. We will consider the patterns of homicide by age, gender and race separately, then discuss their combined effects (Fox and Zawitz 2004).

Age

Persons aged 18 through 24 are most likely to commit homicide or to be a victim of homicide. Persons at the extremes of the age spectrum—those 50 years of age or older or 14 and younger—are the least likely to murder or to be murdered. Recently, the age patterns of offending and victimization are remarkably similar. However, there has been a marked decline in the age of homicide offender, resulting in similar patterns of adolescent (14 to 17 years old) offending and adults 25–34 years old. The probability of committing homicide beyond the age of 35 falls sharply. However, the victimization of persons in the 35 to 49 age range is strikingly similar to that of adolescents aged 14 to 17.

Gender

Males are far more likely to commit homicide or to be a victim of homicide than are females. Males typically commit about 9 in every 10 homicides in the United States and account for about 3 of every 4 of its victims. Most recent data show that males are nine times more likely to commit murder and 3.2 times to be murdered than are females.

The predominate gender pattern is male-on-male homicide, while female-on-female murder is least likely to occur. About 2 of every 3 homicides involves a male offender and a male victim, slightly more than 1 in 5 involve a male offender and a female victim, 1 in 10 a female offender and male victim, and only 2.4 times in every 100 homicides will a female kill another female. Compared to men, women are more likely to be killed by an intimate partner or in a sex related offense.

A young African-American man, the victim of multiple gunshots, struggling for his life in an over-worked hospital emergency room.

Race

Blacks in the United States are seven times more likely to commit murder and six times more likely to be murdered than are whites. Criminal homicide is predominately intraracial. Black offenders are responsible for 94 percent of the homicidal deaths of black victims, and white offenders are responsible for 86 percent of white homicide victims. Drug-related conflicts resulting in homicide are far more common among blacks (66%) than whites (32%), as are felony-murders (59% vs. 39%), gun-related homicides (55% vs. 44%), and arguments (52% vs. 46%).

Age, Gender, and Race

As is evident from the foregoing discussion, black males are at greatest risk of committing homicide and of being victimized by homicide. Black males between the ages 18 through 24 have the highest rates of homicide offending, followed by black males aged 14 to 17, and black males who are 25 years of age or older. Homicide victimization is also highest among black males aged 18 to 24, followed by black males 25 years of age and older, and those aged 14 to 17. Homicide victimization and perpetration is next highest among white males.

As we have seen, homicide is far less common among females. Rates of offending and victimization, however, are markedly higher among black than white females. For both black and white females the highest rates of offending and victimization are for those 18 through 24 years of age, followed by the age categories 25 and older and 14 to 17. In sum, criminal homicide is essentially an intraracial event, disproportionally involving black Americans as both victims and offenders.

Special Populations

Native Americans

Native American and Alaska Native populations constitute a diverse and fragmented array of cultures and traditions. The U.S. Bureau of Indian Affairs recognizes 330 American Indian tribes and 226 Alaska Native villages with a combined total population of approximately 2 million residents. Overall, Native Americans are the targets of acts of violence twice as often as all other residents of the United States. Recent reports show that 124 of every 1,000 Native Americans are victims of nonlethal violent crimes, including assault, rape/sexual assault, and robbery. The corresponding violent victimization rates for blacks (61), whites (49), and Asians (29) are considerably less (Greenfield and Smith 1999).

Age disparity marks much of violent victimization. One-third of all violent attacks on Native Americans are directed toward those aged 18 to 24. One in four Native Americans in this age group are victims of violence in a given year, making it the age group with the highest rate of violent victimization in the United States. Rates of violence are higher for both male and female Native Americans than for their counterparts of other races. For example, Native American women are victims of violence 50 percent more often than are black males (Greenfield and Smith 1999: 38).

Native Americans also exhibit unique patterns of victim–offender relations, use of weapons, and alcohol involvement. Interracial homicide predominates among Native Americans. When Native Americans are murdered, 4 in 10 times the offense is committed by someone of a different race than the offender, 3 in 10 times the offender is white, and 1 in 10 times the offender is black. Similarly, when a Native American is assaulted, about 7 in 10 times the offender is a non-Native American. This pattern of victimization is similar to Asians (68%), but markedly different from blacks (19%) or whites (31%) in the United States (Greenfield and Smith 1999: 38).

Native Americans fall prey to aggravated assault and simple assault far more often than blacks, whites, or Asians. For every Asian who is a victim of aggravated assault, there are almost six Native Americans for every white victim,

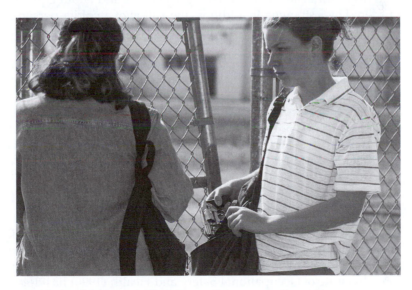

A young woman is about to complete a casual gun buy.

there are almost four Native American victims, and for every black, there are more than two Native American victims. Racial patterns for simple assault are similar. Native Americans are almost five times more likely to be victims of simple assaults than are Asians, and over two times more than whites and blacks (Greenfield and Smith 1999: 21).

Elderly

The elderly are far less likely to be involved in criminal activity either as an offender or victim than are younger persons. Persons over the age of 65 are twelve times less likely to be seriously assaulted than are younger persons. About 1 in 20 homicides claims the life of an elderly person; about 1 in 40 involves an elderly offender. The homicide victimization rate for persons over 65 is 3 per 100,000 persons in this age category, compared to 15 for persons between the ages of 12 and 24, and 11 for those between the ages of 25 and 49 (Klaus 2000).

As with younger persons, the risks of homicide victimization vary widely by gender and race. The rate of homicide victimization is twice as high for older males (4 per 100,000) compared to 2 per 100,000 for females. Older black homicide victimization rates (12 per 100,000) are six times higher than that of older whites, and four times higher than other racial groups combined (Klaus 2000).

However, the elderly are considerably more likely to be killed during the commission of another felony (e.g., robbery, burglary, or larceny) than are younger homicide victims. Up to the age of 50, about 1 in 4 intentional and unjustifiable killings are classified as felony-murders. Between the ages of 50 and 70, felony-murders constitute between 25 and 50 percent of elderly homicidal deaths, and between 50 and 75 percent after the age of 70 (Fox and Zawitz 2004).

Persons over the age of 65 are about twice as likely to be murdered by their relatives or intimates than are younger persons and about equally as likely to be murdered by a stranger. In addition, the killing of an older person is less than half as likely to involve a firearm compared to younger persons (36% vs. 73%) (Klaus 2000: 16).

Patterns of nonfatal forms of violence reflect those of criminal homicide. Among the elderly, higher risks of victimization are found among blacks than whites, males than females, and the divorced or separated than the married or widowed. More specifically, for every 1,000 black males in the general population 15 are victims of a nonfatal form of violence, compared to 6 for white men, 7 for black women, and 4 for white women. And, there are 14 victims of a nonfatal violent attack for every 1,000 elderly persons who are divorced or separated, compared to a rate of 4 for the married or widowed (Klaus 2000: 11).

Workplace Violence

Considerable media attention is given to mass killings in the workplace, and the risk of victimization on the job concerns persons across the country. Each year in the United States two million job-related acts of violence are committed. The National Institute of Occupational Safety and Health (1996) has determined ten risk factors for physical violence in the workplace (see Table 4.1).

Table 4.1 Risk Factors for Physical Violence in the Workplace

---

1. Contact with the public
2. Exchange of money
3. Delivery of passengers, goods, or services
4. Having a mobile workplace such as a taxicab or police cruiser
5. Working with unstable or volatile persons in health, social services, or criminal justice settings
6. Working alone or in small numbers
7. Working late at night or during early morning hours
8. Working in high-crime areas
9. Guarding valuable property or possessions
10. Working in community-based settings

Source: National Institute of Occupational Safety and Health. 1996. *Violence in the Workplace: Risk Factors and Prevention Strategies.* Current Intelligence Bulletin 57. Washington, DC: Author.

The age, race, and gender characteristics of victims and offenders involved in nonfatal workplace violence are markedly similar. Both victims and offenders are predominately male, white, and older. Males constitute 67 percent of the victims and 83 percent of the offenders; 89 percent of the victims and 58 percent of the offenders are white, 29 percent are black (National Institute of Occupational Safety and Health 1996). As shown in Table 4.2, law enforcement officers experience the highest rate of nonlethal violent victimization on the job.

While the vast majority of 1.5 million annual incidence of workplace violence involves simple assault, the most recent data indicate that there are about 396,000 aggravated assaults and 1,000 homicides. Homicide has emerged as the second leading cause of death on the job. Certain occupations increase the risk for victimization in the workplace. Robbery is the primary motive in 7 in 10 of the workplace homicides, making taxicab drivers, with the highest rate of workplace homicide (41.4 per 100,000), particularly vulnerable (Warchol 1999: 5).

Intimate Partner Violence

As we have seen, women are far less likely to be victims of homicide than are men. However, women are decidedly more likely to be victimized by an intimate partner than are men. There are more than 1,800 intimate partner homicides in the United States each year, about 1 of every 9 homicides overall. The rate of intimate partner homicide is relatively low, and declining. Wide gender disparities are, however, evident—the rate of victimization for intimate partner homicide for women (1.2 per 100,000) is about 2.4 times higher than that for men (0.5 per 100,000 for men) (Rennison and Welchans 2000).

Table 4.2   Occupational Risk for Nonlethal Violent Victimization

Occupation	Rate per 1,000 population
Law enforcement officers	306
Private security guards	218
Taxi drivers	184
Prison guards	117
Bartenders	91
Mental health professionals	80
Gas station attendants	79
Liquor store clerks	68
Mental health custodial workers	63
Junior high/middle school teachers	57
Bus drivers	45
Special education teachers	41
High school teachers	29
Elementary school teachers	16
College teachers	3

Source: Warchol, G. (1999) *Bureau of Justice Statistics Special Report: Workplace Violence.* Occupational Safety & Health Administration, U.S. Department of Labor.

Intimate partner homicide is most often committed by a spouse, girlfriend, or boyfriend, and least likely by an ex-spouse. Of all women who are killed each year in the United States, about one-third are killed by an intimate partner—usually a spouse—compared to 4 percent of men who are victimized by their spouse. Women are the victims in 3 of every 4 intimate partner homicides. White women are the most frequent targets for intimate partner homicide, followed by black women, white males, and black males (Rennison and Welchans 2000).

Both intimate partner homicide and nonlethal forms of intimate partner violence have been on the decline in recent years. Yet there are about one million incidents of violent crime each year in the United States committed by intimate partners—spouses, ex-spouses, or boyfriends. Black women are the victims of intimate partner violence about 35 percent more often than white women and 250 percent more than women of all other races. Similarly, black men are the targets of intimate partner violence 62 percent more often than white men and 250 percent more often than men of other races. Young women—aged 20 to 24—are at greatest risk to be assaulted by an intimate partner. Their rate of 21 per 1,000 is seven times higher than the highest rate for men aged 25 to 34 (3 per 1,000). The highest rates of victimization for both women and men are also found among the divorced, separated, and never married. With a rate of victimization over 30 per

AT A GLANCE

Global Patterns and Trends

- Countries with the highest murder rates: (victims per 100,000 persons per year)
  - South Africa   75.3
  - Columbia   64.6
  - Estonia   28.2
  - Brazil   19.0
  - Mexico   17.6
  - Philippines   16.2
  - Taiwan   8.1
- Countries with the lowest murder rates:
  - Japan   0.62
  - Ireland   0.62
  - Spain   0.95
  - Norway   0.97
  - Kuwait   1.01
  - Netherlands   1.11

U.S. Patterns and Trends

- The southern region of the United States has higher rates of homicide and assault and battery than other sectors of the country. More recently, high rates of violent crime are found in the Western states. Relatively low rates exist in the New England, Mountain, and West North Central regions.
- Homicide and assault and battery victimization and offending rates are highest in larger cities with populations above 500,000. Rural areas have the lowest rates of violent crime.
- Minorites—African Americans, Native Americans, and Hispanics—are disproportionately represented among victims and offenders of homicide and assault and battery. For example, African Americans are seven times more likely than whites to be murdered and eight times more likely than whites to commit homicide.
- Homicide and assault and battery typically involve male offenders and male victims.
- Violent crime victimization and offending varies across the age spectrum. The rates increase through the teenage years, crest in the early twenties, and steadily decrease through the remaining years. With few exceptions, this pattern exists for all race, sex, and ethnic groups.

Sources: Bureau of Justice Statistics. 1994. U.S. Department of Justice, Uniform Crime Report, International Comparisons.

1,000, divorced or separated women are six times more likely to be victimized than are their male counterparts (Rennison and Welchans 2000).

In addition, the lower the household income, the greater the risk of intimate partner violence. Women who live in households with the lowest income have the highest rates of victimization (20 per 1,000)—about seven times higher than women from the wealthiest households (3 per 1,000). Related to household income is ability to own a home. Again, the risk of victimization is considerably higher among women and men who live in rental properties. Women who live in rental housing are three times more likely (and men twice as likely) to be assaulted by an intimate partner than are their counterparts who reside in their own homes. Urban women also have higher rates of victimization (9.5 per 1,000) than women who live in the suburbs (7.8) or rural areas (8.1). Little variation is found in the victimization rates of men by size of place (Rennison and Welchans 2000).

In sum, the Bureau of Justice Statistics reports that:

> Among women, black, young, divorced or separated, earning lower incomes, living in rental housing, and living in an urban area were all associated with higher rates of intimate partner victimization. . . . Men who were young, black, divorced or separated, or living in rented housing had significantly higher rates of intimate partner violence than other men (Rennison and Welchans 2000: 3).

Children and Adolescents

More than 2,000 children and adolescents are murdered in the United States each year. With a rate of 3.0 per 100,000 for persons under the age of 18, the United States ranks first among developed nations in child and adolescent homicide (Snyder and Sickmund 1999). Excluding the victimization of infants, children and adolescents are twice as likely to be murdered in the United States than in the developed nation with the next highest child homicide rate, and five times more likely to murdered than in the other twenty-five developed countries combined. Over the later third of the twentieth century, all causes of death of children have declined, except homicide (World Health Organization 1995).

Within the United States, child and adolescent homicides are concentrated in certain geographic areas. Most recently, childhood homicide victimization occurred in only 471 of the nation's 3,141 counties across the nation. That is, 85 percent of the counties in the United States did not have a single child murder, and 8 percent had only one child victim. Child homicide victimization is also disproportionately found in certain major urban areas. One in four childhood homicides are carried out in five urban areas: Los Angeles, Chicago, New York, Philadelphia, and Detroit. Washington DC, for example, had a child homicide rate nine times higher than that for the nation as a whole (Snyder and Sickmund 1999).

Childhood homicide also varies widely by the victim's race, age, and gender. Minority children are the most vulnerable to being murdered. Black children, with a rate of 9.1, are the most apt to being victimized; the rate of Hispanic children (5.0) is next, and white children, with a rate of 1.8, are the least likely to be murdered. Death by homicide in the United States has emerged as one of the five leading causes of death for children, and the second leading cause of death for teenagers. Homicide ranks as the fourth leading cause of death for children aged 1 to 4, third for those aged 5 to 14, and second for those aged 15 to 24. Below the age of 4, infants have the highest rate of victimization. There is a steady decline to the age of 4 when the rate remains very low and stable until the age of 13, when it rises sharply for male adolescents and increases for females, but far less dramatically. In sum, adolescents (12 to 17 years of age) have the highest rate of victimization, followed by very young children (0 to 5 years of age), and children in the middle years (6 to 11) (Snyder and Sickmund 1999: 16).

About 1 in 9 homicide victims in the United States is 17 years of age or younger, 7 in every 10 are male, and 47 percent are black. A firearm is used 56 percent of the time, making it the most usual weapon involved in youth homicide. Victims most often know their perpetrators: 40 percent are family members, 45 percent are acquaintances, and 15 percent are strangers (Finkelhor 1997; Finkelhor and Ormrod 2001a).

Early Childhood. There are distinct differences in homicide victim–offender relations found in early childhood, in the middle years, and in adolescence. The rate of early childhood homicide victimization is 2.6 per 100,000. Boys are somewhat more likely to be killed than are girls (54 vs. 46 percent); but males are considerably more likely than females to be offenders (58 vs. 42 percent). However, when the victim is an infant in the first six days of life, two-thirds of the time the homicide offender is the mother.

Family members kill young children more than 7 in 10 times, usually by battering them with their hands or feet, strangling or suffocating them. Children under the age of 1 are particularly vulnerable to suffocation (Finkelhor 1997; Finkelhor and Ormrod 2001a).

Middle Childhood. Rates of homicide victimization in the middle childhood years (6 to 11) are the lowest of any age group in the United States (0.6 compared to 2.2 for persons 65 and over). Family members commit about 6 in 10 of these murders, half the time with a gun. Half the offenders are over the age of 30, and 1 in 8 are unknown to the victim. A variety of circumstances surround the murder of children in the middle years, including acts of pedophilia, gang murders, negligent homicide by persons playing with guns, and felony-murders (Finkelhor 1997; Finkelhor and Ormrod 2001a).

The Adolescent Years. In the adolescent years, homicide increases dramatically and is markedly different from the victimization of younger persons. Homicide in the teen years is 10 percent higher than for persons at any other age. Patterns of victimization among teens tend to resemble those of adults. About 8 in 10 of the victims and 95 percent of the offenders are male, 86 percent of the homicides are committed with a firearm, but only 1 in 11 involves a family member as the offender. Other teens or young adults are responsible for killing 2 of every 3 adolescents in the United States (Finkelhor 1997; Finkelhor and Ormrod 2001a).

Juvenile Offenders. Juveniles are more likely to commit homicide with other persons than are older offenders. In a given year, about 1,400 homicides are attributed to juvenile offenders in the United States; 1,700 juveniles and 900 adults are involved in these offenses. That is, about 31 percent of the time when a juvenile commits homicide, an adult is involved. Older juvenile offenders have a greater tendency to commit homicide in the company of an adult than do those offenders in the pre- or early teen years (Snyder and Sickmund 1999).

About 93 percent of juveniles who commit homicide are male, 56 percent are black, and 88 percent are between 15 and 17 years of age. Marked gender and age differences in the choice of victims are also found. Male juvenile homicide offenders are most apt to kill an acquaintance (54 percent) or a stranger (37 percent) and least likely to kill a family member (9 percent). Female juvenile homicide offenders, however, are most likely to kill within the family (39 percent) and least likely to victimize a stranger (15 percent). Female offenders are also far more likely to kill a young child (18 percent), compared to male offenders who victimize children under the age of 6 only 1 percent of the time (Snyder and Sickmund 1999).

Teenage male homicide offenders are more likely to use a firearm (73 percent) in the act of homicide than are females (41 percent). Young female offenders are twice as likely (27 percent) to resort to the use of their hands or feet to batter their victims, or to suffocate, drown, or burn them as compared to their male counterparts (13 percent). In addition, they kill their victims with a knife more than twice as often (32 percent) as young male offenders (14 percent) (Snyder and Sickmund 1999).

Minority youth are disproportionately involved in juvenile homicide offending. The homicide offense rate for black youth is about 194, for Asian/Pacific Islanders 44, for Native Americans 34, and whites 30. Gun-related homicides are also more common among young black offenders (72 percent), compared to 67 percent for Asians/Pacific Islanders, 59 percent for whites, and 48 percent for Native Americans (Snyder and Sickmund 1999).

While most juvenile homicide offending is intraracial, there is nonetheless considerable variation across racial and ethnic categories. Overall, more than 8 in 10 of the juvenile homicides involve offenders and victims of the same race or ethnic group. About 9 in 10 times young white offenders victimize another white, 76 percent of the time a black offender will choose a black victim, and 58 percent of Asian/Pacific Islander offenders and 48 percent of Native American offenders commit intraracial homicide (Synder and Sickmund 1999).

Assault and Battery of Children. Analyses of the National Crime Victimization Survey and other data on the criminal victimization of children by David Finkelhor, Director of the Crimes Against Children Research Center at the University of New Hampshire, and his colleagues (Finkelhor and Ormrod 2000b) reveal several striking findings. With the exception of criminal homicide, juveniles (aged 12 to 17) are more than twice as likely to be victimized by crime than adults. The rate of violent victimization for juveniles (92 per 1,000) is 2.9 times higher than the adult rate of 32. One in four victims of a violent act (other than homicide) is a juvenile. Juveniles are also more likely to be assaulted with a weapon (22.9 per 1,000) than are adults (9.0 per 1,000), more likely to sustain an injury (27.1 per 1,000) than adults (8.9 per 1,000), but less likely to have the crime reported to the police. Only 28 percent of the violent crimes committed against juveniles are reported to the police compared to 48 percent for adults (Snyder and Sickmund 1999).

Homicide as a Situated Transaction

In many cases a conflict between two persons begins with verbal taunts, accusations, or threats and escalates into battery, serious injury, or death. David Luckenbill (1977) views this process as a *situated transaction* in which either person may ultimately become the victim or the offender. Luckenbill describes a six-stage process that ends in homicidal death. In the first stage, the eventual offender perceives the victim's actions or verbal communication to be offensive or to compromise his or her sense of respect from important others. In the offender's view the behavior of the victim is intended to provoke an immediate reaction. In stage two, the offender relies on bystanders to confirm his or her judgment about the derogatory behavior of the victim. The offender then responds in stage three with a demand that the victim stop the provoking behavior and makes it clear that action will be taken if the antagonistic behavior does not stop. In stage four the offender continues to convey to the victim the possible dire consequences of the victim's taunting. Preparation for combat occurs in stage five when the offender or victim produces a weapon, or finds one at the scene. The situated transaction now escalates into a violent confrontation, which results in the death of the victim. The homicidal process ends in stage six when the offender either leaves the scene or is detained by witnesses.

To Luckenbill, homicide involves a dynamic series of interactions between the victim and the offender. The victim is an active participant in the commission of a homicide. Interpersonal conflicts are common occurrences; homicide and assault and battery are by contrast far less usual. It is important, therefore, to understand the dynamic interplay between persons who engage in conflict-ridden interactions and how the process by which verbal taunting and physical gesturing culminates in homicidal death. Cultural and ecological considerations also help us to understand the dynamics of homicide. In Luckenbill's study, he found that witnesses were present in 70 percent of the homicides, in 36 percent of the cases the offender was armed prior to the altercation with the victim, and 42 percent of the homicides occurred in public places (bars and taverns, streets, and informal gather places).

Victim-Precipitated Homicide

Marvin Wolfgang (1958) introduced the concept of victim-precipitated homicide while studying patterns of criminal homicide in Philadelphia. **Victim-precipitated homicide** means that the victim was the first one to use physical force against the person who ultimately became the homicide offender. Wolfgang determined that victim-precipitated homicide occurs in 26 percent of all cases of criminal homicide. If verbal aggression were included in the definition of victim-precipitated homicide, it is likely that the victim would have provoked more than half of all intentional and unjustifiable killings.

Theories of Criminal Homicide, Assault and Battery

As with suicide, theories applicable to the understanding of criminal homicide, assault and battery can be considered on two levels of analysis: macro—that is, the societal or group level, and the micro or individual level. When we seek to explain and predict rates of criminal homicide, and assault and battery, we use macro-level theories of analysis. However, when we are interested in understanding individual behavior, we use theories at the micro-level of analysis.

Social Integration

Emile Durkheim's *Suicide* (1951) provides the foundation for Andrew Henry and James Short's (1954) theory of homicide and suicide. Three key variables—status, strength of the relational system, and external restraint—serve to explain and predict homicide and, by extension, assault and battery. Status refers to the influences one has over decisions made by members of a given social group or collectivity. The strength of the relational system is measured by the involvement in networks of social relationships. External restraint refers to the extent to which a person is required to conform to the demands and expectations of others.

Henry and Short hypothesize that as status decreases, the strength of the relational system increases along with external restraints on behavior. Lower status persons are more involved with others, either with neighbors in crowded residential areas or with fellow employees in production and assembly line work, or in other group work settings. As the proximity of others increases, so too does the likelihood of interpersonal conflict and group discord. Lower status also denotes relative powerlessness. That is, lower status persons are often told what to do and when and how to do; rarely are they able to demand that others carry out their wishes. The inability to influence much of their lives is exceedingly frustrating for lower class persons. Simply put, two social conditions follow from being positioned in the lower strata. First, as status decreases, the probability of interpersonal conflict increases. And second, as status decreases, external restraints increase, resulting in elevated levels of frustration. Henry and Short hypothesize that both of these social conditions increase the probability of criminal homicide and, arguably, related forms of interpersonal violence.

Robert K. Merton (1968) also draws on Durkheim's formulation of integration, with particular focus on his concept of anomie or normlessness. To Merton, anomie is a social condition that is obtained when institutionalized means do not lead to the attainment of culturally approved goals. For example, when completing an educational program does not result in getting a job, or when full-time employment does not provide sufficient income to pay one's bills, a condition of anomie is said to exist. As we have seen, Merton has identified five adaptations to the condition of anomie: conformity, innovation, ritualism, retreatism and rebellion. Two adaptations—innovation and rebellion—are particularly applicable to criminal homicide and assaultive behavior. *Innovation* refers to the acceptance of culturally approved goals (e.g., money, status, power), but the rejection of the institutionalized means for attaining them. Innovators may use forms of coercion to gain status within a group; physical force may be used to establish power and dominance over others. Money and material possessions may be taken from others by force.

To Merton, *rebellion* occurs when both the institutionalized means and culturally approved goals are rejected and replaced by alternative means and goals. In a sense, rebellion involves overturning the existing social structure and developing a new order. This new order makes possible the violent acquisition of an infamous, threatening social status. Examples of rebellion fall along a continuum from large-scale political revolutions to the actions of Neo-Nazi and other white supremacist and hate groups.

Social Disorganization

William Wilson (1987) and others have advanced a social disorganization formulation to account for violent behavior, particularly among African Americans in the inner city. To Wilson, the concentration of poverty is key to the understanding of social disorganization within certain sectors of large urban areas. Poverty is endemic among urban African Americans; 38 percent of extremely poor African Americans live in the worst inner city neighborhoods, compared to 7 percent of extremely poor whites in the United States (Sampson and Wilson 1995). These neighborhoods are physically dilapidated areas characterized by high unemployment with few opportunities for job training or employment prospects. A sense of fatalism hangs in the air, and living for the moment is common and intensified. Minor misunderstandings or perceived affronts may quickly escalate into violent altercations. Unable to obtain desired material goods (e.g., clothes, jewelry, etc.) legitimately, they are simply taken by force if necessary.

Elijah Anderson's (1999) investigation of life on the streets of Philadelphia provides considerable insight into daily interactions within the inner city. In his *Code of the Street* (Anderson 1999), he describes in detail the interplay between the social conditions that characterize interactions among the residents of a largely African American neighborhood and the negotiations that are made between the residents and the larger Philadelphia society. Key to the understanding of the *Code of the Street* is the issue of respect. Anderson defines respect as being treated "right" or being granted one's "props" (for proper due) or the deference one deserves (Anderson 1999: 33). Within the street culture, respect is a critical component of social capital, an insulator against being bothered by others or provoked into altercations. The absence of respect from others means that one is always subject to being victimized, being verbally or physically harmed, or having goods stolen or destroyed. Subtle forms of being shown disrespect or being dissed—for example, prolonged eye contact—increase the risk of further disgrace. Respect is a fragile commodity–difficult to gain and to keep: It must be carefully negotiated and guarded.

The interactional dynamics that surround the quest for respect often lead to violent street encounters. Physical prowess is admired and a basis for respect. Challenges from others are common, and physical violence is often required to maintain respect. Any sign of weakness or unwillingness to confront assailants results in the loss of respect. When respect is diminished or lost, its restoration is extremely difficult, often impossible. With few economic resources or marketable skills, the person is relegated to a life among others who view him or her as easy prey.

Routine Activities

Lawrence Cohen and Marcus Felson (1979) contend that three conditions serve to greatly increase the probability of criminal activity. First, there must be a motivated offender to carry out the crime (e.g., criminal homicide, and assault and battery). Second, there must be a suitable target or victim. And, third there must be an absence of a guardian for the potential victim. These three conditions must converge in time and space for criminal activity to occur. As we have seen, social conditions in inner city neighborhoods provide opportunities for criminal behavior not found in other sectors of the city.

In addition, risk-taking behaviors—walking alone late at night in unfamiliar places, drinking to excess in night clubs or bars and flashing large amounts of money, or engaging in provoking and aggressive behavior—understandably place a person at greater risk for violent victimization.

Strain

Robert Agnew (1992) has set forth a strain theory of deviant and criminal behavior of particular relevance to criminal homicide and assaultive behavior. To Agnew, strain is largely generated by negative interpersonal relations. Sustained interaction with others who thwart a person's ability to attain legitimate goals (e.g., educational, occupational, affiliation, and respect), is stressful and typically results in negative emotions. These negative emotions—anger, resentment, jealousy, anxiety, or depression—require the person to develop a coping strategy to alleviate the resultant tension. Conditions in the surrounding social environment may exacerbate the interpersonal tension and serve to reduce the chances of adapting positively to experiences of strain. In the absence of viable outlets for tension reduction or healthy alternatives to destructive behaviors, interpersonal violence becomes more probable.

Frustration-Aggression

In 1939, John Dollard and his colleagues set forth their frustration-aggression hypothesis. The frustration-aggression hypothesis states that frustration always leads to aggression. Frustration occurs when an individual is blocked from the attainment of important needs and goals. If others make it impossible or significantly impede an individual from getting what he or she needs or wants, then frustration is acutely felt. To Dollard and his colleagues, some form of aggression always follows. Aggression may be turned inwardly—directed toward the self in the form of suicidal behavior, mutilation, depression, or addiction. Aggression may also be turned outwardly—directed toward others in the form of homicidal or assaultive behavior, either physical or sexual or both.

Disadvantaged individuals and groups experience a wide range of frustrations in their everyday lives. Frustrations are endemic to life in the lower socioeconomic strata of society. Acute frustrations begin in childhood with limited access to medical and dental resources, inferior clothing and school supplies, and caretakers who themselves are burdened by economic and social deprivation and who are not able to spend the time each child needs to advance in school. The cycle of poverty continues from one generation to the next, so too do the attendant frustrations and ensuing expressions of aggression. Verbal aggression often leads to explosive violence. The possibility of injury or death is always present.

Unreciprocity

Stuart Palmer (1972) reformulates the frustration-aggression hypothesis into the reciprocity and unreciprocity in role relationships. Palmer argues that unreciprocity in role relationships explains and predicts homicide and assaultive behaviors. Unreciprocity is experienced when others in complementary roles—wives and husbands, employers and employees, parents and children—inhibit or render impossible the carrying out of our roles. Unreciprocity is frustrating for an individual and, if experienced over an extended period of time, may well lead to violent behavior.

Social Control

Travis Hirschi (1969) poses the question: Why don't individuals engage in criminal or delinquent behavior? To Hirschi, it is as important to understand individuals' reluctance to commit crimes as it is to understand why they willingly do so. He contends that the greater the integration of the individuals into conventional society, the less likely they are to commit acts of violence toward others. Four bonds that tie an individual to conventional society are used to measure integration. These bonds are attachment, commitment, involvement, and belief. Attachment refers to the willingness of individuals to conform their conduct to the norms of the larger society. Evidence of commitment is found in the investment of time and energy in conventional activities—school, work, family, and civic projects. Involvement is indicated by the intensity in which a person engages in conventional activities. And, belief refers to conviction that there is a common value system and one is morally bound to live in accordance with it.

More recently, Michael Gottfredson and Travis Hirschi (1990) have proposed a general theory of crime. Central to the general theory—intended to account for all forms of crime—is the concept of self-control. The lack of self-control is manifest in various related ways. Gottredson and Hirschi observe that "people who lack self-control will tend to be impulsive, insensitive, physical (as opposed to mental), risk-taking, shortsighted, and nonverbal, and they tend therefore to engage in criminality and analogous risk-taking behavior" (Gottfredson and Hirschi 1990: 89). The overriding benefit of crime, to Gottfredson and Hirschi (1990: 89), "is not pleasure but relief from momentary irritation." Individuals who routinely engage in behaviors that demonstrate their lack of self-control are, understandably, at greater risk for involvement in spontaneous, often explosively violent, attacks on others.

Subcultural Considerations

Various subcultural formulations of crime and deviance inform our understanding of homicidal and assaultive behaviors. Richard Cloward and Lloyd Ohlin (1961) consider both subcultural and opportunity factors in attempting to account for variations in forms crime and violence. Three subcultures identified by Cloward and Ohlin—criminal, violent, and retreatist—serve to structure opportunities for criminal activity. The opportunity to engage in crimes-for-profit—drug dealing, burglary, auto theft, gambling, and so on—depends on integration into a criminal subculture. Sources of drugs, fences for stolen goods, car "chop shops" or dealers in "hot" cars, must be available to the would-be criminal. Violent subcultures arise in places where for-profit criminal activities are less available. Physical force is commonly used to gain respect, status, or a "rep" from others. Physical aggression is also a means to acquire money and goods from others. Retreatist subcultures attract members who do not have opportunities or motivation to engage in a criminal subculture or the physical prowess to use violence to meet their needs. Retreatists tend to withdraw into a lifestyle dominated by substance abuse, psychiatric impairment, demonic rituals, or cult behavior.

As expected, homicidal and assaultive behaviors are most common within violent subcultures. However, criminal subcultures are also marked by considerable interpersonal conflict surrounding the myriad of illicit activities carried out on a daily basis. Disputes over drug sales and markets, theft of stolen goods, and threats of physical harm made to family members or friends must be settled within the neighborhood and among the combatants.

Marvin Wolfgang and Franco Ferracuti (1967) contend that acts of homicide and assaultive behaviors become far more likely with a subculture of violence. To Wolfgang and Ferracuti, subcultures of violence are marked by a constellation of norms and values that support the use of violence to settle interpersonal disputes. The willingness to resort to violence to resolve conflict is a learned response, observed at home and played out on the street. Wolfgang and Ferracuti (1967: 188–189) describe a subculture of violence as:

> Quick resort to physical combat as a measure of daring, courage, or defense of status appears to be a cultural expression, especially for lower socioeconomic class males of both races. When such a culture norm response is elicited from an individual engaged is social interplay with others who harbor the same response mechanism, physical assaults, altercations, and violent domestic quarrels that result in homicide are common.

Explanations of Homicide, Assault, and Battery Rates

Theories and Theorists	Sociological Predictors	Hypotheses
Integration		
• Henry and Short	Prestige	Homicide, assault, and battery increase as the status (prestige) of individuals diminishes.
	External restraints	Homicide, assault, and battery increase as the strength of external restraints increases.
	Relational system	Homicide, assault, and battery increase as the strength of the relational system increases.
• Merton	Anomie	The greater the level of anomie, the greater the possibility of homicide, assault, and battery.
Social Disorganization		
• Wilson	Concentration of poverty	Neighborhoods characterized by concentrations of poverty experience higher homicide, assault, and battery rates.
Opportunity and Subculture		
• Cloward and Ohlin	Opportunity	Individuals who cannot gain access to legitimate opportunity for success seek entrance to illegitimate structures for violence.
		Participation in violent opportunity structures increases the probability that the individual will commit homicide, assault, and battery.
• Wolfgang and Ferracuti	Subcultures for violence	Where deprivation of economic goods is great, subcultures of violence develop.
		Participation in subcultures of violence increases the acceptance of subcultural customs and values for violence as a response to frustrating conditions.
		Acceptance of such values increases the likelihood for committing homicide, assault, and battery.
• Miller	Focal concerns of the lower class: Toughness	The greater the acceptance of the focal concerns, the greater the probability of violent behavior.

(continued)

Theories and Theorists	Sociological Predictors	Hypotheses
	Smartness Excitement Fate Autonomy	
• Sutherland	Differential association	Individuals who are exposed to definitions favorable toward homicide and assault and battery are more likely to commit these offenses.

Social Bonding and Control

• Hirschi	Attachment	The weaker the attachment to conventional society, the more likely the individual will commit homicide, assault, and battery.
	Commitment	The weaker the commitment to conventional society, the more likely the individual will commit homicide, assault, and battery.
	Involvement	The greater the involvement in conventional activities, the less likely the individual will commit homicide, assault, and battery.
	Belief	The stronger the belief in conventional values and norms, the less likely the person will commit homicide, assault, and battery.
• Gottfredson and Hirschi	Self-control	Individuals with high self-control will be less likely to engage in homicide, assault, and battery.
• Agnew	Strain/Stress	The greater the strain, the greater the negative emotional reaction.
		The greater the negative emotional reaction, the more likely an individual will commit homicide, assault, and battery.

Routine Activity

• Cohen and Felson	Suitable targets Motivated offender Guardians	Homicide, assault, and battery are likely to occur when there is a suitable target, a motivated offender, and the lack of capable guardians.

Frustration-Aggression

• Dollard and colleagues	Frustration Aggression	High levels of frustration increase levels of aggression.

		Increased levels of aggression are likely to result in homicide, assault, and battery.
• Palmer	Unreciprocity	Unreciprocity increases levels of frustration.
		Increased levels of frustration result in high levels of aggression.
		This increased aggression is likely to result in homicide, assault, and battery.

In a similar vein, Walter Miller's (1958) conceptualization of the focal concerns of the lower socioeconomic classes help us further understand the dynamics of everyday life that may result in violent altercations and, at times, death. Miller identified six focal concerns of lower class life: trouble, toughness, smartness, excitement, fate, and autonomy. Briefly, trouble refers to the frustrations—financial, social, and legal—faced on an ongoing basis that combine to make life for the economically deprived exceedingly stressful. Toughness—the value of physical prowess and fearlessness—is highly prized. Smartness means the ability to "con" or outwit others or the possession of "street-smarts" or knowledge of survival strategies for life largely unprotected by the police. With few resources, excitement for lower class persons tends to revolve around largely illicit and risk-taking activities such as drug use, fighting, sexual encounters, and gambling. Fate refers to the belief that life events are beyond one's control. Things just happen and there is nothing that can be done about it. A "live-for-the-moment" mentality predominates. While life is subject to uncontrollable forces, there is nonetheless a concern with autonomy or the freedom from restrictions. There is great value placed on being able to act independently of the wishes of others—to be one's own person. These six focal concerns combine to increase the likelihood of violent encounters within the lower socioeconomic strata of society.

Chapter Summary

- Criminal homicide is the intentional killing of one human being by another without justification or excuse.
  - There are two types of criminal homicide:
    - Murder (first and second degree)
    - Manslaughter (first and second degree)
  - Two considerations serve to distinguish between each type and the seriousness of each degree:
    - Premeditation
    - Provocation
- Manslaughter involves less premeditation on the part of the offender and greater victim provocation than murder. Second-degree manslaughter does

not involve the intention to kill, but results from the negligent actions of the offender.

- Homicides where there is no intention to kill nor evidence of wrongful or flagrant carelessness are considered justifiable homicides and excusable homicides.

- Assault is (1) an attempt to commit bodily injury to another human being or (2) putting another in fear of imminent bodily injury. The crime of assault implies the present ability to carry out the assault.

- Battery refers to the actual offensive touching or unwanted physical contact between the assailant and the victim.

- The most serious form of assault and battery is aggravated assault, or an assault committed with the intention of committing an additional crime.

- **ABWDWWITKRSBI**—**A**ssault and **B**attery **W**ith a **D**eadly **W**eapon **W**ith **I**ntent **T**o **K**ill **R**esulting in **S**erious **B**odily **I**njury—is an abbreviation commonly used by law enforcement officers to distinguish between aggravated assault and assaults of a lesser nature.

- While the United States is not the most murderous nation, it does lead the world in gun-related homicides.

- At the beginning of the new millennium an increase in the homicide rate, particularly in urban areas, was evident.

- Homicides vary from urban, suburban, small cities, and rural areas. Homicide is disproportionately committed in large urban areas. As a result, when homicide declines in larger urban places, the rate for the country as a whole falls sharply.

- Persons aged 18 through 24 are most likely to commit homicide or to be a victim of homicide.

- Males are far more likely to commit homicide or to be a victim of homicide than are females.

- Homicide is essentially an intraracial event, disproportionately involving black Americans as both victims and offenders.

- Black males between the ages of 18 and 24 have the highest rates of homicide offending.

- Native Americans are the targets of violence twice as often as all other residents of the United States. When a Native American is assaulted, 7 in 10 times the offender is a non-Indian. Alcohol is most likely to be involved in acts of violence directed toward Native Americans.

- Native Americans fall prey to aggravated assault and simple assault far more often than blacks, whites, or Asians.

- The elderly are far less likely to be involved in criminal activity either as an offender or victim than are younger persons. However, the elderly are considerably more likely to be killed during the commission of another felony (e.g., robbery, burglary, or larceny than are younger homicide victims). Persons over age 65 are twice as likely to be murdered by their relatives or intimates than are younger persons.

- Homicide has emerged as the second leading cause of death on the job. Homicide is the leading cause of job-related death for women. One-half of all injuries to women in the workplace are the result of a fatal attack. Robbery is the primary motive. Taxi drivers have the highest rate of workplace homicide while law enforcement officers are at greatest risk for nonlethal violent victimization on the job.

- Nine risk factors for physical violence in the workplace have been identified:
  - Contact with the public
  - Exchange of money
  - Delivery of passengers, goods, or services
  - Having a mobile workplace such as a taxicab or police cruiser
  - Working with unstable or volatile persons in health, social services, or criminal justice settings
  - Working alone or in small numbers
  - Working late at night or during early morning hours
  - Guarding valuable property or possessions
  - Working in community-based settings

- Overall, women are far less likely to be the victim of a homicide than men, but are more likely to be victimized by an intimate partner than are men.

- Luckenbill's situated transaction is a conflict between two persons involving the escalation of verbal taunts, accusations, or threats to battery and serious injury or death. He describes six stages:
  - The first stage involves offensive actions or verbal communication and the threat to respect from others.
  - In the second stage, bystanders confirm the derogatory behavior.
  - Stage three involves the demand of the offender to stop the provoking behavior.
  - The offender conveys to the victim the dire consequences of the victim's taunting in stage four.
  - A weapon is produced in stage five and the violent transaction takes place.
  - The process ends with stage six when the offender leaves the scene or is detained by witnesses.

- Victim-precipitated homicide, introduced by Marvin Wolfgang, means that the victim was the first one to use physical force against the person who ultimately became the homicide offender.

Key Concepts

Criminal homicide: The intentional killing of one human being by another without justification or excuse.

Justifiable homicide: Court-ordered executions of convicted offenders or the killing of an enemy by a member of the military in the line of duty.

Excusable homicide: The accidental or non-negligent killing of another human being.

Murder: A form of homicide that involves premeditation and malice aforethought on the part of the offender.

Manslaughter: A form of homicide that involves less premeditation or malice aforethought on the part of the offender and greater victim provocation than other forms of homicide.

Premeditation: The act of deliberating or meditating upon, or planning, a course of action.

Malice: The intentional doing of a wrongful act without just cause or legal excuse.

Malice aforethought: An unjustifiable, inexcusable, and unmitigated person-endangering state of mind.

Provocation: The active involvement of the victim, either verbal or physical, in the lethal encounter.

Assault: An attempt to commit bodily injury to another human being; putting another in fear of imminent bodily injury.

Battery: The actual offensive touching or unwanted physical contact between the assailant and victim.

Aggravated assault: An assault that is committed with the intention of committing an additional crime.

Victim-precipitated homicide: Concept introduced by Marvin Wolfgang to descrbibe homicides where the victim was the first one to use physical force against the person who ultimately became the homicide offender.

Critical Thinking Questions

1. Rates of homicide and aggravated assault vary widely among subcultural groupings. Which sociocultural factors might account for a high rate of violence in one subculture and a low rate in another? Discuss two theories that might account for the differences in rates between the two subcultural groups.

2. Choose two explanations for gender differences in violent offending and victimization. What are the advantages and limitations of the theoretical explanations that you have chosen?

3. Identify two sociocultural changes that might bring about a reduction in the violent victimization of children. How might these sociocultural changes affect the incidence and rate of childhood physical and sexual victimization?

4. Marked variations in violent offending and victimization occur across the life span. How does life-course analysis account for age-related differences in violent offending and victimization?

Web Extra

Check out these websites for additional information on homicide:

http://www.ojp.usdoj.gov/bjs

http://www.fbi.gov

http://www.ojp.usdoj.gob/nij

http://www.ncjrs.org

CHAPTER 5

Domestic Violence

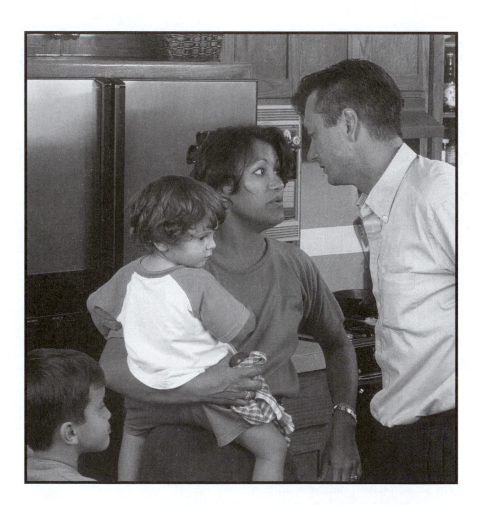

# of Domestic Violence

ELDER ABUSE

- Over the past three years, Mrs. Spencer experienced physical and mental abuse from her daughter and son-in-law. They wouldn't let her leave the house without permission and often parked their cars behind her car so she couldn't drive out of the garage. Her daughter restricted her freedom to cook on the stove or use the toaster oven. At times, her daughter would hide the toaster from her for weeks. On occasion, her daughter would kick her, push her, and threaten to send her to a nursing home. (*Source:* Steinmetz, S., S. Clavan, and K. Stein. 1990. *Marriage and Family Realities: Historical and Contemporary Perspectives.* New York: Harper & Row Publishers, p. 472.)

CHILD ABUSE

- Amy found her 7-month-old son lying face down in his crib. An autopsy determined that his death was caused by SIDS. Hours after the funeral the father, who had been alone with the child, confessed to police that he had suffocated his son with a plastic bag.

His motive was revenge against his wife, whom he resented for not supporting him after his father's death, three years earlier. (*Source:* Fox, J. A. and J. Levin. 2001. *The Will to Kill: Making Sense of Senseless Murder.* Boston: Allyn and Bacon, p. 70.)

INTIMATE ABUSE

- Karen and Peter married while Peter was working on his PhD. To others the couple was intelligent and happy. At home, though, Karen experienced repeated abuse. Peter attempted to choke her; he hit her in the mouth and often threatened to kill her and himself. Karen tried to leave Peter several times but each time he forced her to stay or convinced her to return home. He would beg her to forgive him and apologize for his actions. He promised to change. He never changed, but Karen finally moved out, got a restraining order, and left Peter. (*Source:* The Family Violence Prevention Fund, 2001. Web posted at http://fvpf.org/stories/karen.php3)

LEARNING OBJECTIVES

After reading this chapter you should know:

- ☐ The types and forms of domestic violence.
- ☐ The prevalence of domestic violence.
- ☐ Age, gender, and race characteristics of victims and offenders.
- ☐ Risk factors for domestic violence.
- ☐ Key life-course events that increase the risk of violence between intimates.
- ☐ Why women stay in abusive relationships.
- ☐ The three phases in the cycle of violence.

Introduction

Domestic violence refers to the intentional physical or psychological injury of a family member by another. Family members may be either a victim, an offender, or, in some instances, both. Acts of domestic violence range from assault involving the use of a lethal weapon to witnessing family aggression. Domestic violence ranges from life-threatening offenses to simply an awareness of physical or psychological abuse. Victims of domestic violence around the globe, however, are disproportionately women and children. More powerful members of the family—usually by virtue of their status outside the home, physical dominance, or violent demeanor—habitually victimize the vulnerable members of the household with impunity.

> *You look at these scattered houses, and you are impressed by their beauty. I look at them, and the only thought which comes to me is a feeling of their isolation, and of the impunity with which crime may be committed there. . . . Think of the deeds of hellish cruelty, the hidden wickedness which may go on, year in, year out, in such places, and none the wiser.*
> —Sir Arthur Conan Doyle (1984) (Sherlock Holmes to Dr. John Watson)

Until recent years, violent behavior within the home was largely hidden from public scrutiny. Significant advances have been made in public awareness of the pervasiveness of domestic violence and its debilitating effects; in the passage of domestic violence legislation at the federal, state, and local levels; in the commitment of advocacy groups for women and children; and in innovative law enforcement strategies for protecting the victims of violence and controlling their offenders.

> *The closer the social relationship, the more intense the conflict.*
> —Lewis Coser (1967)

In this chapter we will consider the wide spectrum of domestic violence, patterns of its occurrence, and consequences for its victims. Familial conditions that give rise to domestic violence and serve to ensure its perpetuation are also considered. Finally, we will discuss theoretical formulations that explain the rates or the incidence of various forms of domestic violence.

Legal Definitions

Domestic violence encompasses several forms of abusive behavior–physical, sexual, emotional, or psychological. In the main, domestic violence involves coercion through the use of intimidating, threatening, harmful, or harassing behavior. The Violent Crime Control and Law Enforcement Act (1994) defines domestic violence as "felony or misdemeanor crimes of violence committed by a current or former spouse of the victim, by a person with whom the victim shares a child in common, by a person who is cohabiting with the victim as a spouse, by a person similarly situated to a spouse of the victim under the domestic or family violence laws of the jurisdiction."

Pakistani Women, Divorce, and Honor Killings

A Pakistani woman was killed in her attorney's office by a hit man hired by her mother, father, and paternal uncle. They arranged to have her murdered because she was seeking a divorce from her estranged husband. To a Pakistani, divorce is considered a dishonor that justifies being put to death. "Honor killings" in Pakistan are commonplace following a woman's infidelity or acts of independence, such as attempting to choose her own husband. Violence against women—assault and battery, forcible rape, burning, acid attacks, and mutilation—is endemic in the Pakistani culture. Estimates of spouse abuse range from 70 to 90 percent. Furthermore, acts of domestic violence are largely carried out with impunity. In a study of 215 cases of Pakistani women burned to death at home, only 6 persons were arrested.

Source: www.hrw.org/reports/1999/pakistan/Pakhtml-01.htm

Child Maltreatment

Each state is required to provide both criminal and civil definitions of the forms of **child maltreatment.** While there are variations in the legal definitions across states, there is general consensus about the elements of each of the three forms of child maltreatment. The three forms of child maltreatment are child abuse and neglect, sexual abuse, and emotional abuse (including psychological/verbal abuse/mental injury).

Child abuse and neglect is defined as (1) any act or failure to act on the part of a parent or caretaker that results in death, serious physical or emotional harm, sexual abuse or exploitation, and/or (2) an act or failure to act that presents an imminent risk of serious harm.

Sexual abuse is defined as (1) the employment, use, persuasion, inducement, or coercion of any child to engage in, or assist any other person to engage in, any sexually explicit conduct or simulation of such conduct for the purpose of producing a visual depiction of such conduct or (2) the rape, and in cases of caretaker or interfamilial relationships, statutory rape, molestation, prostitution, or other form of sexual exploitation of children or incest with children.

Emotional abuse refers to acts of omission by the parents or other caregivers that have caused or could cause serious behavioral, cognitive, emotional, or mental disorders. Examples include traumatizing forms of punishment, e.g., being put under the hood of a running car. (CAPTA 2003: 44).

Sociological Definitions

Beyond the legal definitions of the various forms of domestic violence, there are sociological definitions of assaultive behavior in the home. Sociological definitions refer to the meanings and interpretations that individuals attach to their own behavior and to the behavior of persons with whom they interact. We interpret our own behavior: We act for reasons that make sense to us. Similarly, we interpret the motivations of others, for example, as kind or mean, helpful or harmful, appropriate or inappropriate.

Crucial to the sociological definition of domestic violence are those factors that influence the meanings and interpretations attached to the offender's behavior. Women may interpret the violent behavior of their husbands or intimate partners as justifiable or excusable—"I deserved it" or "He was drinking and didn't know what he was doing." Or, they may interpret the violent partner's behavior as vicious and criminal, or the result of a serious mental disorder. Victims of spousal assault construct a "definition of the situation" that takes into account their economic resources and social supports, religious beliefs, and access to legal assistance and protective programs. Women who are economically dependent, who believe divorce is religiously prohibited, who do not gain emotional support from others, or who do not have access to police or legal assistance or protective shelters are less likely to see alternatives to their abusive situation. They tend to define their situation as hopeless, and themselves as helpless to change it.

Learned helplessness characterizes women who find themselves in this situation. Learned helplessness refers to the inability to predict the outcomes of one's actions (Meuer, Seymour, and Wallace 2002). Because battered women find it difficult to know what their abusive partners may do in response to their behavior, they tend to limit themselves to acting in safe ways—asking permission before deciding to do the most mundane things. Learned helplessness results from the development of a "survival" strategy for the battered women (Walker 1979). Battered women's lives tend to focus on devising ways to adapt to their abusive relationship. If an abused woman defines herself as "helpless" and her situation as intractable, then she is less likely to define her abuser as criminal and more likely to be repeatedly victimized.

Extent and Nature of Domestic Violence

Intimate Partner Violence

Intimate partners assault about 1.3 million women and 835,000 men each year in the United States (Rennison and Welchans 2000). For the most part, violence against women is disproportionately committed in the context of domestic violence. Almost two of every three women over the age of 18 who are raped, physically assaulted, and/or stalked during their lifetimes are victimized by a spouse or former spouse, live-in partner, boyfriend, or date. About one in six males are victims of similar offenses (Tjaden and Thoennes 2000). More than nine in ten of the victims of domestic violence are women (BJS 1994), while more than nine in ten of the perpetrators of domestic violence are men (Bachman and Saltzman

1995). The most recent National Violence Against Women Survey shows that 22.1 percent of women and 7.4 percent of men are physically assaulted by their spouse, former spouse, or cohabiting partner, boyfriend, girlfriend, or date in their lifetime. That is, spouses or former spouses, live-in partners, boyfriends, or dates account for three of every four physical assaults or rapes of women 18 years of age or older (Tjaden and Thoennes 2000).

Other annual estimates range from 960,000 to 4 million women who are violently assaulted by their current or former spouse, or intimate partners. Approximately 92 percent of the instances of domestic violence in the United States involve a man assaulting a woman. Women are between five and eight times more likely to be victimized by their intimate partners than are men. When women are the victims of a violent crime, more than one in five times the perpetrator is either her current or former spouse or a boyfriend, compared to one in twenty times for a male victimized by an intimate partner (Greenfeld et al. 1998).

Domestic violence occurs in all racial and ethnic groups, and across all socioeconomic classes (Hotaling and Sugarman 1990). Intimate partner violence occurs in one in three of marriages in the United States (Bachman and Saltzman 1995). Murray Straus and Richard Gelles (1995) estimate that more than one in seven U.S. men batter their wives, and one in three of these violent attacks involve punching, beating up, or are carried out with a knife or gun. American women are victimized by their intimate partners or former partners six times more frequently than by a stranger and are more likely to be injured by their intimate partner than by a stranger (Bachman and Saltzman 1995).

Domestic violence is exceedingly costly for victims and for society as a whole. Overall, four in ten persons who are treated in hospital emergency rooms for injuries due to violence are women; more than eight in ten times the offender is her intimate partner (U.S. Department of Justice 1998). The U.S. Department of Justice reports that an intimate partner victimizes 37 percent of women who go to emergency rooms to be treated for violent injuries (Rand 1997). Put another way, between 22 and 35 percent of women who are treated in emergency rooms are injured by an intimate partner, more than half of them (53 percent) make repeat visits to physicians for traumas related to domestic violence (Abbott et al. 1995; McLeer and Anwar 1989; Randall 1990; and Stark, Flitcraft, and Frazier 1979). Domestic violence accounts for more injuries to women between the ages of 15 and 44 than car accidents, muggings, and rapes (FBI 1991). The financial costs of domestic violence are estimated to be between $5 and $10 billion annually. This includes expenses incurred for medical treatment, the involvement of the police and the courts, shelters and foster care, as well as days away from work and distractions on the job (American Medical Association 1992).

Child Maltreatment

The U.S. Department of Health and Human Services estimates that 903,000 U.S. children are victims of child maltreatment each year. Over half of these children are victims of neglect, about one in four is physically abused, about one in eight is sexually abused, and about one in seventeen is a victim of either medical neglect or psychological abuse (U.S. Department of Health and Human Services 2000).

"I'm in Fear of My Life Right Now."

Sonye Herrera hid in the bathroom. She locked the door. Her heart was pounding. Her father was in another rage, storming around the house. How long before he found her?

Finally, Sonye had decided that she could stand it no more. She had vowed to take him on herself—get him arrested, send him to prison. But she overlooked one immutable reality: She was 15 years old, a child by law and in fact.

Now alone in the bathroom with a cordless phone, she dialed 911. Her father had been drinking. This time he had hit Sonye. Her mother tried to fend him off. But he was talking crazily, and Sonye was on crutches with a sprained ankle, unable to run.

"I'm in fear of my life right now" she told a 911 operator, her voice breaking as she gave her address.

Five minutes ticked by.

Ten minutes.

Twenty minutes.

Still the police did not come.

"What is your name?" the operator asked.

"I'm Sonye Herrera."

"Excuse me?"

"Sonye. Please, I don't have time."

"How old are you?"

"I'm 15, I don't have time. . . . I don't have time. Just come here."

"Are there any weapons in your home at all."

"No."

"No weapons?"

"Spell your name for me"

"S-O-N-Y-E. Please I don't have time to be doing this. Can't you send the cops over here?"

Twenty-eight minutes later, Sonye's mother ran from the house screaming: "Someone help me! Call the cops! He shot my daughter! Help me! Help me!" A few minutes later, Sonye's father shot her mother in the head and then killed himself. Sonye and her mother were buried together.

Source: www.washingtonpost.com/wp-dyn/articles/A36445-2001.Jun7.html

Age, Sex, and Race of the Victims.   Child maltreatment victimization rates are highest for infants through the age of 3 and lowest for teenagers between 16 and 17 years of age. Overall, more than half (51.9 percent) of the victims were female. Child maltreatment rates are lowest for Asians/Pacific Islanders (3.8), followed by whites (8.5), Hispanics (10.6), Native Americans/Alaska Natives (19.8), and highest for African Americans (20.7) (U.S. Department of Health and Human Services 2000).

Age, Sex, and Offender-Victim Relationship. Single offenders predominate among the victimizers of children. Almost nine in ten of child maltreatment cases involve a parent acting alone. However, one in four child maltreatment offenses involve both parents victimizing one or more of their children. Females also make up the majority—about six in ten—of the perpetrators of child maltreatment.

Women offenders are concentrated in the age range between 20 and 39, and they are somewhat younger than men who victimize children. Women perpetrators acting alone account for almost six in ten of the medical neglect cases of child maltreatment, over half of child neglect, and more than one-third of physical abuse cases. Male offenders, however, account for the majority of sexual abuse of children (U.S. Department of Health and Human Services 2000).

Elder Abuse

Considerably less is known about the extent and nature of elder abuse in the United States. Findings from the National Elder Abuse Incidence Study (1996), however, show that:

1. Approximately 450,000 persons over the age of 60 are victims of domestic abuse or neglect.

2. An additional 101,000 persons over the age of 60 experience self-neglect.

3. Elderly women are disproportionately victimized. Women comprise 58 percent of the population over the age of 60, but between 67 and 92 percent of the abused elderly, including 75 percent of the psychologically abused, and 92 percent of the financially abused.

4. Between 52 and 60 percent of the abused elderly are 80 years of age or older—two to three times the proportion of persons over the age of 60 in the general population.

5. About nine in ten times the perpetrator of elder abuse is a member of the victim's family, and two in three times the abuser is a spouse or an adult child.

6. Elderly persons who neglect themselves are most often frail, depressed, and confused.

The Spillover Effect: The Link between Spousal Assault and Child Abuse

There is considerable evidence that homes marked by marital violence are also places in which children are abused or neglected. The U.S. Advisory Board on Child Abuse and Neglect reports that half of the men who batter their wives also assault their children (U.S. Advisory Board on Child Abuse and Neglect 1995). The National Woman Abuse Prevention Project also finds that children who live in homes where marital violence occurs are fifteen times more likely to be victims of physical abuse or extreme neglect. When spousal assault is frequent and severe, children in the home are three times more likely to be physically abused by their mother's batterer (Straus and Gelles 1995). A history of domestic violence is evident in four of ten cases of fatal child abuse. The U.S. Advisory Board concludes that domestic violence is "the single major precursor" of child fatalities that result from abuse and neglect (Pynoos and Nader 1988).

The prevalence of witnessing marital violence by children is well documented. National data on violence between intimates shows that one-half of the female victims of violence have children under the age of 12 in the home. A Gallup Poll shows that between 1.5 and 3.3 million children witness one parent battering the other. Other researchers report that 3.3 million children between the ages of 3 and 17 are exposed to violence between their parents (Jaffe et al. 1990). Straus (1992) estimates that as many as 10 million U.S. children witness marital violence each year and one in three children are exposed to parental battering in their lifetimes.

Similarly, more than one in three mothers who are raped at home have children there who are likely to be aware of her victimization. Maria Roy's study of *Children in the Crossfire* (1988) reports that when boys over the age of 14 attempt to protect their mothers from being battered, about 62 percent of the time they suffer a physical injury.

The Consequences of Domestic Violence

Consequences for Intimate Partners

Spousal assault and other forms of intimate partner violence have both immediate and often long-term negative effects on the victim and children in the home. Partner violence is traumatic for the victim, creating an atmosphere of fear and a sense of helplessness. The initial painful realization that a loved one is capable of a sudden and explosive act of violence is often followed by the victim's experience of anxiety and/or depression, diminished self-worth, substance abuse, and suicidal thoughts (Dutton 1993; Gelles and Harrop 1989; Orava 1996).

The effects of intimate partner violence, however, vary by gender. Women are more likely than men to suffer negative social and psychological effects following their victimization. Murray Straus and Richard Gelles' (1995) second National Survey of Family Violence shows that overall women experience twice the number of negative effects of intimate partner violence than do men. Compared to their male counterparts, more women who are severely abused by their partners spend days in bed because of illness (23 vs. 15 percent); experience psychosomatic symptoms (44 vs. 26 percent); indicate elevated stress levels (61 vs. 34 percent); or feel extremely depressed (58 vs. 30 percent) (Stets and Straus 1990; Straus and Gelles 1995).

There is a dynamic interplay among the consequence of intimate partner violence. Jean Giles-Sims (1998) observes that women who have a sense of powerlessness, hopelessness, and diminished self-esteem tend to suffer from depression and are unable to leave an abusive relationship. Women whose sense of self has been undermined may well turn to alcohol or other drugs as a temporary respite

AT A GLANCE

Domestic Violence

- More than 90 percent of domestic violence victims are women, while as many as 95 percent of domestic violence perpetrators are male.
- More than one in four women around the world suffer violence from an intimate partner. One out of every four U.S. women report that they have been physically abused by a husband or boyfriend at some point in their lives. Thirty percent of Americans say they know a woman who has been physically abused by her husband or boyfriend in the past year.
- While women are less likely than men to be victims of violent crimes overall, women are five to eight times more likely than men to be victimized by an intimate partner.
- Domestic violence is the leading cause of injury to women between ages 15 and 44 in the United States, more than car accidents, muggings, and rapes combined.

Children Who Witness Domestic Violence

- An estimated 3.3 million children are exposed to violence initiated by their mothers or female caretakers each year.
- Boys who witness family violence are more likely to batter their female partners as adults than are boys raised in nonviolent homes. Girls who witness their mothers' abuse have a higher rate of being battered as adults.
- More than six in ten of juvenile offenders incarcerated for murder killed the men who beat their mothers.

Child Abuse

- More than one million substantiated cases of child maltreatment are reported each year.
- In 80 percent of the reported cases, the alleged perpetrator is the child's parent.
- Three of four child victims are female; more than seven in ten child victims are white.

Sources: UNICEF, Bureau of Justice Statistics, U.S. Department of Health and Human Services, U.S. Department of Justice, Lieberman Research INC., New Hampshire Coalition Against Domestic and Sexual Violence (www.NHCADSV.org), National Crime Victimization Survey, National Violence Against Women Survey, Crimes Against Children Research Center, 1999 National Report Series/Juvenile Justice Bulletin: Children as Victims.

from their domestic situation. And the sense that they are hopelessly trapped in a violent relationship may precipitate suicidal behaviors.

Consequences for Children

Children who are the victims of maltreatment or who are physically or sexually abused in their homes are more likely to engage in antisocial behavior, criminal activity, and domestic violence later in life. Abused or neglected children are 53 percent more likely to be arrested as a juvenile, 38 percent more likely to be arrested as an adult, and 38 percent more likely to commit a violent crime (Widom 1992). Maltreated children are also significantly more likely to become abusive husbands and fathers (Daro and Cohn 2000; Edelson 2000; Tolan 2000).

Exposure to parental violence, either as a direct witness or by inference from the threats, screams, and sounds of assaultive behavior, also has pronounced negative effects on children and adolescents (see Table 5.1). Janis Wolak and David Finkelhor (1998) identify behavioral, physical, emotional, and cognitive symptoms of exposure to partner violence. These symptoms may be a direct or an indirect consequence of parental violence (Jaffe et al. 1990). Direct consequences include physical danger to the child; emotional and behavior problems, e.g., posttraumatic stress disorder; fearfulness; isolation; running away from home; and learning to use aggressive behavioral strategies to control situations. Indirect consequences refer to the effects of partner violence on the health and behavior of the child's parents over time. Typical of the indirect consequences are stress-related health disorders of the mother, the father's overt expression of anger and irritability, and the child's being subjected to severe and arbitrary punishment by distraught parents. In addition, exposure to parental violence is associated with suicide attempts by the child, experimentation with alcohol and drugs, teenage prostitution, and engagement in sexually assaultive behavior (Wolfe et al. 1995).

The Risk Factors for Domestic Violence

Key risk factors for becoming a victim of domestic violence have been identified. For both women and men, being a victim of maltreatment in childhood significantly increases the risk of being a victim of domestic violence. And for both women and men, the risk of victimization is significantly greater when there is a disparity in their relative status. That is, when a woman makes more money than her partner, she is at greater risk for victimization. Similarly, when a man's race or ethnicity differs from his partner, he has an elevated risk of being victimized by his spouse. Gerald Hotaling and David Sugarman (1986: 1–13) identify eight risk markers for husbands who victimize their wives:

1. Sexual aggression toward the wife/partner
2. Violence toward the children
3. Witnessing parental violence as a child or teen
4. Working-class status
5. Excessive alcohol usage

Table 5.1   Symptoms of Children
Exposed to Partner Violence

Behavioral

Aggression

Tantrums

Acting out

Immaturity

Truancy

Delinquency

Physical

Failure to thrive

Sleeplessness

Regressive behaviors

Eating disorders

Poor motor skills

Psychosomatic symptoms

Rejection by peers

Emotional

Anxiety

Depression

Withdrawal

Low self-esteem

Anger

Cognitive

Poor academic performance

Language lag

Source: Wolak, J. and D. Finkelhor. 1998. Children Exposed
to Partner Violence. In Jasinski, J. and L. Williams (Eds.),
*Partner Violence: A Comprehensive Review of 20 Years of Re-
search* (pp. 73–111). Thousand Oaks, CA: Sage.

6. Low income

7. Low assertiveness

8. Low educational level

Similarly, for women, the risk of intimate partner violence is significantly
greater when cohabiting versus married, African American versus white, living
with a verbally abusive partner or a partner who controls access to family,

Domestic violence is experienced across socio-economic classes. Children and adolescents who witness parental abuse commonly suffer adverse emotional and behavioral consequences.

friends, or economic resources. Angela Browne's (1987) groundbreaking study of battered women who kill their abusers shows that they differ from other women victims in the following ways:

1. Frequent intoxication by their victims
2. Drug use by their victims
3. Frequent abuse
4. Serious injury at the hands of her victim
5. Rape or sexual victimization by the victim
6. Threats by the victim to kill her
7. Suicide threats by her

Life-Course Risk Factors

Certain key life-course events tend to increase the risk of violence between intimate partners. These life-course events include dating and courtship, the early years of marriage, and separation and divorce (Jasinski and Williams 1998).

Dating and Courtship. Dating and courtship are marked by a considerable degree of sexually and physically aggressive behavior. Analyses of violence among dates and acquaintances in colleges and universities across the United States show that about half the women report being the victim of sexual aggression—one in four of the attacks legally constitute rape or attempted rape (Koss et al. 1987). Meta-analysis of seventeen studies of violence among college students shows that one in three undergraduates engage in either sexual or physical dating violence (Sugarman and Hotaling 1989). Factors that increase the risks of dating and courtship violence include societal norms in support of violence, witnessing violence in their family of origin, divorce of their parents, and situational factors—stress and alcohol and other drug use (Foo and Margolin 1995; Riggs and O'Leary 1989; Sugarman and Hotaling 1989; Tondonato and Crew 1992).

Women Lift the Veil on Abuse

When she heard about the slaying last summer, Naila knew it was time to escape.

Another young Pakistani bride, Shahpara Sayeed, had been set afire in the Uptown neighborhood, allegedly by her husband of 2½ years. Police said he poured gasoline in a taxi and lit a match on North Glenwood Avenue in broad daylight.

After Naila's brother-in-law saw news of the slaying on television, he taunted her.

"I'll burn you," Naila said he told her. I'll do the same to you as Shahpara Sayeed."

According to the World Health Organization, domestic violence occurs among all races, classes, and ethnic groups across the globe with striking similarity. Yet immigrant women in the United States may be at increased risk because of their social isolation and cultural barriers to seeking help. Separated from the support of family and friends at home, and reluctant to seek legal aid within the United States, many immigrant women are particularly vulnerable to domestic violence.

Source: www.vachss.com/help_text/archive/women_lift.html.

Dating and courtship violence does not preclude later marriage. In a study of the first year of marriage, 31 percent of men and 44 percent of women report engaging in courtship violence, and 30 percent of them eventually married their courtship abuser (O'Leary et al. 1989).

Early Years of Marriage.   The early years of marriage are marked by a relatively high risk for partner violence. Daniel O'Leary and his colleagues (O'Leary et al. 1989) find that in the first year and a half of marriage 27 percent of men and 36 percent of women admit being involved in spousal aggression. Intimate partner violence is particularly prevalent among younger married persons. Married couples under the age of 30 are more likely to engage in domestic violence, with the highest incidence being reported by couples between the ages of 18 through 24 (Straus 1980). Among young couples, the risk of intimate partner violence is increased when the husband abuses alcohol, expresses hostility toward his wife, is dissatisfied with the marriage, or thinks drinking excuses his violent behavior (Leonard and Senchak 1993).

Separation and Divorce.   The circumstances that surround the ending of a marriage are extremely stressful. The consequences of stress are particularly acute for the partner who does not want the marriage to be terminated. During the time of the marital dissolution, there is a heightened risk of sexual and physical aggression, and the risk of violent victimization is greater for women than for men. Even when divorced persons remarry, intimate partner violence is twice as likely to occur in the new marriage compared to never-divorced couples (Browne 1987; Feld and Straus 1990; Finkelhor and Yllö 1985; Wilson and Daly 1993).

Why Do They Stay?

The obvious question is: Why do women stay in abusive relationships? Richard Gelles (1987) argues that there are three factors that influence the decision of a woman to remain in an abusive relationship. First, women tend to stay in abusive relationships in which they are assaulted less frequently and less severely. As expected, women who are repeatedly and severely victimized tend to leave the relationship. Second, the more a woman was physically abused as a child, the more likely she is to stay with an abusive husband. Abused children appear to view violent behavior as normal and learn to tolerate it. And third, women who stay with an abusive partner tend to be less educated and either unemployed or holding low-paying jobs. Women with few resources are more likely to endure an abusive relationship and less likely to seek assistance from others.

Women face many obstacles when deciding whether to stay in an abusive relationship (Meuer, Seymour, and Wallace 2002). Table 5.2 presents thirteen of these obstacles.

Table 5.2 Why Women Stay: Obstacles to Leaving an Abusive Relationship

---

1. Economic dependence on the abuser.
2. Fear for her safety and the safety of her children and/or other members of the family.
3. Isolation from a support system.
4. Low self-esteem, resulting from the degradation of the abuse.
5. Beliefs about family—all problems should be resolved within the family, no one else needs to know.
6. Beliefs about marriage—marriage is sacred and forever.
7. Belief that she is the only person who can stop the abuser—reinforced by the abuser's plea that the victim is the only one who understands him.
8. Belief that he will find her if she tries to leave.
9. Lack of options and resources.
10. Fear of being seriously hurt or killed if she attempts to leave.
11. Threats against others if the victim leaves.
12. Health concerns—the victim physically unable to leave.
13. Society's ageist response to elder victims—complaints of abuse by elderly tend to be dismissed.

Source: Meuer, T., A. Seymour, and H. Wallace. 2002. "Domestic Violence" Chapter 9 in A. Seymour, M. Murry, J. Sigmon, M. Hook, C. Edmunds, M. Gaboury, and B. Coleman (Eds.), *National Violence Assistance Academy Textbook.* Office for Victims of Crime.

The Cycle of Violence

To Lenore Walker (2000) the concept of a **"cycle of violence"** describes the process that characterizes intimate partner violence. She outlines three phases in the cycle of violence, each varying in intensity and duration. *Phase One* is marked by a buildup of tension and hostility in the relationship. The eventual abuser becomes increasingly negative toward his partner; the victim tends to withdraw from him to avoid a confrontation. The abuser may perceive the victim's avoidance as a threat to leave him, which triggers increased oppressiveness, jealousy, and possessiveness. In *Phase Two* the actual battering occurs. The violent episode may only take a few minutes, but is followed by an extended period of adaptation to the shocking behavior of the batterer. The emotional fallout for the victim—feelings of helplessness, depression, and malaise—is usually evident between 24 and 48 hours after the assault. *Phase Three* is considered the "honeymoon phase" in which the abusive partner attempts to convince his victim of his sorrow for his actions and pleads for forgiveness. He makes extraordinary efforts to be kind and solicitous toward his abused partner. He may elicit the help of friends or family members to aid in his attempt to convince the victim that he can be trusted and deserves her love and understanding. Nonetheless, he does believe that the battering has served a purpose and that he may not have to engage in further violence toward his partner.

Corporal Punishment

The use of corporal punishment is pervasive in U.S. families. Approximately one-third of infants and 94 percent of toddlers are spanked, a practice that for about one-third of them continues into the early teen years (Straus and Donnelly 2001: 23–24). For example, four in ten 14-year-olds and one in four 17-year-olds experience corporal punishment (Straus and Donnelly, 2001: 24). Corporal punishment is, for the most part, intended to correct the unruly behavior of children. Until recently pediatricians and social scientists have overlooked the adverse consequences of the use of corporal punishment (Straus 2001).

Murray A. Straus, founder of the Family Research Laboratory at the University of New Hampshire, began investigating the use of corporal punishment and its various effects on children and adolescents. His findings and those of other researchers have provided considerable evidence that the use of corporal punishment has deleterious effects on subsequent behavior of children and adolescents and on their emotional well-being and cognitive development. Conversely, not spanking a child has beneficial consequences for a child. Straus and Donnelly (2001: 4) defines **corporal punishment** as "the use of physical force with the intention of causing a child to experience pain, but not injury, for the purpose of correction or control of the child's behavior." Straus, Sugarman, and Giles (1997) report that children who are spanked are significantly more likely to continue their antisocial behavior—e.g., lying, trouble at school, deliberate misbehavior two years later. Furthermore, the more the child is spanked, the greater the frequency of antisocial behavior in the future. These findings hold even when taking into account the child's sex, race or ethnicity, level of antisocial behavior prior to the use of corporal punish-

The psychological trauma of verbal and physical violence extends far beyond the initial incident.

ment, the socioeconomic status of the family, the emotional support of the parents, and the cognitive stimulation provided in the home. In short, it does not matter if the child is male or female, white or nonwhite, particularly unruly prior to the use of corporal punishment or not, from a well-to-do or poor home, or was given emotional support or cognitive stimulation at home, corporal punishment increases the risk a child's emotional disorder and antisocial behavior.

Corporal punishment is also linked to fighting in school. Evidence is available that kindergarten children who are spanked are twice as likely to physically attack another child at school within six months. And, children who are administered severe forms of corporal punishment—more than a slap or a tug on an arm—are four times more likely to assault another kindergarten student. An additional recent study shows that the more children are subjected to corporal punishment, the more likely they are to engage in fighting in school five years later. The link between corporal punishment and antisocial behavior is evident for both boys and girls at all ages and races (Gunroe and Mariner 1997; Straus 2000b).

Children who are slapped by a parent have a greater probability of assaulting a parent a year and a half later. Child-to-parent assault is more likely even when taking into account the race, the family's socioeconomic status, the child's physical size, attitude toward aggression, and attachment to the parent (Brezina 1999). Corporal punishment of boys is also linked to their use of violence in a dating relationship. The use of physical force on a girlfriend is far more common among boys who have been hit by a parent (Simons et al. 1998).

A national study of 960 U.S. children shows that corporal punishment tends to restrict cognitive development of children. Cognitive ability in the early stages of development (children aged 1 to 4) is measured by body part recognition,

Ten Myths About Corporal Punishment

1. Spanking works better.
2. Spanking is needed as a last resort.
3. Spanking is harmless.
4. One or two times won't cause any damage.
5. Parents can't stop without training.
6. If you don't spank, your child will be spoiled or run wild.
7. Parents spank rarely or for only serious problems.
8. By the time a child is a teenager, parents have stopped.
9. If parents don't spank, they will verbally abuse their child.
10. It is unrealistic to expect parents never to spank.

Source: Straus, M., and D. Donnelly. 2001. *Beating the Devil Out of Them: Corporal Punishment in American Families and its Effects on Children.* New Brunswick, NJ: Transaction Publishers, pp. 149–162.

memory for locations, and motor and social development. The effect of several variables—mother's education; mother's age at the time the child was born; the child's age, gender, and birth weight; father's presence in the home; mother's supportiveness and cognitive stimulation; ethnicity; number of children in the home—is controlled in an attempt to isolate the impact of corporal punishment on cognitive development. The results show that cognitive development of children is impeded by the use of corporal punishment (Straus and Paschall 1998).

Using data from a national sample of 6,002 U.S. families, Straus and Kantor (1994) investigate the possible link between corporal punishment of teenagers and adverse behavioral and psychological effects later in life. They hypothesize that the more teenagers experience corporal punishment, the more likely they are to be depressed, have suicidal thoughts, abuse alcohol, and assault their wives or children later on.

Theories of Domestic Violence

Exchange/Social Control Model

Richard Gelles (1979, 1994) has integrated exchange and social control formulations to account for violence in the family. Exchange theory posits that human social behavior is motivated by the desire to maximize rewards and minimize

The More Corporal Punishment a Child Experiences, the More Likely He or She is To:

In Childhood

- Hit other children.
- Act out aggressively in other ways, such as hitting parents.
- Experience less rapid cognitive development.

In Adulthood

- Be depressed or suicidal.
- Physically abuse children or spouse.
- Engage in other violent crimes.
- Have a drinking problem.
- Be attracted to masochistic sex.
- Not achieve a high occupation or income.

Source: Straus, M., and D. Donnelly. 2001. *Beating the Devil Out of Them: Corporal Punishment in American Families and its Effects on Children.* New Brunswick, NJ: Transaction Publishers, pp. 165–166.

punishment or costs associated with certain actions. If others provide benefits to an individual for behaving in a certain way, then he or she will tend to continue that behavior. The continuation of the social interaction, then, depends on the extent of reciprocity involved. However, if there is an absence of reciprocity between the interacting parties, then interpersonal conflict and violence may well ensue.

Gelles (1994: 274) notes that: "A central (and perhaps a greatly oversimplified) proposition of an exchange/social control theory of family violence is that *people hit and abuse other family members because they can.*" If the perceived benefits for assaulting a family member—exertion of control and dominance and the immediate release of tension—outweigh the potential costs—public disgrace, arrest or abandonment—then domestic violence is more probable. In addition, the social control formulation proposes family violence is more likely when there is an "absence of social controls which would bind people to the social order and negatively sanction family members for acts of violence" (Gelles 1994: 275).

Gelles (1994: 275-276) summarizes his exchange/social control formulation in the following three propositions:

1. Family members are more likely to use violence in the home when they expect the costs of being violent are less than the rewards.

2. The absence of effective social controls over family relations decreases the costs of one family member being violent toward another.

3. Certain social and family structures serve to reduce social control in family relations and therefore reduce the costs and/ or increase the rewards of being violent.

Gelles (1994) also argues that three social conditions increase the likelihood of violence within the home: privacy, inequality, and the cultural link between violence and being a "real man."

Privacy.   What occurs in the confines of the U.S. home is largely a private matter. Wide discretion in the forms that interaction between family members may take is socially and legally permissible. Wives and husbands, children and grandparents may act toward one another in the privacy of their homes in ways that would be inappropriate in a public setting and legally sanctioned if directed toward someone outside the family.

Domestic privacy, then, limits the extent of social control over family interaction. Both formal and informal means of control are used less frequently and with less severe sanctions in matters involving domestic violence. Except in rare instances, neighbors are reluctant to interfere in family altercations; law enforcement agencies are restricted by specific guidelines for dealing with calls involving domestic violence. As a consequence, there is an absence of social controls over intrafamilial matters that increase the opportunity for assaultive behavior in the home.

Inequality.   Families are typically characterized by inequality among their members. Status differences between spouses flow from the economic resources of husbands and wives—husbands often have a higher paying job with more social prestige than their wives. Wide status differences are evident between parents and their offspring—children are most often physically weaker, economically dependent, and without ready access to guardians outside the home. These inequities serve to structure offender–victim relations in domestic violence. The victimization of women and children is not only more frequent, but the physical and psychological consequences are more severe. Women, and by extension their children, often lack the economic resources to seek legal assistance or to leave the hostile situation. They may also be so intimidated by the threat of more severe beatings that they are reluctant to take advantage of publicly supported programs for battered women and children. As a result, men can act violently toward their wives and children with impunity.

Violent Behavior and the "Real Man."   The U.S. culture provides considerable support for the belief that "real men" are also violent men. Men are culturally expected to be decisive, act aggressively, and appreciate competitive and violent sports. This is particularly true for men who live in "subcultures of violence," where violence is seen as a viable means to settle disputes (see Wolfgang and Ferracuti 1967). In the home, men are considered the "head of the household" and as such they control important decisions; they expect to be treated with deference and respect. When these cultural expectations are not met, wives and children may well be dealt with in a violent manner. The link between manliness and the willingness to use violence to establish dominance and control underlies much of domestic violence (Gelles 1994).

Power and Dominance

Murray A. Straus and his colleagues (1995) in the Family Violence Research Program at the University of New Hampshire have developed a balance of power/gender inequality formulation of domestic violence. In families characterized by an asymmetrical power structure—where typically the husband's wishes take precedence over those of his wife—the probability of domestic violence is increased. The dominance of men within the family is played out in the larger context of the social conditions that affect family interactions.

The experience of stress in everyday life impacts life within the family. Stress and conflict experienced in the workplace or school, in the neighborhood or community, or in the larger society may well affect the behavior of family members toward one another. The consequences of socioeconomic inequity add further to the stress generated by daily interactions outside the family. The lack of job opportunity or stability is a primary source of stress within the family. Marital conflict often is precipitated by financial problems with few prospects for economic recovery or stability.

Yet, Straus and his colleagues (1995) argue that stress experienced by family members does not adequately account for domestic violence. When husbands and wives have also been violently victimized or witnessed violence in their family of origin, or when the family is immersed in a "subculture of violence" that legitimates the use of violence, the chances that familial stress will erupt in a violent altercation are greatly increased.

Power theory takes into account a myriad of social conditions that generate stress for family members. It also recognizes the stressful consequences of gender inequality and sexism for husband–wife interaction. However, power imbalance theory is not limited to issues related to gender inequality in attempting to account for domestic violence.

Feminist Theory

Feminist theorists focus their attention on the patriarchal structure of society to explain the violence of men toward their female intimate partners (Dobash and Dobash 1988; Yllö 1984; Yllö and Bograd 1988). Male dominance is the key to understanding the victimization of wives and paramours. Men, it is argued, set expectations for the behavior of their intimate partners. When these women fail to live up to these expectations, men resort to violence to establish their position of dominance in the relationship. The Dobashs (1988), a husband and wife team of feminist researchers from Wales, argue that men learn to use physical force largely by participating in a violent male subculture.

Kersti Yllö (1984, 1988) argues that issues related to gender and power are critical to understanding domestic violence. Male dominance within the family is viewed as a reflection of the power structure of the larger society. Simply put, men resort to violence to exert coercive control over women. Feminist theorists argue that men batter women because they gain considerably from doing so. Not only does violence result in the domination of a woman at the time it is carried out, but it also establishes gender differences in the social relationship.

Subculture of Violence

Marvin Wolfgang and Franco Ferracuti's (1967) subculture of violence formulation helps us understand the context in which domestic violence may occur. Families in neighborhoods that are characterized by norms and values that support the use of violence to settle interpersonal disputes are more likely to resort to violence to resolve family conflicts. The family then models the behavior that is prevalent within its surrounding subculture. Children witness violent outbursts in the home and are often the targets of parental assault. Violent behavior becomes a learned response—an appropriate, expected, and effective way to get what you want immediately or to control the behavior of other people.

Routine Activities

The tenets of Lawrence Cohen and Marcus Felson's (1979) routine activities approach to understanding criminality are particularly applicable to violence within the family. Cohen and Felson argue that criminal activity requires: (1) a motivated offender to carry out the offense, (2) a suitable target or victim, and (3) an absence of a guardian for the potential victim. When these three conditions converge in time and space, criminal offending becomes more probable.

As Richard Gelles (1994) points out family violence differs from other forms of assaultive behavior. Men who have accepted the cultural view that real men use violence to maintain dominance over their wives and children carry out intrafamily violence in the privacy of the home, often characterized by an inequitable spousal relationship. Men who believe that the use of violence against wives and children is a mark of their manliness are certainly *motivated offenders.* Wide disparities in economic and other resources of wives and by extension their children—characteristic of inequitable relations between husband and wives—provide *suitable targets* for family violence. And the privacy of the home virtually ensures the *lack of a guardian* for the intended victim.

Strain

Strain theory, set forth by Robert Agnew (1992), focuses on negative interpersonal relations as a primary source of stress for the individual. Sustained family conflict has been found to generate particularly devastating negative emotions, e.g., jealousy, rage, resentment, and depression. Healthy coping strategies are required if an individual is to reduce the resultant tension. Prior experiences with family violence, either as a witness or a victim, and integration into a subculture of violence may impede the development of effective coping strategies and increase the likelihood of domestic violence. The use of violence tends to worsen the strained relations within the family, resulting in the perpetuation of negative emotional states for both the victim and offender. In brief, the cycle of negative familial relations leads to negative emotions that may erupt in acts of violence toward family members. However, violence within the family further strains the fragile relations among the family members and sets in motion a new wave of negative emotions with which to cope.

Frustration–Aggression

The frustration–aggression hypothesis of John Dollard and his colleagues (1939) states that the experience of frustration always leads to aggression. Frustration may be seen as a blockage to goal attainment. Certainly the behavior of family members often involves impediments to one another's goals—husbands have expectations for their wives, and wives for their husbands that may not be met; parents expect their children to behave in ways that are disregarded; and children's demands may well be in conflict with their parents' willingness or ability to grant. In short, family life is fraught with frustrating experiences. The aggression that follows may be verbal—shouting, threatening, and at times abusive. But, it may soon escalate into pushing, shoving, slapping, or more severe forms of physical aggression. The inability to control the situation by violence or the threat of violence is itself frustrating, leading to the recurrence of assaultive behavior.

Unreciprocity

Stuart Palmer (1972) has recast the frustration–aggression hypothesis in role terms. He argues that unreciprocity in role relationships accounts for aggressive and violent behavior. Unreciprocity is experienced when others in complementary roles (e.g., wives and husbands, parents and children), interfere with the roles' performance. Husbands may attempt to control their wives' behavior or access to economic resources, thereby impeding their opportunities to socialize outside the family or to be able to adequately care for the children. Wives may make inordinate demands on the husband's time or economic resources. Unreciprocity in familial relations is marked by controlling and domineering behavior or manipulative or relentlessly demanding behavior. If unreciprocity in the relations among family members persists, then some form of aggression is highly likely. As aggressive behaviors escalate, physical violence may well follow.

Self-Control

In their General Theory of Crime, Michael Gottfredson and Travis Hirschi (1990) argue that the lack of self-control predicts involvement in all forms of criminal activity. Persons who lack self control tend to be "impulsive, insensitive, physical

Explanations of Domestic Violence Rates

Theories and Theorists	Sociological Predictors	Hypotheses
Power Dominance Theory		
• Straus	Power Imbalance Stress Conflict	Broad social-structural conditions produce stress and conflict in family systems. When stress is coupled with violent childhood experiences, domestic violence is more probable.
Feminist Theory Gender/Inequality Theory		
• Yllö • Dobash and Dobash	Patriarchy	Patriarchy teaches men how and when to use violent techniques. Men maintain power and control through violence against women.
Subculture Theory		
• Wolfgang and Ferracuti	Subcultures of Violence	Participation in subcultures of violence increases the acceptance of subcultural customs and values for violence as a response to frustrating conditions. Acceptance of such values increases the likelihood of committing domestic violence.

Individual Level Explanations of Domestic Violence

Theories and Theorists	Sociological Predictors	Hypotheses
Social Learning Theory		
• Akers	Differential Reinforcement	Individuals who hold attitudes that disapprove of domestic violence are less likely to commit domestic violence. The greater the costs for domestic violence, the less likely the individual is to commit domestic violence.
• Glaser	Differential Identification	Individuals are more likely to commit domestic violence if they identify with another person who views domestic violence as acceptable.

(continued)

Routine Activities Theory

• Cohen and Felson	Motivated Offender Suitable Target Absence of Guardian	Domestic violence is likely to occur when there is a suitable target, a motivated offender, and a lack of a capable guardian.

Control/Exchange Theory

• Gelles	Inequality Privacy Social Control	Family members are more likely to use violence in the home when they expect that the costs of being violent are less than the rewards. The absence of effective social controls over family relations decreases the costs of one family member being violent towards another.
		Certain social and family structures serve to reduce social control in family relations, and therefore reduce the costs and/or increase the rewards of being violent.

General Strain Theory

• Agnew	Strain/Stress	The greater the strain experienced by an individual, the greater the experience of negative emotions. The greater the negative emotional experience, the more likely an individual will commit domestic violence.

Self-control Theory

• Gottfredson and Hirschi	Self-control	The greater the individual's self-control, the lower the probability of engaging in domestic violence.

Frustration-Aggression Theory

• Dollard and colleagues	Frustration Aggression	High levels of frustration increase levels of aggression.
		Increased levels of aggression are likely to result in domestic violence.

Unreciprocity

• Palmer	Unreciprocity	Unreciprocity increases levels of frustration.
		Increased levels of frustration are likely to result in higher levels of domestic violence.

(as opposed to mental), risk-taking, shortsighted, and nonverbal, and they tend therefore to engage in criminality and analogous risk-taking behavior" (Gottfredson and Hirschi 1990: 90). To Gottfredson and Hirschi (1990: 90), criminal offending provides "relief from momentary irritation." Often, husband and wives assault one another simply to end an explosive encounter—an argument that neither side is willing to negotiate—or to assert control over the other person or the present situation. When self-control is weak conflict between spouses or parents and their children may erupt into acts of aggression and violence.

Social Learning Theory

Ronald Akers's (1994) social learning formulation considers factors that generate both the either deviant or conforming behavior. To Akers, learning deviant or conforming behaviors involves four related processes: differential association, definitions, differential reinforcement, and imitation. Differential association means interaction with persons who favor the violation of the law far more so than with persons who advocate conformist behavior. The more time an individual spends with others who condone the use of violence in the home—"to keep wives and children under control"—the more likely that person is to engage in wife battering and child abuse. *Definitions* refer to the meaning that is assigned to certain behaviors. Akers (1994: 97) notes that they are "the orientations, rationalizations, definitions of the situation, and other evaluative and moral attitudes that define the commission of an act as right or wrong, good or bad, desirable or undesirable, justified or unjustified." When spousal assault and severe corporal punishment are defined as normative, necessary, and justifiable, they will be routinely carried out in the home. Differential reinforcement of a given behavior is a consequence of the rewards received or anticipated. Behaviors that are positively rewarded will tend to be repeated. Domestic violence may be positively rewarded by the compliance of the victim with the wishes of the perpetrator. Wives may acquiesce to the demands of their husbands; children may carry out the wishes of their parents or forego expecting their parents to condone their behavior. When acts of violence against family members result in a desirable outcome for the offender, they will be reinforced and most often repeated. Imitation means simply that individuals model or copy the behavior of others. Children who have witnessed violence between their parents or who have been the victims of abuse at the hands of their caretakers may learn that these behaviors are effective means for controlling others and for immediate gratification. Because it seemed to work for their parents, it becomes a viable strategy for dealing with their own wives and children.

Differential identification, introduced by Daniel Glaser (1956) is closely related to the concept of differential reinforcement. He points out that a deviant may well identify with another who is likely to condone her or his behavior. The concept of differential identification helps us to understand why not all children who are exposed to violent behavior in the home batter their wives or abuse their children. If children or adolescents do not identify with a violent parent, then they are less apt to see violence as an acceptable strategy for controlling members of their family. Their lack of identification with an abusive parent may result in abhorrence for violence either within the home or outside of it. Differential identification is then another element in the complex process of learning patterns of behavior.

Chapter Summary

- Domestic violence is coercive behavior through the use of intimidating, threatening, harmful, or harassing behavior. Domestic violence includes:
  - Physical abuse
  - Sexual abuse
  - Emotional or psychological abuse
- Domestic violence occurs in all racial and ethnic groups, and across socio-economic classes.
- Women are more likely to be victimized by their intimate partners than are men.
- Women who are separated or divorced are 150 percent more likely to be assaulted by an intimate partner than their male counterparts.
- Women are more likely than men to suffer negative social and psychological consequences following victimization.
- Being a victim of child maltreatment significantly increases the risk of being a victim of domestic violence. Also, the risk of victimization is significantly greater when there is a disparity in the relative status between victim and offender. In addition, intimate partner violence is significantly greater for those who are cohabitating versus married, African American versus white, living with a verbally abusive partner, or one who controls access to family, friends, or economic resources.
- Certain key life course events tend to increase the risk of violence between intimates. These include:
  - Dating and courtship
  - Early years of marriage
  - Separation and divorce
- Victims of spousal assault construct a "definition of the situation" that takes into account their economic resources and social supports, religious beliefs, and access to legal assistance and protective services. If an abused women defines herself as "helpless" and her situation as intractable, then she is less likely to define her abuse as criminal and more likely to be repeatedly victimized.
- Women tend to stay in abusive relationships:
  - If they are assaulted less frequently or less severely
  - If they were abused as a child
  - If they are less educated and are either unemployed or hold low-paying jobs

- The "cycle of violence" characterizes intimate partner violence. It includes three phases:
  - Phase one: A buildup of tension and hostility
  - Phase two: The actual battering
  - Phase three: The abusive partner attempts to convince his victim of his sorrow for his actions and pleads for forgiveness
- Four forms of child maltreatment are generally agreed upon:
  - Physical abuse
  - Neglect
  - Sexual abuse
  - Emotional abuse
- Approximately 903,000 U.S. children are victims of child maltreatment each year. Most of these children are victims of neglect, followed by physical abuse, sexual abuse, and either medical neglect or psychological abuse.
- Child maltreatment victimization rates are highest for infants through the age of 3 and lowest for teenagers between 16 and 17 years of age.
- Child maltreatment rates are lowest for Asians/Pacific Islanders, followed by whites, Hispanics, Native Americans/Alaska Natives, and highest for African Americans.
- Most child maltreatment cases involve one parent acting alone. The majority of the perpetrators of child maltreatment are female. Male offenders account for the majority of sexual abuse of children.
- There is considerable evidence that homes marked by violence between spouses are also places in which children are abused or neglected.
- Children who are the victims of maltreatment or who have been physically or sexually abused in their homes are more likely to engage in antisocial behavior, criminal activity, and domestic violence later in life.
- Considerable evidence exists to support the idea that corporal punishment has deleterious effects on subsequent behavior of children and adolescents and on their emotional well-being and cognitive development. Conversely, not using corporal punishment has beneficial consequences for a child.
- Less is known about the extent and nature of elder abuse.
  - Approximately 450,000 persons over the age of 60 are victims of domestic abuse or neglect.
  - Elderly women are disproportionately victimized.
  - Between 52 and 60 percent of the abused elderly are 80 years of age or older.

Key Concepts

Domestic violence: The involvement of any family member in the intentional physical injury of another; coercion through the use of intimidating, threatening, harmful, or harassing behavior.

Child maltreatment: Child abuse and neglect, sexual abuse, and emotional abuse.

Child abuse and neglect: Any act or failure to act on the part of a parent or caretaker that results in death, serious physical or emotional harm, sexual abuse or exploitation; an act or failure to act that presents an imminent risk of serious harm.

Sexual abuse: The employment, use, persuasion, inducement, or coercion of any child to engage in any sexual behavior, including rape, statutory rape, incest, molestation, prostitution, or other form of sexual exploitation of children.

Emotional abuse: Acts or omission to acts by the parents or other caregivers that have caused, or could cause serious behavioral, cognitive, emotional, or mental disorders.

Learned helplessness: The inability to predict how an abuser will react to one's actions; a process that results in devising ways to adapt to an abusive relationship.

Cycle of violence: The term coined by Lenoir Walker to describe the process that characterizes intimate partner violence.

Corporal punishment: The use of physical force with the intention of causing a child to experience pain, but not injury, for the purpose of correction or control of the child's behavior.

Critical Thinking Questions

1. What is the link between involvement in domestic violence either as an offender or a victim and the likelihood of engaging in violent behavior outside the home?

2. What are the sociocultural roots of domestic violence, including child and elder victimization? What are the intrafamilial conditions that exacerbate an adverse sociocultural milieu?

3. Jim is 10 years old, and he and his 6-year old sister Sally have witnessed their father beating their mother on many occasions. They, too, have suffered physical injury repeatedly at the hands of their father. It is now twelve years later and Jim and Sally are each employed as unskilled laborers and will be married in the same year. In the next four years, Jim and Sally will each have three children. Describe the domestic life for Jim and Sally. What are the factors that will increase or decrease the likelihood of domestic violence?

4. Discuss the sociopolitical conditions that serve to perpetuate the forms of violent behaviors that occur in the home. What factors serve to significantly reduce the occurrence of domestic violence?

Web Extra

Check out these websites for additional information on domestic violence:

http://www.ncadv.org

http://www.unh.edu/frl

http://www.unh.edu/ccrc

CHAPTER 6

Suicide and Life-Threatening Behaviors

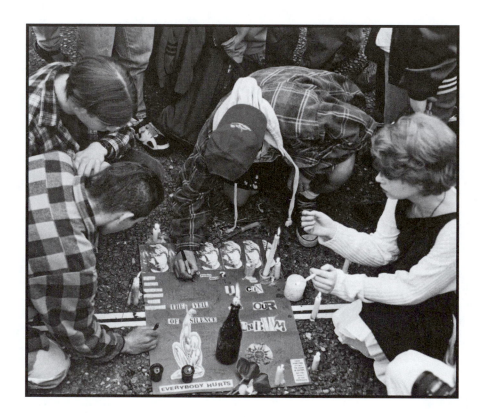

Portraits of Suicide

- Many places around the world are known as "suicide spots"—well-known places where people go to kill themselves. These include bridges, such as The Golden Gate Bridge, buildings, and volcanoes. Aokigahara, a forest near Mt. Fuji, is a well-known suicide spot in Japan. The dense vegetation, mountain dogs, and underground magnetic field that disrupt compasses make it difficult for searches and rescues. As a result, the site attracts suicidal people who don't want their bodies to be recovered. During an annual search, police recovered 73 bodies. Police further calculate that as many as 40 people attempt suicide in the forest each year. (*Source:* Kattoulas, V. 1998. "Japan's Suicide Spot" *Newsweek,* October 27. Web posted at www .newsweek.com:10/27/98.)

- A Duke University student posted suicide instructions on the Internet that included forty methods for suicide. A 14-year-old boy downloaded those instructions and followed method number 14. He jumped in front of a train. At the time of his suicide, he was carrying a notebook with the instructions that suggested he go for decapitation to ensure his death rather than a broken spine. (*Source:* The Associated Press. 1999. "Online Suicide Instructions Evoke Anger" *USA Today,* January 26. Web posted at www.usatoday.com: 1/26/99.)

LEARNING OBJECTIVES

After reading this chapter you should know:

- ☐ The medical, legal, and cultural definition of suicide.
- ☐ Patterns and trends of suicide in the world and in the United States.
- ☐ Age, gender, and race patterns of suicide.
- ☐ Precipitating factors, risk factors, and protective factors of suicide.
- ☐ Current prediction, prevention and intervention methods for suicide in the United States.
- ☐ Special topics including homicide followed by suicide, suicide by cop, and assisted suicide.

Introduction

Suicide and other acts of self-destruction represent a complex set of behaviors, some intentional and deliberate, others ambivalent and reckless. Wide cultural differences exist in the meanings attached to suicidal behavior and its appropriateness as a form of death. The decision to end one's own life may be viewed as morally reprehensible and religiously prohibited, permitted under well-defined circumstances, or an expected form of death for some members of society.

Suicidal behavior tends to be structured by age, gender, and race as are other forms of violent behavior. In this chapter we will consider the diversity of suicide and self-destructive behavior across the globe, the differential involvement of various segments of society, and theoretical understandings of the influence of social structural arrangements, cultural meanings, and values given to suicidal behavior and its various precipitants.

Medical/Legal Definitions of Suicide

Suicide is typically defined as the willful, deliberate, and voluntary termination of one's life. Medical examiners, coroners, and public health officials in the United States rely on the definition of suicide provided by Centers for Disease Control and Prevention (CDC) in Atlanta. The CDC (1988) defines suicide as a "death from injury, poisoning, or suffocation where there is evidence (either explicit or implicit) that the injury was self-inflicted and that the decedent intended to kill himself/herself."

> *There is but one truly serious philosophical problem, and that is suicide. Judging whether life is or is not worth living amount to answering the fundamental question of philosophy.*
>
> —Albert Camus.[1]

The World Health Organization (WHO) provides a broad, yet succinct, definition of suicide. The WHO (1995) defines suicide as "a suicidal act with a fatal outcome"; a suicidal act is considered to be a "self-injury with varying degrees of lethal intent." These medical-legal definitions of suicide provide considerable latitude in their interpretation.

> *Mostly, I have been impressed by how little value our society puts on saving the lives of those who are in such despair as to want to end them. It is a social illusion that suicide is rare. It is not.*
>
> —Kay Jamison (1999: 310).

The intention to end one's life is an essential element in the determination of suicide. Suicidal intention may be either *explicit*—as in the case of suicide notes, powder burns on the hand of the victim, or *implicit*—inferences drawn from autopsy results or toxicological tests, reports of the victim's emotional state prior to death, expressions of the desire to die, and making plans to carry out a suicide (Jamison 1999).

According to the guidelines set forth by the CDC, self-inflicted death may be determined by pathologic (autopsy), toxicologic, investigatory, and psychologic evidence and by statements of the decedent or witnesses. Intent to kill oneself is evident if: "at the time of injury, the decedent intended to kill himself/herself or wished to die and that the decedent understood the probable consequences of his/her actions" (CDC 1988).

In many cases circumstantial evidence provides the only clue about the cause of death. Therefore, the final determination by the medical examiner or coroner may well be influenced by political expediency, family intervention, or lack of medical certainty on the part of the medical examiner or coroner. Accidental deaths or involvement in reckless and high-risk behaviors that result in one's death are not included among deaths by suicide (CDC 1988).

---

[1]Albert Camus posted at www.websyntax.com/camus/quotes/bysubject.asp

Forensically trained medical examiners, for the most part, are found in large urban areas and medical school settings. It is still the case in the United States that decisions about the case of death are made by medical doctors without forensic training or by coroners without medical training. The misclassification of the cause of death, particularly in the case of suicide, may be problematic. Deaths due to drug overdose, drowning, falls, and one-car accidents are particularly difficult to classify. Estimates of misclassification range from 50 percent in earlier studies to 10 percent more recently (Jamison 1999).

In short, while the medical/legal definition of suicide is accepted across the United States, the availability of forensic pathologists who serve as medical examiners is limited. This shortage of forensically qualified medical doctors is far more pronounced outside the United States.

Suicide around the World and in the United States

The suicide rate is calculated as the number of deaths caused by suicide per 100,000 persons in the general population. Keeping in mind the caution with regard to the under-reporting of suicide across the world and within the United States, suicide rates are known to vary widely. Approximately one million people kill themselves each year around the world. That is, for every 100,000 persons in the world 16 will take their own lives, or one person every 40 seconds. Over the past 45 years, suicide across the world has increased by 60 percent, making it one of the three leading causes of death in the world for those aged 15 through 44 (WHO 1992).

Except for The People's Republic of China, suicide rates for males exceed those for females. Chinese women killed themselves at a rate (17.9) slightly above the world rate, while the male suicide rate (14.3) was below the world rate. However, in all other countries for which the World Health Organization (WHO) has collected recent data on suicides, national male rates of suicide are typically two to five times higher than those for females. Exceedingly high rates of male suicide are found in Lithuania (73.7), the Russian Federation (72.9), and Kazakhstan (51.9). The highest rates of female suicide are found in The People's Republic of China (17.9), Sri Lanka (16.6), and Hungary (15.6), which also has a particularly high rate of male suicide (49.2) (WHO 1992).

Countries with the lowest rates of male suicides are Egypt (0.1), the Syrian Arab Republic (0.2), and Iran (0.3). Interestingly, Egypt, the Syrian Arab Republic, and Iran each report a suicide rate for women of (0). Other countries for which the suicide rate for women is (0) are: Antigua and Barbuda, Bahamas, Dominican Republic, Honduras, Jordan, Saint Kitts and Nevis, Saint Vincent and The Grenadines, and Seychelles. In a very few societies—Andaman Islanders, the Yahgan of Tierra del Fuego, and some Aborigine tribes—suicide is said never to occur (WHO 1992).

Rate of Suicide in the United States

Suicide is the eighth leading cause of death in the United States. In recent years more than 30,000 deaths each year are attributed to suicide, for a rate of 11 per 100,000 persons. There is a completed suicide in the U.S. every 15 minutes. Suicides are attempted, however, approximately every 60 seconds. There are more deaths due to suicide in the U.S. than homicide. For every three suicides there are two homicides (www.cdc.gov.).

Males are four times more likely to kill themselves than are females. But females are between two and three times more likely to attempt suicide than are males (Cannetto and Sakinofsky 1998). Rates of suicide are much higher among white Americans than non-whites and among older persons than the younger persons (www.cdc.gov).

White males commit more than seven in ten of all suicides in the United States. An additional 18 percent are white females. Whites then account for about nine in every ten suicides in the United States. Particularly among white Americans, suicide tends to increase with age. Suicide rates are highest among persons 65 years of age and older. Among older Americans, males account for 83 percent of all suicides. For males between 20 and 64, the suicide rate remains fairly constant. After the age of 65, however, their suicide rate increases significantly. For women, suicides tend to rise rapidly between the ages of 40 and 54 and peak again after the age of 75 (www.cdc.gov).

Compared to other forms of death, suicides account for relatively few deaths. About 1.4 percent of all deaths are attributed to suicide, while 32 percent are caused by heart disease, 23 percent cancer, and 7 percent stroke. However, suicide ranks as the second leading cause of death for college students, the third for persons between the ages of 15 and 34, and fourth for persons between the ages of 10 and 14 (www.cdc.gov).

Suicide rates are rising fastest among the young. Over the past half century, suicide among males ages 15 to 24 tripled; for women ages 15 to 24, the rate doubled. For children ages 10 to 14, the suicide rate has more than doubled in the past two decades. The alarming increase in suicide among the young is evident among young black males, a traditionally lower risk group for suicide. In the past fifteen years, suicide among black males (15–24) has increased by more than 66 percent (www.cdc.gov). Similarly, the most recent data show that the suicide rate among Native Americans (including Native Americans and Alaska Natives) is 1.5 times higher than that for the United States as a whole. Approximately 64 percent of all Native American suicides are committed by males between the ages of 15 and 24 (www.cdc.gov).

Regional Differences in the United States

The overall rate of suicide in the United States has been relatively stable during the past twenty years, hovering between 11 and 12 per 100,000. However, rates of suicide vary widely across the United States. Suicide rates are highest in the West (14.1), followed by the South (13.1), Midwest (11.4), and lowest in the Northeast (9.3). Methods for carrying out a suicide also vary by geographical region. Firearm-related suicides are most prevalent in the South, while drug overdoses are most common in the Western states (www.cdc.gov).

Special Populations

Women

As we have seen, women are far less likely to kill themselves than are men, but are far more likely to attempt suicide than are men. Every 90 minutes in the United States a woman will kill herself, but every 78 seconds a woman will attempt to kill herself. Alarming increases have been noted in recent years among young women. Over the latter decades of the twentieth century, the suicide rate for women 15 to 24 doubled, tripled for white girls ages 10 to 14, and quadrupled for African American girls (www.afsp.org/index-1.htm).

Suicidal behavior is more common among single, separated, divorced, or widowed women. Loss of family ties or crises in interpersonal relations are among the leading precipitants of suicide attempts in women. Mood disorders, including depression, dysthymia, and seasonal affective disorder, are more common in women and have been cited as underlying factors in their suicidal behavior (www.afsp.org/index-1.htm).

Native Americans

The rate of suicide among Native Americans is reported to be higher than for any other ethnic group. The Native American suicide rate tends to be highest among young adults and declines with age. The suicide rate of young Native Americans (15 to 24 years of age) is three to four times higher than any other ethnic group. The typical Native American suicide is a young male who is unemployed, drinks heavily, and ends his life either with a firearm or by hanging. Young Native American females are more likely to attempt suicide, typically by drug overdoses, than to complete suicide (Bachman 1992; EchoHawk 1997).

Ronet Bachman (1992: 120) in her in-depth investigation of violent death among Native Americans finds that "economic deprivation has a significant and positive impact on suicide within reservation communities." Suicide rates on the reservation increase with unemployment, dropout, and poverty rates. Bachman also observes that the suicide rate is highly correlated with the homicide rate.

> It is apparent that suicide is related to the structural circumstances within communities, such as unemployment and poverty. When communities provide little opportunity for economic self-sufficiency, frustrations appear to be manifest in acts of violence. These acts tend to be non-discriminatory and are directed both toward the self in acts of suicide or toward others in acts of assault that are often lethal (Bachman 1992: 120–121).

The highest rates for both suicide and homicide are found among Native Americans who live in the southwestern United States, the northern Rocky Mountains, the Plains states, and Alaska. Suicide rates vary widely—as much as 150 per 100,000—between Native American tribes (Berlin 1987).

Elderly

Among white Americans, the risk of suicide tends to increase with age. Persons over the age of 65 are significantly more apt to end their own lives than younger persons. Men disproportionately account for elderly suicides, more so than other age groups. Older men are at greatest risk to end their own life. Among elderly men, the divorced or widowed are 2.7 times more likely to kill themselves than are those who are married, and 1.4 times more likely than the never-married. Similarly, elderly women who are divorced or widowed are 1.8 times more likely to commit suicide than are elderly married women and 1.4 times more likely than their never-married counterparts (www.cdc.gov).

While separation, divorce, or widowhood elevate the risk of suicide in general, other risk factors set the elderly apart from the young. Physical illness,

Elderly Suicides

- While the elderly are about 12 percent of the population, they account for about 18 percent of all suicides.

- Older white males have the highest rate of suicide, about 35 per 100,000, or over three times the rate for the U.S. population as a whole.

- Older persons attempt suicide less frequently than do younger persons, but they complete the suicidal act. For persons over the age of 65, there is one completed suicide for every four attempts.

- Older men account for 85 percent of elderly suicides, 5.5 times more than for elderly women suicides.

- Beyond undiagnosed or untreated depression, common risk factors for elderly suicide include:

  - The recent death of a loved one
  - Physical illness, uncontrolled pain, or the fear of a prolonged illness
  - Perceived poor health
  - Social isolation and loneliness
  - Major changes in social roles (e.g., retirement)

Sources: www.cdc.gov; www.suicidology.org; www.nimh.nih.gov

depression, and social isolation are more pronounced among the elderly. The elderly are also more apt to have sought medical attention just prior to their suicide. While the elderly make fewer suicide attempts, they tend to use more lethal methods (Pearson, J. L., et al. 1997; www.cdc.gov).

A global epidemic of elderly suicide is underway. The World Health Organization (WHO 1995) reports that Hungary has one of the highest rates of elderly suicides worldwide (168.9 for men and 60 for women). Rural China also has an exceedingly high rate of elderly suicide (142.6 for men and 100.8 for women). By contrast, the rates for elderly (over 75) males and females in the United States are 50.7 for men and 5.6 for women, and in Canada the elderly male and female rates are 26.6 and 3.7 respectively (WHO 1995).

Youth

Recent decades have witnessed alarming increases in the rates of suicide among adolescents and young adults. Persons under the age of 25 account for about 1 in 6.7 suicides in the United States. Over the past four decades adolescent and young adult suicide has nearly tripled. For persons between the ages of 15 and 24, suicide is the third leading cause of death, behind intentional injury and homicide. More teenagers and young adults die from suicide than from cancer,

The stresses of life often over-whelm college and university students. Conflicting demands on their time and energy increasingly lead to self-medication—drug and alcohol abuse—and other self-destructive behaviors. Suicide is the second leading cause of death among undergraduates.

heart disease, AIDS, birth defects, stroke, pneumonia and influenza, and chronic lung disease combined (www.cdc.gov).

While the risk of suicide is greatest among young white males, the suicide rate among young black males is rising dramatically. Over the past few decades, the suicide rate among black male teenagers (15–19) has more than doubled. The increase in the black male suicide rate is almost ten times higher than the rate increase for 15- to 19-year-olds in general. In addition, the suicide rate for pre- and early teens (10–14), while lower than the rate for older teenagers, is now more than double what it was a few decades earlier (CDC 1998).

Increases in youth suicide are also evident across the globe. The highest rates of youth suicide—more than 30 per 100,000—are found in Finland, Latvia, Lithuania, New Zealand, the Russian Federation, and Slovenia. Japan and countries in Western Europe tend to have youth suicide rates below 15 per 100,000. Overall, the suicide rate for young males (15–24) exceeds that for their female peers by a ratio of 11 to 1; in Ireland the ratio is 2 to 1. In Sweden females are as equally likely to commit suicide as males (WHO).

Precipitants of Suicide

Several factors are known to increase the risk of suicidal behavior. These factors may be considered on three levels: social structural positioning (e.g., age, race, gender, marital status), life circumstances (e.g., stress, social losses, and relationship crises), and individual (e.g., mental or physical illness, alcohol and drug abuse, perceptions of helplessness and hopelessness).

Social Structural Positioning

As we have seen throughout this chapter, suicidal death is not distributed uniformly across the social structure. Rather, suicide varies by age, race and ethnicity, gender, and marital status. Older persons, whites, males, and the unmarried, particularly the recently separated and divorced, are more vulnerable to suicide.

Youth Suicides in the United States

- Suicide ranks as the third leading cause of death for young people (15–24); only accidents and homicide occur more frequently.

- About eleven persons between the ages of 15 to 24 commit suicide each day, or one every 2 hours and 15 minutes.

- Over the past sixty years, the suicide rate for young males (15–24) rose by 400 percent and doubled for young females.

- Males between 15 and 19 years of age are 4.8 times more likely to commit suicide than are their female peers, and males between the ages of 20 and 24 are 6.6 times more likely to kill themselves.

- For every complete suicide among the young, there are an estimated 100 to 200 attempted suicides.

- Suicide is the second leading cause of death for college students.

- One in twelve college students has made a suicide plan.

- College students with a mental health problem are at highest risk for suicide. Males, Asians, and Hispanics, and students under the age of 21 are at particularly high risk for suicide.

Sources: www.cdc.gov; www.suicidology.org; www.nimh.nih.gov

It follows that older white men would have the highest rate of suicide and younger nonwhite females would have the lowest rates. Being divorced or separated tends to increase the risk of suicide for all social structural groupings.

Suicide also varies considerably by occupational status and occupational history. Suicide tends to be higher among persons in high-prestige occupations (e.g., professional and managers) and low-prestige occupations (e.g., farm workers, laborers, and operatives) (Palmer and Humphrey 1990). A consistent finding is that persons who occupy mid-level occupations (e.g., school teachers, clerical workers, career bureaucrats) are less prone to suicide. For persons at the extremes of the occupational prestige continuum either much can be lost or little can be gained. When control over one's life circumstances is lost, the resulting frustration may result in a sense of overwhelming futility. Suicide may then ensue.

Life Circumstances

For many of us everyday life may be turbulent at times, a wild and unpredictable series of tragic events that leave us with the sense that life is hopeless and we are helpless to do anything about it. If this sense of hopelessness and helplessness persists, it begins to significantly compromise our problem-solving ability. Farber (1968) has observed that when hope is lost, our sense of competence is also lost. Competency means that we have control over what happens to us, that we can influence the circumstances of life that most matter to us. When this is lost and a strong sense of hopelessness and helplessness take hold, persistent thoughts of suicide may follow. A plan to put those thoughts into action may seem to be needed.

Jack Gibbs (1968: 17) asserts that the fundamental etiological factor in suicide is the "disruption in social relations." Disruption in social relations refers to an interruption in a regular pattern of social interaction. Gibbs (1968: 17) sets forth two propositions on the link between disruptions in social relations and suicide: (1) "The greater the incidence of disrupted social relations in a population, the higher the suicide rate of that population; and (2) all suicide victims have experienced a set of disrupted social relations that is not found in the history of non-victims." Disruption in social relations typically refers to the loss of an important social role, (spouse, parent, job or occupation, close friend, etc). Social losses, particularly of persons close to us through death, abandonment, or rejection, may well precipitate our sense of hopelessness and helplessness. When loss

---

AT A GLANCE

Global Trends and Patterns

- In the past forty-five years, the world suicide rate has increased 60 percent. Worldwide suicide is the thirteenth leading cause of death and among the three leading causes of death among those aged 15 to 44 years.
- Approximately one million people die from suicide each year, a global rate of 16 per 100,000 persons, or one suicide every 40 seconds.
- Females worldwide experience a lower suicide rate than males with the exception of the People's Republic of China.

U.S. Trends and Patterns

- More than 30,000 persons commit suicide each year in the United States.
- About one-half million persons who attempt suicide are treated in emergency rooms each year.
- About 1.5 times more people die from suicide than from homicide.
- Overall, suicide is the eleventh leading cause of death for all Americans, and is the third leading cause of death for young people aged 15 to 24.
- For each completed suicide there are an estimated sixteen attempted suicides. More than 5 million living Americans have attempted to kill themselves.
- Nearly 3.6 times as many teen boys commit suicide as girls, but girls are more likely to attempt suicide.

Sources: The WHO (http://www.who.mt.mental_health/pages/suicide.html); Statistics on Suicide (http://www.rochford.org/suicide/resource/stats/); U.S. Public Health Service, *The Surgeon General's Call to Action to Prevent Suicide.* Washington, DC: 1999; Centers for Disease Control and Prevention, Suicide and Attempted Suicide, MMWR 2004:53:471–498; http://www.afsp.org; http://www.nimh.nih.gov; http://www.suicidology.org

is final, when there is no chance for recovery of the lost person, job, reputation, or status in the community, suicide may appear to provide the ultimate solution.

Attempted Suicide

Attempted suicide is far more common than is completed suicide. While there are no official national data on attempted suicide, it is estimated that there are more than three-quarters of a million attempted suicides in the United States each year (NIMH 2003). For every completed suicide there are an estimated 18 to 20 attempted suicides (Mosiciki 1996). Five million Americans are now alive who have attempted to kill themselves (American Association of Suicidology, www .suicidology.org).

Females are between two and three times more likely to attempt suicide than are males. Women, particularly younger women, are more likely to attempt suicide than are men. In the United States, females account for about nine in every ten adolescent suicide attempts. Overall the ratio of a female-to-male suicide attempts is between two and three to one (Stephens 1987).

Suicide has been called a "cry for help" (Farberow and Schniedman 1961). This is especially the case for suicide attempters who for the most part are trying to call attention to a problematic life situation and to elicit others in changing it. An attempt to manipulate one's life circumstances, rather than to cause one's death, influences the lethality of means and the location of the attempt. Less lethal means are typically used in a suicide attempt (e.g., drug overdoses, wrist slashing, or gas poisoning) (Peck 1985–1986). The timing of the attempt and the place it occurs are chosen to maximize the chances of a rescue.

Suicide attempters are typically more ambivalent about living or dying than are persons who complete suicide. Their uncertainty is reflected in the high incidence of warnings, often vague and mostly ignored. Suicide attempts also use less lethal means to kill themselves than do suicide completers. Typically, suicide attempters will overdose on sleeping pills, cut their wrists, or try to asphyxiate themselves (Peck 1984, 1985–1986).

Ronald Maris's (1981) comparison of suicide completers, nonfatal suicide attempters, and natural deaths shows that suicide attempters tend to be young depressed females who use less lethal methods (e.g., poisoning and cutting), but are prone to make multiple attempts. Rigidity of thought, reliance on others for emotional support, feelings of helplessness, and the inability to see alternatives to life circumstance or solutions to current problems are common among suicide attempters (Clifton and Lee 1995).

Psychiatric Illness and Suicide

To Kay Jamison, M.D. (1999) healthy people do not kill themselves. Persons with one or more psychiatric symptoms account for an estimated 90 to 95 percent of all suicides. About one in ten schizophrenics die at their own hand. About three in ten persons suffering from a psychotic disorder will attempt suicide in their lifetimes; more than 42 percent of those suffering from schizo-affective disorder or a major depressive disorder will attempt suicide in their lifetime (Radomsky et al. 1999).

Jamison (1999: 104) contends: "Psychiatric illness, depression and particularly depression combined with alcohol and drugs are the major causes of suicide." She further observes that an estimated 30 to 70 percent of people who kill themselves are victims of mood disorders; the rate is even higher when depression coexists with alcohol or drug abuse. Simply put, *depression+drugs=suicide* (Jamison 1999: 104).

Certain forms of psychiatric illness elevate the risk of suicide. Suicide attempters are thirty-eight times more likely to kill themselves, those suffering from mood disorders (depression) twenty times more likely, manic-depressives fifteen times more likely, and schizophrenics more than eight times more likely (Harris and Barraclough 1997). Jamison (1999: 102–103) notes that:

> Two things seem to be true: First, although there are exceptions, almost everyone who has a physical illness and subsequently commits suicide also has a psychiatric illness. Second, most of the medical conditions that do show a significant increase in the rate of suicide—temporal lobe epilepsy, Huntington's disease, multiple sclerosis, spinal cord injury, HIV/AIDS, head and neck cancer—originate or strongly influence the brain and the rest of the nervous system. These medical disorders can cause extreme mood swings, and in some instances dementia.

Maris (1981) also finds that suicide victims in Chicago are more likely to have a history of mental disorder than persons who die of natural causes. He reports that 40 percent of suicide victims and 50 percent of suicide attempters have been hospitalized for psychiatric illness in their lifetime compared to 3 percent of persons who die of natural causes.

Risks for Suicide

While risk factors do vary by age, gender, and ethnicity, certain individual attributes and behaviors are known to elevate the probability of suicide. Among these risk factors are the co-occurrence of mental disorders (e.g., depression and alcohol abuse, impulsivity and aggression, the use of highly lethal means in attempting suicide) (Brent et al. 1994; Cornelius et al. 1995; Henriksson et al. 1993).

To Jamison (1999), the symptoms of suicide are well established. These symptoms are outlined in Table 6.1. She points out that the symptoms of suicide vary in severity and in duration. Rarely do individuals manifest all of the symptoms, but several may be experienced at a given time. If for example, a person has feelings of guilt, hopelessness, helplessness, worthlessness and is experiencing fatigue or loss of interest in ordinary activities and is abusing drugs and/or alcohol and these symptoms last more than two weeks, then the risk of suicidal behavior is greatly increased.

In addition, Christine Sadowski of the Mayo Clinic notes that warning signs of suicide include: suicidal threats—saying, for example, "I wish I had never been born" or "Everyone would be better off if I were dead"—are to be taken seriously. It is not true that people who threaten suicide do not carry it out; **withdrawal,** the unwillingness to communicate or desire to be left alone; **mood swings,** rapid changes in personality, **self-destructive behavior,** including risk-taking behaviors and pronounced drug or alcohol use, **experience of a life crisis or trauma,** usually involving the loss of an important status or social role (See http://www.mayohealth.org/mayo/9709/htm/suicide.htm.).

Table 6.1   Symptoms of Suicide

- Disruptive sleeping or eating patterns
- Ruminative feelings of guilt, hopelessness, helplessness, worthlessness
- Persistent sad or depressed mood, especially for no obvious reason
- A noticeable loss of pleasure in activities and little enjoyment in things that used to bring much enjoyment
- Fatigue or loss of interest in ordinary sex activities, including sex
- Difficulty concentrating and indecisiveness
- Irritability, with increased crying, anxiety, and/or panic attacks
- Increased use or abuse of drugs and/or alcohol
- Persistent physical symptoms or pains that do not respond to treatment
- Rapid loss or gain in weight
- Preoccupation with death; thought or talk of self-destruction or suicide
- Increased visits or calls to friends or relatives
- Putting one's affairs in order and giving things away
- Suddenly happier and calmer

Source: Jamison, K. 1999. *Night Falls Fast*. New York: Alfred Knopf.

Clues to Suicide

Suicidal persons typically provide clues of their intention to kill themselves. These clues may be subtle behavioral changes (e.g., putting one's affairs in order or oft handed remarks, "No one would care if I were not here any more.") Most often suicide is not an impulsive act, but is carefully planned. Clues are given but are often missed by those close to the victim (Leenarrs 1999). Edwin Shneidman (1996) finds that 90 percent of persons who commit suicide give verbal or behavioral clues within a week of their deaths.

About 75 percent of suicide victims visit a doctor in the last four months of their lives. Suicidal persons often present themselves to a physician as helplessness and hopelessness, yet these feelings tend to be overlooked. Shneidman (1996: 353) also notes that: "All verbal indications should be taken seriously." Actual suicide attempts are most common among completed suicide. About eight in ten suicide victims have previously attempted suicide. While suicide attempts may appear to be "attention-getting" ploys, they are more often attempts to change an intolerable life situation. If the attempt does not result in a change in the conditions of one's life, then repeated and typically more serious attempts may be made.

The Suicide Process

Jerry Jacobs (1967) contends that persons who end their own lives must in some way resolve the social prohibitions of suicide. He describes the process that provides the rationalization for suicide in the following way:

1. A person experiences a series of overwhelming and seemingly unsolvable problems.
2. These problems are viewed as part of a never-ending and progressively worsening pattern of personal tragedies.
3. Death is seen as the only way to free one's self from the continual misery.
4. Because supportive others are unable to be found, the person becomes increasingly more socially isolated.
5. Ways are sought to overcome their perceived sense that society condemns suicide as immoral.
6. Social isolation facilitates the withdrawal from any social prohibitions against suicide.
7. The decision to commit suicide is rationalized as not a denunciation that life is sacred but its affirmation despite the desire to end the misery of one's life.
8. The suicide victims tend to view life's problems as not of their making and can only be resolved by self-inflicted death.
9. Once suicide becomes inevitable, the person no longer feels responsible or guilty for the decision to end his or her own life.
10. To ensure they will not be condemned in the afterlife, they ask God for forgiveness or request in a note that their survivors pray for them (Jacobs 1967).

The Contagion of Suicide

The contagion of suicide or suicide clusters, particularly among the young, is well publicized. However, the contagious nature of suicidal behavior is centuries old. Suicide epidemics are documented in Ancient Greece and among the Romans 600 years before Christ. More recently reports of suicide clustering, for the most part, involve teenage and young adult victims. Analyses of suicide clusters among adolescents find that imitation is a key factor; however, suicide victims tend to have a history of suicide attempts, threats, and other self-destructive behaviors. The suicide of persons admired by the victim, may legitimate the suicide of an adolescent. Or, the desire for revenge or instant recognition may prompt an adolescent to end his or her own life (Jamison 1999).

Special Topics

Suicide Notes

Edwin Shniedman (1996), a pioneer in the analysis of suicide notes, observes that they are usually written at the time of the suicide, just before killing oneself. Suicide notes must be understood, therefore, in the context of the suicidal act, filled with the emotions that attend the taking of one's own life. What can be learned from notes left by suicide victims?

Suicide notes are used in an attempt to discover the underlying dynamics of suicide or to gain particular insight into the suicidal mind. Feelings of love and hate, fear and rejection, shame and humiliation are commonly expressed in suicide notes (Schniedman et al. 1994). Suicide notes are then valuable sources of information about the thinking and feeling of the victim at the time of the suicide; the stress of ending one's own life necessarily limits the complexity of the note; and in the context of the victim's life history, suicide notes provide insights into the events that led to the ending of one's own life (Schniedman et al. 1994).

Homicide Followed by Suicide

Suicide committed by a person who has just killed someone else is a rare event. Yet there is considerable variation across cultures and at different times in history. For example, suicide followed homicide 42 percent of the time in Denmark, 33 percent in England, 22 percent in Australia, 11 percent in Israel, 10 percent in Edmonton, Winnipeg, and Calgary, and 4 percent in the United States (Landau 1975; Silverman and Mukherjee 1987; West 1966). Stack (1997: 436) hypothesizes that the variation in **homicide–suicide** may be due to "the extent to which cultures foster self-blame and the extent to which murderers experience guilt after a homicide."

D. J. West's (1966) classic study of homicide followed by suicide in England compares 148 homicide–suicide cases with 148 homicides. He reports that homicides are quite similar to the general population in terms of occupation status, while the homicide offenders alone are most often drawn from the lower occupational groupings. In addition, West finds that the suicide offenders are more likely to kill family members, to kill multiple victims (particularly their children), to be young females (41%), and to be less likely to have a criminal record than the homicide-only offenders. In the United States, Wolfgang finds that white homicide offenders are more likely to kill themselves than are black offenders. About one in four of the homicide offenders in Wolfgang's study are white while half of the homicide–suicide cases involve white offenders. One-third of the suicide offenders have an arrest record, compared to two-thirds of the homicide-only offenders. Unlike West's study in England, Wolfgang (1958) finds that the homicide-only offenders (92 percent) are overwhelmingly male.

In sum, homicide offenders who kill themselves soon after the murder are far more likely to be emotionally tied to their victims than are offenders who do not commit suicide. West (1966: 46) observes:

> As far as they go, the statistics available in these three communities all fit the hypothesis that murderers who kill themselves, compared with murderers in general, form a less socially deviant group, and that their relationships to their victims are more often close and intimate.

Steven Stack (1997) has outlined eight patterns that characterize homicide-suicides. These patterns are frustrated personal relationship, ambivalence, jealousy and morbid jealousy, separation, depression, helplessness, and guilt. **Frustrated personal relationships** refers to the chaotic nature of the personal relationship found between the victim and offender in homicide–suicide cases. The relationship is fraught with abuse, separations, and chronic upheaval (Rosenbaum 1990). *Ambivalence* is an integral part of the chaotic relationship that pre-existed the homicide–suicide. An emotionally charged love–hate relationship is evident along with strong dependency on the person who is both adored and despised. *Jealousy and morbid jealousy* refers to the fear that one's romantic partner is unfaithful. Within the context of an otherwise discordant relationship the added stress of infidelity significantly increases the risk of a homicide–suicide (West 1966). *Separation* is a key precipitating event in a homicide–suicide. *Depression* typically follows separation and is closely linked to suicide. *Helplessness* is a consequence of the combination of a rage sparked by the irreversible loss of a person on whom the offender is dependent. Caught in the conflict of emotions, the offender chooses to end the life of his partner and himself. *Guilt* floods in immediately following the homicide of a partner. The murder of someone loved deeply, albeit chaotically, renders life unbearable. Self-inflicted death becomes the only way to end the offender's overwhelming sense of guilt.

Stack (1997) provides analyses of 16,245 homicide cases in Chicago between 1965 and 1990, involving 265 homicides followed by the offender's suicide. In cases of homicide–suicide both the offender and victim are somewhat older than in the cases of homicide-only. The mean age of the homicide–suicide offenders is 39.7 compared to 28.7 for the homicide-only cases. The mean age of the homicide–suicide victims is 35 compared to 32 for the homicide-only cases. The victim in homicide–suicides is overwhelmingly female (78.5 percent) compared to 18 percent for the homicide-only cases; male (97 percent) compared to 86 percent and Caucasian (36 versus 15.5 percent). By contrast, homicide–suicide offenders are only somewhat more likely to be Caucasian (32 versus 28.7 percent). In addition, the victims in homicide–suicide cases are far more likely to be spouses (45 vs. 9 percent) girlfriend/boyfriend (11.7 vs. 3 percent) an ex-lover (8 vs. 0.9 percent), or a child (7.6 vs. 2 percent).

Stack (1997) hypothesizes that when an offender kills someone emotionally close to him or her, guilt or self-blame is most likely. His findings show that the odds of a homicide–suicide is 12.68 times greater in cases of ex-spouses/lover; 6.11 times greater for current boyfriend/girlfriend; and 1.88 times greater for friends compared to nonintimate homicides. When a child is the victim, the odds are 10.28 times greater that the offender will commit suicide compared to nonintimate homicides.

Assisted Suicide

On October 27, 1997, Oregon became the only state to legalize physician-**assisted suicide.** The *Death with Dignity* (Oregon Revised Statutes 1997) statute established certain criteria that must be met before a physician can assist in the termination of life. The person must:

- Be terminally ill.
- Have six months or less to live.
- Make two oral requests for assistance in dying.
- Make one written request for assistance.
- Convince two physicians that she or he is sincere, is not acting on a whim, and that the decision is voluntary.
- Not have been influenced by depression.

- Be informed of "the feasible alternatives, including but not limited to, comfort care, hospice care and pain control."
- Wait for 15 days.

Wide cultural differences are evident in the practice of physician-assisted suicide. In Switzerland, physician-assisted suicide has been legally condoned for more than sixty years. Both physician and laypersons are permitted to assist in a suicide. Known as EXIT practices, Swiss law requires that to be eligible for an assisted suicide, a person must be a Swiss resident, 18 years of age, mentally competent, and with "intolerable health problems." In addition, the application must be made in person, and there must be evidence that there is no coercion or influence by a third party. A single physician can make the decision to grant permission for an assisted suicide. But in difficult cases, a team composed of a lawyer, psychiatrist, and a physician must grant permission (Schaer 1996).

Physician-assisted suicide is also permitted in the Netherlands. A recent study of 114 cases of physician-assisted suicide and 535 cases of euthanasia in the Netherlands shows that more problems occur during the completion of a physician-assisted suicide than with the completion of euthanasia. In 18 percent of the cases the physician-assisted suicide patients are unable to take the medication—the physician must administer the fatal dose (Dutch Study 2000).

Forms of assisted suicide are practiced in Australia, Japan, and Holland. While physician-assisted suicide per se is not permitted, in Australia active euthanasia is condoned under controlled conditions. In Japan mercy killings are permitted under four conditions: (1) the patient is suffering from unbearable pain, (2) death is inevitable and imminent, (3) all possible measures have been taken to eliminate the pain with no other treatment left open, and (4) the patient has clearly expressed his or her will to approve the shortening of his or her life. Holland legally prohibits euthanasia; however, as of 1993 physicians cannot be

Jonathan Grenz, who contracted throat cancer, was assisted in suicide by Dr. Jack Kervorkian, the alleged "Doctor Death."

prosecuted for its practice. Physicians can, therefore, assist in the suicide of a patient if: (1) the patient is in intolerable pain (including emotional pain), (2) the patient has repeatedly and lucidly asked to die, (3) two doctors agree on the procedure, (4) relatives are consulted, and (5) the death is reported (Knickerbocker 1998; www.euthanasia.com).

Suicide by Cop

Suicide by cop refers to an event in which an individual's behavior constitutes an imminent danger of serious injury or death and is intended to cause a law enforcement officer to use fatal force to defend him- or herself. Goals of the victims of "suicide by cop" are either instrumental or expressive. A goal is instrumental when victims attempt: (1) ". . . to escape or avoid the consequences of criminal or shameful actions; (2) using a forced confrontation with police to reconcile a failed relationship; (3) hoping to avoid the exclusion clauses of life insurance policies; (4) rationalizing that while it may be morally wrong to commit suicide, being killed resolves the spiritual problem of suicide; or (5) seeking what they believe to be a very effective and lethal means of accomplishing death" (Mohandie and Meloy 2000: 384–389). Victims who focus on expressive goals are communicating: "(1) hopelessness, depression, and desperation; (2) a statement about their ultimate identification as victims; (3) their need to save face by dying or forcibly overwhelmed rather than surrendering; (4) their intense power needs; (5) rage and revenge; (6) their need to draw attention to an important personal issue" (Mohandie and Meloy 2000: 384–389).

In Los Angeles, 13 percent of fatal police officer shootings and 11 percent of all police officer–involved shootings are situations of suicide by cop. The researchers report that virtually all the suspects are males (98%), with a criminal record (70%) and/or a drug and alcohol problem (65%) or a history of psychiatric illness (63%). Almost eight in ten of the victims (78%) verbally communicate that they want to commit "suicide by cop." Approximately half the time the victims

Suicide by Cop

A well-mannered 19-year-old college student addressed this note to police before he got himself shot to death. Earlier that day he bought goodbye cards for family and friends and a toy gun. Later, when stopped by police for speeding and erratic driving, he pulled his toy gun and advanced toward officers. After ignoring repeated commands, the officers fired their weapons, shooting him three times. Police then learned that he was carrying a toy gun and that he had planned his death. In the goodbye cards, family, friends, and police learned of his depression over a $6,000 gambling debt.

Sources: Eltman, F. 1997. "Student Commits Suicide-by-Cop." *The Detroit News,* November 18. Stincelli, R. "Suicide-by-Cop" Web posted at www.suicidebycop.com.

point a gun at the police officer—15 percent of the time the gun is fired and about 30 percent of the time the victim threatens the police officer with a knife (Hutson et al. 1998).

Theories of Suicide

Theories of suicidal behavior may be divided into those that explain and predict either rates of suicide or the self-destructive behavior of individuals. At times theoretical formulation primarily intended to account for rates of suicide have been used in studies of individual behavior. However, this chapter considers the various theories at either the macro (societal or social collectivity) or micro (individual) level of analysis.

Explanations of Suicide Rates

Social Integration.   Attempts to explain and predict rates of suicide are greatly indebted to the pioneering work of Emile Durkheim (1951) in the latter part of the nineteenth century. Durkheim, a founding father of sociology, conducted one of the first theoretically based empirical studies of suicide. In his book *Suicide,* Durkheim advances the theory that the degree of integration of a society or social grouping explains its rates of suicide. Integration refers to the understanding and acceptance of values considered essential to social life. Societies and social collectivities may be characterized by high levels of social integration, that is, widespread adherence to common values, low integration or few, if any values held in common, or changes in the degree of value acceptance. Based on the extent and nature of social integration, Durkheim argues that there are three basic types of suicide: altruistic, egoistic, and anomic. *Altruistic suicide* occurs in societies or social collectivities that are characterized by excessively high levels of social integration. Individuality is lost to the collective interests. A person lives for the good of his or her society and is willing to sacrifice everything, even life itself, for the welfare of others. For example, kamikaze pilots in World War II were willing to dive bomb their planes into enemy ships to assist the Japanese war effort. *Egoistic suicide,* on the other hand, occurs when a society is characterized by little social integration. Members of society are essentially disconnected from one another; social ties are weak or broken; and individualistic behavior predominates. In the absence of involvement with others, life may lose meaning and suicide may ensue. *Anomic suicide* occurs when there is rapid change in the social integration. This sudden change may be the result of economic chaos, either positive or negative, widespread social mobility, or unpredicted upheavals in life circumstances. Individuals are thrown into disarray; norms or guides for their behavior either nonexistent or are no longer applicable. Persons who suddenly find themselves bankrupt, unemployed, abandoned, or friendless experience what Durkheim terms *anomie* or a state of normlessness. Integration into social life is suddenly disrupted. Individuals are left without viable guides for their behavior.

Durkheim adds a fourth form of suicide, fatalistic, to his typology. *Fatalistic suicide* refers to the condition of overregulation of individual behavior. When individual behavior is tightly controlled by others and personal autonomy is rendered impossible, a sense of powerlessness may ensue. Under conditions of inordinate regulation of behavior, fatalistic suicide may result.

Sociologists Jack Gibbs and Walter Martin (1964) propose an innovative conceptualization of social integration. They contend that status integration and the related concept of role conflict are key factors in understanding the link between social integration and suicide. Status integration refers to the frequency that a set of statuses is found in a population, (e.g., male engineer, female nurse, etc.). Unusual configurations of statuses are a measure of the lack of status integration (e.g., female airline pilots, or male preschool teachers). The absence of status integration leads to role conflict or clash of expectations of one role with another (e.g., being a mother and a medical doctor). The more unusual is the configurations of one's statuses, the greater the experience of role conflict and the more likely suicide becomes.

Drawing on the work of Durkheim, anthropologist Andrew Henry and sociologist James Short (1954) contend that rates of suicide are predicted by three key variables: prestige, strength or the relational system, and the level of external restraint. Prestige typically refers to the status within any social grouping. Status denotes influence over group decisions or extent of deference granted to persons of higher social ranking. The strength of the relational system means the extent to which persons are involved in networks of social relationships with others. External restraint refers to the extent to which a person is required to conform to the demands and expectations of others.

To Henry and Short, the interplay of these three variables serves to explain and predict rates of suicidal behavior. As status increases, the strength of the relational system tends to decrease. That is, persons of higher status are less likely to interact with a wide range of other people, limiting their social contacts to a carefully chosen few. Also, as status increases, the need to comply with the demands and expectations of others decreases. The less the involvement with others and the more removed from their restraints, the less other persons are to be blamed when frustration is experienced. Put another way, persons who are low in status, highly involved in the lives of others, and must meet the demands and expectations of many others have several external targets to blame for life's frustrations. In the absence of these external causes for problematic events or circumstances, the self must bear the burden of frustration. In the extreme, suicide becomes more probable.

Robert K. Merton (1957), a founding structural-functional theorist in sociology, attempts to define more specifically what Durkheim meant by anomie. To Merton, anomie refers to the disjunction between culturally approved goals and the institutionalized means for attaining them. It is assumed that persons within a given culture are socialized to strive for the same goals—status, economic well-being, leisure, and so on—but for many the means to reach these goals—advanced education, occupational prestige and social opportunities, economic fortune—may not be available or may not lead to the culture's most prized goals. This may lead to what Merton terms *retreatism* or the rejection of the culturally approved goals and the institutionalized means for pursuing them. Retreatism may take the form of alcohol or drug addiction, depression and mental disorder, an alternative lifestyle (e.g., joining a cult, or becoming a marginally employed drifter, or in the extreme suicidal behaviors).

Social Conflict.   Social conflict theorists argue that the status arrangements and resultant power in society tend to precipitate varying forms of suicide. As status increases or decreases so too does a person's relative power and influence. Sociologist Alex Thio (1983) contends that suicide among the more powerful members of society is a voluntary act, while among the less powerful it is coerced. With increased power come higher expectations for a life of ease and comfort; tolerance for adversity is lowered. The prospect of a life of hardship—economic, social, or physical—is unthinkable. Suicide may provide the only solution to impending misery. Among the powerless, however, suicide is more a consequence of the experience of everyday deprivation and uncertainty. Access to needed resources—medical, educational, job opportunities—is limited by the power structure of society. The powerless are largely dependent on available employers close at hand. Lives are played out in the factories, fields, and mines of their employers. Alternatives are few and rarely sought. Life's circumstances may combine to coerce the decision to kill one's self.

Explanations of Suicide Rates

Theories and Theorists	Sociological Predictors	Hypotheses
Integration		
• Durkheim	Integration	The greater the social integration, the lower the suicide rate.
	Anomie	The greater the level of anomie, the higher the suicide rate.
• Gibbs and Martin	Status Integration	The greater the degree of status integration, i.e. role conflict, the lower the suicide rate.
	Role Conflict	
• Henry and Short	Prestige	As prestige of individuals becomes greater, the suicide rate increases.
	External Restraints	As the external restraint placed on behavior decreases, the suicide rate increases.
	Relational System	As the strength of the relational system decreases, the suicide rate increases.
• Merton	Anomie	The greater the level of anomie, the greater the possibility of retreatism and suicide.
	Retreatism	
Conflict		
• Thio	Power and Status Groups	Higher-status, more powerful individuals are more likely to voluntarily commit suicide while lower-status individuals are more likely to be coerced into committing suicide.

Explanations of Individual Behavior

Theories and Theorists	Sociological Predictors	Hypotheses
Social Bonding and Control		
• Hirschi	Attachment	The weaker the attachment to conventional society, the more likely the individual will commit suicide.
	Commitment	The weaker the commitment to conventional society, the more likely the individual will commit suicide.
	Involvement	The greater the involvement in conventional activities, the less likely the individual will commit suicide.
	Belief	The stronger the belief in conventional values and norms, the less likely the person will commit suicide.
Strain		
• Agnew	Strain/Stress	The greater the strain, the greater the negative emotional reaction.
		The greater the negative emotional reaction, the more likely an individual will commit suicide.
Social Learning		
• Akers	Definitions of Behavior	Individuals who hold attitudes that disapprove of suicide are less likely to commit suicide.
	Differential Reinforcement	The greater the punishment for suicide, the less likely an individual is to commit suicide.
Rational Choice		
• Clarke and Cornish	Cost/Benefit Analysis	The greater the cost or benefit associated with suicide, the more likely an individual is to commit suicide.
Imitation		
• Phillips	Imitation	If an individual observes a suicide, then he/she is more likely to commit suicide.
Phenomenological		
• Douglas	Meaning	If a person views suicide as a form of revenge, then he/she is more likely to commit suicide.
		If a person views suicide as a way of gaining sympathy from others, then he/she is more likely to commit suicide.

Explanations of Individual Suicidal Behavior

Various explanations of the suicidal behavior of the individual have been advanced. Some are drawn from Durkheim's integration-regulation formulation and others from social strain, social learning, rational choice, and phenomenological approaches.

Social Bonding and Control. Travis Hirschi (1969) sociological theory of deviant behavior draw on Durkheim's (1951) formulation of social integration. Hirschi argues that integration can be conceptualized as a set of four bonds between the individual and the larger society: attachment, commitment, involvement, and belief. *Attachment* refers to the extent to which individuals internalize the norms of society and are affected by others' reactions to their behavior. *Commitment* means the individual places great importance on engaging in conventional behavior and advocating highly prized cultural values. *Involvement* refers to the amount of time and effort an individual spends on conventional activities intended to contribute positively to others as opposed to involvement in idiosyncratic, self-serving behaviors. *Belief* connotes the person's deeply held conviction that their culture's values are essential for the functioning of society and must be strongly supported. When the individual's bonds to society are weakened or nonexistent, external controls of their behavior are largely absent. This lack of control over behavior leaves the individuals without normative guides and supports. Engagement in self-destruction may well follow.

Social Strain. Robert Agnew (1992) also draws on the work of Durkheim (1951) and Merton (1957) in formulating his strain theory of deviant behavior. To Agnew *strain* refers to the discrepancy between an individual's aspirations and expectations and their goal attainment. Strain results when our relations with other people are so disruptive that we are unable to achieve important goals (e.g., going to school, work, caring for our children, etc.). Strain causes negative emotions—fear, anger, anxiety and depression—that must be dealt with by the individual. When coping strategies are no longer effective, self-destructive behaviors may emerge.

Social Learning. Social learning theory may also be used to account for an individual's suicidal behavior. Ronald Akers (1985), a pioneering sociological theorist, argues that most deviant behavior can be explained by social learning. He notes that whether a person engages in suicidal or other forms of deviance depends, in large part, on the meanings attached to behavior and the rewards anticipated from engaging in it. Individuals tend to repeat behaviors that provide desired rewards and benefits—behaviors that are reinforced by others. All behaviors are not equally rewarded or result in benefit to the individual. To Akers, *differential reinforcement*—the rewards and benefits that attend certain behaviors but not others—explains why individuals engage in certain forms of deviant behavior while others do not. By assigning positive value to suicidal behavior, others may reinforce an individual's involvement acts of self-destruction. To the extent to which suicidal acts are differentially reinforced—rewarded more so than nonsuicidal behaviors—more often repeated.

Rational Choice. Rational choice formulations of deviant and criminal behavior are founded on the central tenets of the Classical School of Criminology established in the mid-eighteenth century. Social philosophers Caesar Beccaria (1963 [1764]) and Jeremy Bentham (1948 [1780]) were among the first to advance the hedonistic principle as an explanation for human social behavior. They argue that individuals are fundamentally rational beings, endowed with free will, who consciously and deliberately decide to engage in certain behaviors and not others. When deciding what course of action to take, individuals evoke the hedonistic principle. Simply put, the hedonistic principle posits that individuals seek to maximize their pleasure and minimize their pain when deciding on a certain behavior. The relative benefits versus costs of engaging in a behavior are rationally assessed and a choice is then made. Suicide is the outcome of the process of weighing the alternatives of choosing to live or to die at one's own hand.

David Phillips (1974) and Jack Douglas (1967) set two further innovative conceptualizations of individual suicidal behavior forth. Phillips' groundbreaking work on the link between imitation and suicide informs much of the subsequent research in the United States, Germany, and Japan (Ishii 19912; Jonas 1992; Stack 1996). The *imitation* approach to the understanding of an individual's decision to commit suicide is simply that suicides that receive much media attention, either in print or television coverage, and thus tend to precipitate increased suicidal behavior. The more the media attention, the more probable are "copycat" suicides. Related to the phenomenon of imitation is the concept of differential identification. *Differential identification* refers to the varying effects the characteristics of the suicide victim have on the imitation process. That is, widespread media attention to a suicide of a well-known person (e.g., a political leader or entertainment celebrity) may result in more imitation or copycat suicides than the suicide of an unrecognized person (Wasserman 1984). Philips argues that suicides of highly visible persons are more likely to prompt imitation suicides.

Finally, sociologist Jack Douglas provides an alternative way of understanding a person's suicidal behavior. Taking the *phenomenological approach* to the explanation of suicide, Douglas focuses on the meanings that an individual attaches to his or her behavior. The meanings attached to behavior serve to guide individual action. To understand suicidal behavior, Douglas contends, it is necessary to reconstruct the personal meanings of suicide that lead to self-inflicted death. Douglas (1967: 284–319) offers four broad categories for the meanings of self-inflicted death:

- "As a means of transforming the soul from this world to the other world."
- "As a transformation of the substantial self in this world or in the other world."
- "Suicide is a means of achieving fellow-feeling (sympathy)."
- "As a means of getting revenge."

The phenomenological approach seeks to understand the decision to end one's life from the vantage point of the victim. It informs us about the processes involved in finding meaning and value in the act of suicide. Suicide is viewed as beneficial to the victim: it must take on a positive meaning to be carried out.

Chapter Summary

In this chapter we have considered the global nature of suicide, its cultural and structural variations, and theoretical understandings of suicidal behaviors. We have also reviewed special topics on suicide: minority, including Native

American, involvement, the rise in self-destructive acts among the young and among the elderly, physician-assisted suicide, and suicide by cop. We have learned that:

- Suicide is one of the three leading causes of death in the world for people 15 to 44 years of age.
- Males typically have higher suicide rates than females.
- Whites have higher suicide rates than other racial or ethnic groups.
- Suicide rates are rising fastest among the young.
- Similar rises are seen among Native American populations.
- Suicide rates are highest in the Western United States.
- The South, however, leads the nation in the use of firearms for suicide.
- More people attempt a suicide each year than actually complete a suicide.
- Suicide is more common among the single, the divorced, and the widowed.
- The risk of suicide tends to increase with age. Older men have an elevated risk of suicide. Elder suicide is not uniformly experienced around the globe.
- Social structural positioning, life circumstances, previous suicide attempts, and psychiatric illness are precipitating factors for suicide.
- The warning signs for suicide have been well established. Suicide threats, withdrawal from others, mood swings, self-destructive behavior, and the experience of life crisis or trauma are common warning signs of suicide.
- Suicide notes are valuable source of information about the thinking and feeling of the victim at the time of the suicide. Common themes found in suicide notes include hate, love, shame and disgrace, fear (particularly of insanity), and traumatic rejection and self-abnegation.
- Homicide followed by suicide is a rare event that varies considerably across cultures. Eight patterns that characterize these suicides include: frustrated personal relationships, ambivalence, jealousy and morbid jealousy, separation, depression, helplessness, and guilt. Homicide–suicide offenders are more likely to be emotionally tied to their victims than are offenders who do not commit suicide.
- Oregon is the only state in the United States to legalize physician-assisted suicide. Physician-assisted suicide is permitted in such countries as The Netherlands, Australia, Japan, and Holland.
- Suicide by cop refers to an event in which an individual's behavior constitutes an imminent danger of serious injury or death and is intended to cause a law enforcement officer to use fatal force to defend him or herself.

Key Concepts

Suicide: The willful, deliberate, and voluntary termination of one's life.

Withdrawal: The unwillingness to communicate or desire to be left alone.

Mood swings: Rapid changes in personality.

Self-destructive behavior: Risk-taking behaviors and pronounced drug or alcohol use.

Experience of a life crisis or trauma: The loss of an important status or social role.

The suicide process: Process that provides the rationalization for suicide and resolves the social prohibitions of suicide.

Homicide–suicide: Suicide committed by a person who has just killed someone else.

Frustrated personal relationships: The chaotic nature of the personal relationship found between the victim and offender in homicide–suicide cases.

Assisted suicide: Suicide act by which a physician can assist in the termination of life.

Death with Dignity **Act:** Oregon statute that established certain criteria that must be met before a physician can assist in the termination of life.

Suicide by cop: An event in which an individual's behavior constitutes an imminent danger of serious injury or death and is intended to cause a law enforcement officer to use fatal force to defend him- or herself.

Critical Thinking Questions

1. The medical/legal definition of suicide is complex and often subject to individual interpretation. Describe in detail three cases in which an "actual" suicidal death could be misclassified. How might the medical/legal errors be averted in the determination of cause of suicidal death?

2. Except for China, what accounts for the otherwise universal high male than female rate of suicide? Why is the male–female suicide ratio different in China?

3. Why is there such a marked gender difference in involvement in homicide followed by suicide? What kinds of social processes precede a male-perpetrated "homicide followed by suicide" and a female-perpetrated "homicide followed by suicide" event?

4. Is the taking of one's own life ever justified? Discuss at least three key reasons for your decision to either reject suicidal death as unjustified under any conditions, or provide three reasons and circumstances in which suicide is justifiable.

Web Extra

Check out these websites for additional information on suicide:

http://www.nimh.nih.gov

http://www.cdc.gov

http://www.AFSP.org

http://www.suicidology.org

Mental Illness

P O R T R A I T S

of Mental Illness

MENTAL ILLNESS IN BALI

- Mental illnesses in different cultures, such as those on the Indonesian island of Bali, present themselves quite differently than in Western cultures such as the United States. Anthropologist Robert Lemelson studies these differences. In the course of his research, he meets Gede, a Balian with obsessive-compulsive behavior. Gede has many other obsessions and compulsions and is often overtaken with such strong feelings of anxiousness that it makes him want to die. "Whenever a piece of glass—a window, say, or a light bulb—breaks, Gede Sudiasih opens the notebook that lies on his living room table and makes an entry. He writes down what the glass was and the exact time, the day, and the year that it broke. He then checks and rechecks his entry. Only after he is assured the information is accurate can he close the notebook and return to his daily routine." In addition to recording broken glass, Gede keeps track of every person who passes his house. Gede's obsessive and compulsive behaviors are not diagnosed or treated, as they would be if he lived in Western society. Lemelson describes Gede as an anxious, but hardworking man. Despite the mental disorder, Gede shows up for work every day as a government employee and is treated no differently than his fellow villagers. (*Source:* R. Lemelson. 2001. "Strange Maladies," *Psychology Today* (December), pp. 61–64.)

CREATIVITY, SUCCESS, AND MENTAL ILLNESS

- According to some studies, mental illness, success, and creativity often go hand in hand. Many well-known artists, writers, and musicians have experienced mental disorders and have received therapy or hospitalization for such disorders. A large proportion of these people committed or attempted to commit suicide as a result. Ernest Hemingway, Virginia Woolf, Walt Whitman, Sylvia Plath, Vincent Van Gogh, Marilyn Monroe, and Kurt Cobain are just a few who had depressive disorders and committed suicide. An increasing number of celebrities, including Ted Turner, Greg Louganis, Alanis Morissette, Carrie Fisher, Jean-Claude Van Damme, Tipper Gore, and Roseanne, are now publicly announcing their struggles with mental illness. (*Sources:* Druckman, A., and C. Maday. 1999. "Celebrity Meltdown." *Psychology Today* (December), 46–52; Goodwin, F., and K. Jamison. 1990. *Manic-Depressive Illness.* New York: Oxford University Press.)

LEARNING OBJECTIVES

After reading this chapter you should know:

- ☐ The nature of mental illness.
- ☐ The cultural, social, and medical definitions of mental illness.
- ☐ The forms and prevalence of mental illness including the sociodemographic variations in prevalence.
- ☐ The medical and sociocultural explanations for mental illness.

Introduction

Considerable controversy surrounds the definitions of mental illness, its etiology, and treatment. Competing biological, psychological, and sociological definitions and explanations of mental illness are found around the world. Cultural variations in the forms and prevalence of mental illness must be understood. This chapter considers the intricate sociocultural dimensions of mental disorder across the globe as well as theoretical formulations of the incidence and prevalence of mental illness.

Nature of Mental Illness

Behaviors labeled as mental illness have evolved over the centuries. Nearly all forms of disruptive or disapproved behavior were once believed to stem from demonic possessions. Immorality and a wanton lifestyle were considered the underlying cause of mental disorders. In the eighteenth century "lunatics" or "the insane" were beaten, publicly displayed, or put away in asylums. Public viewing of caged and chained lunatics was held on Sundays in many of these asylums. It was believed that nothing could be done for the insane; they were irreparably damaged and permanently impaired (Mumford 1983).

> *. . . the best [psychiatric] diagnoses are provisional and somewhat fictional.*
>
> —Barry Nurcombe, director of child and adolescent psychiatry at Vanderbilt University (posted at http://www.mentalhealthfacts/quotes.htm)

> *Over the years it [the National Committee for Mental Hygiene] has championed for the promotion of "mental health" despite the fact that nobody knows what it is or how to do it.*
>
> —E. Fuller Torrey, psychiatrist

With the advent of psychotherapeutic drugs in the mid-twentieth century, physicians and others associated with institutions for the mentally ill began treating their patients more humanely. The medical model emerged as the dominant explanation and treatment strategy for those afflicted with a mental disease. Organic causes were sought for the mental illness. Highly effective drug therapies replaced confinement, which was often under brutal conditions. For the first time, a decline occurred in the number of patients housed in mental hospitals, and this resulted in the ability to successfully treat them in a community setting (Mumford 1983).

Definition of Mental Illness

Multiple, often conflicting, definitions of mental illness are offered. Legal and medical professionals as well as laypersons interpret and define mental illness according to different values, goals, and interest group affiliations. As with other forms of deviance, the definition of mental illness is influenced by the social and cultural context in which it occurs and also by the value judgments of mental health practitioners. Consequently, the meanings attached to mental illness continually change, new forms are recognized, and other forms redefined or eliminated over time.

Cultural Definitions

Societies share "particular historical traditions, challenges, opportunities and stresses that provide a common experience. These experiences create a distinctive context that influences how basic psychological processes are expressed within a given culture" (NIMH 1999a). **Culture**—the values and norms of a society—affects conceptions of behavior and the definition of mental illness. Normative behaviors in one culture may be viewed as symptomatic of a mental disorder in another (Lemelson and Winters 2001). **Cultural relativism** refers to cross-cultural variation in the social construction of reality. Manifestations of mental disorder are socially and culturally constructed. For example, in the United States and other developed countries, persons who hallucinate are considered to be mentally ill. In other cultures, however, individuals who experience visions or hear voices are honored.

> In rural Laos, unprovoked assaultive or destructive behavior, social isolation, self-endangerment due to neglect or self-destructive acts, nonviolent but disruptive or inappropriate behavior, and inability to do productive work characterized natives who were called insane. But hallucinations are rarely used by Laotians to identify insanity (Mumford 1983: 416).

The Dobu of the South Pacific provide another example of cultural relativism. With a limited food supply, the Dobu are a highly paranoid and suspicious people who typically distrust their fellow tribesmen. Dobu who are not distrustful and constantly vigilant are considered mentally ill (Palmer and Humphrey 1990).

Some mental disorders and responses to mental disorders are *culture-bound*, that is, unique to the culture in which they are found. In Japan, cultural-bound neuroses stem from an "overwhelming sense of obligation and dependence. Shinkeishitsu (nervous temperament), for example, involves hypersensitivity, perfectionism, social withdrawal or total discomfort in unfamiliar surroundings" ("Increasing Signs of Stress" 1983: 67). Table 7.1 provides a description of several other **culture-bound disorders.**

Treatment methods reflect cultural differences as well. Because the Japanese culture places value on work and service to others, many of the treatment methods are aimed at "getting patients back to work." Morita explains one such therapy.

> For a week patients are confined to bed, with no visitors, no TV and no reading matter. Forced to wallow in their own thoughts, they come to see that action is better than endless self-obsession. Patients then work outdoors for two weeks, going from light to heavy labor. They also attend indoctrination lectures. No talk about the self is allowed ("Increasing Signs of Stress" 1983: 67).

Another Japanese therapy, Naikan (introspection) is a directed meditation program where the therapist urges those in treatment to focus on their ingratitude toward the sacrifices of important persons in their life. The therapist then instructs that the only escape from mental anguish is to plunge oneself into acts of service ("Increasing Signs of Stress" 1983).

Table 7.1 Culture-Bound Syndromes

Syndrome	Culture	Symptoms
Amok	Malaysia, Laos, Papua New Guinea, Puerto Rico, Navajos	Brooding, followed by violent behavior, persecutory ideas, amnesia, exhaustion. More often seen in men than women.
Ataque de nervios	Latin America	Uncontrollable shouting, crying, trembling, heat in the chest rising to the head, verbal or physical aggression, seizures, fainting.
Ghost sickness	Native Americans	Nightmares, weakness, feelings of danger, loss of appetite, fainting, dizziness, hallucinations, loss of consciousness, sense of suffocation.
Koro	Malaysia, China, Thailand	Sudden and intense anxiety that the penis (in males) or the vulva and nipples (in females) will recede into body and cause death.
Latah	East Asia	Hypersensitivity to sudden fright, trancelike behavior most often seen in middle-aged women.
Susto	Mexico, Central America	Appetite disturbances, sleep disturbances, sadness, loss of motivation, low self-worth, following a frightening event. Sufferers believe their soul has left their body.
Taijin kyofusho	Japan	Intense fear that one's body displeases, embarrasses, or is offensive to others.

Source: R. Carson and J. Butcher. 1992. *Abnormal Psychology.* 9th edition. Glenview, Il: Scott Foresman.

Social Definitions

Sociologists offer many definitions of mental disorder and theoretical explanations for its occurrence. While conflicting conceptualizations are evident, it is generally conceded that key to the understanding of mental illness is social perception. The definition of mental illness is essentially based upon (1) value judgments made by mental health professionals, (2) normative expectations and reactions of society, and (3) differing beliefs about the causes of mental illness (Clinard and Meier 1998; Mechanic 1968).

Value Judgments. Psychiatrists and mental health professionals—clinical psychologists, psychiatric social workers, and counselors—variously define mental illness. *The Diagnostic and Statistical Manual* (1994) of the American Psychiatric Association provides a set of criteria for the diagnoses of mental illness. However, the judgments of practitioners are often guided by their individual values and beliefs. As a result, assessments of behavior vary; similar symptoms may receive different diagnoses by different practitioners. Diagnostic decisions are often influenced by prior experience with the symptoms or an "idealized" view as to what constitutes normal behavior (Clinard and Meier 1998: 414). The individual's

Political Dissenters and Forced Psychiatric Hospitalization

It is disturbing to hear that political dissenters and protesters are being confined in psychiatric hospitals and declared mentally ill by government officials or others in powerful positions. It is not uncommon though. Evidence of this was once seen in the former Soviet Union and more recently in rural China. Huang Shurong, a 42-year-old Chinese woman, spent 210 days of the past three years involuntarily committed to several psychiatric hospitals in rural China. Government officials forced her into the hospitals after she protested a local land dispute. During her confinement, she was subjected to drug and electroshock therapy, although her friends, family, and even some psychiatrists insisted she was not mentally ill. She was finally discharged when doctors could no longer justify keeping her hospitalized. Ms. Huang is not the only political dissenter forcefully hospitalized. While confined, Ms. Huang roomed with five other political dissenters.

Source: Rosenthal, E. 2002. "In Rural China, Mental Hospitals Await Those Who Rock the Boat." *New York Times,* February 16. Web posted at (http://www.nytimes.com/2002/02/16/international/asia/16CHIN.html?ex=1014879719&ei=1&en=89f1ecc9c9cf65c7).

emotional state, physical illnesses, stressful life events, and social and occupational functioning may also be taken into account when evaluating his or her mental health (Atkinson et al. 1996).

Normative Expectations, Societal Reactions, and Labeling.   Sociologists tend to define mental illness as a departure from normative guidelines or expectations for behavior. *Normative violations*—behaviors that are disruptive, offensive, or highly unusual—may evoke a societal reaction. These behaviors and the individuals who express these behaviors may then be labeled as mentally ill and responded to as such. Societal reactions and labeling produce new social roles for those considered mentally ill. Over time, the stigmatized person may fully adopt the mentally ill role. Norms and the violation of norms, along with societal reactions and the subsequent processes of societal labeling, are therefore crucial processes in defining mentally ill behavior.

Beliefs about Mental Illness.   The work of David Mechanic (1968) and others (Schnittker et al. 2000) focuses on how mental illness is differentially perceived across cultures and forms of social organization. Mental illness is either viewed as a behavior that can be controlled by the afflicted person or viewed as beyond the will of the individual to control. These conflicting views on mental illness often shape how groups define and treat mentally ill behavior. However contradictory, both of these views are usually accepted as definitions of and explanations for mental illness.

A young Albanian boy on the floor of a room occupied by several patients in the El-basan Psychiatric Hospital.

Medical Definition

Most psychiatrists, psychologists, and other medical professionals refer to mental illness as a disease resulting from some genetic abnormality or inherited vulnerability. According to the **medical model,** mental disorders are comparable to physical disorders, requiring medical diagnoses and treatment. *The Diagnostic and Statistical Manual* (1994) of the American Psychiatric Association **(DSM-IV)** provides standard criteria for the diagnosis and treatment of specific mental disorders. Table 7.2 presents fifteen categories of mental disorders listed in the manual. Each main category includes numerous subcategories. Over 450 specific mental disorders are included in the latest revision of the *DSM-IV.*

Mental disorders are classified as either **organic disorders** (Alzheimer's disease, senile psychosis, and paresis), which originate from physiological difficulties and organic causes or **functional disorders,** which include several related disorders whose underlying causes are less well known. Sociological explorations of mental illness tend to focus on the functional disorders. These disorders take many forms but are traditionally known as **psychoses** and **neuroses.** Psychoses are the most debilitating disorders and often require long-term treatment. Neuroses are minor disorders, typically characterized by anxiety, depression, and maladaptive behavior. These disorders rarely require hospitalization. Some of the most common and well-known functional disorders are outlined below (see DSM-IV).

Depression.   **Unipolar (major) depression** is classified as a serious mood disorder and is distinguished from "normal depressive moods." Feeling down or "blue" as everyday stresses, losses, or life changes occur is usually temporary and fades away within a few weeks. The American Psychiatric Association considers depression "abnormal only when it is out of proportion to the event and continues past the point at which most people begin to recover" (Atkinson et al. 1996: 524). In addition to emotional symptoms, such as a depressed mood, a depressive disorder is marked by cognitive, motivational, and physical symptoms. Some of these symptoms include dissatisfaction and anxiety; changes in appetite, sleep, and psychomotor functions; loss of interest and energy; feelings of guilt; thoughts of death; and diminished concentration.

Table 7.2 Main Diagnostic Categories (DSM-IV)

1. Disorders usually first diagnosed in infancy, childhood, or adolescence
2. Delirium, dementia, amnesic, and other cognitive disorders; mental disorders due to a general medical condition
3. Substance abuse disorders
4. Schizophrenic disorders
5. Mood disorders
6. Anxiety disorders
7. Somatoform disorders
8. Dissociative disorders
9. Sexual and gender identity disorders
10. Factitious disorders
11. Eating disorders
12. Sleep disorders
13. Impulse-control disorders
14. Personality disorders
15. Adjustment and other disorders

Source: Adapted from DSM-IV.

Bipolar Disorder. **Bipolar disorder,** also known as **manic-depression,** differs from unipolar depression in that the former involves pronounced mood swings from depression to uncontrolled mania, while persons with unipolar disorder experience depression only. Manic behavior is recognized by elevated mood, increased psychomotor activity, and racing thought processes. Persons in the manic phase of their bipolar disorder experience a sense of omnipotence, coupled with a pronounced lack of judgment about the consequences of their actions. They do not think they need to sleep or eat, but they feel that they can continue to function for extended periods of time at an increasingly accelerated pace. Table 7.3 shows the differing patterns in manic and depression behavior found in bipolar disorder.

Personality Disorders. **Personality disorders** are characterized by "long-standing patterns of maladaptive behavior that constitute immature and inappropriate ways of coping with stress or solving problems" (Atkinson et al. 1996: 513). An individual diagnosed with these types of disorders may express manipulative behavior, disorganized and unstable mood or behavior, and thought disturbances. Personality disorders are usually recognizable during childhood, and many have a lifetime or near-lifetime duration. Symptoms of these disorders may not become evident, however, until the individual encounters an extremely stressful situation. Personality disorders often co-occur with other mental disorders, most commonly mood disorders.

    Antisocial, narcissistic, histrionic, schizotypal, dependent, and borderline are a few of the different types of personality disorders. Many of the personality disorders share common features, which are easy to confuse with one another. In

Table 7.3 Differing Patterns in Manic and Depressive Behavior

	Manic	**Depressive**
Emotional Characteristics	Elated, euphoric	Gloomy, hopeless
	Very sociable	Socially withdrawn
	Impatient at any hindrance	Irritable
Cognitive Characteristics	Racing thoughts	Slowness of thought processes
	Flight of ideas	
	Desire for action	Obsessive worrying
	Impulsive behavior	Inability to make decisions
	Positive self-image	Negative self-image, self-blame
	Delusions of grandeur	Delusions of guilt and disease
Motor Characteristics	Talkative	
	Hyperactive	Decreased motor activity
	Does not become tired	Tired
	Needs less sleep	Difficulty sleeping
	Increased sex drive	Decreased sex drive
	Fluctuating appetite	Decreased appetite

Source: I. Savagon and B. Savagon. 1996. *Abnormal Psychology: The Problem of Maladaptive Behavior.* Upper Saddle River, NJ: Prentice Hall.

general, though, personality disorders are distinguished from one another by odd and eccentric behavior; dramatic, emotional, or erratic behavior; and anxious or fearful behavior.

Schizophrenia. Schizophrenia and related schizophrenic disorders are the most chronic, severe, and disabling of the mental disorders. The psychotic behavior associated with schizophrenia involves alterations in thought, perception, and consciousness; these alterations are often referred to as hallucinations or delusions. Individuals with schizophrenia may hear voices that are not there, exhibit disorganized speech and behavior, or seem to lose touch with reality. The symptoms of schizophrenic disorders take either positive or negative forms. A positive symptom reflects an excess of normal functions such as suspiciousness and delusional behavior. Negative symptoms involve a loss or decrease in normal functioning, including flat affect or lack of emotion, loss of motivation or initiative, loss of energy, and the inability to experience pleasure.

Anxiety Disorders. Anxiety disorders include panic disorder, obsessive-compulsive disorder, post-traumatic stress disorder, generalized anxiety disorder, and phobias. In each of these disorders, "an anxiety disorder may be said to exist if the anxiety experienced is disproportionate to the circumstance, is difficult for the individual to control, or interferes with normal functioning" (U.S. Department of Health and Human Services 1999a: Chapter 7). Anxiety disorders may stem from very specific situations or objects, as in the case of phobias, or

AT A GLANCE

Global Patterns

- Mental disorders account for five of the ten leading causes of disability worldwide.

- Unipolar depression is the leading cause of disability worldwide among persons 5 years of age and older.

- Reports show that psychiatric and neurological conditions could increase their share of the total global disease burden by almost half, from 10.5 percent to almost 15 percent by 2020.

United States

- An estimated 22.1 percent of Americans aged 18 and older—about one in five adults (44.3 million people)—suffer from a diagnosable mental disorder.

- About 3 percent of the U.S. population experiences co-occurring mental disorders.

- Depressive and anxiety disorders are the most common types of mental illness, affecting approximately 19 million U.S. adults each year.

- Schizophrenia is considered the most chronic and disabling of the mental disorders, affecting about 1 percent of the U.S. population aged 18 and older.

- Over 20 percent of children and adolescents in the United States are estimated to have mental disorders.

- Anxiety disorders affect as many as 13 percent of young people and are the most common mental health problems that occur in children ages 9 to 17 years old.

- In the United States, one in ten children and adolescents suffers from mental illness severe enough to cause some level of impairment.

Sources: Murray, C. and A. Lopez (eds.) 1996. *The Global Burden of Disease.* Cambridge, MA: Harvard University School of Public Health on behalf of the World Health Organization and the World Bank, Harvard University Press; NIMH. 2001a. *The Impact of Mental Illness on Society.* Web posted at http://www.nimh.nih.gov/publicat/burden.cfm.;

Satcher, D. 1999a. *Mental Health: A Report of the Surgeon General.* Department of Health and Human Services; NIMH. 2001b. *The Numbers Count: Mental Disorders in America.* Web posted at http://www.nimh.nih.gov/publicat/numbers.cfm;

Satcher, D. 1999b. *Mental Health: Culture, Race and Ethnicity.* A supplement to *Mental Health: A Report of the Surgeon General.* Department of Health and Human Services;

NIMH. 2001c. *Women hold up half the sky: Women and mental health research.* Web posted at http://www.nimh.nih.gov/publicat/womensoms.cfm;

Let's Talk Facts about Mental Health of the Elderly. 1997. Washington, DC: American Psychiatric Association. Web posted at http://www.psych.org/public_info/elderly.cfm.

NIMH. 1999b. *Brief Notes on the Mental Health of Children and Adolescents.*

A patient confined in a psychiatric institution near Moscow, Russia.

more diffuse, nonspecific circumstances. The latter are characterized by chronic and excessive worrying, restlessness, and tension. Some additional signs of anxiety include feeling of fear or dread, rapid heart rate, lightheadedness or dizziness, perspiration, cold hands/feet, and shortness of breath. These symptoms may be related to separation, animals, social fears, or nature fears. For example, individuals may fear being in crowds or being alone, or they may be afraid of snakes or heights.

The Epidemiology of Mental Illness

While the manifestations of mental illness vary from culture to culture, most societies possess some concept of mental disorder. A wide range of epidemiological studies show "severe psychoses seem to be recognized and to occur, everywhere" (Murphy 1976: 1019). Cross-cultural studies of schizophrenia conducted by the World Health Organization (WHO 1991) show similar types of symptoms and prevalence in the following culturally diverse countries: Colombia, the former Czechoslovakia, Denmark, England, India, Nigeria, the former Soviet Union, Taiwan, and the United States. Cultural differences are found in symptom expression, tolerance, and course of the illness. The reluctance to diagnose a person as depressed and variations in tolerance for mentally ill behavior account for much of the differences in prevalence of mental illness around the world (Murphy 1976). Cultures that share common concepts of mental illness often share similar rates of mental illness (U.S. Department of Health and Human Services 1999b).

Prevalence of Mental Disorders in the United States

Approximately one in five adults or 44 million Americans over the age of 18 have a diagnosable mental disorder (U.S. Department of Health and Human Services 1999a: Chapter 2). Co-occurring disorders are found in 3 percent of the adult pop-

Table 7.4   Prevalence of Common Anxiety Disorders

Anxiety Disorder	Percentage of U.S. Adults, ages 18–54
Panic Disorder	1.7
Social Phobia	3.7
Specific Phobia	4.4
Agoraphobia	2.2
Obsessive-Compulsive Disorder	2.3
Generalized Anxiety Disorder	2.8
Posttraumatic Stress Disorder	3.6

Source: National Institute of Mental Health. 2001a. The Numbers Count: Mental Disorders in America. Bethesda, MD: National Institute of Mental Health.

ulation. About 6 percent of adults have a serious mental illness and experience some significant functional impairment. Four of the ten leading causes of disability in the United States are mental disorders, particularly major depression, bipolar disorder, schizophrenia, and obsessive-compulsive disorder (Murray et al. 1996). Anxiety disorders are the most prevalent form of mental illness, affecting more than 19 million American adults (NIMH 2001a). Table 7.4 shows the prevalence of the more common forms of anxiety disorders. Almost 10 percent of the U.S. population has a depressive disorder in a given year (NIMH 2001a). Unipolar depression is more prevalent than bipolar depression. For every one person with bipolar depression, five others have unipolar depression. Studies of the U.S. general population estimate the prevalence of personality disorders to be between 10 and 14 percent (Weisman et al. 1993). Schizophrenia is one of the least common mental disorders in the United States with approximately 2.2 million adults diagnosed (about 1 percent of the general population) (NIMH 2001a).

Sociodemographic Variations in Prevalence

Sex.   According to most research, men and women in the general population are *equally likely* to have some form of mental disorder. Differences are found, however, in patterns or varying forms of mental illness (Tansella 1998). Studies such as those of the World Health Organization show "men have more problems related to alcohol, drug abuse and antisocial behavior, while women suffer more from anxiety, depression and eating disorders" (Tansella 1998: 26). Anxiety, depression, and some personality disorders are twice as prevalent among females than males. A recent survey shows that women are at greater risk than men for developing posttraumatic stress disorder (PTSD) following a traumatic life event (NIMH 2001c). Of the depressive disorders, women are twice as likely to experience unipolar depression, while both sexes are equally likely to experience bipolar depression (NIMH 2001c). Men and women also experience schizophrenic disorders with equal frequency (Robbins and Regier 1991).

Age. The overall prevalence of mental disorders in the United States is approximately 15 to 25 percent for every age group (U.S. Department of Health and Human Services 1999a: Chapter 2). However, mental disorders are more common among adults aged 18 to 54. It is well documented that young adults experience some of the highest rates of mental illness. Depressive disorders and schizophrenia are usually diagnosed in the early to mid-twenties. Cross-national cohort studies show an increase of major depression among younger individuals (Cross National Collaborative Group 1992).

Youth. Children and adolescents are affected by many of the same mental disorders as adults. Studies in the United States and other countries find that one in ten children has a mental disorder (NIMH 1999b). Of this age group, 13 percent are affected by an anxiety disorder (Shaffer et al. 1996). In addition, disruptive disorders such as attention deficit disorder and conduct disorder affect approximately 10 percent of children and adolescents ages 9 to 17. Schizophrenic disorders are thought to be extremely rare in children (U.S. Department of Health and Human Services 1999a: Chapter 2).

Elderly. Elderly people—those aged 65 and older—are at greater risk for some mental disorders than young people (*Let's Talk Facts* 1997). It is estimated that as many as 25 percent of people in this age group have a mental disorder. It is further thought that many more cases are untreated or misdiagnosed. For example, because signs of depression often mimic dementia, many physicians attribute the symptoms to old age. As a result, experts estimate that depression afflicts up to 15 percent of the elderly age group. The World Health Organization finds that worldwide, "236 elderly people per 100,000 suffer from mental illness, compared to 93 per 100,000 for those aged 45 to 64, the next younger group" (*Let's Talk Facts* 1997: 1).

Race. Racial differences for overall rates of mental illness are not clear. Ethnic groups often experience culture-bound syndromes, which account for some variation in the prevalence of mental disorders. Culture-bound syndromes seen in Hispanic Americans include *susto* (fright), *nervios* (nerves), *mal de ojo* (evil eye), and *ataque do nervios* (nervous/panic attacks). Symptoms of an *ataque do nervios* may include screaming uncontrollably, crying, trembling, verbal or physical aggression, dissociative experiences, seizure-like or fainting episodes, and suicidal attempts (U.S. Department of Health and Human Services 1999b). Racial groups who live in similar communities and share similar lifestyles appear to have similar rates of mental illnesses. Certain segments of minority populations including Native Americans, Latino and Hispanic Americans, and African Americans are "over-represented in high-need populations that are particularly at risk for mental illness" (U.S. Department of Health and Human Services 1999b:). These include refugees, the homeless, the incarcerated; those on welfare or in foster homes; and those exposed to violence, alcohol, or substance abuse.

Racial differences are found, however, when assessing the prevalence of specific disorders. Members of these high-need populations have higher rates of both lifetime histories and active disorders than do other groups. Somatization, i.e., hypochondria, is more common among African Americans than among white Americans. African Americans are more likely to have phobias and schizophrenia, but less likely to have depressive disorders (Clinard and Meier 1998). Findings on Native American populations indicate that rates of mental illnesses, including disruptive behavior, substance abuse disorders, and comorbid disorders, run extremely high compared to whites (Beals et al. 1997). Differences in specific disorders are also found among Hispanic Americans. The surgeon general's report on mental health, race, and ethnicity outlines these differences (U.S. Department of Health and Human Services 1999b):

- Adult Mexican immigrants have lower rates of mental disorders than Mexican Americans born in the United States, and adult Puerto Ricans living on the island tend to have lower rates of depression than Puerto Ricans living on the mainland.

- Studies have found that Latino youth experience proportionately more anxiety-related and delinquency problem behaviors, depression, and drug use than do white youth.

- Regarding older Hispanic Americans, one study found over 26 percent of its sample were depressed, but depression was related to physical health; only 5.5 percent of those without physical health problems said they were depressed.

Marital Status. A number of studies find that being married is associated with good mental health and low incidence of mental illness. The divorced or separated, the widowed, or the never married often exhibit the poorest mental health. With regard to sex, the effects of marriage on mental health are not consistent. In some studies, it is hypothesized that the positive effects of marriage are mainly limited to males (Bernard 1982). Other studies conclude that the marriage relationship is stronger for females (Gove et al. 1972). The Midtown Manhattan Study (Srole and Fischer 1978) finds that married men experience the lowest rates of mental illness, followed by single men, and last divorced men. Women exhibit a different pattern. Single women show the lowest rates of mental illness, followed by the married. The highest rates are again found among the divorced.

Social Status. Studies of the effect of social status, i.e., class, socioeconomic status, and educational level, on mental illness show that severe psychiatric disorders are disproportionately concentrated in the lowest social classes (Dohrenwend et al. 1992; Dohrenwend and Dohrenwend 1975; Hollingshead and Redlich 1958; Kessler and Cleary 1980; Miech et al. 1999; Nordenmark and Strandh 1999; Weich and Lewis 1998; Wheaton 1980). In contrast, members of the upper socioeconomic strata are more likely to experience minor disorders such as neuroses. One explanation is that people with mental illness are less likely to be consistently employed. Their mental illness impairs social mobility and status attainment. Consequently, those with mental illness tend to drift downward because of unemployment and financial strain (Dohrenwend et al. 1992). Persons in the lower socioeconomic strata also are subjected to more severe life stresses than those with more social resources. Poverty, low income, and a low standard of living are accompanied by few resources for coping with such stressors. The accumulation of social stressors may well trigger the onset of a mental disorder

(Dohrenwend et al. 1992). Labeling and attribution theorists contend that persons in the upper socioeconomic group typically react to the aberrant behavior of members of the lower social classes as indicative of mental illness. Commonly held beliefs about the causes of mental illness within the lower classes influence their prevalence of mental disorders. For example, lower-class persons may attribute their social status, health, and life chances to fate, bad luck, and other forces beyond their control (Wheaton 1980).

Special Topics in Research

Sociological research on mental illness tends to focus on sociodemographic variations in the prevalence of mental disorders, the social processes that may precipitate mental illnesses, and the everyday experiences of the mentally ill. Sociologists examine value judgments, normative expectations, and cultural beliefs associated with mental illness.

Family Experience, Inherited Vulnerabilities, and Stressful Life Events

It is commonly accepted that at least some forms of mental illness are a result of inherited vulnerabilities. Schizophrenia and manic-depressive disorder are two diagnoses thought to be associated with genetic components. Brain scans, genetic markers, and studies of drug effectiveness provide evidence that genetic factors predispose some individuals to mental illness.

Inherited vulnerabilities and genetic predispositions to mental illness operate in conjunction with stressful life events (Matsumoto 1997). Family experiences, including marital discord, divorce, role conflicts, and childhood trauma, become major sources of stress for individuals and are associated with the prevalence of mental illness (Paykel 1974). Parent-child relationships characterized by conflict and stress also relate to the development of mental illness. Debilitating conditions in their family of origin may contribute to one's mental illness later in life. For example, parents who themselves are mentally ill, or who practice domineering, rejecting, and overprotecting styles of parenting, may well increase the vulnerability of their children to mental illness. Theodore Lidz (1965: 362) and his colleagues propose three such conditions that may affect the development of children in this way:

1. A deficiency in parental nurturing of the child, which leads the child to have severe difficulty in achieving autonomy in the sense of adequate independence and ability to take responsibility.

2. Defective socialization of the child by the family as a social institution. The integrated development of the child, the learning of appropriate age and sex roles, and the achievement of an integrated ego structure are consequently blocked.

3. Defective transmission by the family of basic communicative and other instrumental cultural techniques to the child.

Depressive and anxiety disorders as well as schizophrenia are disproportionately found among individuals who experience these types of stressors within parent–child relationships.

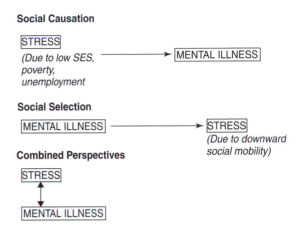

Figure 7.1 Social Causation and Social Selection Traditions— The role of stress as a cause and a consequence of mental illness. (*Source:* Adapted from B. Dohrenwend et al. 1992. "Socioeconomic Status and Psychiatric Disorders: The Causation-Selection Issue." *Science.* 255: 946–952)

Stress may also result from adverse life circumstances and events. Dohrenwend and Dohrenwend (1975) find that persons—most notably of lower social status—who experience economic deprivations and chronic job disruptions are more vulnerable to mental disorders. Stress, however, does not by itself produce mental illness. People experience and withstand considerable stress, yet do not become mentally ill. In many cases, mental illness results from maladaptive perceptions and responses to stressful life events.

Social Causation versus Social Selection. The **social causation tradition** focuses on the role of social stressors in the etiology of mental illness. Social causation theorists argue that the stress of poverty, unemployment, and low socioeconomic status actually produces mental illness. The **social selection tradition** examines social stressors that result as a consequence of mental disorder. Advocates of the social selection approach contend that the stress inherent in being mentally ill itself precipitates downward mobility and diminished economic opportunities (Dohrenwend et al. 1992; Miech et al. 1999). This perspective views mental illness as impairment to status attainment. Those who have mental disorders find it difficult or almost impossible to complete their education or even to find and maintain employment. In the face of diminished resources, their ability to cope with the problems inherent in their mental illness is severely compromised.

Both traditions are generally accepted as plausible causes and consequences of mental illness. Neither has been sufficiently refuted in the literature. Most studies find that the relationship between stress and mental illness is bidirectional. That is, stress may lead to mental illness that may produce a more stressful life situation (Acharya 2001). Figure 7.1 illustrates the tenets of each approach.

Labeling, Societal Reaction, and Social Roles

The process involved in the societal labeling of mental illness produces unintended consequences. Central to the labeling approach is Robert Merton's (1957) concept of a "self-fulfilling prophesy." That is, the process of labeling a person as mentally ill results in the very behavior that portends mental illness. The person is viewed as being what he or she is labeled. When a negative label is assigned to an individual, their behaviors are interpreted as being consistent with that label.

Otherwise "normal" behaviors—an expectant mother singing to her unborn child on a bus—may be viewed as evidence of a mental disorder.

The Myth of Mental Illness.   Psychiatrist Thomas Szasz (1974) views mental illness not as real, biological illness, but as a myth. Illness, he argues, is "a condition of the body, . . . a structural or functional abnormality of cells, tissues, organs, or bodies" (Vatz and Weinberg 1993: 62). Accordingly, he opposes the classification of thoughts, feelings, and behaviors as diseases. While Szasz acknowledges that mental illness does exist, he holds that society labels individuals as mentally ill because their behavior is morally or otherwise unacceptable to the group. Mental illness, therefore, does not lie within the individual. Rather, it is a societal response to such behavior.

In the *Myth of Mental Illness,* (1974) Szasz describes societal responses to mental illness within the framework of a "game-playing model of human behavior" where players—the mentally ill and psychiatrists—act out certain behaviors socially defined by their roles. He describes the roles as impersonations that may be calculated and deliberate. Individuals may act mentally ill in an effort to elicit help from others or to escape sanctions for criminal actions.

Szasz (1974) argues that psychiatrists also perform roles. Psychiatrists socially construct a view of mental illness in such a way that the public rarely disputes the legitimacy of psychiatric diagnoses. The act of diagnosing or labeling behavior as mentally ill is one way that medical professionals exert control over such behaviors. Szasz (1974: 37) offers five reasons for why psychiatrists make diagnoses:

1. Scientific—To identify the organs or tissues affected and perhaps the cause of the illness.
2. Professional—To enlarge the scope, and thus the power and prestige, of a state-protected medical monopoly and the income of its practitioners.
3. Legal—To justify state-sanctioned coercive interventions outside of the criminal justice system.
4. Political-economic—To justify enacting and enforcing measures aimed at promoting public health and providing funds for research and treatment on projects classified as medical.
5. Personal—To enlist the support of public opinion, the media, and the legal system for bestowing special privileges (and impose special hardships) on persons diagnosed as (mentally) ill.

Accordingly, psychiatrists are given authority to label mental illness. This authority leads to the depriving of freedoms for some, and the relieving of individual responsibility for others.

The Mentally Ill Role.   Thomas Scheff's (1966) examination of mental illness also focuses on the process of societal labeling and the role-playing model. He begins his analysis with a definition of mental illness, which is derived from the labeling perspective. Mental illness, or the symptoms of mental illness, is seen as residual rule-breaking or *residual deviance*—any nonconforming, disruptive behavior that is not otherwise defined as criminal. As a consequence of their behavior, rule-breakers are labeled as mentally ill.

Explanations of Rates of Mental Illness

Theory	Sociological Predictors	Hypotheses
Integration		
Durkheim	Social Integration	The greater the social integration, the lower the rate of mental illness.
Social Disorganization and Anomie		
Merton	Anomie	The more anomic social life is, the greater the likelihood that mental illness will occur.
Conflict		
Thio	Power Status	High-status, more powerful individuals are more likely to experience neurotic forms of mental illness while low-status, less powerful individuals become psychotic.
Sellin	Culture Conflict	If a society is characterized by culture conflict, then there is a greater likelihood that mental illness will occur.

Explanations of Individual Levels of Mental Illness

Theorist	Sociological Predictors	Hypotheses
Strain		
Agnew	Strain	If an individual cannot escape or adapt to strain, then he or she may become angry and frustrated. This frustration may lead to mental illness.
Labeling and Societal Reaction		
Scheff	Societal Reaction Labeling	If an individual engages in nonconforming behavior that is not considered criminal, then he or she may be labeled mentally ill. If an individual is labeled mentally ill, then he or she may eventually assume that exact role.
Szasz	Societal Reaction Labeling	If an individual's behavior is immoral or unacceptable to the group, then he or she may be labeled mentally ill.

Unlike Szasz, Scheff is interested in how individuals come to play the mentally ill social role. Scheff proposes that stereotypes, learned at an early age, and other cultural expectations of the mentally ill help labeled persons play the role of a mentally ill person. He offers three propositions pertaining to the acceptance of this role. First, "labeled deviants may be rewarded for playing the stereotyped deviant role" (Scheff 1966: 84). Second, "labeled deviants are punished when they attempt to return to conventional roles" (Scheff 1966: 87). Last, "in the crisis occurring when a residual rule-breaker is publicly labeled, the deviant is highly suggestible, and may accept the proffered role of the insane as the only alternative" (Scheff 1966: 88). In summary, those labeled as mentally ill usually accept the role as their own, either because of rewards and punishments or because they believe there is no alternative role available to them.

Being Sane in Insane Places.   D. L. Rosenhan (1973) and Erving Goffman (1961) provide analyses of the role of institutionalized mental patients and of how they are treated by the hospital staff. Hospitalized mental patients must conform their behavior to the role expectations of the staff. Behavior that is inconsistent with these expectations is viewed as evidence of psychiatric illness.

Rosenhan's (1973: 251) experiment questions traditional psychiatric diagnoses and how "diagnosis betrays little about the patient but much about the environment in which an observer finds him." His experiment involves nine professionals, all of sound mind, who pose as mental patients. Their objective is to determine if hospital staff can distinguish between those who are sane and those who are not.

Each pseudopatient gains entrance into the psychiatric ward complaining of hearing voices. Accurate information is offered as to their life history, relationships with family, and work and school experiences. Upon secret admission, each pseudopatient stops displaying any symptoms of abnormality and behaves as he might in any other setting. Without knowing what to expect, the pseudopatients assume that their experiment will be recognized and that they will be discharged from the hospital. Everyday behaviors such as writing in a notebook, however, are documented as evidence of psychological disturbance. Despite being perfectly sane, none of the pseudopatients are immediately released from the mental hospital.

Goffman provides an insightful analysis of life within a mental hospital and the moral career of mental patients. He observes that the role as mental patient begins with a set of mortifying experiences, i.e., restricted free movement, communal living, and diffused authority of hospital staff. Patients define their roles by these experiences and are socialized to accept the role of a mentally ill person. Doing so ensures rewards rather than punishments and eventual discharge from the hospital. Patients who are easily managed, who submit to hospital routines, and who follow staff directives are labeled by the hospital staff as mentally healthy; patients who are not submissive and compliant are viewed as mentally ill.

Theoretical Explanations of Mental Illness

As shown in the previous sections of this chapter, medical explanations for mental illness are commonly accepted. Mental disorders are thought to result from physical processes within the body, most often chemical imbalances or brain dysfunctions. Individuals may possess hereditary vulnerability to mental disorders. More often, biological and genetic factors are compounded by stress and other environmental factors to produce mental illness in certain individuals. Stressful life events may trigger the onset of a psychotic episode, acute anxiety, or sudden depression. Psychiatrists, psychologists, and other mental health professionals consistently adopt the medical model for the diagnoses, treatment, and understanding of mental illnesses.

Sociocultural explanations also contribute to the explanation of mental illness. The societal reaction or labeling perspective provides insight into how mental illness is defined and used to socially control deviant individuals, or those who are labeled as mentally ill. Szasz (1974; 1994) and Scheff (1966) offer two theories of mental illness from this perspective. Additional sociological theories, including integration, strain, and conflict theories, can be applied to the study of mental illness. In addition to explaining why individuals experience mental illness, these theories help explain rates of mental illness in societies.

Integration Theories

Emile Durkheim's (1951) theory implies that extremely high or low levels of societal integration can give rise to anxiety and mental disorders. In cases of low integration, members of society are detached from the group. Rates of mental disorders and levels of anxiety are high due to uncertainty in life and low social support. In cases of high integration, society members are extremely emerged in the group. Rates of mental illness and anxiety may be lower due to greater social supports and predictability. Stress, depression, and repressed aggression may also be experienced, however, because individuality is discouraged and emphasis is placed on group cohesion. Suicide rates in these types of societies are often high.

Social Disorganization and Anomie

Robert Merton's (1957) theory of social disorganization and anomie focuses on the stress that results from the inability to reach culturally defined goals, a condition he terms anomie. Societies who experience these anomic conditions react in various ways to the stress and are often characterized by high rates of mental illness.

Robert Agnew (1992) furthers this idea by examining individual adaptation to anomic conditions. For some, he contends, opportunities to reach culturally defined goals are blocked by anomic conditions, the loss of something positive, or the presence of negative events. These blocked opportunities are in themselves a source of stress. Individual maladaptation to such stress may lead to mental illness.

Conflict

Culture conflict theories such as that of Thorsten Sellin (1938) suggest that deviance results from the clash of norms and values between different cultures over what is acceptable behavior. Societies characterized by culture conflict may also foster mental illness. Individuals caught between two cultures experience uncertainty over appropriate behavior. Uncertainty alone may produce stress. But in the case of an individual who exhibits inappropriate behavior, he or she may be labeled as peculiar or, in some cases, mentally ill. According to Sellin, culture conflict arises between cultures and within cultures, for example, middle-class versus lower-class norms.

Alex Thio (1978) proposes a power conflict theory of mental illness. In his view, powerful members of society exploit the less powerful members in their quest for power. This quest for power leads to neurotic behavior disorders. To draw attention away from these disorders and toward the reactions of the powerless to exploitation (e.g., aggression), the powerful label the powerless as psychotic. The powerless lack treatment for their psychoses and do not possess the authority to dispute the label. As a result, the psychoses of the powerless are perpetuated and viewed as culturally more severe than neuroses.

Chapter Summary

- Although the nature and definitions of mental disorders vary from country to country and over time, some form of mental illness is seen across the globe. Disorders are most common among the young, the lower socioeconomic classes, the divorced or separated, and certain high-risk populations.

- The medical model of mental illness dominates what is known and accepted about mental disorders. Psychiatrists and mental health professionals diagnose and treat mental disorders according to set criteria in the *Diagnostic and Statistical Manual (DSM-IV)*. Organic and functional disorders along with psychoses and neuroses are defined. Numerous specific disorders are also included. Some of the most common and well-known disorders include:
  - depression
  - bipolar disorder
  - anxiety disorders
  - personality disorders
  - schizophrenia
    - Depression and anxiety are the most common forms of mental illness. Each affects 19 million adults per year.
    - Schizophrenia affects relatively few people, but it is considered one of the most chronic and severe mental disorders known today.

- Much is also known and accepted about the relationship between stress and mental illness. Stressful life circumstances such as unemployment, poverty, and family dysfunction are thought to play a major role in the etiology of mental illness. Stressful life events are considered to be both a cause and a consequence of mental illness.

- Mental illness is socially and culturally defined with regard to the norms, values, and beliefs of a given society. As a result, some disorders are culturally bound, while others are seen in almost every culture.

Key Concepts

Culture: The norms, values, and beliefs of a given society or group.

Cultural relativism: Cross-cultural variation in the social construction of reality.

Culture-bound disorders: Mental disorders that are unique to the culture in which they are found.

Medical model: Mental disorders are attributed to some genetic abnormality or other inherited vulnerability.

Diagnostic and Statistical Manual (DSM-IV):   Publication of the American Psychiatric Association used to diagnose mental disorders according to standardized criteria.

Organic disorders: Mental disorders that originate from physiological or organic causes.

Functional disorders: Group of related disorders whose causes are less well known.

Psychoses: The more severe forms of mental disorders; often require long-term treatment.

Neuroses: The less severe disorders such as depression and anxiety; often referred to as minor disorders.

Unipolar (major) depression: Serious mood disorder classified in the DSM-IV; characterized by emotional, cognitive, motivational, and physical symptoms.

Bipolar (manic-depression) disorder: Serious mood disorder classified in the DSM-IV; characterized by episodes of manic and depressive behavior.

Personality disorders: Maladaptive, immature, and inappropriate ways of coping with stress or solving problems, manipulative behavior, disorganized and unstable mood or behavior, and thought disturbances.

Schizophrenia: Severe and chronic mental disorder classified in the DSM-IV; characterized by alterations in thought, perception, and consciousness, for example, hallucinations or delusions.

Anxiety disorders: Anxiety that is disproportionate to the circumstance, that is difficult for the individual to control, or that interferes with normal functioning.

Social causation tradition: Idea asserting the role of social stressors in the etiology of mental illness.

Social selection tradition: Idea asserting that social stressors are a consequence of mental disorders.

Critical Thinking Questions

1. The manifestations of mental disorder vary widely around the world, yet there are a limited number of medically recognized psychiatric diagnoses. What might account for this seemly incongruous finding?

2. Consider the efficacy of the "myth of mental illness." Is mental illness a social construction fabricated by psychiatric professions, or are psychiatric diagnoses as legitimate as any other medical diagnoses?

3. What sociocultural conditions and social processes are most likely to generate high rates of psychotic vs. less debilitating forms of mental disorder?

4. Depression is the most prevalent form of mental illness found around the world. What accounts for the prevalence of depression across widely disparate cultures? Why do women suffer from depression more so than men worldwide?

Web Extra

Check out these websites for additional information on mental illness:

http://www.nimh.nih.gov

http://www.samhsa.gov

http://www.apa.org

CHAPTER 8

Alcohol Abuse

PORTRAITS

of Substance Abuse

ALCOHOLICS COME FROM ALL WALKS OF LIFE

- Peggy was a heavy drinker for fourteen years, yet she never thought of herself as an alcoholic. Her drinking and occasional prescription drug abuse occurred within the confines of the upper middle class home where she lived with her husband and three young children. Peggy started drinking at age 23 to ease tensions and boost her self-esteem. She was able to deny her addiction for a long time because she looked fine on the outside. Every morning, despite a hangover, she would prepare her kids for school, participate in community activities, and fulfill normal housewife duties. However, there wasn't a day during those fourteen years that she didn't drink or get drunk.

SOURCES OF ADDICTION

- Wendy had her first drink at age 12. By 16, she was a full-fledged alcoholic. Her parents did not intervene because alcoholism was a way of life to them. Her mother died at age 35, her father died at age 39 from drinking, and both her father's parents were alcoholics. Wendy refuses to blame her alcoholism on her parents. She is an alcoholic because she chose to drink and cope with life through drinking. She liked what it did for her, because it took her from reality and put her wherever she wanted to be.

Source: PBS. *Moyers on Addiction: Close to Home.* Web posted at: (http://www.pbs.org/wnet/closetohome/stories/html.)

LEARNING OBJECTIVES

After reading this chapter you should know:

- ☐ Definitional issues related to alcohol abuse.
- ☐ The nature and prevalence of alcohol abuse worldwide and in the United States.
- ☐ Differences in alcohol abuse among various gender, age, race/ethnic groups, and special populations.
- ☐ The influence of culture on alcohol abuse.
- ☐ The effect of religious practices and spirituality on alcohol abuse.
- ☐ The disease concept of alcohol dependence.

Introduction

Excessive drinking, particularly among the young, is a global phenomenon. The processes of globalization may accelerate excessive drinking practices (Stares 1996). This chapter considers definitional issues related to alcohol and illicit drug consumption and the extent and social structural patterns of use across the world and in the United States. Substance use among special populations including Native Americans, college students, and the elderly is also considered. Attention is given to the impact of culture, religion, and spirituality on drinking practices and illegal drug use. Finally, theoretical explanations of rates of substance abuse and individual precipitants are provided.

Definitions

Since Swedish physician Magnus Huss introduced the concept of **alcoholism** in 1849, its definition has undergone several changes. To Dr. Huss, alcoholism simply meant a disease caused by excessive alcohol consumption (Keller and Doria 1991).

> *What was once called the "American Disease" is fast becoming a global habit.*
> —Paul B. Stares (1996)

Scientific advances, cultural and religious perspectives, and legal considerations have contributed to numerous reinterpretations of alcoholism. The National Council on Alcoholism and Drug Dependence and the American Society of Addiction Medicine (cited in Flavin and Morse 1991: 266–271) define alcoholism as:

> *Underage drinking has reached epidemic proportions in America.*
> —Joseph A. Califano, Jr., CASA Chairman and President (2002)

a primary, chronic disease with genetic, psychosocial, and environmental factors influencing its development and manifestations. The disease is often progressive and fatal. It is characterized by continuous or periodic impaired control over drinking, preoccupation with the drug alcohol, use of alcohol despite adverse consequences, and distortions in thinking, most notably denial.

This definition of alcoholism is consistent with the diagnosis of substance dependence provided in the *American Psychiatric Association's Diagnostic and Statistical Manual (DSM-IV)* (1994) and the International Classification of Diseases, tenth edition. The *DSM-IV* sets forth the criteria for substance dependence. At least three of the following criteria must occur during a twelve-month period:

- Substance is often taken in larger amounts or over longer period than intended.

- Persistent desire or unsuccessful efforts to cut down or control substance use.

- A great deal of time is spent in activities necessary to obtain the substance, use the substance, or recover from its effects.

- Important social, occupational, or recreational activities given up or reduced because of substance abuse.

- Continued substance use despite knowledge of having a persistent or recurrent psychological or physical problem that is caused or exacerbated by the use of the substance.

The National Institute on Alcohol Abuse and Alcoholism (www.niaaa
.nih.gov) notes that **"alcohol dependence syndrome"** is marked by:

- *Craving:* A strong need or compulsion to drink.

- *Loss of control:* The frequent inability to stop drinking once a person has
begun.

- *Physical dependence:* The occurrence of withdrawal symptoms, such as
nausea, sweating, shakiness, and anxiety, when alcohol is stopped after a
period of heavy drinking. These symptoms are usually relieved by drinking
alcohol or by taking another sedative drug.

- *Tolerance:* The need for increasing amounts of alcohol in order to get
"high."

Alcohol Use around the World

Regions with the highest level of economic development tend to have the highest per capita consumption of alcohol (Mayor 2001). Europeans as a whole have
the highest per capita consumption of alcohol in the world (Setterobulte,
Jensen, and Hurrelmann 2001). However, wide variations in drinking behaviors
are found across the globe. The World Health Organization provides data on
the per capita consumption of alcohol for persons over the age of 15 in 153
countries. The countries with the highest annual per capita consumption
(in liters) include the following: Slovenia (15.15), Republic of Korea (14.40),
Luxembourg tied with Czech Republic (14.35), Guyana (14.03), and France
(13.74). The countries with the lowest annual per capita consumption are In-
donesia (0.13), Yemen (0.15), Gambia (0.16), Guinea (0.17), and the Democratic
Republic of the Congo (0.21). By contrast, the United States (8.9) ranks thirty-
two on the list, behind other English-speaking countries: the Bahamas (12.09),
Ireland (11.90), and the United Kingdom (9.41) (Setterobulte, Jensen, and
Hurrelmann 2001).

The World Health Organization (WHO) estimates that there are 140 million
people in the world who are alcohol dependent (Mayor 2001). While alcohol consumption is declining among adults across Europe and much of the Western
world, binge drinking is surging among the young. A recent investigation of
drinking practices of European youth shows two patterns of alcohol consumption. The first pattern is that drinking is a common practice among the young;
however, fairly small amounts are usually consumed. The second drinking pattern is that, on certain occasions, excessive amounts of alcohol are consumed in a
binge-drinking fashion with the sole intent of becoming intoxicated. Teenage
drinking is most common in the Czech Republic, Denmark, Ireland, Malta, and
the United Kingdom. Drinking among teenagers in Eastern Europe is increasing,
particularly in Lithuania, Poland, Slovenia, and Slovakia. Teenage drunkenness is
highest in Denmark, Finland, Ireland, and the United Kingdom. And binge drinking (five or more drinks on any one occasion) is most prevalent in Denmark,
Ireland, Poland, and the United Kingdom (Mayor 2001).

Alcoholism as a Disease

E. M. Jellinek, a pioneer in alcoholism research, takes the view that excessive drinking may involve an underlying disease process. His typology of alcoholism includes four distinct categories, two of which are disease related. The disease-related forms are gamma alcoholism and delta alcoholism. Gamma alcoholism involves physiological processes resulting in increased alcohol tolerance and progressive loss of control over its use. Delta alcoholism also involves metabolic and other biochemical changes but is characterized by the *inability to abstain* from alcohol rather than the *loss of control* over its use.

Two nondisease forms of alcoholism are termed alpha and beta. Alpha alcoholism is characterized by excessive drinking that results in a psychological rather than a physical dependence. Alpha alcoholics do not typically suffer from physical illnesses associated with their drinking. Beta alcoholism, however, does involve physical deterioration but is not marked by either physical or psychological dependency.

Jellinek identifies a four-phase process in the development of the disease of alcoholism:

- *Phase I* is the prealcoholic stage in which drinking becomes progressively more excessive. Increasingly larger amounts of alcohol are needed to achieve a state of well-being.

- *Phase II* is the early alcoholic stage marked by defensive attitudes toward drinking, such as denial of a drinking problem or rationalization for increasing consumption. Physical symptoms—blackouts, shakes, loss of memory—are also evident in the early alcoholic stage.

- *Phase III* is known as the crucial phase in the development of alcoholism. In this stage there is a loss of control over drinking and a physical need for alcohol. Drinking is no longer a matter of personal choice but becomes a necessary part of daily life.

- *Phase IV* is the chronic stage in the development of the disease. In all respects this is the terminal phase of alcoholism. The alcoholic goes on drinking sprees that last for days at a time; physical deterioration, including malnutrition, cirrhosis, and neurological damage, is pronounced. If left untreated, the alcoholism may result in a complexity of medical problems that often result in premature death.

Source: Jellinek, E. M. 1960. *The Disease Concept of Alcoholism.* New Haven, CT: College and University Press.

Substance Use in the United States

Findings from the most recent *National Survey on Drug Use and Health* provide a profile of substance use among persons 12 years of age and older in the United States. Considering alcohol use, the survey shows that:

- About half (50.1 percent) of Americans had at least one drink in the previous month.
- Almost 23 percent report binge drinking (five or more drinks during a single occasion) in the previous month.
- About 7 percent admit to heavy drinking (five or more drinks during a single occasion on five or more days in the previous month).
- About half of the residents of large metropolitan areas drink at least occasionally, compared to 46 percent of the residents of small metropolitan areas and 40 percent of those living in rural areas.
- Sixty-five percent of college-educated persons drink, compared to about 54.6 percent of persons 18 to 22 years of age who were not enrolled in college.
- College graduates (26 years of age or older) drink less heavily than similar aged persons who have not graduated from college.
- Excessive alcohol use—binge and heavy drinking—markedly decreases with age (SAMHSA 2004).

Alcohol consumption increases through age 25, then it begins to decline. The reduction in alcohol use across the life span is evident for both genders and all races and ethnic groups. For example, binge and heavy drinkers are most often found among persons between 21 to 25 years old and least common among persons over the age of 60. About 45 percent of persons 21 years of age engage in binge drinking and 17 percent drink heavily, compared to fewer than 10 percent of persons over the age of 60 who binge or drink heavily.

Regional Differences in the United States

The western region of the United States leads the nation in per capita alcohol consumption. Across the nation, per capita consumption of alcohol has declined markedly over the past two decades. While the decline is most pronounced in the western region, the per capita consumption (more than 2.3 gallons per year) is still higher than in the southern, midwestern, and northeastern regions (each less than 2.1 gallons per year) (Nephew et al. 1999).

The West leads the nation in the per capita consumption of beer (more than 1.3 gallons per year), followed by the Midwest and South (1.2 to 1.3 gallons per year) and the Northeast (less than 1.1 gallons per year). Per capita wine consumption is also highest in the West (more than 0.43 gallons per year) followed by the Northeast (0.38 gallons per year). The South and Midwest have a similarly low preference for wine (0.22). Distilled spirits are being consumed at a per capita level that is strikingly similar (between 0.6 and 0.7 gallons per year) across the four major regions of the country (Nephew et al. 1999).

States in the United States (including the District of Columbia) with the highest per capita rates of alcohol consumption (in gallons) are New Hampshire (4.08), District of Columbia (4.01), Nevada (3.96), Delaware (2.88), and Wisconsin (2.88). The states with the lowest per capita alcohol consumption (in gallons) include Kentucky and Kansas (1.73), Oklahoma (1.67), West Virginia (1.60), and Utah (1.29). Considering only persons who drink, the states (including the District of Columbia) with the highest annual levels of individual consumption (in gallons) are the District of Columbia (9.17), New Hampshire (6.66), Tennessee (6.49), Arizona (6.30), and Nevada (6.29). The states with the lowest levels of consumption per drinker are Iowa (3.49), Virginia (3.50), Michigan (3.56), Connecticut (3.57), and Washington (3.62) (Nephew et al. 1999).

Age, Race, and Gender

Men are more apt to drink (62.4 percent) than are women (46 percent). However, among teenagers gender differences are negligible: Girls are slightly more likely to drink (18.3 percent) than boys (17.1 percent). Whites are most likely to drink (54.4 percent) and blacks are least likely to use alcohol (37.9 percent). Persons of mixed race (44.4 percent) and Native Hawaiians or Other Pacific Islanders (43.3 percent) only slightly exceed the proportion of drinkers found among Native Americans or Alaska Natives (42.0 percent), Hispanics (41.5 percent) and Asians (39.8 percent) (SAMSHA 2004).

Among Americans who use alcohol about 17 percent drink heavily (more than one ounce of ethanol per day), 38 percent drink moderately (between 0.22 to less than one ounce of ethanol per day), and 44 percent are light drinkers (at least 12 drinks in the past year to less than 0.22 ounces per day). White men and women tend to consume more alcohol than their black counterparts. White men are most likely to engage in heavy drinking, followed by black men, white women, and black women. Whites also predominate among moderate and light drinkers (SAMHSA 2001).

Culture and Alcohol Use

Wide variations exist in the cultural patterns of alcohol use, its integration into everyday life, and the meanings associated with it. Culture shapes all aspects of alcohol use, including its physical and social consequences. D. B. Heath (1982) notes that sociocultural factors are as critical to the understanding of the influence of alcohol on behavior as are physiological or psychological considerations. Culture, in short, exerts a powerful influence over the use of alcohol across the globe.

In cultures where drinking is an integral part of everyday life, alcohol dependency is low. R. H. and E. M. Blum (1969: 188–227) observe: ". . . In those cultures where drinking is integrated into religious rites and customs, where the place and manner of consumption are regulated by tradition and where, moreover, self-control, sociability, and 'knowing how to hold one's liquor' are matters

Sex and Substance Abuse

Recently the National Center on Addiction and Substance Abuse at Columbia University conducted a study of the possible link between sexual activity and substance abuse among teenagers. While sexual activity does not "cause" substance abuse, nor does substance abuse "cause" sexual activity, the study finds a strong link between the two forms of behavior. Among the key findings are:

- "Compared to teens with no sexually active friends, teens who report half or more of their friends are sexually active are:
  - More than six and one-half times likelier to drink
  - 31 times likelier to get drunk
  - 22.5 times likelier to have tried marijuana
  - More than five and one-half times likelier to smoke

- Teens who spend 25 or more hours a week with a boyfriend/girlfriend (compared to teens who spend less than 10 hours a week with a boyfriend/girlfriend) are:
  - Two and one-half times likelier to drink
  - Five times likelier to get drunk
  - 4.5 times likelier to have tried marijuana
  - More than 2.5 times likelier to smoke

- Girls with boyfriends two or more years older (compared to girls whose boyfriends are less than two years older or who do not have a boyfriend) are:
  - More than twice as likely to drink
  - Almost six times likelier to get drunk
  - Six times likelier to have tried marijuana
  - Four and one-half times likelier to smoke"

Source: Adapted from The National Center on Addiction and Substance Abuse (CASA) at Columbia University. 2004. *National Survey of American Attitudes on Substance Abuse IX: Teen Dating Practices and Sexual Activity* New York: Author. Web posted at: www .casacolumbia.org/Absolutenm/Articlefiles/380-August_2004_CH_Teen_Survey.pdf.

AT A GLANCE

Global Patterns and Trends

- The age of initiation into alcohol/drug use is declining across the globe.
- There has been an increase of alcohol use among women. Women are also at higher risk for alcohol-related harm than men.

U.S. Patterns and Trends

- About half of the U.S. population 12 years of age and older used alcohol in 2003; 22.6 percent participated in binge drinking, and 6.8 percent were considered heavy drinkers.
- 29 percent of underage persons (aged 12 to 20) report drinking alcohol.
- Binge drinking is concentrated in the age range 18–25 (41.6%); and 47.8% at age 21.
- College students are more likely than their peers not in college to drink, binge drink, and drink to excess.
- Approximately 14 million Americans meet the diagnostic criteria for alcohol dependence.
- Persons who are alcohol dependent are four times more likely to have started drinking before the age of 15.

Sources: The National Center on Addiction and Substance Abuse. 2002. "Teen Tipplers: America's Underage Drinking Epidemic," New York: Columbia University; Mayor, S. 2001. "Alcohol and Drug Misuse Sweeping the World, says WHO," *British Medical Journal,* 322: 7284; Settertobulte, W., B. B. Jensen, and K. Hurrelmann. 2001. "Drinking Among Young Europeans," World Health Organization-Regional Office for Europe; *United Nations World Drug Report 2000.* 2000. Oxford: Oxford University Press; Substance Abuse and Mental Health Services Administration (SAMHSA). 2004. *Overview of Findings from the 2003 National Survey on Drug Use and Health.* Rockville, MD: U.S. Department of Health and Human Services.

of manly pride, alcohol problems are at a minimum, provided no other variables are overriding." Two cultures, Italian and Jewish, illustrate the importance of the integration of drinking practices into everyday life. To anthropologist Donald Heath (1995), the low rates of alcoholism among Italians and Jews are a consequence of effective cultural socialization.

> . . . children are introduced to alcohol as part of their regular family life and learn to drink moderate amounts while still young. In both countries, alcohol is commonly drunk with meals and is considered a natural and normal food. Most people agree that alcohol in moderation, for those who choose to drink, is necessary, and that abuse is unacceptable and results in immediate sanctions.

In their classic study of Jewish drinking practices, sociologists Bruce Berg and Barry Glassner (1980) identify four cultural processes that reduce problematic alcohol use. First, alcohol abuse is linked with being a non-Jew. Second, early in life, children learn that drinking in moderation is part of religious and family customs and carries symbolic importance to a Jew. Third, Jews who drink moderately tend to associate with other Jews who do the same. Fourth, Jews learn techniques to avoid being pressured into drinking excessively.

Findings from several cross-cultural studies provide remarkably consistent conclusions about the use of alcohol. N. E. Zinberg (1981) identifies five cultural conditions that promote nonproblematic drinking practices:

- Group drinking is clearly differentiated from drunkenness and associated with ritualistic or religious celebrations.
- Drinking is associated with eating, preferably ritualistic feasting.
- Both sexes and several generations are included in the drinking situation, regardless of whether all drink.
- Drinking is divorced from the individual's effort to escape personal anxiety or difficult (intolerable) social situations.
- Inappropriate behavior when drinking (aggression, violence, overt sexuality) is absolutely disapproved, and protection against such behavior is offered by the "sober" or less intoxicated.

Religion, Spirituality, and Substance Use

The possible effect of religion and spirituality on the use of various substances is the focus of a recent report issued by the National Center on Addiction and Substance Abuse at Columbia University. Religion is defined as "a set of particular beliefs about God or a higher power shared by a group of individuals, and the practices, rituals, and forms of governance that define how those beliefs are expressed" (National Center on Addiction and Substance Abuse 2001). Spirituality refers more to a personal expression of belief and is defined as "a deeply personal and individualized response to God, a higher power, or an animating force in the world" (National Center on Addiction and Substance Abuse 2001). It is possible, therefore, to be spiritual without having an affiliation with a particular church or religious organization.

Analyses of national data collected in three separate studies show:

- Adults who deny that religious beliefs are important to them are one and one-half times more likely to drink, three times more likely to binge drink, four times more likely to use illicit drugs, and six times more likely to use marijuana than adults who report that religious beliefs are important to them.
- Adults who do not participate in religious services are two times more likely to drink, five times more likely to use illicit drugs, seven times more

Bill Wilson co-founded Alcoholics Anonymous to recover from his addiction to alcohol.

likely to binge drink, and eight times more likely to use marijuana than adults who participate in religious services at least once a week.

- Teenagers who deny that religious beliefs are important to them are three times more likely to drink and binge drink, four times more likely to use marijuana, and seven times more likely to use illicit drugs than teenagers who report that religious beliefs are important to them.

- Teenagers who do not participate in religious services are two times more likely to drink, more than three times more likely to use marijuana and binge drink, and four times more likely to use illicit drugs than teenagers who participate in religious services at least once a week.

- Substance-dependent persons are more likely to become drug free if they participate in a spiritually based program such as Alcoholics Anonymous or Narcotics Anonymous (www.casacolumbia.org).

More than six decades ago, Bill Wilson and Dr. Bob Smith co-founded **Alcoholics Anonymous** (*Alcoholics Anonymous* 2001). Arguably, Alcoholics Anonymous is the most successful recovery program for alcoholics worldwide. Alcoholics Anonymous is a spiritually based rehabilitation strategy that combines group support, individual mentoring, and personal awareness and commitment. A fundamental precept of Alcoholics Anonymous is the alcoholic's recognition that he or she is, in fact, an alcoholic. Alcoholics in the program must also accept that they are powerless over their alcoholism and that they desire to stop drinking. Fearless and uncompromising self-examination is coupled with a willingness to compensate those whom they have injured. By active participation in this program, recovering alcoholics are guided through their recovery—"one day at a time."

The Twelve Steps of Alcoholics Anonymous

Step One: Admitted we were powerless over alcohol—that our lives had become unmanageable.

Step Two: Came to believe that a Power greater than ourselves could restore us to sanity.

Step Three: Made a decision to turn our will and our lives over to the care of God "as we understood Him."

Step Four: Made a searching and fearless moral inventory of ourselves.

Step Five: Admitted to God, to ourselves, and to another human being the exact nature of our wrongs.

Step Six: Were entirely ready to have God remove all these defects of character.

Step Seven: Humbly asked Him to remove our shortcomings.

Step Eight: Made a list of all persons we had harmed and became willing to make amends to them all.

Step Nine: Made direct amends to such people wherever possible, except when to do so would injure them or others.

Step Ten: Continued to take personal inventory and when wrong promptly admitted it.

Step Eleven: Sought through prayer and meditation to improve our conscious contact with God "as we understood Him," praying only for knowledge of His will for us and the power to carry that out.

Step Twelve: Having had a spiritual awakening as the result of these steps, we tried to carry this message to alcoholics and to practice these principles in all our efforts.

Source: Alcoholics Anonymous Comes of Age: A Brief History of A.A. 1970. New York: Alcoholics Anonymous World Services. The Twelve Steps are reprinted with permission of Alcoholics Anonymous World Services, Inc. (A.A.W.S.) Permission to reprint the Twelve Steps does not mean that A.A.W.S. has reviewed or approved the contents of this publication, or that A.A.W.S. necessarily agrees with the views expressed herein. A.A. is a program of recovery from alcoholism only—use of the Twelve Steps in connection with programs and activities which are patterned after A.A., but which address other problems, or in any other non-A.A. context, does not imply otherwise.

Special Populations

College Students

Drinking on college campuses has long been pervasive, often excessive, and more recently linked to risky behaviors and dire health consequences (Wechsler 1995). About eight in ten college undergraduates drink at least occasionally, 44 percent binge drink (five drinks in a row for men, and four in a row for women), and 23 percent binge drink frequently (Wechsler et al. 2000). Undergraduate males are more likely to engage in binge drinking (50 percent) than are their female counterparts. Compared to their peers who are not students, undergraduates are more likely to engage in binge drinking. Binge drinking is associated with the significantly greater risks of health problems, car accidents, personal injury, aggressive behavior, and sexual assault and victimization (Wechsler 1995).

The onset of drinking and other drug use typically occurs in adolescence (Gledhill-Hoyt et al. 2000). For almost seven in ten marijuana smokers, initiation into its use began while in high school. However, one in three regular users of marijuana began using the drug after the age of 18, usually as a college student. Occasional drinking behaviors tend to begin before entrance into college and continue during the undergraduate years. Less than one in three college students (about 28 percent) began drinking, or engaged in binge drinking, after the age of 18.

The use of multiple substances is common among undergraduate students. Typically, binge drinking accompanies marijuana smoking or the use of other drugs. About nine of every ten college students who smoke marijuana also binge drink or use other illicit drugs. Similarly, 87 percent of undergraduates who use illicit drugs other than marijuana also binge drink or use multiple illicit drugs (Gledhill-Hoyt et al. 2000). Put another way, the more frequently an undergraduate binge drinks, the more likely the student will also be to smoke marijuana, use cocaine, or other illicit drugs (Jones et al. 2001).

The physiological and mind-altering effects of alcohol and most psychotropic drugs are affected by several factors, including an individual's physical health, level of fatigue, emotional state, and social circumstances surrounding the use of the drug (Hanson and Venturelli 2001). Distinct differences in the ways that men and women metabolize alcohol are also well known. Women become intoxicated more quickly than men, and they remain intoxicated for a longer time. Women also become dependent on alcohol more readily than men (Alexander and La Rosa 1994). One of the most common methods of determining the effects of alcohol on an individual's ability to function dependably considers three factors: gender, body weight, and amount of alcohol consumed. An individual's blood alcohol concentration (BAC) is a function of these three variables taken together.

Native Americans

There is considerable evidence that Native Americans as a whole have a disproportionately high rate of alcohol dependency (May 1996). It is important to note that there is wide variation in alcohol abuse among the 300 Native American tribes with more than 2 million members. Estimates range from 30 to 84 percent of tribal members who drink alcohol, compared to about 67 percent in the general population. Overall, problematic drinking is about twice as common among Native American men than among women. Alcohol abuse is implicated in more than one in four deaths of Native American men compared to about one in seven deaths of tribal women (Moran and Moran 1995).

Distinct patterns of drinking behaviors can be found among Native Americans both young and old. Typically, all available alcohol—usually considerable quantities—is consumed in a relatively brief period of time. What there is to drink is shared among the members of the group in a "binge drinking" fashion (May 1996).

Two types of Native American drinkers have been identified: "Anxiety drinkers" become intoxicated on a regular basis and manifest a range of alcohol-related medical and interpersonal problems. High unemployment rates are evident among the anxiety drinkers, and they typically succumb to a premature death caused by their excessive drinking. "Recreational drinkers" are more occasional users of alcohol than the anxiety drinkers, but when they do drink they do so with the intention of becoming intoxicated. Car accidents, fighting, driving under the influence, and other forms of disorderly conduct are common among recreational drinkers. It is estimated that recreational drinkers account for about two of every three Native Americans who abuse alcohol (May 1996).

Various explanations are offered to account for high rates of alcohol abuse among Native Americans. The anomic conditions of tribal life characterized by widespread blockage to educational and occupational opportunities found in the larger society are thought to precipitate excessive drinking and other drug use (Jessor et al. 1968). Social disorganization—the disintegration of cultural traditions and upheavals within the family—is also viewed as generating conditions conducive to substance abuse (Bachman 1991). Related to a disorganized social milieu is the sense that cultural identity has been lost, and along with it a feeling of self-worth and social determination (Bachman 1992).

Criminologist Malcolm D. Holmes and Native American researcher Judith A. Antell (2001) offer an alternative view of Native American drinking patterns. They contend that Native Americans and whites devise differing "symbolic-moral universes" to explain deviant behavior. These social constructions provide two conflicting frameworks for understanding the etiology of Native American drinking behaviors and effective methods of altering them. The symbolic-moral universe of Native Americans focuses on their collective experience of exploitation and cultural decimation at the hands of white intruders. The consequences of white expansion into Native American habitats and their disregard for promises made and for the integrity of tribal cultures is now experienced as widespread economic deprivation and despair. To combat their destructive drinking practices, Native Americans advocate the reestablishment of their tribal identity and cultural heritage. At the same time they argue that educational and economic opportunities must be made available to Native Americans. In addition, cultural identification is viewed as consistent with economic

Explanations of Rates of Alcohol Abuse

Theory and Theorists	Sociological Predictors	Hypotheses
Social Integration		
• Merton	Anomie	The greater the disjunction between institutionalized means and culturally approved goals, the higher the rate of alcohol abuse.
	Retreatism	The greater the rejection of institutionalized means and culturally approved goals, the greater the retreatist behavior in society. The greater the retreatist behavior in society, the higher the rate of alcohol abuse
Subcultural Opportunities		
• Cloward and Ohlin	Retreatism Subcultures	The fewer the subcultural opportunities—either legitimate or illegitimate—for success, the more likely retreatist subcultures will emerge. The more retreatist subcultures in a given society, the higher the rate of alcohol abuse.
• Bales	Cultural Tension	As tension and stress increase in a given culture, and as effective means of tension reduction decrease, the higher the rate of alcohol abuse.
Cultural Integration		
• Blum and Blum	Cultural Integration	The more drinking is integrated into the customs of daily life, the lower the rate of alcohol abuse.

progress and will serve to ameliorate the problematic substance use of Native Americans.

Elderly

Alcohol consumption tends to decline with an increase in age. Among the elderly about 52 percent of men and 68 percent of women abstain from the use of alcohol. However, about three in ten of the 10 million alcoholics in the United States are over the age of 60 (Gupta 1993). Estimates of alcoholism among the elderly range from 2 to 10 percent of the general population (Egbert 1993). The onset of alcoholism occurs in later life about one-third of the time, while two-thirds of the older alcoholics developed their dependence earlier in life (Rigler 2000). Experiences of later life—loss of health, death of friends and family members, depression—may trigger late-onset alcoholism. Women and minorities are more apt to develop an alcohol dependency later in life (Gomberg 1995; Mulford and Fitzgerald 1992).

Explanations of Alcohol Abuse

While numerous theories have been offered to explain alcohol and drug dependence, particular attention will be given here to sociological and social psychological formulations. Much attention has been given in recent years to the biological roots of the excessive use of alcohol and other drugs. However, issues related to the processing of alcohol in the human body and the biochemical underpinnings of addiction are beyond the scope of this book.

Rates of Alcohol Abuse

Culture and Subculture. Sociologist Robert Bales (1946) focuses on the cultural basis for excessive drinking behavior. He argues that cultures may generate various levels of stress and tension, typically accompanied by related negative emotions of anger, resentment, and depression. The use of intoxicants is also culturally defined as either an appropriate or inappropriate way to relieve stress. If the use of alcohol is condemned in a given culture, then alternative means of tension reduction may be provided. To the extent that a culture positively sanctions the use of alcohol or other drugs to alleviate stress and fails to provide other effective methods of stress reduction, that culture will experience high rates of alcohol and other drug dependence.

Richard Cloward and Lloyd Ohlin (1960) argue that subcultural opportunity structures may account for distinct patterns of deviant behaviors. Cloward and Ohlin consider three distinct subcultures: criminal, violent, and retreatist. The retreatist subculture has particular relevance for the understanding of variations in rates of alcohol and drug dependence. When opportunities to engage in lucrative criminal behaviors are blocked and violent means to status and recognition are not available, retreatist subcultures may emerge. Individuals who have otherwise blocked alternative deviant opportunities may gravitate to subcultures that have ready access to illicit drugs and alcohol. Retreatist subculture provides the opportunity and social supports necessary for the progressive use of intoxicants.

Social Integration. Robert Merton (1968), a colleague of Richard Cloward and Lloyd Ohlin, offers a related formulation. Retreatism is one of Merton's five responses to anomie, a disjunction between institutionalized means and culturally approved goals in society. When the institutionalized means do not lead to culturally approved goals, there may be a widespread rejection of both means and goals. To avoid the stress and tension that follows from anomic social conditions, one may retreat into the solace provided by drug and alcohol abuse.

Cultural Integration. To the extent that drinking is integrated into everyday life, alcohol use is regulated by social norms and cultural traditions. Drinking is positively sanctioned, expected behavior for all members of the family. Drinking commonly accompanies a meal or is part of a religious ritual. Excessive drinking is abhorrent, a violation of the culture's time-honored values and traditions.

Explanation of Individual Alcohol Abuse

Theory and Theorists	Sociological Predictors	Hypotheses
Social Strain		
• Agnew	Stress/Tension	As stress and tension increases, negative emotions increase. As negative emotions increase, the likelihood of alcohol dependence increases.
Self-Derogation		
• Kaplan	Self-Derogation	The greater the self-derogation, the greater the likelihood of alcohol dependence.
Social Learning		
• Akers	Differential Association Definitions Differential Reinforcement Imitation	The greater the primary association with persons who define substance abuse as justifiable and pleasurable, the more likely those definitions will be reinforced and substance abuse behaviors imitated. The more involvement in the substance abuse learning process, the more likely will alcohol dependence occur.

Persons who violate norms and customs that surround the use of alcohol may be severely sanctioned or ostracized from their family and close friends (Blum and Blum 1969).

Individual Alcohol Abuse

Self-Derogation. Howard Kaplan's (1995) formulation of self-derogation provides a social psychological perspective on the etiology of substance abuse. Kaplan argues that the desire for self-esteem is a primary motivation for individual behavior. Self-esteem or a positive attitude toward one's self is contingent upon the following: personal characteristics or abilities that are highly valued by the individual, positive response by significant others, and the ability to deflect negative responses and accept positive responses from others as valid. If these conditions for the development of self-esteem cannot be met, then the processes of self-derogation may ensue. Self-derogation or negative attitudes toward one's self tend to undermine the individual's motivation to conform to the norms of conventional society and increase motivation to engage in forms of deviant behavior that may provide an escape from their experiences of social devaluation. Commonly, a devalued person will reject the norms of those groups that are the source of his or her negative self-attitudes and seek membership in less conventional groups. Deviant group membership provides a respite from attacks on one's self-esteem and thereby provides opportunities for alternative forms of self-enhancing behaviors. In the short term, drinking to excess or the use of mind-altering drugs may provide the user with a way to counter the processes of self-derogation and establish a sense of well-being.

Social Strain.   Sociologist Robert Agnew's (1992) formulation of social strain points out that negative social relations typically give rise to particularly stressful emotional states. Persons entangled in adverse interpersonal relationships commonly feel anxiety, depression, anger, and futility. Mood-altering substances, alcohol, and a variety of drugs may be resorted to in order to relieve acute emotional distress. Often the effects of alcohol and other drugs, both licit and illicit, exacerbate the situation. As interpersonal relations further deteriorate, the use of intoxicants may well increase.

Social Learning.   Central to Ronald Akers' (1985) social learning formulation are four interrelated concepts: *differential association, definitions, differential reinforcement,* and *imitation.* These concepts provide a framework for the process of learning to engage in deviant forms of substance use. The concept of differential association, drawn from Edwin Sutherland's (1947) theory by the same name, refers to the extent of interaction with members of groups that advocate deviant substance use. Definitions of substance use as justifiable, desirable, and pleasurable are learned in the context of primary group interaction. Differential reinforcement refers to the anticipation that the rewards of alcohol abuse markedly exceed any possible negative sanctions. Excessive drinking is differentially reinforced when the expected pleasure overshadows any adverse social or legal response. Imitation is simply modeling one's behavior after that of others.

Chapter Summary

- Wide variations in excessive drinking practices are found around the world and in the United States. Alcohol abuse is particularly prevalent among the young worldwide.
- Definitional issues related to substance dependence are considered:
  - Tolerance refers to either the need for increased amounts of the substance in order to achieve intoxication (or the desired effect) or a marked diminished effect with continued use of the same amount.
  - Substance dependence occurs when at least three of the following criteria are met during a twelve-month period:
    - Substance is often taken in larger amounts or over a longer period than intended.
    - Persistent desire or unsuccessful efforts are made to cut down or control substance use.
    - A great deal of time is spent in activities necessary to obtain the substance, use the substance, or recover from its effects.
    - Important social, occupational, or recreational activities are given up or reduced because of substance abuse.

- Continued substance use occurs despite knowledge of having a persistent or recurrent psychological or physical problem that is caused or exacerbated by the use of the substance.

• When drinking practices are integrated into everyday life, alcohol dependency tends to be low. Notable examples are: Italian, French, and Jewish cultures.

• When drinking practices are not integrated into everyday life, alcohol dependency tends to be high. Notable examples are the Irish, Native American, and youth cultures.

• The disease concept of alcohol dependence dominates research on the etiology and treatment of substance abuse.

Key Concepts

Alcoholism: A primary, chronic disease with genetic, psychosocial, and environmental factors that influence its development and manifestations; often progressive and fatal.

Alcohol Dependence Syndrome: As noted by the National Institute on Alcoholism and Alcohol Abuse, a syndrome characterized by craving, loss of control, physical dependence, and tolerance as each relates to the use of alcohol.

Craving: A strong need or compulsion to drink.

Loss of control: The frequent inability to stop drinking once a person has begun.

Physical dependence: The occurrence of withdrawal symptoms such as nausea, sweating, and anxiety when a drug is no longer used.

Tolerance: Either a need for increased amounts of the substance in order to achieve the desired effect, or marked diminished effect with continued use of the same amount.

Alcoholics Anonymous: Founded by Bill Wilson and Dr. Bob Smith as a spiritually based recovery program and support group for alcoholics.

Critical Thinking Questions

1. The use of alcohol is common around the world. Yet, consumption levels vary markedly as do rates of alcoholism. What accounts for the apparent disconnect between the amount of alcohol consumed in a given culture and its rate of alcoholism?

2. Is the process of becoming addicted to alcohol linked in any way to the process by which an individual seeks to recover from that addiction? Put another way, are the same social circumstances and motivations that brought about the person's addiction involved in the recovery process?

3. Compare the socialization process that tends to increase or decrease the likelihood of becoming addicted to alcohol. What accounts for persons whose family members or close friends are substance abusers and they are not?

Web Extra

Check out these websites for additional information on Alcohol Abuse:

http://www.niaaa.nih.gov

http://www.samhsa.gov

http://www.casacolumbia.org

http://www.aa.org

CHAPTER 9

Illicit Drug Use

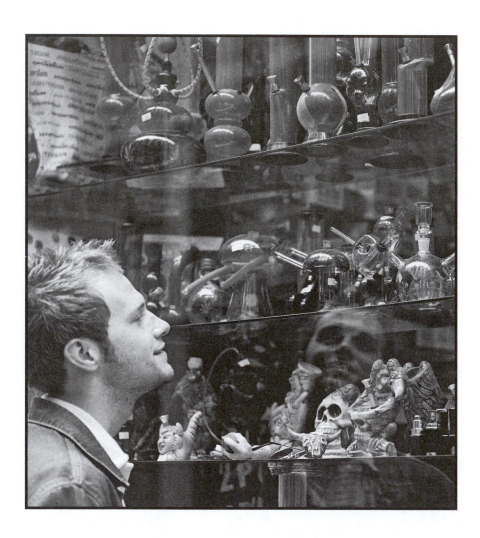

P O R T R A I T S

of Illicit Drug Use

- As a full-time housewife and mother, Sue hardly fits the stereotypical picture of a heroin addict. But for a year and a half of her adult life, she, along with her husband, was consumed with getting high on heroin. Sue decided to start using heroin after a friend vowed it would help ease the headaches and muscular pain from epileptic seizures she had suffered since she was 15. Sue quickly became addicted. Her heroin addictions took a toll on her home, her relationships, and her family. Buying drugs became a family affair. Her two children went along for the ride. Too impatient to wait out the 20-minute ride home, Sue and her husband would find a dark street corner and shoot up (with their kids in the back seat).

- Louis started using heroin at 19. Eventually, he became addicted to cocaine. He thought drugs would help him cope with anger, anomie, and feelings of powerlessness as well as his troubled life. Before becoming addicted, Louis ran away from home at age 16, lived on the streets of New York, and joined a gang before being sent to prison for 18 months. Louis says he didn't choose to become an addict; he chose to experiment, to escape. His efforts to stop using drugs always failed. While the pleasure of the high was gone, he felt powerless to give up drugs. He does whatever he has to do to support his habit.

Source: PBS. *Moyers on Addiction: Close to Home.* Web posted at: http://www.pbs.org/wnet/closetohome/stories/html.

LEARNING OBJECTIVES

After reading this chapter you should know:

- ☐ Definitional issues related to illicit drug use.
- ☐ The nature and prevalence of illicit drug abuse worldwide and in the United States.
- ☐ Differences in alcohol and drug use among various gender, age, race/ethnic groups.
- ☐ The influence of education and employment status on illicit drug use.
- ☐ Explanations of rates of and individual involvement in illicit drug use.

Introduction

Illicit drug use, like excessive alcohol consumption, is a global phenomenon. It is estimated that the annual worldwide expenditure on illicit drugs exceeds $321 billion. That is, more money is spent on illicit drugs each year than the Gross Domestic Product (GDP) of 88 percent of the countries worldwide (United Nations, 2005). The annual wholesale value of illicit drugs marketed across the globe ($94 billion) far exceeds the wholesale market value, for example, of wine ($17.3 billion), wheat ($16 billion), and coffee ($5.7 billion) (United Nations, 2005).

> *"So long as large sums of money are involved—and they are bound to be if drugs are illegal—it is literally impossible to stop the traffic, or even to make a serious reduction in its scope."*—Milton Friedman, Recipient of the Nobel Prize for Economics (Friedman and Friedman 1984).

This chapter considers definitional issues related illicit drug use and the extent and social structural patterns of use across the world and in the United States. In addition, theoretical explanations of rates of substance abuse and individual precipitants are provided.

Definitions

Several related terms must be understood before discussing the use of illicit drugs. First, the concept of a **drug** must be considered. A physical substance may be classified as a drug if it causes recognizable physical or psychological effects (Stephens 1987). It is often assumed that a physical substance classified as a drug consistently produces recognizable physiological effects and that those effects are predictable from one user to the next. Sociologist Eric Goode (2005), however, points out that the classification of a substance as a drug, its legal status, and its physical or psychological effects are largely matters of social and cultural definition.

> *"Penalties against possession of a drug should not be more damaging to an individual than the use of the drug itself."*
> —Jimmy Carter, U.S. President. (Message to Congress 1977).

The legal status of a drug is contingent upon the social perception that its use may impede an individual's ability to perform essential roles—caregiver, student, employee—or its use may prompt wanton and threatening behavior (Tittle and Paternoster 2000). In the absence of any therapeutic value, a substance may be rendered illegal; its use and distribution are then considered criminal offenses. Physiological and mind-altering effects of a drug are also affected by the sociocultural context of its use. Expected effects of a drug and the effects that are actually experienced are largely learned from other drug users and become socially defined and interpreted (Becker 1963; Goode 2005) (See Table 9.1).

The second term is **addiction.** Addiction refers to a physiological dependence on a substance. When the substance is not available, the addicted person experiences pronounced distress, known as a withdrawal or abstinence syndrome. Addiction may also involve psychological dependence, a strong emotional need for the substance in the absence of a physical dependence on it (Abadinsky 1989; Granfield and Cloud 1996; Tittle and Paternoster 2000).

Sociologist Ronald Akers (1991) argues that addiction involves two processes: dependence and **tolerance.** Dependence results from the physical effects of the substance that are sustained only with its continual use. The sudden cessation of the use of certain drugs, notably heroin, morphine, or methamphetamines, may cause severe physical and psychological discomfort. A long-time drug user who stops using drugs may become extremely agitated, nervous, depressed, or unable to sleep or eat. Physical symptoms typically accompany a general feeling of emotional distress. The former drug user may develop stomach ailments, an elevation in temperature, and other symptoms that commonly accompany severe influenza. Dependence on certain drugs is, in part, related to the desire to avoid **withdrawal** symptoms that follow an interruption in drug use (Lindesmith 1947, 1968).

Over time a drug user may develop a tolerance to a particular drug. That is, the drug user must increase the amount of drug consumed to achieve the desired effect. The physiological advantages that accompany the use of the drug are lost unless taken in sufficient quantities. The inability to stave off the ill effects of withdrawal is another drawback of drug tolerance. The drug user must maintain a certain level of intake to ensure that the symptoms of withdrawal do not occur. In short, drug tolerance sets up a vicious cycle of the increasing need for a drug—a need that may well exceed the user's physical ability to sustain (Tittle and Paternoster 2000).

Illicit Drug Use around the World

Information about illicit drug use across the globe is subject to interpretation. Much of what is known is extrapolated from a wide variety of sources. The United Nations Office on Drugs and Crime, however, has led the way to an increasingly accurate picture of drug production, trafficking, and use across the globe. It is estimated that there are 200 million illicit drug users worldwide, or about 5 percent of all persons between the ages of 15 and 64 (*United Nations, 2005 World Drug Report,* p. 23). Cannabis or marijuana is clearly the most frequently used drug across the globe. Cannabis is used by eight of every 10 illicit drug users (160.9 million) around the world. More than 26 million persons use amphetamines, about 16 million use opiates, and an estimated 13.7 million people use cocaine worldwide. Nonetheless, active drug users represent a relatively small percentage of the world's population. Cannabis is used by only 4 percent of persons around the globe, while amphetamines are used by 0.6 percent, opiates by 0.4 percent, and cocaine by 0.2 percent (*United Nations, 2005 World Drug Report,* p. 23).

Illicit Drug Use in the United States

About 14 million people in the United States (6.3 percent of the population) use illicit drugs. The most common drug is marijuana, used by three of every four illicit drug users. About six in ten illicit drug users limit their consumption to

Table 9.1 Commonly Abused Drugs

Substance: Category and Name	Examples of Commercial and Street Names	DEA Schedule[*]/ How Administered[**]	*Intoxication Effects*/Potential Health Consequences
Cannabinoids			*euphoria, slowed thinking and reaction time, confusion, impaired balance and coordination*/cough, frequent respiratory infections; impaired memory and learning; increased heart rate, anxiety; panic attacks; tolerance, addiction
hashish	boom, chronic, gang-, ster, hash, hash oil, hemp	I/swallowed, smoked	
marijuana	blunt, dope, ganja, grass, herb, joints, Mary Jane, pot, reefer, sinsemilla, skunk, weed	I/swallowed, smoked	
Depressants			*reduced anxiety; feeling of well-being; lowered inhibitions; slowed pulse and breathing; lowered blood pressure; poor concentration*/fatigue; confusion; impaired coordination, memory, judgment; addiction; respiratory depression and arrest, death
barbiturates	*Amytal, Nembutal, Seconal, Phenobarbital*; barbs, reds, red birds, phennies, tooies, yellows, yellow jackets	II, III, V/injected, swallowed	
benzodiazepines (other than flunitrazepam)	*Ativan, Halcion, Librium, Valium, Xanax*; candy, downers, sleeping pills, tranks	IV/swallowed, injected	*Also, for barbiturates—sedation, drowsiness*/depression, unusual excitement, fever, irritability, poor judgment, slurred speech, dizziness, life-threatening withdrawal.
flunitrazepam[***] (Club Drug)	*Rohypnol*; forget-me pill, Mexican Valium, R2, Roche, roofies, roofinol, rope, rophies	IV/swallowed, snorted	*for benzodiazepines—sedation, drowsiness*/dizziness
GHB[***] (Club Drug)	*gamma-hydroxybutyrate*; G, Georgia home boy, grievous bodily harm, liquid ecstasy	I/swallowed	*for flunitrazepam*—visual and gastrointestinal disturbances, urinary retention, memory loss for the time under the drug's effects
methaqualone	*Quaalude, Sopor, Parest*; ludes, mandrex, quad, quay	I/injected, swallowed	*for GHB*—drowsiness, nausea/vomiting, headache, loss of consciousness, loss of reflexes, seizures, coma, death
			for methaqualone—*euphoria*/depression, poor reflexes, slurred speech, coma

Substance: Category and Name	Examples of Commercial and Street Names	DEA Schedule[*]/ How Administered[**]	*Intoxication Effects/Potential Health Consequences*
Dissociative Anesthetics			*increased heart rate and blood pressure, impaired motor function/memory loss; numbness; nausea/vomiting*
ketamine (Club Drug)	*Ketalar SV;* cat Valiums, K, Special K, vitamin K	III/injected, snorted, smoked	
PCP and analogs	*phencyclidine;* angel dust, boat, hog, love boat, peace pill	I, II/injected, swallowed, smoked	*Also, for ketamine—at high doses, delirium, depression, respiratory depression and arrest*
			for PCP and analogs—possible decrease in blood pressure and heart rate, panic, aggression, violence/loss of appetite, depression
Hallucinogens			*altered states of perception and feeling; nausea; persisting perception disorder (flashbacks)*
LSD (Club Drug)	*lysergic acid diethylamide;* acid, blotter, boomers, cubes, microdot, yellow sunshines	I/swallowed, absorbed through mouth tissues	
mescaline	buttons, cactus, mesc, peyote	I/swallowed, smoked	*Also, for LSD and mescaline—increased body temperature, heart rate, blood pressure; loss of appetite, sleeplessness, numbness, weakness, tremors*
psilocybin	magic mushroom, purple passion, shrooms	I/swallowed	*for LSD—persistent mental disorders*
			for psilocybin—nervousness, paranoia
Opioids and Morphine Derivatives			*pain relief, euphoria, drowsiness/nausea, constipation, confusion, sedation, respiratory depression and arrest, tolerance, addiction, unconsciousness, coma, death*
codeine	*Empirin with Codeine, Fiorinal with Codeine, Robitussin A-C, Tylenol with Codeine;* Captain Cody, Cody, schoolboy; (with glutethimide) doors & fours, loads, pancakes and syrup	II, III, IV/injected, swallowed	*Also, for codeine—less analgesia, sedation, and respiratory depression than morphine*
fentanyl and fentanyl analogs	*Actiq, Duragesic, Sublimaze;* Apache, China girl, China white, dance fever, friend, goodfella, jackpot, murder 8, TNT, Tango and Cash	I, II/injected, smoked, snorted	*for heroin—staggering gait*

(continued)

Table 9.1   *Continued*

Substance: Category and Name	Examples of Commercial and Street Names	DEA Schedule[*]/ How Administered[**]	*Intoxication Effects*/Potential Health Consequences
heroin	*diacetylmorphine;* brown sugar, dope, H, horse, junk, skag, skunk, smack, white horse	I/injected, smoked, snorted	
morphine	*Roxanol, Duramorph;* M, Miss Emma, monkey, white stuff	II, III/injected, swallowed, smoked	
opium	*laudanum, paregoric;* big O, black stuff, block, gum, hop	II, III, V/swallowed, smoked	
oxycodone HCL	*Oxycontin;* Oxy, O.C., killer	II/swallowed, snorted, injected	
hydrocodone bitartrate, acetaminophen	*Vicodin;* vike, Watson-387	II/swallowed	

Stimulants

			increased heart rate, blood pressure, metabolism; feelings of exhilaration, energy, increased mental alertness/rapid or irregular heart beat; reduced appetite, weight loss, heart failure, nervousness, insomnia
amphetamine	*Biphetamine, Dexedrine;* bennies, black beauties, crosses, hearts, LA turnaround, speed, truck drivers, uppers	II/injected, swallowed, smoked, snorted	
cocaine	*Cocaine hydrochloride;* blow, bump, C, candy, Charlie, coke, crack, flake, rock, snow, toot	II/injected, smoked, snorted	*Also, for amphetamine—rapid breathing*/tremor, loss of coordination; irritability, anxiousness, restlessness, delirium, panic, paranoia, impulsive behavior, aggressiveness, tolerance, addiction, psychosis
MDMA (methylenedioxymethamphetamine) (Club Drug)	Adam, clarity, ecstasy, Eve, lover's speed, peace, STP, X, XTC	I/swallowed	*for cocaine—increased temperature*/chest pain, respiratory failure, nausea, abdominal pain, strokes, seizures, headaches, malnutrition, panic attacks
methamphetamine (Club Drug)	*Desoxyn;* chalk, crank, crystal, fire, glass, go fast, ice, meth, speed	II/injected, swallowed, smoked, snorted	
methylphenidate (safe and effective for treatment of ADHD)	*Ritalin;* JIF, MPH, R-ball, Skippy, the smart drug, vitamin R	II/injected, swallowed, snorted	*for MDMA—mild hallucinogenic effects, increased tactile sensitivity, empathic feelings*/impaired memory and learning, hyperthermia, cardiac toxicity, renal failure, liver toxicity
inhalants	*Solvents (paint thinners, gasoline, glues), gases*	not scheduled/ inhaled through	

Substance: Category and Name	Examples of Commercial and Street Names	DEA Schedule[*]/ How Administered[**]	Intoxication Effects/Potential Health Consequences
	(butane, propane, aerosol propellants, nitrous oxide), nitrites (isoamyl, isobutyl, cyclohexyl); laughing gas, poppers, snappers, whippets	nose or mouth	*for methamphetamine—aggression, violence, psychotic behavior*/memory loss, cardiac and neurological damage; impaired memory and learning, tolerance, addiction
			stimulation, loss of inhibition; headache; nausea or vomiting; slurred speech, loss of motor coordination; wheezing/unconsciousness, cramps, weight loss, muscle weakness, depression, memory impairment, damage to cardiovascular and nervous systems, sudden death

[*]Schedule I and II drugs have a high potential for abuse. They require greater storage security and have a quota on manufacturing, among other restrictions. Schedule I drugs are available for research only and have no approved medical use; Schedule II drugs are available only by prescription (unrefillable) and require a form for ordering. Schedule III and IV drugs are available by prescription, may have five refills in 6 months, and may be ordered orally. Most Schedule V drugs are available over the counter.

[**]Taking drugs by injection can increase the risk of infection through needle contamination with staphylococci, HIV, hepatitis, and other organisms.

[***]Associated with sexual assaults.

Source: Web posted at (http://www.nida.nih.gov/DrugPages/DrugsofAbuse.html).

marijuana, 17 percent combine marijuana with another drug, and 24 percent use drugs other than marijuana. Of 5.7 million persons who are non-marijuana drug users, two of every three use psychotherapeutic drugs illegally—pain relievers, tranquilizers, stimulants, and sedatives. Far less commonly used drugs are cocaine (1.2 million), including about 265,000 crack users; hallucinogens (1 million); and heroin (130,000). However, new forms of drug use, commonly referred to a "club drugs" are on the rise. For example, about 6.4 million persons in the United States have experimented with MDMA (Ecstasy) at least once (SAMHSA 2001).

Regional Variations

Variations in illicit drug use are evident across the United States. The western region has the highest rate of illicit drug use (8.0 percent), followed by the Northeast (6.6 percent), the Midwest (5.7 percent), and the lowest rate is found in the South (5.5 percent). Rates also vary by size of place—that is, metropolitan areas

Global Illicit Drug Markets

The *United Nations' 2005 World Drug Report* provides detailed estimates of the monetary value of illicit drug markets around the world. Drug markets may be considered on three levels: producer, wholesaler, and retailer. Most recent global data show that in the equivalent of U.S. dollars:

- Illicit drug producers netted $12.8 billion annually.
- Illicit drug wholesalers realized the $94 billion—more than seven times the monetary value of illicit drug production.
- Illicit drug retailers gained $321.6 billion—or, more than 3.4 times illicit drug wholesalers, and 25 times more than the producers of illicit drugs.

For example, consider that cannabis is the most profitable drug marketed worldwide. On the retail market, the sale of cannabis accounts for more than $113 billion, that is, about 1 of every 3 dollars spent by illicit drug users around the world. However,

- Cannabis growers gain only 1/13th of the profit from its retail sale, and
- Cannabis wholesalers make slightly more than 26 cents for every retail sales dollar.

Cocaine is the second most profitable illicit drug worldwide with annual retail sales of $70.5 billion. As with cannabis, the illicit drug retailers realize an inordinate percent of the profits. For example,

- Cocaine producers make about $500 million annually, or $1 for every $141 realized by the cocaine retailers.
- Cocaine wholesalers make $18.8 billion annually, or $1 dollar for every $3.75 made by retailers, but more than 37 times more than cocaine producers.

Source: Adapted from United Nations. 2005. Office on Drugs and Crime, *2005 World Drug Report.* Vienna, Austria, 2005, p. 17.

have the highest rates of illicit drug use (about 6.5 percent) and rural and small town areas, the lowest (3.9 percent and 4.5 percent, respectively). Variations by size of place are less pronounced among younger drug offenders. Rates among the young tend to be somewhat lower in less urbanized areas (8.0 percent), and higher in small cities in non-metropolitan places (11.5 percent). Drug use among the young in large cities (9.4 percent) falls between that found in more rural areas and in smaller cities (SAMHSA 2001).

Poppies being harvested in Afghanistan. Following the fall of the Taliban, poppy growing became the primary means of livelihood for a significant segment of the Afghanistan population.

AT A GLANCE

Global Patterns and Trends

- The use of illicit drugs is increasing in many developed countries.
- New drugs and new forms of drugs are emerging. The intentional inhaling or "huffing" of volatile solvents is an increasing problem. Also, "club drugs" are extremely common. It is estimated that 1 million people in the United Kingdom take Ecstasy each week.
- An estimated 15 million people worldwide incur a significant risk to their health as a result of using drugs.

U.S. Patterns and Trends

- Over 110 million Americans report trying illegal drugs at some point in their lives.
- More than 4 in 10 Americans have used marijuana or hashish.
- More than 1 in 8 Americans have tried cocaine.
- 1 in 5 Americans have used nonprescribed psychotherapeutics.
- 3 in 10 Americans have used an illicit drug other than marijuana.
- Huffing and club drugs are also popular among American teens. More than one in four teens reports huffing.

Sources: Mayor, S. 2001. "Alcohol and Drug Misuse Sweeping the World, says WHO," *British Medical Journal,* 322: 7284; *United Nations World Drug Report 2000.* 2000. Oxford: Oxford University Press; Substance Abuse and Mental Health Services Administration (SAMHSA). 2004. *Overview of Findings from the 2003 National Survey on Drug Use and Health.* Rockville, MD: U.S. Department of Health and Human Services.

The Fall of the Taliban and The Rise of Poppy Production

Several independent sources have documented the resurgence of opium poppy production in Afghanistan in recent years. The sap from poppies is processed into heroin and morphine in small mobile drug labs around the country and shipped to drug markets worldwide. With the demise of the Taliban (who banned poppy production on religious grounds) and the devastation of the peasant economy following the regime change, the small farmers began growing poppies to survive. Afghanistan is now a leading supplier of heroin and morphine across the globe.

- Opium poppies are grown in 28 of the country's 32 provinces, with more than 1.7 million people employed.
- Three-quarters of the world's opium is produced in Afghanistan—about 3,600 tons grown on 200,000 acres.
- In 2003, $2.3 billion were realized from drug production in Afghanistan.
- 90 percent of the heroin sold throughout Europe comes from Afghanistan.
- The World Bank estimates that drug production accounts for half of the country's economy.

Sources: Time Magazine, August 9, 2004; PakTribune posted at: www.paktribune.com/news/index.php?id=79951; www.pbs.org/newshour/bb/asia/afghanistan/aug03/drigs/html.

Age, Gender, and Race

Age. Illicit drug use is most common between the ages of 14 and 34, declining rapidly after the age of 44. Persons between the ages of 18 and 20 are most likely to use illicit drugs (19.6 percent), compared to 9.7 percent of youth between 12 and 17; about 3 percent of 12- and 13-year-olds use illicit drugs. As might be expected, persons over the age of 65 are decidedly unlikely to use illicit drugs of any kind. Among 12- and 13-year-olds, psychotherapeutic use is the most common form of illicit drug offending, followed by marijuana, inhalants, and cocaine. After the age of 14, the use of marijuana far exceeds the use of any other drug, with psychotherapeutics less than half as likely (SAMHSA 2001).

Gender. Overall, illicit drug use tends to be more common among men than women. In the United States about 7.7 percent of men and 5.0 percent of women use drugs illegally. Men and women are, however, approximately equally likely to use psychotherapeutic drugs without prescription. The gender difference is largely absent among younger drug users. Between the ages of 12 and 17, males

Three very young Jamaican girls smoking ganja—a form
of marijuana—while other children look on.

(9.8 percent) and females (9.5 percent) have similar rates of drug use. The choice
of drugs does vary among young users. Boys are somewhat more likely to use
marijuana; girls are more apt to use psychotherapeutic drugs (SAMHSA 2001).

Race and Ethnicity. In the United States, drug use is most common among Native Americans/Alaskan Natives (12.6 percent) and persons of mixed race (14.8
percent), with Puerto Ricans next (10.1 percent). Whites and blacks (6.4 percent)
are equally likely to use illicit drugs, followed by Mexicans (5.5 percent), Central
and South Americans (4.1 percent), Cubans (3.7 percent), and Asians (2.7) with

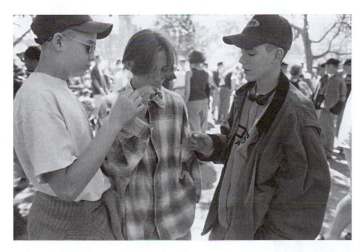

Adolescent boys smoking marijuana in plain view while
other students mill around.

A recent college graduate finds
that the combination of wine
and marijuana ease the stresses
of the day.

the lowest rate. Native Americans/Alaskan Natives between the ages of 12 and 17 have the single highest rate of illicit drug use (SAMHSA 2001).

Education and Employment Status

Illicit drug use is inversely related to education and employment status. While college graduates are more likely than high school dropouts to have experimented with drugs (44.6 percent versus 28.9 percent), they have the lowest rate of current illicit drug use (4.2 percent) compared to 6.3 percent for high school dropouts. College-aged persons (18 to 22), whether enrolled in school or not,

The anguish and futility of drug
use experienced by estranged
youth around the world.

have similar rates of illicit drug use (about 18.2 percent). Persons who are employed full-time are far less likely to use illicit drugs (6.3 percent) compared to the unemployed (15.4 percent) and part-time employees (7.8 percent). However, about three of every four illicit drug users in the United States are employed (SAMHSA 2001).

The use of multiple substances is common among undergraduate students. Typically, binge drinking accompanies marijuana smoking or the use of other drugs. About nine of every ten college students who smoke marijuana also binge drink or use other illicit drugs. Similarly, 87 percent of undergraduates who use illicit drugs other than marijuana also binge drink or use multiple illicit drugs (Gledhill-Hoyt et al. 2000). Put another way, the more frequently an undergraduate binge drinks, the more likely the student will also be to smoke marijuana, use cocaine, or other illicit drugs (Jones et al. 2001).The physiological and mind-altering effects of alcohol and most psychotropic drugs are affected by several factors, including an individual's physical health, level of fatigue, emotional state, and social circumstances surrounding the use of the drug (Hanson and Venturelli 2001).

Explanations of Illicit Drug Dependence

While numerous theories have been offered to explain drug dependence, particular attention will be given here to sociological and social psychological formulations.

Rates of Illicit Drug Dependence

Richard Cloward and Lloyd Ohlin (1961) identify three subcultural opportunity structures: criminal, violent, and retreatist. The retreatist subculture emerges when the opportunities for financial gain from criminal activities are not available, and social status can not be achieved by violent means. The retreatist subculture may provide access to illicit drugs and a supportive environment for their use. The participants in a retreatist subculture are socialized into the use of illicit drugs, taught various justifications for their use, and given a safe haven from detection by legal authorities.

Social Integration. To Robert Merton (1968), retreatism is an adaption to anomie, a disjunction between institutionalized means and culturally approved goals in society. When the institutionalized means do not lead to culturally approved goals, both means and goals may be rejected. Individuals may seek to retreat to the illicit drug use to blunt the effects of the emotional turmoil of an anomic life.

Social Conflict. Alex Thio (1983), an influential power-control theorist, contends that members of the more powerful strata of society foster the stereotype of an illicit drug user as a lower-class person who would rather use drugs than work and one who is largely a burden on society. This view deflects attention from drug use among the members of the upper socioeconomic groups. There is then in Thio's terms "high consensus" about who will be publicly labeled a "drug addict" and relatively low consensus about illicit drug use among the corporate and professional elite.

Explanations of Rates of Alcohol and Illicit Drug Dependence

Theory and Theorists	Sociological Predictors	Hypotheses
Social Integration		
• Merton	Anomie	The greater the disjunction between institutionalized means and culturally approved goals, the higher the rate of illicit drug use.
	Retreatism	The greater the rejection of institutionalized means and culturally approved goals, the greater the retreatist behavior in society. The greater the retreatist behavior in society, the higher the rate of illicit drug use.
Subcultural Opportunities		
• Cloward and Ohlin	Retreatism Subcultures	The fewer the subcultural opportunities—either legitimate or illegitimate—for success, the more likely retreatist subcultures will emerge. The more retreatist subcultures in a given society, the higher the rate of illicit drug use.
Social Class/Power		
• Thio	High Consensus/ Low Consensus Deviance	The higher the consensus about the social characteristics of illicit drug users, the higher the publicly defined rates among the lower socioeconomic groups in society.

Explanation of Individual Illicit Drug Use

Theory and Theorists	Sociological Predictors	Hypotheses
Social Strain		
• Agnew	Stress/Tension	As stress and tension increases, negative emotions increase. As negative emotions increase, the likelihood of illicit drug use increases.

Self-Derogation

• Kaplan	Self-Derogation	The greater the self-derogation, the greater the likelihood of illicit drug use.

Euphoria, Cognitive Association, and Seduction

• McAuliffe and Gordon	Euphoria	The greater the desire to experience euphoria associated with illicit drug use, and the greater the desire to avoid prolonged periods without euphoria, the greater the likelihood of illicit drug use.
• Lindesmith	Cognitive Association	The greater the association between the severe distress of drug withdrawal, the more likely illicit drug use will continue.
• Katz	Seduction	The greater the feeling of excitement, thrill, or adrenaline "rush" associated with illicit drug use, the more likely illicit drug use will occur.

Social Learning

• Akers	Differential Association	The greater the primary association with persons who define illicit drug use as justifiable and pleasurable, the more likely those definitions will be reinforced and illicit drug use will be imitated. The more involvement in the illicit drug use learning process, the more likely illicit drug will occur.
	Definitions	
	Differential Reinforcement	
	Imitation	
• Becker	Learning Process	If the substance abuse learning process involves effective socialization techniques for its use and the ability to associate pleasure from its use, then substance dependence becomes more likely.

Self-Control

• Gottfredson and Hirschi	Self-Control	The lower the individual's self-control, the greater the likelihood of illicit drug use.

Illicit Drug Use

Self-Derogation.   Howard Kaplan (1995) argues that self-derogating individuals are particularly prone to deviate from the norms of conventional society. Self-derogation—or negative self-attitudes—result from the perception of social de-valuation. As such, they are a persistent source of stress for the individual. The use of mind-altering substances provides an escape from the pains of perceived rejection by others and the accompanying derogation of one's self.

Social Strain.   Robert Agnew (1992) argues that negative social relations commonly result in emotional distress. Feelings of anxiety, depression, anger, and futility are typical among persons mired in adverse interpersonal relationships. Mood-altering drugs may provide a respite from their negative emotional state. Illicit drug use is viewed as an immediate, albeit short-term solution to an intractable interpersonal problem.

Cognitive Association, Euphoria, and the Seduction of Substance Use.   Key to Alfred Lindesmith's (1947, 1968) view of substance dependency is the association of severe distress with the cessation of drug use. If an individual believes that physical or emotional disorder can only be averted if he or she continues to engage in substance use, then dependency is more likely to ensue.

Two additional theoretical formulations can be applied to the onset and continuation of alcohol and other drug use. William McAuliffe and Robert Gordon (1974) contend that the euphoria associated with drug use, particularly heroin, is the key factor that sustains its use. Withdrawal resulting from the interruption of substance use, they contend, is a consequence of the absence of euphoria, more so than the fear of experiencing distress from the discontinuation of its use. Similarly, sociologist Jack Katz's (1988) attention to the seduction of crime is consistent with McAuliffe and Gordon's view. Katz argues that individuals are attracted to criminal and deviant behavior simply because it is inherently exciting. Risk-taking behaviors, such as underage drinking and illicit drug use, provide an adrenaline "rush" or "high" apart from the effects of the substance itself. Engaging in illicit substance use or drinking to excess is tantamount to a flagrant disregard for conventional social behavior.

Social Learning.   Learning theorists in the sociological tradition, principally Ronald Akers (1985, 1992) and Howard Becker (1963), point out that drug and alcohol use involves a process of learning appropriate methods of substance use and learning to associate its effects with a sense of pleasure.

Central to Ronald Akers's (1985) social learning formulation are four interrelated concepts: *differential association, definitions, differential reinforcement,* and *imitation.* These concepts provide a framework for the process of learning to engage in deviant forms of substance use. The concept of differential association, drawn from Edwin Sutherland's (1947) theory by the same name, refers to the extent of interaction with members of groups that advocate deviant substance use. Primary drug-using groups provide a social milieu that facilitates learning to use various drugs. Definitions of substance use as justifiable, desirable, and pleasurable are learned in the context of primary group interaction. Differential reinforcement refers to the anticipation that the rewards of drug use markedly exceed any possible negative sanctions. Deviant substance use is differentially reinforced when the expected pleasure overshadows any adverse social or legal response. Imitation is simply modeling one's behavior after that of others. Novel forms of acting, use of language and dress, and music and entertainment are readily imitated by the young.

In his classic study, *Becoming a Marijuana User* (1963), Howard Becker provides an analysis of the process of learning to use marijuana and learning to associate its effects with a sense of pleasure. Rather than assuming that drug users are suffering from a psychological disorder, Becker argues that the introduction into marijuana use, for example, occurs largely by chance. Friends make marijuana available, encourage the newcomer to try it, and provide instruction in its use.

Given certain conditions, experimental drug use may escalate into more routine involvement with drugs. To Becker there are three stages in the process of becoming a regular marijuana user. The first stage, *learning the technique*, assumes that a novice marijuana smoker must be taught the techniques necessary to achieve a "high" and to associate that feeling with pleasure. The second stage, *learning to perceive the effects*, follows from mastering the techniques necessary to use marijuana effectively. Once the novice user is able to experience the effects of marijuana, he or she must then recognize the effects and associate them with the use of the drug. It is possible to be "high" on marijuana without being aware of it. The novice user must learn to recognize the symptoms of being "high" and to associate those symptoms with use of marijuana. The continued use of marijuana depends on achieving the third stage in the process, *learning to enjoy the effects*. The effects of marijuana tend to involve a mix of sensations, some pleasurable, others not. The user must be able to differentiate the ill effects of the drug's use from desirable experiences. One novice marijuana user observes:

> It started taking effect, and I didn't know what was happening, you know what it was, and I was very sick. I walked around the room, walking around the room trying to get off, you know; it just scared me at first, you know. I wasn't use to that kind of feeling (Becker 1963: 53).

As experience with marijuana use increases, so too does the ability to control its deleterious effects. Fellow users are able to interpret the sensations that accompany a marijuana "high" as pleasurable and desirable, rather than frightening and repugnant.

Self-Control. Gottfredson and Hirschi's General Theory of Crime (1990) posits that low self-control is the central precipitant of criminal behavior. Several elements of low self-control—impulsivity, risk-taking, and short-sightedness—place an individual at particularly high risk for illicit drug use. The inability to defer immediate gratification tends to accompany low self-control. Given the opportunity to engage in illicit drug use, a person with hedonistic tendencies and low self-control is vulnerable to experimenting with mind-altering substances.

Chapter Summary

- Wide variations in the use of illicit drugs and excessive drinking practices are found around the world and in the United States. Substance abuse is particularly prevalent among the young worldwide. The processes of globalization tend to increase the availability of mind-altering substances.

- Definitional issues related to substance dependence are considered:
  - A drug is defined as a physical substance that causes recognizable physical or psychological effects.
  - Addiction refers to a physiological dependence on a substance, that, in its absence, involves pronounced distress, known as a withdrawal or abstinence syndrome. Addiction may also involve psychological dependence, or a strong emotional need for the substance in the absence of a physical dependence on it.
  - Tolerance refers to either the need for increased amounts of the substance in order to achieve intoxication (or the desired effect) or a marked diminished effect with continued use of the same amount.

Key Concepts

Drug: A physical substance may be classified as a drug if it causes recognizable physical or psychological effects.

Addiction: A physiological or psychological dependence on a substance and accompanying withdrawal symptoms when its use is discontinued.

Tolerance: Either a need for increased amounts of the substance in order to achieve the desired effect, or marked diminished effect with continued use of the same amount.

Withdrawal: Physical and emotional distress that accompanies the cessation of alcohol and other drug use.

Critical Thinking Questions

1. Are illicit drug users markedly different across the socioeconomic class spectrum? Does the social class of illicit drug users affect their motivations and rationalizations for using controlled substances?

2. How does the sociopolitical structuring of society influence the definition of illicit drug use and attempts to control it?

3. How would you differentiate between experimental or recreational drug users and persons who are addicted to illicit drugs?

4. To what extent does the availability of illicit drugs account for the prevalence of their use? Put another way, does the availability of certain illicit drugs determine the number of people in a given population who use illicit drugs, or simply the kinds of drugs that are used?

Web Extra

Check out these websites for additional information on Drug Abuse:

http://www.nida.nih.gov

http://www.samhsa.gov

http://www.whitehousedrugpolicy.gov

http://www.drugpolicy.org

CHAPTER 10

Sexual Offending

of Sexual Offending

DATE RAPE DRUGS

Samantha, age 15, two 14-year-old girlfriends, and four guys they'd just met went to a party. Samantha was handed a soft drink. Her best friend drank what she believed to be orange juice and vodka. Both girls became extremely sick, vomiting, and ultimately losing consciousness. Samantha died as a result of a drinking a GHB-laced soda. Four boys were charged with her death.

GHB and rohypnol are central nervous system depressants, which are ten times more powerful than Valium, and often used as "date rape" drugs. Because these drugs are often colorless, tasteless, and odorless, they can be added to beverages, ingested unknowingly, and used to incapacitate victims and prevent them from resisting sexual assault. Both of these drugs are illegal in the United States. Legislation, including the "Drug-Induced Rape Prevention and Punishment Act of 1996," is used for increased penalties for use of any controlled substance to aid in sexual assault. Nevertheless, emergency departments report nearly 5,000 GHB and 500 rohypnol-related mentions year each. (*Source:* "Four to be Tried in 'Date-Rape Drug' Death: Girl died after drinking GHB-laced soda." (January 30, 2000). Web posted at http://www.apbnews.com. See also Infofax—Club Drugs. Web posted at http://165.112.78.61/Infofax/clubdrugs.html, http://www.whitehousedrugpolicy.gov/publications/factsht/gamma/index.html, http://www.whitehousedrugpolicy.gov/publications/factsht/rohypnol/index.html and http://www.usdoj.gov/ndic/pusb4/4532/4532p.pdf.)

FALSE ALLEGATIONS OF CHILDHOOD SEXUAL ABUSE

Nadean Cool, Beth Rutherford, Vynnette Hammane, and Elizabeth Carlson are all victims who became aware of childhood sexual abuse during therapy. Repressed memories of satanic cult participation, rapes, sexual assaults, and murder surfaced during hypnosis. One woman remembered during therapy that "her father, a clergyman, had regularly raped her between the ages of 7 and 14 and that her mother sometimes helped him by holding her down." She later recalled that her father impregnated her twice and forced her to abort the fetus herself with a coat hanger. Her father was forced to resign his clergy post after the allegations were made public. These victims, however, were not victims of childhood sexual assault, but the victims of therapists who planted false memories of childhood sexual abuse. Each of the therapists was sued and the victims received settlements ranging from $1 million to $2.67 million for their ordeals. (*Source:* E. Loftus. "Creating False Memories." In *Perspectives: Social Psychology*, M. Acker, ed. Boulder, CO: Coursewise Publishing, Inc. (1997), pp. 12–17.)

LEARNING OBJECTIVES

After reading this chapter you should know:

☐ Definitions, prevalence, and victim/offender characteristics of rape, sexual assault, and child sexual abuse.

☐ Types of rapists and juvenile sexual offenders.

☐ Definitions, prevalence, and types of prostitutes.

☐ Nature of online sexual victimization of youth and consequences of childhood sexual abuse.

☐ Theoretical understanding of criminal sexual deviance.

Introduction

Most countries around the world define some forms of sexual behavior as deviant. There is, nonetheless, considerable variation in the kinds of sexual acts that are considered criminal. Sexual behaviors that are considered criminal in some societies are accepted forms of cultural ritual in others. This chapter focuses on criminal sexual offending—rape, child sex abuse, and prostitution—from a global perspective. Variations in prevalence, victim and offender characteristics, and issues related to each form of criminal sexual offending are examined. Theoretical explanations of the incidence and prevalence of criminal sexual offending and victimization are discussed.

> *In reference to sexual trafficking of women and children, a UN spokesperson states: "There is less law enforcement . . . The earnings are incredible. The overhead is low—you do not have to buy cars or guns. Drugs you sell once and they are gone. Women can earn money for a long time."*
>
> (Bertone 2000: 4).

> *"My life was like an animal's. I was sold three times. I begged my boss to let me go home, but she said I owed much money and must pay it back. Every day I had to sleep with men. I was not allowed to leave even during menstruation. I was told if I escaped, they would track me, kill me—and my parents, too."*
>
> —A former Thai prostitute (Leuchtag 1995: 12).

Definitions of Criminal Sexual Offending

Various sources of data on criminal sexual offending and victimization in the United States principally—the National Crime Victimization Survey (NCVS), the Uniform Crime Reports (UCR), and the National Incident-Based Reporting System (NIBRS)—differ somewhat in their definitions of rape, sexual assault, and sex offenses. The age of the victim may determined whether a sexual act is considered a crime. Forcible rape, statutory rape, a variety of sexual assaults, and other sexual offenses of lewd acts, sodomy, fondling, and molestation are examples. Other "hands-off" or nonviolent sexual offenses include exhibitionism and voyeurism. Prostitution and related forms of sexual deviance, discussed later in the chapter, are also examples of criminal sexual offending.

Rape

As defined by the UCR, "**forcible rape** is the carnal knowledge of a female forcibly and against her will" (Federal Bureau of Investigation 2000). Assaults and attempts to commit rape are also included in this definition. Rape, as defined by the NCVS, is defined as "forced sexual intercourse in which the victims may be either male or female and the offender maybe of a different sex or the same sex as the victim" (Greenfeld 1997: 30). This definition also includes attempts and threats to commit rape; however, victims must be at least 12 years old. The NIBRS definition of forcible rape includes both male and female victims and rapes committed without the use of force where the victim is incapable of giving consent, i.e., temporary or permanent mental or physical capacity.

Severe Assault and Severe Injury Perpetraion Between Dating Partners at Universities Around the World (in Rank Order)[1]

In the 16 countries studied, women were more likely to severely assault their dating partners in 19 universities, but men were more likely to severely injure their dating partners in 21 universities.

Severe Assault Perpetration (%)			Severe Injury Perpetration (%)		
Site	**Male**	**Female**		**Male**	**Female**
INDIA-PUNE	12.5	25.8	INDIA-PUNE	8.7	13.9
USA-Louisiana	18.0	22.5	CANADA-Loudon	10.3	7.8
USA-Mississippi	20.0	20.6	USA-Louisiana	15.4	3.8
KOREA-Pusan	9.9	22.2	USA-Indiana	13.6	5.1
CANADA-Loudon	13.8	16.9	USA-Texas	9.7	3.7
MEXICO-Juarez	12.8	15.9	USA-Cincinnati	9.0	1.2
USA-Indiana	18.6	11.5	KOREA-Pusan	2.5	5.6
CANADA-Toronto	8.5	11.4	USA-Mississippi	8.3	3.4
USA-Texas	11.8	12.8	CANADA-Toronto	3.7	3.1
Hong Kong	5.8	15.0	USA-Texas	5.0	1.6

[1] Severe assault refers to: "Used a knife or gun on my partner, punched or hit my partner with something that would hurt, choked my partner, slammed my partner against a wall, beat up my partner, burned or scalded my partner on purpose, kicked my partner."

Adapted from: Straus M. 2004. "Prevalence of Violence Against Dating Partners by Male and Female University Students Worldwide," Violence Against Women, 10: 790–811.

Date rape is forcible rape that involves romantic partners or acquaintances in a dating relationship. Sexual assault and rape in the context of a date typically involve the various forms of verbal or physical coercion, the inebriation of the victim, or the use of a date rape drug to subdue the victim. The ability of the victim to give consent to her dating partner is a key issue in the determination of the criminality of the act (Koss and Cleveland 1997).

Sexual Assault

Sexual assault "includes a wide range of victimizations involving attacks in which unwanted sexual contact occurs between the victim and offender" (Greenfeld 1997: 31). The Federal Bureau of Investigation broadly defines **sex offenses** as acts "against chastity, decency, morals, and the like" (Greenfeld 1997: 31). Victimizations may include sodomy, sexual assault with an object, fondling, molestation and indecent liberties, and **incest.** The NIBRS provides the following definitions of sexual assault:

> *Forcible sodomy:* Oral or anal sexual intercourse with another person, forcibly and/or against that person's will.
>
> *Sexual assault with an object:* Use of an instrument or object to unlawfully penetrate the genital or anal opening of the body of another person, forcibly and/or against that person's will.
>
> *Forcible fondling:* The touching of the private body parts of another person for the purpose of sexual gratification, forcibly and/or against that person's will, including indecent liberties and molestation.
>
> *Incest:* Nonforcible sexual intercourse between persons who are related to each other within the degree wherein marriage is prohibited by law (see Greenfeld 1997: 31).

Nonviolent Sexual Offenses

Voyeurs or "peeping toms" achieve sexual gratification by spying on others, usually strangers. They particularly enjoy watching other people have sex. **Exhibitionists** repeatedly expose their genitals to unsuspecting people, usually women and children, in public places as a way of experiencing sexual arousal. Nonviolent sexual offenses such as voyeurism and exhibitionism are typically not physically harmful to victims. Victims, however, may experience psychological or emotional trauma or, at the least, become disturbed by such events (Greenfeld 1997; Sarason and Sarason 1996: 228).

Sexual offenders often engage in fondling, caressing, and other nonviolent behaviors. **Frottage** describes the touching or rubbing against a nonconsenting person for sexual arousal (Righthand and Welch 2001). For example, an offender may brush shoulders with another person in passing. In these instances, the victim is usually unaware that frottage has occurred.

Stalking refers to "a course of conduct directed at a specific person that involves repeated visual or physical proximity, nonconsensual communication, or verbal, written or implied threats, or a combination thereof, that would cause a reasonable person fear" (Violence Against Women Grants Office 1998: 6). Specifically, stalking victims may be followed, receive unwanted phone calls or letters, or be threatened. Stalkers may vandalize property or simply watch the victims without their consent.

Sexual Offenses against Children

Statutory rape is defined as "the carnal knowledge of a person without force or the threat of force when that person is below the statutory of age of consent" (Greenfeld 1997: 31). The age of consent varies by jurisdiction across the United States. The NIBRS designates statutory rape as a separate sexual offense category. The UCR includes statutory rape as a sex offense, while the NCVS does not include reports on victims under the age of 12.

Sexual assaults of children, excluding forcible or statutory rape, are described as "lewd acts with children." These acts are similar to sexual assaults of adults, but apply specifically to children. Fondling, indecent liberties, immoral practices, molestation, and other indecent behaviors with children are included.

Pedophilia, sexual abuse, and child molestation are terms used interchangeably to describe sexual offenses against children. No generally accepted definition exists to describe each term. As a result, much confusion exists surrounding the understanding of pedophiles and the prevalence of child sexual abuse. According to the American Psychiatric Association's *Diagnostic and Statistical Manual of Mental Disorders*, **pedophilia** includes intense and recurrent sexual urges and sexually arousing fantasies involving some form of sexual activity with a prepubescent child (American Psychiatric Association 1994). Definitions of **child molestation** and sexual abuse may include, but are not limited by, the definition of pedophilia. The American Medical Association recommends that the definition of sexual abuse of children include: "exploitation of a child for gratification or profit of an adult" (Murray 2000: 211). Pedophilia, child molestation, and child sexual abuse may take a variety of forms, ranging from exhibition, fondling, sexual intercourse, or use of a child in pornographic material. Pedophiles and child molesters are often defined by their use of manipulation, persuasion, and friendship to sexually assault children.

Offenders groom their victims rather than use force. **Grooming** refers to attempts to manipulate or coerce someone into performing sexual acts for a proposed reward (Office for Victims of Crime 2001). The offender tries to build the trust of a child in order to get what he or she ultimately wants from the child. For example, an offender may give or let a victim borrow an item such as candy, a book, a magazine, or a toy in return for engagement in sexual acts.

Prostitution

Prostitution refers to any sexual exchange for money or other reward (Meier and Geis 1997). Varying sexual acts may be exchanged, including oral and anal sex; sadistic, masochistic, and exhibitionist acts; as well as traditional forms of sexual relations. Male or female prostitutes may perform these acts.

Although legal in certain parts of the world, prostitution, the solicitation of prostitutes, and commercial vice are often considered criminal, dehumanizing,

Prostitutes, Pimps, and Violence

Many prostitutes enter the business with dreams of making good money. A closer analysis of what actually results in this illegal business is that pimps are the ones who benefit the most from prostitution. After paying the pimps, many prostitutes receive only 10 to 20 percent of a night's earnings. "It is estimated that over 90 of street prostitutes are controlled by pimps." Pimps can be fathers, mothers, brothers, establishment owners, drug dealers, men or women. All lure, kidnap, or sell young girls—particularly homeless runaways—into prostitution. Recently, fourteen alleged pimps were arrested in Atlanta, Georgia for luring girls as young as 10 into prostitution.

Coyotes, people who conduct others illegally across the U.S./Mexican border, also act as pimps or sexual traffickers. For example, Maria, a Honduran woman looking for work in the United States, was approached by a Honduran coyote who befriended her and promised good jobs and safe passage into the United States. Once in the United States, the coyote demanded $450 from her. When she couldn't pay, she was sold to a cantina owner and forced to work as a cantina girl, sitting and dancing with male customers, until she could pay off her debt.

In addition, many are forced into prostitution by their families, sold to pimps for a price of $1,000. In some third-world countries, young girls are sold for only $17. Once bought, a prostitute becomes indebted to the pimps and finds it extremely difficult to escape. Pimps, through violence and fear, physically, emotionally, and financially control prostitutes. Prostitutes are raped, beaten, and tortured. One prostitute states, "He had a six-foot bullwhip and he hit me in the head with it . . . We got home and he beat me with that bullwhip and told me to go to sleep."

Governments act as international pimps for the sex tourism industry in Thailand. Tour agencies recruit customers from Germany, the Netherlands, Japan, Saudi Arabia, Australia, and the United States with brochures advertising Thai women as "slim, sunburnt, and sweet . . . masters of the art of making love by nature" and as "little slaves who give real Thai warmth." Banks, airlines, hotels, and bar and brothel owners form a network of agents who extract profits from the $4 billion-a-year multinational sex tour industry.

Sources: M. Hornblower, "The Skin Trade," Time, 141 (25) (June 21, 1993), p. 44(8); A. Leuchtag, "Merchants of Flesh," *The Humanist,* 55 (2) (March-April 1995), p. 11(6); H. Jei, "The Flesh Trade's Empty Promises," *Connexions,* 46. (Summer 1994), p. 11(1); N. Katyal, "Men Who Own Women: A Thirteenth Amendment Critique of Forced Prostitution," *Yale Law Journal,* 103 (3). (December 1993), pp. 791–826; and "Pinch on the Pimps," *Time,* 157 (11) (March 19, 2001), p. 63.

There are more than one million children held as sex slaves and prostitutes in Asia, principally in Vietnam, China, Cambodia, Thailand, and the Philippines.

and immoral. Consequently, efforts are made to socially control and legally respond to prostitution and related behaviors. In places where prostitution is permitted, there are certain restrictions as to where prostitutes may solicit customers. For example, Nevada allows licensed brothels to operate under strict legal arrangements. In Great Britain, prostitution is permitted, but prostitutes are not allowed to solicit customers on the streets.

Kingsley Davis (1976), a noted social theorist, views prostitution as functional for society. He argues that prostitution contributes to the preservation of the moral order, the integration of society, the purity of marriage, and feminine virtue among non-prostitutes. Immoral, stigmatized females are given work while men away from home or those who desire deviant sexual activity can buy the services of prostitutes.

Sexual Trafficking of Women and Children. In many countries, prostitution is associated with large-scale operations of **sexual trafficking.** Trafficking occurs when women or children are

> illicitly engaged (recruited, kidnapped, sold, etc.) and/or moved, either within national or across international borders; [or when] intermediaries (traffickers) during any part of this process obtain economic or other profit by means of deception, coercion and/or other forms of exploitation under conditions that violate the fundamental human rights (Bertone 2000: 4).

In essence, women and children are traded, exchanged, or sold often against their will into sexual slavery and prostitution services. Countries such as India, Thailand, Brazil, and the Philippines are especially well known for the illicit trafficking of women and children. Many women in these countries hold attitudes favorable toward prostitution and see it as an opportunity to make money for their families. The relatives of young girls and women encourage a permissive view of prostitution, and often sell female family members into the sex industry for payment and future profits.

Rates of Criminal Sexual Offending

Around the World

Conflicting views of sexual offending make it difficult to estimate the prevalence of rape, child sex abuse, and prostitution around the world. Much is known, however, about these types of offenses in many of the industrialized countries— the United States, Canada, Australia, and England and Wales. Rates of rape and child sex abuse are similar in these countries. However, England and Wales report lower overall rates of sexual offending than the United States (Langan and Farrington 1998). Alarmingly high incidents of rape abuse are reported in South Africa where the rape rate is double that of the United States (Amanpour 1997). The number of rape and child sex abuse cases in some Southeast Asian countries is also considerably higher than reported in most other regions of the world (International Crime Victimization Survey).

In the United States

In a given year, there are over 200,000 rape and attempted rape victims in the United States. An additional 183,000 sexual assault victimizations are reported each year (U.S. Department of Justice 2001). Put another way, there are approximately two rape and sexual assault victims for every 1,000 U.S. adults age 12 and older. Estimates of date rape are less certain. The Stanford Rape Education Project and other studies suggest that as many as one in three female and one in ten male students are victims of date rape (Clinard and Meier 1998: 177). The National Violence against Women Survey finds that one in twelve women and one in forty-five men are stalked at some point in their lives (Fisher et al. 2002; Tjaden and Thoennes 1998).

In recent years, the National Child Abuse and Neglect Data System provides evidence of a decline in substantiated and reported cases of child sex abuse in the United States (Jones and Finkelhor 2001). Data show that more then 100,000 cases of child sex abuse are substantiated each year; twice as many cases are reported each year. A study of sexual assault in young children finds that over two-thirds of all victims of sexual assault reported to law enforcement are juveniles under the age of 18. With the exception of forcible rape, children below the age of twelve account for about half of the cases of forcible fondling, forcible sodomy, sexual assault with an object, and forcible rape reported annually in the United States (Snyder 2000).

Police make nearly 18,000 arrests for forcible rape in a given year, a rate of 9.8 per 100,000 inhabitants. More than 61,000 arrests are made for sex offenses (Federal Bureau of Investigation 2000). Annual surveys of correctional populations estimate that over 88,000 sex offenders are incarcerated in state prisons, accounting for almost 10 percent of the inmate population. Of incarcerated violent offenders, one in five is considered a sexual offender. Of incarcerated sex offenders, six in ten are convicted of sexual assault while four in ten are convicted of forcible rape. Thus, for every one convicted rapist, there are three convictions for other sexual assaults. The largest category of convicted sexual assault offenders is made up of inmates serving time for criminal fondling, molestation, and other sexual assaults committed against persons other than children. About two out of every three convictions for sexual assault are for fondling, molestation, and other forms of sexual misconduct. Less than 2 percent of convicted sex offenders are serving time for lewd acts with children and statutory rape. Relatively few sex offenders are serving time for the forcible rape of a child (Greenfeld 1997).

Characteristics of Criminal Sexual Offending

Victim Characteristics

While most victims of violent crime are male, females predominate among victims of rape and sexual assault. For adults, over 90 percent of rape or sexual assault victims are female, approximately ten female victims for every one male victim (Greenfeld 1997). In the United States, three females are raped or sexually assaulted per every 1,000 adults age 12 and older (U.S. Department of Justice 2000: 189). In recent years there has been an increase in the prevalence of male rape victimization. Males now constitute between 5 and 10 percent of rape victims in the United States (Scarce 1997).

Victims of child sexual abuse are more likely to be female than male, although the ratio of male to female victims is generally smaller. Under the age of 12, less than 70 percent of sexual assault victims are female, approximately six females for every one male victim. Sexual assault with an object and forcible fondling are also more likely to involve females, while the majority of victims of forcible sodomy are male (Snyder 2000).

Juvenile rape and sexual assault victims represent approximately two-thirds of all victimizations reported to law enforcement agencies. Self-reports of convicted rape and sexual offenders show that four in ten offenders victimize children age 12 or younger. In addition, one in seven victims of sexual assault are under the age of six. Overall, 14-year-olds constitute the greatest risk for becoming a victim of a sexual assault known to a law enforcement agency. For victims under the age of 12, 4-year-olds are at greatest risk is for sexual assault. For most offenses—forcible sodomy, forcible rape, sexual assault with an object, and forcible fondling—the risk of victimization peaks at age 4 and again between the ages of 13 and 14, then drops significantly (Snyder 2000).

A greater number of rape and sexual assault victims are white females, followed by black females, white males, and black males. Rates of victimization, however, are highest among black females. Nearly five black females are victims of rape or sexual assault for every 1,000 U.S. adults age 12 and older, 1.5 times greater than the rate for white females (U.S. Department of Justice 2000: 188, 191).

Special populations experience extremely high rates of rape and sexual assault victimization. A study by the American Indian Women's Chemical Health Project reported that 75 percent of Native American women have experienced some type of sexual assault in their lives. Similarly, Alaska Natives experience the highest rates of sexual victimization in United States. For the past twenty years, the Alaska Native Women Sexual Assault Committee formed by the FBI finds that the rape rate in Alaska is the highest in the United States (National Sexual Violence Resource Center 2000).

Offender Characteristics

As expected, males commit nearly all officially recorded forcible rapes (99 percent). Females rarely rape and commit relatively few other sexual offenses (approximately 7.5 percent) (Greenfeld 1997). A study of 115 sexually assaulted males shows that men assault 87 percent of men. Furthermore, a man and a woman together assault 6 percent of men, and a lone woman assaults 7 percent of the male victims. Females sexually assault other females in less than 1 percent of the cases (King and Woollett 1997). Overall, 6 percent of offenders who sexually assault juveniles are female. Female offenders are most common in assaults of children under the age of 6 (Snyder 2000).

The majority of rape and sexual assault offenders are ages 18 and over with four out of every ten incidents involving offenders over age 30. About a quarter of the incidents reported to law enforcement agency involve offenders under age 21. Juvenile offenders assault only 4 percent of adult victims (Greenfeld 1997; Snyder 2000).

Of sexual crimes committed against juveniles, 23 percent involve juvenile offenders under the age of 18 and 16 percent under the age of 12. Juvenile sex offenders tend to victimize a greater proportion of younger victims. Nine out of ten offenders under 18 victimize someone younger than 18 years. Juveniles victimize 40 percent of victims under the age of 6. Young offenders, however, are seldom involved in forcible rapes of young children (Snyder 2000).

White offenders account for more than 63 percent of the arrests for rape (FBI 2000). Minority offenders, however, experience higher rates of arrest for rape than white offenders. The highest rates are found among Native Americans. The National Sexual Violence Research Center reports that "the average annual rate of rape and sexual assault among American Indians is 3.5 times higher than for all races" (National Sexual Violence Resource Center 2000: 4).

Social and Situational Characteristics of Sexual Offenses

Victim-Offender Relationship.   Sexual offenders and their victims are likely to have a prior relationship, either as family members or acquaintances. Between 8 and 11 percent of adults are victimized by family members. Adults (those over 18) are seven times more likely to be victimized by an acquaintance than a family member. Victims over the age of 30 are more likely to be raped or sexually assaulted by a stranger than are children, by a ratio of 12 to 1 (Greenfeld 1997).

Nearly nine in ten of the youngest victims of rape (those under 12) know their rapist. In 43 percent of the cases, family members are responsible for the rape or sexual assault of children (Snyder 2000). Other cases involve professional caretakers, teachers, recreational leaders, and babysitters (Finkelhor and Ormrod 2001b). Only 14 percent of offenders are strangers to children. This is especially

AT A GLANCE

Global Patterns

- The highest rates of sexual victimization are found in South and Southeast Asia and South Africa. Sexual trafficking, child prostitution, and child pornography are extremely common in these countries as well as the former Soviet Union, Israel, Turkey, and Germany.
- More than one million children annually are estimated to be victims of sexual abuse worldwide.
- Industrialized countries such as the United States, Australia, the United Kingdom, and Canada report similar rates of rape, sexual assault, child victimization, and prostitution.
- Native Americans and Alaska Natives are victims 3.5 times more often than other ethnic and racial groups.

United States Trends and Patterns

- Nearly all cases of sexual assault involve male perpetrators and female victims.
- Black females are especially vulnerable to rape and sexual assault.
- Victims of rape and sexual assault are usually between the ages of 16 and 19.
- Most sex offenders are over the age of 18.
- Juvenile sexual offenders disproportionately victimize persons of a similar age.
- In most cases—especially those of young children—victims and offenders know each other.
- College students are at particularly high risk for involvement in sexually assaultive behavior, both as victims and offenders.
- Internet sexual solicitation of children and child pornography are among the more rapidly increasing forms of sexual offending.

Sources: Snyder, H. 2000. *Sexual Assault of Young Children as Reported to Law Enforcement: Victim, Incident, and Offender Characteristics.* Washington, DC: U.S. Department of Justice, Office of Justice Programs, and Bureau of Justice Statistics; Greenfeld, L. 1997. *Sex Offenses and Offenders: An Analysis of Data on Rape and Sexual Assault.* Washington, DC: U.S. Department of Justice, Office of Justice Programs, and Bureau of Justice Statistics); Fisher, B. et al. 2000. *The Sexual Victimization of College Women.* Washington, DC: National Institute of Justice; National Sexual Violence Resource Center. 2000. *Sexual Assault in Indian Country: Confronting Sexual Violence.* Enola, PA: Author; Office for Victims of Crime. 2001. *Internet Crimes Against Children.* Washington, DC: U.S. Department of Justice, Office of Justice Programs, and Office for Victims of Crime; Amanpour, C. 1997. "South Africa copes with skyrocketing rape, abuse rates," CNN. February 23. Web posted at http://www.cnn.com/WORLD/9702/23/safrica.rapes/; Bray, M. 2001. "Call for crackdown on child sex laws," CNN. November 22. Web posted at http://www.cnn.com/2001/WORLD/asiapcf/southeast/11/22/asia.childsex/index.html; CNN. 2002. "Dozens arrested in child porn probe: 50 more arrests expected by week's end." March 19. Web posted at http://www.cnn.com/2002/US/03/18/fbi.child/porn/?related.html.

true for the youngest victims, where only 3 percent of the offenders are strangers to the victims (Snyder 2000).

Location. Victimization rates of rape and sexual assault are high in the Northeast and Western regions of the United States and somewhat lower in the Midwest and the South. Urban areas, as opposed to suburban and rural areas, experience higher rates of rape and sexual assault victimization (U.S. Department of Justice 2000: 188, 195).

Distinct regional patterns of arrest for rape are evident across the United States. Arrests rates for rape are highest in the Midwest and lowest in the West. In contrast, Western states report a substantially higher rate of arrests for sexual offenses than other regions of the United States. Urban areas report the highest arrest rates for both rape and sexual offenses than suburban or rural areas. Cities with populations of 250,000 and over report the highest rates (FBI 2000).

Nearly 60 percent of rape and sexual assaults occur in private residences. Over one-third occurs in the victims' homes. Other residences include the homes of friends, neighbors, or relatives. Rapes and sexual assaults that occur in residences are most likely to be perpetrated by a family member and least likely by a stranger (FBI 2000). Snyder (2000) also reports that:

- Younger victims are more likely to be victimized in a residence than older victims (77 percent versus 55 percent).
- Juvenile male victims are more likely to be sexually assaulted in a residence than are juvenile female victims (77 percent versus 69 percent).
- Sexual assaults (other than rape)—forcible sodomy, sexual assault with an object, and forcible fondling—are more likely (75 percent) to occur in a residence.

Of the rapes and sexual assaults that occur away from the home, victims report that more than half occur less than one mile from their home, either on the street, in a parking lot/garage, or another location. Sexual assaults that occur in nonresidential locations are most common in roadways, fields/woods, schools, commercial/office buildings, parking lots, and hotels/motels (Greenfeld 1997; Snyder 2000).

Time. Victims report that most rapes and sexual assaults is most likely to occur between 6 P.M. and 6 A.M. (43 percent). The time of day when sexual assaults occur, however, is related to the age of the victim. Most adult victims are sexually assaulted between 8 P.M. and 2 A.M. Sexual assaults of young children peak around 3 P.M. and near the traditional mealtime hours of 8 A.M., noon, and 6 P.M. Rapes and sexual assaults are most common Saturdays and least common on Wednesdays, with the largest number of rapes occurring between 8 P.M. Friday and 8 A.M. Saturday. Rape is also most likely to be reported to law enforcement in August; and least likely to be reported in December (Greenfeld 1997; Snyder 2000).

Reporting Rape, Sexual Assault, and Child Sexual Abuse

According to Greenfeld (1997), one-third of rape and sexual assault victims report their victimization to a law enforcement agency. A study of gender differences in rape reporting concludes that:

- Male victims are less likely to report a rape or sexual assault to police than females.

- Sexual assaults are almost twice as likely to be reported when the offender is a stranger.

- Sexual assaults are nearly five times as likely to be reported if something was stolen during the assault.

- The odds of reporting increase if injuries are sustained or if the victim requires medical attention.

- The presence of a weapon also increases rape/sexual assault reporting.

- To a lesser extent, higher levels of education and lower levels of income were related to rape/sexual assault reporting (Pino and Meier 1999: 979).

Gender differences in likelihood of reporting rape are related the perceived seriousness by the victim. Female victims typically view personal injury, the presence of weapons, unknown perpetrators, and acts of theft as particularly serious. Victims who are assaulted under these circumstances are therefore more likely to report a rape to the police. Males, on the other hand, only perceive a rape as serious enough to report when bodily injury occurs (Pino and Meier 1999).

Victims fail to report rapes to police in an effort to avoid the emotional and humiliating experience of being questioned by investigators and prosecutors. Many withhold reports because they fear that the police will do nothing to help them. Rape victims are often accused of precipitating the assault with provocative actions, clothing, or circumstances (Pino and Meier 1999).

The age of child sexual abuse victims often mitigates the reporting of the offense. Reports of childhood rape and assault, however, are frequently made later in life. One study of sexually assaulted males shows that victims who are assaulted before age of 16 are likely to delay reporting the incident for more than seventeen years (King and Woollett 1997). Both children and adults are responsible for false allegations of childhood sexual abuse. For example, some cases of daycare and teacher abuse often result in false allegations of sexual abuse of children. Elizabeth Loftus (1997), a psychologist who specialized in distortions of memory, finds that suggestion and imagination can create childhood memories of sexual abuse that never occurred.

Typology of Rapists

Several typologies of rape offenders are offered, many are based on the motivation of the offender and issues of power, anger, and aggression. Nicholas Groth (1983) identifies three motivations for rape: power, anger, and sadism. Murray

Cohen and colleagues (1977) offer a similar typology, which describes rapists as sexual aim, aggressive aim, or sexual-aggression defusion rapists. Each type of rapist reacts in such a way that sexuality becomes an expression of conquest, a hostile act, or an erotic expression of anger and power.

Another typology, formulated by Richard Rada (1978), identifies rapists according to (1) situation stress, (2) masculine identity conflict, (3) sadistic tendencies, (4) sociopathic personality, or (5) psychotic personality. A situational stress rapist responds to severe disruption in personal life, such as job conflicts, family dysfunction, and financial difficulty. Masculine identity conflict, sadistic, and sociopathic offenders rape because of sexual uncertainty, violent tendencies, and sexual desires. Robert Hazelwood and Ann Burgess (1995) offer an additional typology, which includes four types of rapists: power-assertive rapists, power-reassurance rapists, anger-retaliatory rapists, and anger-excitation rapists (see Table 10.1 for a summary of these typologies).

Table 10.1 Types of Rapists

A. Nicholas Groth, Murray L. Cohen et al., Richard T. Rada, and Robert R. Hazelwood and Ann Burgess rely on strikingly similar theoretical concepts to construct their typologies of rapists. This table links the type of rapists with patterns of assaultive behavior.

Groth	Cohen, et al.	Rada	Hazelwood & Burgess	Description of the Offender's Behavior
Power Rape	Aggressive aim	Situational stress	Power-assertive	Seduce victims, plan their crimes, and use a great deal of force. Assert their masculine power through the act of rape.
Anger Rape			Anger-retaliatory	Attack by surprise and subdue victims with direct or physical force. Act out of anger; rape becomes the expression of anger.
	Sexual aim	Masculine identity	Power-reassurance	Attack strangers, select victims in advance through stalking, and often contact victims after the rape. Act out of a sense of social or sexual inadequacy.
Sadistic Rape	Sexual-aggression defusion	Sadistic tendencies	Anger-excitation	Involve strangers, planning, and careful execution. Stimulated by the infliction of pain toward victim. Often record activities and keep a souvenir of the attack.
		Sociopathic		Primarily motivated by sexual desires
		Pyschotic personalities		Severe psychiatric impairment associated with rape and sexual assaultive behavior

---

Sources: Groth, N., Rape: Behavioral Aspect, in *Encyclopedia of Crime and Justice*, vol. 4, S. Kadish (ed.), New York: Free Press (1983); Cohen, M. et al. The Psychology of Rapists, in *Forcible Rape: The Crime, The Victim and the Offender*, D. Chappell et al. (ed.), New York: Columbia University Press (1977). Rada, T., *Clinical Aspects of the Rapist*, New York: Grune and Stratton (1978), Hazelwood, R. and A. Burgess (eds.), *Practical Aspects of Rape Investigation: A Multidisciplinary Approach*, New York: CRC Press (1995).

Dennis Stevens (1999) offers a typology of rapists based on premeditation factors, victim selection, style of the attack, and the degree of violence. To Stevens, there are three primary motives for rape: righteous rape, peer rape, and fantasy rape. Righteous rapists justify their actions and view their victims as responsible for the attacks. They contend that in some way their victims consented to sex. Peer rapists blame their attacks on current friendships, described as "bad company." And, fantasy rapists are motivated to rape by "some imaginary goal that had been a part of their past" (Stevens 1999: 50). Diana Scully (1990) presents a similar broad typology of admitters and deniers. Similar in nature to righteous rape, deniers contend that sexual relations with victims are consensual. Scully's work with Joseph Marolla (1996) examines how deniers justify and admitters excuse rape accounts. Five themes are identified with regard to rape justifications. Scully defines these themes as: (1) women as seductresses; (2) women mean "yes" when they say "no"; (3) most women eventually relax and enjoy it; (4) nice girls don't get raped; and (5) raping as being guilty of a minor wrongdoing. Each theme is an attempt to discredit and blame the victim while the rapist tries to present his actions as justified in the context. Three themes are found in the excuses of admitters: (1) the use of alcohol and drugs, (2) emotional problems, and (3) nice guy image. Each excuse tries to explain the rape in a way that allows the rapists a semblance of moral integrity.

Juvenile Sexual Offenders

A few research studies attempt to classify juvenile sex offenders based on the type of offense and the characteristics of the victims. These characteristics include the offenders' social competence, antisocial behavior and impulsivity, degree of sexual preoccupation, and extent of contact with victims (Righthand and Welch 2001). Such typologies outline juvenile sexual offenders as pedophilic, child molesters, rapists, sexually reactive children, fondlers, and paraphilic offenders. Pedophilic juveniles, child molesters, and sexually reactive offenders victimize younger children (under the age of 12). There is typically a three- to five-year difference in age between offenders and victims. Juveniles described as sexual assault, rapists, or fondlers often assault somewhat older children. Groups of undifferentiated and unclassifiable offenders commit mostly "hands-off" assaults including exhibitionism and obscene phone calls.

Prostitution

Extent of Prostitution

The extent of prostitution in the United States and around the world can only be estimated. The UCR indicates that more than 61,000 prostitute-related arrests are made each year, for a rate of 34 arrests per 100,000 inhabitants. Women are almost twice as likely to be arrested for prostitution as are men. However, nearly 38 percent of the arrests for prostitution are of males. Patterns of arrests show that a substantial number of arrests are made starting at age 18 and then decreasing after the age of 40. The greatest number of arrests for prostitution is made in the 25 to 40 age range. While the highest rate of arrests for prostitution is found in the Midwest, the Western region makes a greater number of arrests compared to all other regions. Nearly the all arrests for prostitution are in large cities with populations over 250,000. The urban rate of arrest as is 137 per 100,000 inhabitants, or four times the total prostitution arrest rate (FBI 2000). Almost one-fourth of these arrests are of the "johns"—customers of prostitutes (Meier and Geis 1997).

Arrest data provide notoriously poor indicators of the number of prostitutes actually operating and give no indication of other aspects of the sex trade industry. It is estimated that 500,000 prostitutes work in the United States each year. However, as many as 5 million women in the United States age 18 to 64 may have prostituted themselves at some point in their life. Additionally, 16 to 20 percent of adult men report having had some experience with prostitutes (Clinard and Meier 1998; Janus and Janus 1993).

Prostitution, sex tourism, and sexual trafficking are extremely prevalent in many Asian countries such as Thailand, Japan, and South Korea. Sexualized work developed during periods of wartime and is now common in South and Southeast Asia. Military and local police allow a variety of types of prostitution to continue, disregard evidence of sexual trafficking, and rarely punish law-breakers. In addition to the Asian experience, women from Eastern Europe, the former Soviet Union, Israel, Turkey, Italy, and Germany work sexual trafficking routes around the world. In the former Soviet Union, abducted women are placed on auction blocks, partially naked, and sold for an average price of $1,000 (Bertone 2000).

Estimates of underage prostitution indicate that 800,000 underage prostitutes work in Thailand, 400,000 in India, 250,000 in Brazil, and 60,000 in the Philippines. UNICEF reports provide estimates that nearly one-third of sex workers in these areas are child prostitutes. More than 90,000 underage prostitutes provide sexual services in the United States. The child sex industry brings in billions of dollars a year, making up about 15 percent of Thailand's gross national product (Bray 2001).

Typology of Prostitution

Prostitutes are classified according to their methods of operation, their degree of privacy, and their income. Three major types of prostitutes include streetwalkers, bar girls, and call girls (Clinard and Meier 1998). Most prostitutes are considered **streetwalkers** who solicited clients in relatively public places, e.g., on the street corner, in mainly large urban areas, generally within established territories. Streetwalkers provide the cheapest type of prostitution services available and often possess long arrest records for prostitution. **Call girls** are well-paid, high-status prostitutes who work largely away from public scrutiny, with little interference from the police. They serve wealthy clients who are referred by known and trusted sources. Call girls typically go to the hotel room or residence of their clients. **Bar girls** solicit clients in public bars, either working alone, in groups, or with pimps. The bar girl, or B-girl, is present in the bar in the guise of a patron.

Prostitute soliciting a patron on
a city street.

Prostitution is also commonly practiced in massage parlors, photographic studios, or commercial escort agencies (Cavan 1970).

Street Life, Drugs, and Prostitution

Complex interrelationships exist among life on the street, drugs, and prostitution (Potterat et al. 1998). Homeless and runaway youth engage in prostitution as **survival sex**—exchanging sexual favors for food, shelter, and other basic necessities. Many of these youth are from middle-class backgrounds. Both girls and boys engage in heterosexual and homosexual survival sex (Arena 2001).

Illicit drug use among prostitutes often occurs before entry into sexualized work. Studies show that the majority of prostitutes are involved in illicit drug

Prostitutes in upscale restaurants and bars discretely solicit customers, many of whom are in the city on business or for a convention.

Street solicitation may well be detached, sophisticated, and highly selective.

use; more than half began using drugs prior to becoming prostitutes. However, prostitutes are not always lured by drugs into their work and do not continue to work to support a drug addiction. Poverty and violent victimization often act as antecedents to drug use as well as prostitution (Goldstein 1979; Gossop et al. 1994; Potterat et al. 1998; Silbert et al. 1982).

Online Sexual Solicitation and Pornography of Youth

Recent reports and surveys of online sexual solicitation and pornography of youth note that because so many children are online today, predators can easily find and exploit them. To meet children and gain their trust, sexual predators may present themselves as someone of a different age, gender, or occupation. On-line predators victimize children and teenagers by:

- Enticing them through online contact for the purpose of engaging them in sexual acts.
- Using the Internet for the production, manufacture, and distribution of child pornography.
- Using the Internet to expose youth to child pornography and encourage them to exchange pornography.
- Enticing and exploiting children for the purpose of sexual tourism (travel with the intent to engage in sexual behavior) for commercial gain and/or personal gratification (Office for Victims of Crime 2001:2).

Completed Internet seductions and **aggressive sexual solicitations** (actual offline contact, attempts for offline contact, and requests for offline contact between victim and offender through regular mail, telephone, or in person) are very serious types of victimization. A recent study of online victimization shows that 1 in 33 youth surveyed received an aggressive sexual solicitation. A special type of online victimization involves **traveler cases,** where adults or youth travel to physically meet and have sex with someone they first came to know on the Internet. These offenses are estimated to be less common than stranger sexual assaults or intrafamily sexual abuse. The National Center for Missing and Exploited Children estimates that nearly 800 traveler cases, confirmed or under investigation, have been identified by law enforcement sources (Finkelhor, Mitchell, and Wolak 2001).

Physical contact between the child and the perpetrator does not have to occur for a crime to be committed. **Sexual solicitations** refer to "requests to engage in sexual activities or sexual talk or give personal sexual information that was unwanted or, whether wanted or not, were made by an adult" (Mitchell et al. 2001: 3011). The online victimization survey also shows that "approximately one in five youth surveyed received a sexual solicitation over the Internet in the last year" (Finkelhor, Mitchell, and Wolak 2001: 1).

Demographic and other risk factors are associated with online sexual solicitation. Girls are more likely to be solicited online than boys of a similar age. Older youth (age 14 to 17) tend to be at greater risk primarily because they spend more time on the Internet, often unsupervised, or at households other than their own. Because Internet use is related to computer ownership, many child victims are from middle class homes. Additionally, participation in chat rooms, risky online behavior, and talking to strangers online put youth at greater risk for victimization. Risk is higher for troubled or rebellious teens and emotionally vulnerable youth who may be dealing with issues of sexual identity. Alienated or depressed youth are also more vulnerable to online solicitation by strangers (Mitchell et al. 2001).

With regard to online offenders, recent survey results show that other youth and females account for much of the offending behavior (Mitchell et al. 2001). For example, one survey finds that 48 percent of the offenders are youth, while one in four of the aggressive episodes is initiated by females (Office for Victims of Crime 2001). Internet pedophiles and other online sexual predators who are arrested include law enforcement officers, nurses, teachers, and school bus drivers (CNN 2002).

Law enforcement agencies including the FBI as well as legislators from around the world are currently responding to various forms of Internet victimization (CNN 1997, 2002). Committees from the United Nations and UNICEF are calling for action against child sexual abuse and the 23,000 Web sites that have already been detected as advocating sex with children (CNN 1999b). Local and national level special operations target child pornography rings and Internet pedophiles in efforts to expand the knowledge base about the types of crimes, the victims, and the offenders. A recent FBI investigation ("Operation Candyman"), which focused on an online child pornography web group, identified 7,000 email addresses linked to the group, with 4,600 in the United States and 2,400 in other countries. This investigation led to the arrest of 40 individuals from 20 states. Previous arrests were made through similar investigations. "Operation Rip Cord" led to more than 120 arrests in the United States, Germany, and the United Kingdom for child pornography, trading pictures of minors, or soliciting child sex over the Internet. Other arrests have been widely publicized in South Korea and Japan (CNN 1997, 2001, 2002; Reuters 2000b).

Investigations, which involve officers who "decoy" themselves as youth to try to catch online offenders, offer great potential for capturing Internet pedophiles and child pornographers. In one such investigation, an agent pretending to be a teenage girl entered a chat room limited to twenty-three children. All twenty-two other youths turned out to be adults seeking improper contact with other children (CNN 1998).

Consequences of Childhood Sexual Victimization

There is considerable evidence that childhood sexual victimization has immediate traumatic effects and may well have pronounced negative consequences later in life. Consequences of victimization include behavioral and psychological problems such as acting out, running away, truancy, conduct disorder, delinquency, promiscuity, and inappropriate sexual behavior. Increased rates of psychiatric disorders—including depressive disorders, anxiety disorders, and alcohol and drug abuse, as well as sexual problems—are seen in adult life and are cited as some of the most common long-term effects of childhood sexual abuse (Mullen 1991; Ryan et al. 1996; Widom 1995).

Studies are now at odds as to whether childhood sexual abuse is linked with the development of criminal behavior later in life (Browne and Finkelhor 1986). Longitudinal studies of abuse victims find that, compared to nonvictims, victims are at higher risk of arrest for committing crimes as adults, including sex crimes (Widom 1995). The most frequent type of crime associated with childhood victimization is prostitution. Studies of prostitutes, however, find that prostitute and nonprostitute samples do not differ significantly in prior experience with childhood sexual abuse (Nadon et al. 1998).

Sex offenders have often been sexually victimized as children. Nearly 35 percent of sexual assault offenders and over 20 percent of rapists report childhood sexual victimization (Greenfeld 1997). Among juvenile sexual offenders, nearly 40 percent are victims of sexual abuse (Ryan et al. 1996). Similarly, a self-report study of pedophiles finds that 42 percent of these offenders are sexually abused during childhood (Murray 2000). Pedophiles report choosing victims who are the same age as they were at the time of their childhood sexual abuse. It remains, however, that two-thirds of convicted sex offenders are not victims of childhood sexual abuse (Greenfeld 1997). Furthermore, the vast majority of child sex abuse victims are not arrested for sex crimes or any other crimes as adults (Widom 1995).

Explanations of Criminal Sexual Offending

Theoretical Explanations

Several sociological and social psychological theories of deviant behavior explain the prevalence or incidence of sexually violent and exploitive behavior, including prostitution. The psychological perspective has, however, dominated the understanding of child sexual offenders. Therefore, pedophilia and child molestation are viewed as a mental health problem as well as a criminal offense. Two conflicting views of sexual crimes against women are evident. The first holds that forcible rape and sexual assault are motivated by the offender's need to exert power, control, and dominance over the victim; the second considers rape to be driven by innate, sexual desires.

Explaining Rates of Criminal Sexual Offending

Anomic conditions and areas characterized by social disorganization and conflict often produce high rates of criminal sexual offending. Robert Merton's (1968) theory holds that members of society react to anomie, the disjunction between cultural goals and structured means for achieving goals, either through conformity or deviance. Deviant reactions result in a rejection of culturally prescribed goals and/or means. Frustrated by blocked opportunities for legitimate cultural success, members may adopt a sexually deviant lifestyle as a means of achieving some form of success. Prostitutes may earn substantial amounts of money while rapists and sexual offenders acquire a sense of power and control over victims.

Culture conflict theory as proposed by Thorsten Sellin (1938) suggests that crime is nothing more than a disagreement over what constitutes acceptable behavior. As a result, certain types of crime may occur in one society but not in another. Conduct norms, or definitions of what is and is not deviant, provide the basis for acceptable behavior in specific group settings. A clash of values, customs, and definitions of behavior may produce deviance. Rape and sexual assault can therefore occur because the conduct norms of one group clash with those of another. These behaviors, according to Sellin, are considered primary conflict, or a fundamental clash of cultures. Sellin, however, considers prostitution as a form of secondary conflict, or conflicts between smaller groups within the larger culture, e.g., class conflicts. Prostitution is often viewed by lower-class groups as an acceptable way of life; members are not condemned for participating in prostitution. Middle-class values, however, form the basis for most criminal laws. Since the act of prostitution is opposed to middle-class standards, it becomes criminal.

Alex Thio (1978) further explains the conflict between higher-status, powerful groups and lower-status, less powerful groups. Power theory holds that the powerful condemn the lower-class offenders in an effort to maintain control and power. Lower-class sexual deviance becomes criminal while the coercive sexual exploitations of the upper class are unrecognized as rape or sexual assault. Similarly, streetwalkers and common prostitutes experience more attention in the

Explanations of Rates of Criminal Sexual Deviance

Theories and Theorists	Sociological Predictors	Hypotheses
Sociobiological Perspectives		
• Thornhill and Palmer	Sexual motivation	The greater the sexual motivation in a given population, the higher the rate of rape and sexual assault.
Feminist Perspective		
• Straus et al.	Power and Dominance	The more prevalent the belief that men should exert power and dominance over women, the higher the rates of rape and sexual assault.
• Yllo; Dobash and Dobash	Patriarchy	The greater the belief in patriarchy, the higher the rates of rape and sexual assault.
• Brownmiller	Power, control, dominance	The greater the need of men to maintain power, control, and dominance over women, the higher rates of rape and sexual assault.
Integration		
• Merton	Anomie	The greater the level of anomie, the greater the higher the rates of sexual offending.
Subcultural		
• Wolfgang and Ferracuti	Subcultures of violence	The more pervasive is a subculture of violence, the greater the probability that violent sexual offending will occur.
• Miller	Focal concerns: Trouble Toughness Smartness Fate Autonomy	The greater the acceptance of focal concerns of the lower class, the greater the rates of rape and sexual assault.
Conflict		
• Sellin	Cultural Conflict Primary Secondary	The greater the ratio of primary to secondary culture conflict, the higher the rates of criminal sexual offending.
• Thio	Power, status groups	The lower the social status and power of members of a group, the greater the probability of criminal sexual offending.
Integrated Theories		
• Barron and Straus	Gender Inequality Social Disorganization Subcultural Support	The greater the gender inequality, social disorganization, and support for legitimate violence, the higher the rates of rape and sexual assault.

Individual Level Explanations of Sexual Offending

Theories and Theorists	Sociological Predictors	Hypotheses
Social Learning		
• Sutherland	Differential Association	The more an individual is exposed to definitions favorable toward acts of sexual offending, the more likely he or she will engage in sexually deviant behaviors.
• Glaser	Differential Identification	The more an individual identifies with another who views acts of sexual offending as acceptable, the more likely he or she is to engage in sexually deviant behaviors.
• Philips	Imitations	The more often an individual observes or is victimized by childhood rape or sexual assault, the more likely he or she is to engage in sexually deviant behaviors.
Routine Activities		
• Cohen and Felson	Motivated offender Suitable target Absence of guardian	The greater the probability that a suitable target, a motivated offender, and a lack of a capable guardian will co-occur, the greater the likelihood that an individual will engage in predatory sexual offending.
Control-Exchange		
• Gelles	Inequality Privacy Social Control	The greater the gender inequality, the less the costs of interpersonal violence, and the more likely individual family members will engage in sexual assaultive behaviors.
		The greater the privacy of a family, the more likely individual family members will engage in sexual assaultive behaviors.
		The less effective social controls over family relations become, the less the costs of interpersonal violence, and the more likely individual family members will engage in sexual assaultive behaviors.
Rational Choice		
• Cornish and Clarke	Cost-Benefit Analysis	The greater the benefit anticipated from sexually deviance, the more likely an individual is to engage in sexual offending.
Strain		
• Agnew	Strain/Stress	The greater the strain experienced by an individual, the greater the experience of negative emotions. The greater the experience of negative emotion, the more likely an individual will engage in sexual deviance.
Frustration-Aggression		
• Dollard et al.	Frustration	The greater the frustration experienced by an individual, the greater the probability that the individual will engage in acts of aggression.
		The greater the number of acts of aggression, the greater the likelihood of involvement in rape and sexual assault.

way of criminal punishment than call girls and prostitutes who work for upper-class clientele.

Subcultural theories of Walter Miller (1958) and Marvin Wolfgang and Franco Ferracuti (1967) help to explain how the acceptance of subcultural values results in violent behavior. Miller's subcultural formulation centers on the focal concerns of the lower class—trouble, toughness, smartness, excitement, fate, and autonomy. He proposes that lower-class focal concerns provide a path for subculturally recognized success. This path of trouble, toughness, and excitement may include involvement in criminal sexual deviance. Wolfgang and Ferracuti similarly argue that some subcultures see violence as a way of life and therefore support violent reactions and adaptations to life circumstances. The violent adaptations are learned within the context of the group and come to be an expected means for settling disputes and maintaining prestige within the group. The advantages of engaging in violent behavior are emphasized, legitimized, and accepted.

Feminist theorists argue that patriarchy, or male dominance, teaches men that violence is an acceptable means to socially control women and maintain power and control over them. Men are viewed as naturally aggressive and are socialized to believe that male aggression is normal, even in the context of rape and coerced sexual relations. Susan Brownmiller (1975) is one of the first feminist theorists to assert that rape is an act of power and violence. Similar theories provided by Kersti Yllö (1984; Yllö and Bograd 1988) and the Dobashes (1988), as well as Catherine MacKinnon (1989) and Andrea Dworkin (1981), view rape as an unnatural behavior that has nothing to do with sex. This view is now one of the most widely accepted explanations for why men rape. Feminist theorists also tend to consider prostitution a consequence of the power of men to sexually exploit women.

Similar types of theories focus on patriarchy, power, and dominance to explain rape, sexual assault, and other forms of violence in the family context. Murray Straus's (1983) power dominance theory explains violence within the family context, why husbands and fathers use violence to socially control their wives and children. The acceptance of violence in the family is prescribed by the larger society and then translated into the family system. Stress and frustrations make violence more probable. Straus also argues that violence within the family is more likely if the stress is coupled with violent childhood experiences of the parent.

Larry Barron and Murray Straus (1989) offer an integrated theory of rape, which combines elements from gender inequality, social disorganization, and subcultural theories. Areas with high levels of gender inequality and social disorganization are often characterized by support for legitimate violence. In contrast, areas where the status of women is higher and marked by economic parity between men and women, rape rates tend to be lower.

Individual Level Explanations of Criminal Sexual Offending

According to social learning theorists, all behavior, including crime, is learned. Edward Sutherland (1947) first introduced differential association, the process of learning criminal values. Learning crime occurs in interaction with others who hold definitions favorable to crime and who advocate involvement in criminal activity. Rapists, sexual offenders, and prostitutes may learn specialized techniques, motives, and rationalizations for committing crime during this process.

Victims of childhood sexual abuse may later imitate this behavior and victimize others (see Phillips [1974]).Childhood victims of sexual abuse, however, do not always become sexual offenders or rapists. Glaser's (1960) theory of differential identification explains how an individual is more likely to commit rape or sexual assault if he identifies with another person who views such behavior as acceptable. If a person who has been a victim of sexual abuse does not identify with his or her assailant, then he or she is less likely to perpetuate the cycle of sexual offending.

Strain theory holds that individuals experience a negative emotional reaction to stress and strain. According to Robert Agnew (1992), strain may result from blocked opportunities for success, the loss of something positive in one's life, or the presence of negative events. As a result of this emotional reaction, individuals may engage in rape, sexual assault, or prostitution in an effort to cope with or adapt to a stressful life situation.

Dollard and his colleagues (1939) propose that crime, specifically aggressive types of behavior, is a response to frustration. The frustration-aggression thesis suggests that high levels of frustration increase levels of aggression. Direct aggression toward others is the most likely consequence. Aggression may also be displaced on someone who is not the source of aggression.

Rapists, sexual offenders, and prostitutes often rationally choose criminal sexual offending by weighing the costs and benefits of doing so (Cornish and Clarke 1987). If the benefits outweigh the costs, then an individual is more likely to engage in that behavior. Prostitutes may find that the associated income is greater than the costs involved, or a sexual offender may believe the costs of being caught or reported to the police are extremely low.

Cohen and Felson's (1979) routine activity theory suggests that crime is most likely to occur when there is a (1) suitable target, (2) motivated offender, and (3) lack of a capable guardian. Incidents of rape and sexual assault often occur in secret, when no one is around to intervene. Offenders choose targets that are easy to physically control or manipulate. Children, women of small stature, and anyone with emotional or cognitive deficits are therefore suitable and attractive targets for some sexual predators.

Richard Gelles' (1983) control-exchange theory explains how sexual offending occurs within families. The costs and benefits of using violence, rape, or sexual assault are first assessed. Family members are more likely to rape or offend other members if the costs are less than the rewards. The lack of effective social controls decreases the costs associated with rape and sexual assault of another family member. Social control also decreases as the privacy within the family increases. Privacy allows for more opportunities to commit sexual offenses without being caught. Inequalities among family victims and offenders reduce the costs associated with offending. Powerful family members are then able to exert control over weaker members.

Chapter Summary

- Forms of sexual deviance are found around the world, although all are not considered criminal. Those that are may not be punished or legally controlled to any great extent.

- The prevalence of sexual deviance is largely unknown. Research shows, however, that certain types of victims and offenders are more likely to be involved in sex crimes.
  - Women and girls are more likely than men to be victims.
  - Men are almost always the offenders.
  - Victims are usually between the ages of 16 and 19.
  - Offenders are more likely to be over the age of 18.
  - Juvenile sexual offenders victimize other youth a majority of the time.
  - Most victims and offenders know one another.

- One-third of victims report a rape or sexual assault.
  - Males are less likely to report rape than females.
  - Differences in reporting are related to the perceived seriousness of the offense.

- Typologies of rapists are on motivations to rape. Rapists may:
  - Exert power or masculinity over women.
  - Act out of a sense of sexual inadequacy.
  - Express anger through rape.
  - Be stimulated by the infliction of pain toward a victim.

- Righteous rapist or deniers contend that sexual relations are consensual.

- Juvenile sexual offenders are classified according to characteristics of the offense, age of victim, and offender traits such as social competence, antisocial behavior and impulsivity, and degree of sexual preoccupation.

- Prostitution, sexual trafficking, and sex tourism are found across the globe, but are considered extremely prevalent in many Asian countries such as Thailand, Japan, and South Korea.

- Prostitutes are classified according to methods of operation, degree of privacy in work, and incomes. Three types are offered.
  - Streetwalkers
  - Call girls
  - Bar girls

- Internet pedophiles, online solicitation of youth, and child pornography are of special interest to law enforcement and legislators.

- It is estimated that one in five children receives a sexual solicitation online. A few solicitations are considered aggressive.

- Risk factors for online sexual solicitation are identified. Girls; those ages 14-17; those who engage in risky online behavior; and troubled, rebellious, and emotionally disturbed youth are at greatest risk. Youth and females account for much of the online offending.

- Studies are at odds as to whether childhood sexual victimization is associated with later criminal deviance. Prostitution is commonly associated with childhood sex abuse.

Key Concepts

Forcible rape: Forced sexual intercourse in which the victim may be either male or female and the offender of a different sex or the same sex as the victim.

Date rape: A forcible rape that occurs in the context of a dating relationship.

Sexual assault: A variety of victimizations in which unwanted sexual contact occurs between the victim and offender as described in the National Crime Victimization Survey.

Sex offenses: Unwanted sexual contacts as described by the FBI Uniform Crime Report.

Incest: Nonforcible sexual intercourse between persons who are related to each other within the degree wherein marriage is prohibited by law.

Voyeurs: Those who achieve sexual gratification as they spy on others; peeping toms.

Exhibitionists: Those who repeatedly expose their genitals to unsuspecting people in public places as a way of experiencing sexual arousal.

Frottage: The touching or rubbing against nonconsenting persons for sexual arousal.

Stalking: Repeated visual or physical proximity, nonconsensual communication, or verbal, written, or implied threats that would cause fear in a reasonable person.

Statutory rape: Sexual intercourse with a person below the statutory age of consent.

Pedophilia: Intense and recurrent sexual urges and sexually arousing fantasies involving some form of sexual activity with a prepubescent child.

Child molestation: Any sexual abuse of a child where the child is exploited for the gratification or profit of an adult.

Grooming: Attempts to manipulate or coerce someone into performing sexual acts for a proposed reward.

Prostitution: Any sexual exchange for money or other reward.

Sexual trafficking: The trading, exchanging, or selling of persons against their will into sexual slavery and prostitution services.

Streetwalkers: Prostitutes who solicit clients on the street; provide the cheapest type of prostitution services.

Call girls: Well-paid, high-status prostitutes who serve wealthy clients.

Bar girls: Typically solicit clients in public bars, massage parlors, or photographic studios.

Survival sex: Exchanging sexual favors for food, shelter, and other basic necessities.

Aggressive sexual solicitation (online):   Internet solicitations of children in which actual offline contact, attempts for offline contact, and requests for offline contact are made through regular mail, telephone, or in person.

Traveler cases: Cases where adults or youth travel to physically meet and have sex with someone they first came to know on the Internet.

Sexual solicitation (online):   Requests to engage in sexual activities or sexual talk or give personal information that were unwanted regardless of whether made by an adult.

Critical Thinking Questions

1. Write a script for a date between college students who have been dating for two months. Describe where they will meet and the places they will go. Consider the interaction between the two students, when they are with others and when they are alone. Give examples of their verbal and nonverbal communication that might lead to misunderstanding about their intentions. How might the interpretation of the situation differ between the male and female student? What are the possible consequences of this misinterpretation?

2. Imagine that two total strangers—a male and female—meet by chance at a party. Neither of them knows anything about the other. However, the male has engaged in forced sexual relations on several occasions with his "dates" and the female has been a victim of sexual assault. Describe the interaction between the two strangers. How would their interaction differ if the female had not been a victim of sexual assault?

3. What differentiates sexual predators who victimize adults from those who victimize children? What are the social situations, motivations, and rationalizations that give rise to the sexual victimization of adults compared to children?

4. How do the theoretical formulations of rates and the incidence of sexual offending? Are the explanations of the prevalence of sexual offending in a given group incompatible with the explanations of individual involvement in such behavior?

Web Extra

Check out these websites for additional information on sexual offending:

http://www.nsvrc.org

http://www.unh.edu/ccrc

CHAPTER 11

Property Crimes

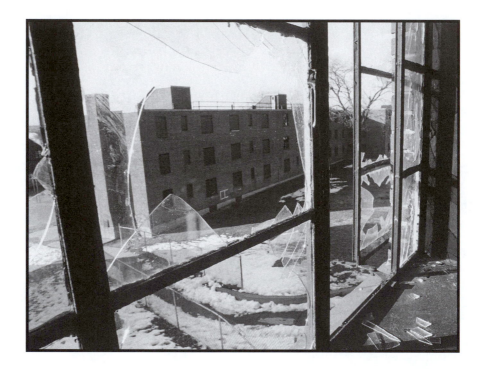

PORTRAITS

of Property Crimes

SPONTANEOUS ROBBERY

"We were just sitting there chillin', and I asked one of the guys do he got a cigarette . . . About this time, he says 'nah,' and he says 'but I bet you this dude got one coming down the street.' So, I went over there and, you know, asked the dude for a cigarette. One of them dudes comes runnin' across the parking lot and hit him—just Boom! So, when he hit him, [he] hit the ground, and just immediately we started kicking him. While we was beating him, others got going to his pockets gettin' everything he got." *Source:* Cromwell (2004: 305)

PROPERTY CRIME AS WORK

"But I do work for my living. Most crime—unless it's the senseless, petty thieving sort—is quite hard work, you know. Planning a job, working out all the details of the best way to do it—and then carrying it out, under a lot of nervous strain and tension—and having to run round afterwards, if it's goods, fencing the stuff, getting a good price for it, delivering it to the fence, and so on—all this needs a lot of thinking and effort and concentration. It certainly is 'work,' don't kid yourself about that." *Source:* An English career criminal in McCaghy, Skipper, and Lefton (1968: 181)

LEARNING OBJECTIVES

After reading this chapter you should know:

- ☐ The nature and definitions of property crimes including burglary, robbery, and larceny-theft.
- ☐ The prevalence of property crimes around the world and the United States.
- ☐ The characteristics of victims and offenders of property crimes.
- ☐ The elements of criminal decision making including planning and target selection.
- ☐ The types of thieves and be able to distinguish among professional, persistent, and occasional thieves.

Introduction

Property crime is found to a greater or lesser extent across the globe. Larceny is the most common crime, reported followed by burglary, then robbery. Strikingly similar rates of robbery are found in cities worldwide. This chapter considers the most prevalent forms of property crime, variations in rates of offending, and characteristics of the offenders and offenses. Attention is also given to the emergence of technologically sophisticated methods for the commission of property offenses and the precipitants of the prevalence and incidence of property crimes.

Legal Definitions

Property crimes involve the "illegal taking or damaging of property, including cash and personal belongings" taken from individuals, motor vehicles, residences, and businesses (FBI 2002a). **Burglary, robbery** and **larceny-theft,** are examples of property crimes. **Fraud, vandalism,** and **arson** are also considered property crimes.

> *". . . stickups have major elements in common. The first is a radical redefinition of the situation—of who has the power—for everyone concerned, especially if a gun is involved. The second is social exchange—'your money or your life.'"*
>
> —Elijah Anderson (1999: 125)

Robbery

Robbery is defined as the "taking of property or cash directly from a person by force or threat of force" (FBI 2002a).The crime of robbery is both a property and violent crime in that it involves direct contact with the victim. Robbery can occur on the street or other outdoor location, take place in a private residence, or happen in a commercial establishment. **Personal crimes** or personal robberies involve specific individuals or occur in personal residences, while **institutional robberies** occur in commercial settings, e.g., banks and convenience stores. Robberies take several forms: **highway robbery, strong-arm robbery,** and **armed robbery.** Highway robbery, sometimes referred as a "mugging," occurs in a public place. Strong-arm robbery does not involve the use of a weapon, while the brandishing of a weapon is an essential element in the commission of an armed robbery. Robberies and attempted robberies can occur with or without injury to the victim. Almost half of all felony murders, however, occur during the commission of a robbery (FBI 1999a).

> *"Burglary is easy, man. I've done about 500 [burglaries] and only been convicted one time."*
>
> —Billy, a juvenile burglar. Cromwell (2004: 297)

Burglary

Burglary is defined as the unlawful or forcible entry or attempted entry of structures, i.e., residences and businesses, with the intent to commit an offense therein (FBI 2002a). Burglars may use forced entry, attempt forced entry, or enter with no force. The offense of burglary usually involves theft, while illegal entry without force is usually referred as criminal trespass. Burglaries are distinct from robberies, although the terms are often mistakenly interchanged. Homes or businesses are burglarized where as people are robbed. A burglary may become a robbery if the offender confronts the homeowners or residents at the time of the burglary. This is termed a **home invasion** or **household robbery.** Burglaries of residences that occur at night are considered more serious and are punished more severely than daytime burglaries because homeowners and residents are usually home during this time (Schmalleger 2002).

Larceny

Larceny is the theft or attempted theft of property or cash without using force or illegal entry (FBI 2002a). Purse snatching and pickpocketing are two types of personal larceny. In each case, property is taken directly from the victim, but without force or threat of force. Household larceny, shoplifting, and employee theft along with motor vehicle theft and theft from motor vehicles are common types of larceny. The dollar value of the property taken determines the legal gravity of the larceny (U.S. Department of Justice 2000).

Fraud

Fraud does not involve the actual taking of property or money directly from the victim (Conklin 1992). Rather, deception is used to receive money or donations or to sell misrepresented or nonexistent products to unwary victims. Examples of fraud include insurance, check, or credit card scams; identity theft; and tax evasion. Advancing technology creates more opportunity for fraud and other high-tech property crimes. Many white-collar, corporate, and government crimes are also considered fraud. These types of property crimes are discussed later in the chapter.

Property Destruction

Vandalism and arson are property crimes that involve the unlawful destruction of property without the knowledge of the owner (Conklin 1992). Forms of vandalism range from graffiti or broken windows to the defacement of a motor vehicle or the destruction of a valuable piece of artwork. Arson applies to the burning or attempted burning of any dwelling, house, public building, motor vehicle or aircraft, or personal property of another (FBI 2002a).

Property Crimes around the World

Property crime, although on the decline in many countries, remains the most prevalent type of criminal activity in the world. Larceny and burglary make up over one-third of all crime. Robbery is less common, accounting for less than 3 percent of all crime in most countries (Neuman 1999).

Inconsistent findings are reported on the prevalence of property crime around the world. Higher rates of property crime are found in highly developed, industrial countries and in countries experiencing economic hardship and high levels of poverty (Neuman 1999). For example, the United States, Canada, Australia, New Zealand, and the United Kingdom report particularly high rates of property crime. Some Eastern European countries with developing economies, such as Poland and Estonia, and urban areas in South America and Africa report equally high rates of property crimes (van Dijk 1994). A notable exception is Japan where property crime rates are low despite high levels of industrialization and economic development (Conklin 1992; Tsushima 1996).

Around the world, the rate at which people commit property crimes or are victims of crime varies with age and sex. Victimization surveys show that men are more likely to be victims of property crimes and robbery than are women

(U.S. Department of Justice 2000). Men are also more likely to commit these types of offenses (FBI 2000). In societies where gender roles are increasingly equal, female crime rates are shown to increase and in some instances are similar to those of men (Clifford 1976). Adolescents and young adults commit most criminal offenses and are more likely to be victims of crime than older persons. Beginning in the mid-to-late twenties, arrest and victimization rates continually decrease with age (FBI 2000; U.S. Department of Justice 2000).

Rates in the United States

In the United States, there are two sources of data on the prevalence of property crimes: the National Crime Victimization Survey (NCVS) and the Uniform Crime Reports (UCR) (U.S. Department of Justice 2000, 2001; FBI 2000). The National Crime Victimization Survey is conducted twice each year by the Bureau of Justice Statistics in more than 50,000 households across the United States. Respondents 12 years of age or older are asked about their criminal victimization during the past six months. The Uniform Crime Report, published annually by the Federal Bureau of Investigation, is a compilation of data provided by police and sheriff's departments in the United States. Data included in the Uniform Crime Report include: the crimes reported to the local law enforcement agencies and found to be valid, arrest rates, and demographic information on persons arrested for major criminal activity. Although the methods of data collection differ, the NCVS and the UCR allow researchers to compare reports of the incidence and prevalence of criminal victimization and offending across the United States.

Victims of Property Crimes

Victimization rates for property crimes and robbery continue to decline in the United States (www.ojp.usdoj.gov/bjs). Property crimes of burglary and larceny-theft, however, account for more than 75 percent of all reported crimes. Annually, there are 178 property crime victimizations in the United States per 1,000 persons age 12 and older per year. The most recent findings from the National Crime Victimization Survey (NCVS) indicate that for every 1,000 adults (those age 12 and older) there are 3 robbery, 32 burglary, and 138 larceny victims in a given year (Rennison 2001).

Regionally, the highest rates of victimization are reported in the West, where there are 223 victims per 1,000 adults age 12 and older. The Northeast reports the lowest rates of property victimizations with a rate of 144 victims per 1,000 adults. Victimization rates are higher in urban than suburban or rural areas of the country. Urban areas in the West report the highest victimization rates compared to all other areas and regions. Data from the NCVS also indicate that burglary and robbery rates are higher for victims with lower incomes and victims who rent rather than own their homes. Victims with higher incomes experience higher rates of larceny-theft than victims lower incomes (Rennison 2001).

Sex, Age, Race, and Ethnicity of Victims.   The NCVS (U.S. Department of Justice 2000) finds that men are victimized at higher rates than women for property crimes and robbery. For every 1,000 male adults (age 12 and older) five are victims of robbery. This is more than twice the rate for females. Males are victims of burglary and larceny-theft at rates somewhat higher than those for females (U.S. Department of Justice 2001).

Persons in the 12-to-24 age group experience a higher rate of property crime victimizations than all other age group. The victimization rate for 18- to 24-year-olds is the highest of all age groups. According to a recent report on juvenile victims of property crime, juveniles age 12 to 17 are victimized at a rate about 40 percent higher than adults (about one out of every six juveniles each year is the victim of a property crime). Larceny accounts for most of the property crime victimizations for this age group. The robbery victimization rate is more than twice the rate for adults (9 versus 4 per 1,000), while motor vehicle theft and burglary victimization rates are lower for juveniles than for adults (Finkelhor and Ormrod 2000).

Property crimes and robbery are the most common forms of criminal victimization among persons age 65 or older. Nine in ten crimes against the elderly are property crimes, while less than four in ten crimes against persons age 12 to 24 are property crimes. Robbery accounts for a quarter of the violent crimes against persons 65 and older, but less than an eighth of the violent crime against those age 12 to 64. Each year elderly persons are the victims of 2.5 million property crimes as well as 46,000 purse snatchings and pocket pickings (U.S. Department of Justice 2000).

Regardless of the type of property crime, blacks' victimization exceeds that for any other race. For example, the rate of property crime victimization per 1,000 persons is 212 for blacks, compared to 173 for whites. Rates of black victimization for robbery, burglary, and larceny are 8, 48, and 151 respectively, while comparable victimization rates for whites are 3 for robbery, 29 for burglary, and 136 for larceny (Rennison 2001; U.S. Department of Justice 2001). Hispanic victims experience higher rates of property crimes and robbery than non-Hispanic victims. These victims are almost twice as likely to be robbed and are over twice as likely to have a motor vehicle stolen than non-Hispanics (Rennison 2001).

Property Crime Arrests

Similar to victimization rates, arrest rates for property crime offenses are falling. Arrest rates for property crimes and robbery are lower than reported victimization rates but remain among the most prevalent types of arrests. According to the Uniform Crime Reports, for every 100,000 inhabitants 146 persons are arrested for robbery, 746 for burglary, and 2,446 for larceny-theft. Regionally, arrest rates for property crimes are highest in the South and lowest in the Northeast. Arrest rates for each region vary by the type of offense. For example, the South has the highest arrest rates for robbery, burglary, larceny, and motor vehicle theft (FBI 2000).

Sex, Age, and Race of Persons Arrested. According to the latest Uniform Crime Reports, men are overwhelmingly more likely to be arrested for property crimes and robbery (FBI 2000). Males account for over 70 percent of the arrests for property crime. For the crimes of robbery and burglary, men comprise nearly 90 percent of all persons arrested. Almost 36 percent of all persons arrested for larceny are female arrests, making it the most frequent crime for which females are arrested.

Arrests for property crimes and robbery begin to climb at age 10 and sharply increase after age 12. Arrests continue to increase until ages 17 or 18 and then begin a steady decline. Persons under age 25 are arrested for property offenses far more often than older persons; a substantial number are between the ages of 18 and 24. Juveniles under the age of 18 are most often arrested for property crimes than any other offense, with larceny-theft being the most frequent offense for which juveniles are arrested. The elderly (those age 65 and older) are arrested for property crimes and robbery markedly less often than younger age groups (FBI 2000).

Victim–Offender Relationship

Robbery tends to involve offenders and victims who do not know one another. More than three-fourths of all robbers are strangers to their victims (Timrots and Rand 1987). John Conklin's (1992: 37) research on robbery shows that:

> Because thieves have access to the property of people they know well, they do not need to use force to steal from them. They can simply take the property by stealth in a larceny. In addition, a potential robber's need for cash can be explained to those with whom he or she is close, and so the would-be robber may be given or loaned the necessary money rather than having to steal it. Concern for people whom they know well may lead robbers to think that if they must use force to steal, they might as well use that force against strangers rather than against relatives or friends. Moreover, strangers are less likely to be able to identify them to the police.

When acquaintances are robbed, it is often because the victim is also involved in criminal activity. In an ethnographic study of armed street robbers, Richard T. Wright and Scott H. Decker (1997) find that six out of ten robbers target others who are involved in illegal activities. Because the robber victims are also breaking the law, they are unlikely to report their victimization to the police. A recent study of acquaintance robbery finds that such robberies may be expressions of grievances or revenge, while others may involve inside information about what the victim is carrying. Further evidence suggests that while acquaintances can identify their robbers, they are reluctant to report incidents to the police (Felson et al. 2000).

The relationship between larceny victims and offenders usually depends on the nature of the offense. Personal larceny is typically not committed against a person whom the offender knows personally. Because larceny is often a crime of opportunity, offenders and victims are most likely to be strangers. One survey of larceny victims indicates that as many as nine in ten personal thefts are committed by strangers (Hindelang 1976).

Unlike robbery or larceny, burglaries are most often committed by someone known to the victim. About half of all burglary offenders select residences familiar to them, but rarely target homes of close friends or relatives (Wright and Decker 1994). Burglars typically do not need to break in a friend or family member's home to steal property or cash. Would-be burglars, however, are able to

AT A GLANCE

Global Patterns and Trends

- Rates of property crimes continue to fall in most industrial countries.
- Theft, followed by burglary, is the most common crime reported to police. Theft rates are higher for industrial countries than nonindustrial countries.
- Robbery accounts for a minority of all reported crime in the United States and in most cities around the world.
- The prevalence of property crimes and robbery is related to problems of economic hardship. The level of some property crimes (e.g., vehicle or bicycle theft) is related to ownership rates.
- In developing countries, rates of property crime are highest in sub-Saharan Africa and Latin America and lowest in Asia.
- Of industrialized countries, Austria, Sweden, Norway, and Northern Ireland have the lowest rates of robbery and burglary crime. The United States, Canada, England and Wales, and Spain have some of the highest rates.

United States Patterns and Trends

- According the Uniform Crime Reports, the rate of robbery and property crime continues to decline. Motor vehicle theft is one property crime that is on the rise.
- Property crimes account for over 75 percent of all crimes reported to the police. Robbery accounts for 3.5 percent.
- For every 1,000 people in the United States (age 12 and older), there are 3 robbery victims, 32 burglary victims, and 138 victims of larceny each year.
- Each year in the United States, one in ten robberies and one in twenty burglaries result in an arrest.
- Men are more often arrested for robbery and property crimes than females. Blacks are more often arrested for robbery than whites. However, whites are more likely to be arrested for burglary and larceny-theft than are blacks.
- Blacks report being victims of robbery and property crimes at higher rates than whites. Hispanics are more likely to be victims of robbery and property crimes than non-Hispanics. Persons age 65 or older are disproportionately affected by property crimes compared to other age groups.

Sources: Mayhew, P. and J. J. M. van Dijk, *Criminal Victimization in Eleven Industrialized Countries: Key Findings from the 1996 The International Crime Victims Survey (ICVS)*, The Hague: Ministry of Justice, WODC, 1997; Newman, G. (ed.), *Global Report on Crime and Justice.* New York: Oxford University Press, 1999; U.S. Department of Justice, *The National Crime Victimization Survey (NCVS)* 2000, Washington, DC: U.S. Department of Justice and Bureau of Justice Statistics, 2000; Rennsion, C., *Criminal Victimzation, 2000: Changes 1999–2000 with Trends 1993–2000*, Washington, DC: U.S. Department of Justice, Bureau of Justice Statistics, 2001; Federal Bureau of Investigation, *Crime in the United States, 2002*, Washington, DC: USGPO, 2000; Office for Victims of Crime, *Victims of Fraud and Economic Crime: Results and Recommendations from an OVC Focus Group Meeting*, 2000. Web posted at http://www.ojp.usdoj.gov/ovc/publications/infores/fraud/victfraud.txt.

familiarize themselves with the daily routines of acquaintances well enough to break and enter successfully.

Two scenarios are common when friends or family members' homes are targets for burglaries. The first involves either an alleged wrongdoing on the part of the victim. Revenge, for example, motivates the burglar more than economic gain. The second scenario is played out when the burglary is in a desperate need for money (Wright and Decker 1994). Many burglary offenders repeatedly exploit family and friends by asking for personal loans. When these loans are not repaid, family and friends become less willing to offer assistance. Offenders may then see burglary as a viable option (Shover and Honaker 1996).

Criminal Decision Making

The decision to commit a crime is influenced by the offender's assessment of risk and perception of available opportunities for its commission. The nature of the offense and its method of execution are also key considerations in the decisions to commit a crime. Planning and target selection are essential elements of property crimes. Target selection depends upon the type of crime along with attractiveness and opportunity to carry out the crime. The attractiveness of a particular target is influenced by the location of the target and the lifestyle of the victim.

Planning

Robbery is typically a crime of opportunity. As a result, most robberies are carried out with little planning (Feeney 1986). One study shows that more than 40 percent of juveniles and 25 percent of adults who commit robberies do not intend to do so until the opportunity arises (Feeney and Weir 1974). Rather, robbery is usually committed when the offender has a desperate need for money or is motivated by revenge. Many robbery offenders are not sure that a crime will really be committed until the last minute. Robbers utilize improvisation skills and communicative signals. Thus, conversations are short and criminal intent is left unspoken. When asked about any conversations before the robbery, one robber replied, "Well, there wasn't much of a conversation to it, really. . . . I asked him if he was ready to go, if he wanted to go do something, you know. And he knew what I meant. He wanted to go make some money somehow, any way it took" (Shover and Honaker 1996: 91). Commercial robbery, however, does involve considerably more planning to be successful (Feeney 1986).

Unlike robberies, burglaries are usually planned ahead of time, although most are not carefully or extensively planned (Wright and Decker 1994). In planning, burglars examine building structure and layout for ease of entry and escape. Burglars also check out alarm systems, occupants, and any nearby witnesses, police, or security patrols. Most of the time planning for a burglary is spent in carefully selecting targets (Reppetto 1974).

Larceny, like robbery, is a crime of opportunity. Amateur shoplifters rarely plan their crimes, but decide to act on the spur of the moment. Access to attractive targets, temptations for theft, and the emergence of an opportunity are important considerations in the decision to commit a theft. Professional shoplifters, however, carefully plan their crimes; much thought is given the goods to be stolen, methods of concealment, and strategies for avoiding apprehension (Cameron 1964).

Target Selection

An attractive target most often sparks a spontaneous robbery, burglary, or larceny. Selected targets include those that are readily available and easily accessible, along with those that present themselves at ideal times and locations. Thus, situational factors and social circumstances influence the likelihood of becoming a victim of robbery, burglary, or larceny.

Robbers target victims who share common vulnerabilities. Many times robbers assume and accept notions about certain types of individuals based on characteristics and vulnerabilities. Selected targets of personal robberies often include those who carry large amounts of cash. This is the case for many illegal immigrants, Hispanics, and known drug dealers (Wright and Decker 1997). Illegal immigrants may carry large amounts of cash because many do not have social security numbers and are unable to acquire bank accounts. Because drug dealers are involved in illegal activities, they are attractive targets for robbers. People who frequent automatic teller machines and people who count their money in public are also targeted in many robberies (Shover and Honaker 1996). Other selected targets include individuals who are unlikely to report robberies to police (Felson et al. 2000). These may include anyone involved in illegal activities or those without the resources, knowledge, or contacts to make such reports. These individuals often live and work in areas with high population densities, high unemployment, and low social cohesion—social conditions that foster robbery (Felson 1998).

Neighborhood and store characteristics are assessed before carrying out robberies in retail locations. Staffing, store hours, cash handling policy, customer activity, and the presence of security precautions are important considerations for commercial robbers. Commercial robbers most often target liquor stores, taverns, and pawnshops where large amounts of cash are readily available. Older, poor neighborhoods are often targeted repeatedly for robbery because stores in these areas cannot afford the necessary security precautions to deter crime (Hendricks et al. 1999).

Seasonal variations show that robbery is distinctly higher in the winter than in the summer. The number of dark hours during the day in winter and mass shopping during the holiday season provide greater opportunities for robbery and a greater need for money among potential robbers. For example, winter robberies are most frequent in the month of December (van Koppen and Jansen 1999).

Attractive targets for burglary include homes with single-adult occupants and those that have younger heads of households (Sampson and Wooldredge 1997). These residences often lack the necessary security systems and therefore make attractive targets. Areas characterized by low population density are also frequent targets for burglars. Houses located in low density areas have more space between them, more trees, bushes, gardens, and large yards as well as numerous points of entry that make it easy for burglars to enter and escape a residence without detection (Felson 1998).

Burglars select residences or retail locations based on their knowledge of the occupants and thorough observation of potential targets (Wright and Decker 1994). Research on criminal decision making finds that occupancy and surveillance are the biggest deterrents against entering a property. Alarms and dogs are effective security deterrents for private homes (Association of British Insurers 1999).

Because burglars want to avoid contact with household occupants, business owners, and witnesses, more residences are burglarized during the day when occupants are usually out of the home; retail locations, however, are more often burglarized at night. Burglaries are thought to be more frequent during the summer months and during good weather when most people are out of their homes. Vacations and outdoor activities result in homes left unguarded for extended periods of time (U.S. Department of Justice 2000).

Victims of personal theft are less likely to be older, married men, while women and individuals with higher socioeconomic status are more often selected as potential targets (Sampson and Wooldredge 1997). High levels of street activity and high population density along with high levels of family disruption and low social cohesion create higher victimization risks for personal and motor vehicle theft (Felson 1998).

Shoplifters select targets based on a variety of factors including the location of the store, security precautions, the ease of picking up merchandise, and their ability to exit the store (Weiner 1970). For example, a study of middle-class

Pickpockets commonly target distracted tourists.

shoplifters shows that these shoplifters select stores in areas where lower class people shop. One shoplifter explains that: "store detectives and clerks pay little attention to clean, neat, well-mannered people downtown because they are so concerned with trouble from poorer, more suspicious-looking shoppers" (Weiner 1970: 217).

Types of Thieves

Offenders vary by their level of professionalism, their specializations, and the frequency with which they commit crimes. Three broad categories of property crime offenders are widely accepted and are most often classified as professional, persistent, or occasional thieves.

Professional, Persistent, and Occasional Thieves

Edwin Sutherland's (1956) classic study of **professional thieves** defines this type of offender as one who "makes a regular business of stealing." Professional thieves differ from other thieves in their careful planning and knowledge of technical skills and methods. These offenders move from locale to locale in their criminal pursuits in order to avoid capture and to select targets with large payoffs. Neil Shover (1996) adds that professional criminals spend long periods of their lives in criminal pursuits although they spend little time incarcerated. **Persistent thieves,** on the other hand, commit a variety of property offenses without specializing to any significant degree. Unlike professionals, persistent thieves are less successful despite their persistence. John R. Hepburn (1984) and others (Wright and Decker 1994) offer another category of property criminals—**occasional thieves.** These offenders are defined by the nature and character of their offenses rather than their frequency of offending. Occasional thieves commit crimes in favorable situations, that is, when the opportunity for theft, burglary, or robbery arises. The crimes "occur on those occasions in which there is an opportunity or situational inducement to commit the crime" (Hepburn 1984: 76). Their crimes do not involve planning, do not involve prior experience or skills, and usually are committed by a lone offender.

Gibbons (1968) offers an additional typology of property crime offenders that ranges from the most professional to the unprofessional. Gibbons' status hierarchy of offenders includes: (1) professional heavies, (2) professionals, (3) semiprofessionals, and (4) amateurs. Professional heavies are considered experts at large-scale burglary and robbery operations. Heavies usually work in groups, each member exhibiting specialized, technical skills of their trade. The group consists of highly successful professional criminals. One level down from the heavies is the professional. These offenders fall into property crime as a way of life, but seldom obtain the large amounts of money from their crimes, as do the heavies. Semiprofessionals are persistent property offenders, who possess few skills and rarely plan their crimes. These offenders may view themselves as professionals, but because they lack criminal knowledge and skills, are more often arrested and incarcerated. Amateur property offenders commit a variety of offenses, but do not possess the same level of criminal skills as do other groups of offenders. These offenders usually hold conventional jobs, typically do not have a criminal record, and rarely define themselves as criminals.

Robbers

Based on interviews with 67 convicted robbers, Conklin (1972) offers a fourfold typology of robbery offenders: (1) professionals, (2) opportunists, (3) addicts, and (4) alcoholics. Professional robbers are committed to crime as a source of livelihood and obtain a major portion of their income from illegal activities. As a result, professional robbers select targets based on the likelihood of a high monetary return. Professional robbers usually plan and organize their crimes prior to committing them and often work in loosely organized groups. Members of the group maintain different roles for carrying out the robbery. The "wheel man" may steal a car, map out an escape route, or drive to and from the robbery site. The "wheel man" or another member of the group may act as the "lookout" or the "peek man." On occasion members of the group are hired to help with the robbery for set percentage of the profits, usually 10 percent. These members, referred to as "10 percenters," often later become full-time members of the robbery group.

Opportunist, addict, and alcoholic robbers do not plan robberies and are not committed to a career of robbery. Rather, they prey on readily available targets usually when they the need for money arises. Opportunists typically obtain less than twenty dollars in each robbery. Addict robbers commit robberies in order to support a drug habit or while under the influence of drugs. Addicts would rather commit burglaries or thefts, but resort to robbery when they become financially

Armed robbery in progress. The intent is to complete the robbery as quickly as possible to ensure a safe "get away."

desperate. Alcoholic robbers typically commit robberies following an unrelated assault precipitated by excessive drinking. Intoxicated robbery offenders are motivated less by monetary gain than by their need to aggress against any available person, often with little or no provocation.

Burglars

Michael Maguire (1982) offers a basic typology of burglary types that includes (1) low-level burglars, (2) middle-range burglars, and (3) high-level burglars. Low-level burglars, typically juveniles, work in unsophisticated groups and commit burglaries based on opportunity and attractive targets. Security devices such as alarms and locks are often deterrents for these types of burglars. Typically, the property or monetary value of the items stolen is insignificant. Low-level burglars tend to grow out of their criminal pursuits as they get older and therefore do not depend on burglary for a livelihood. Middle-range burglars are generally older than low-level burglars and are often involved with alcohol and drugs. Quite often these offenders fluctuate between legitimate work and criminal pursuits. Because these offenders select targets based on their anticipation of a significant payoff, they are not as easily deterred by security precautions. In some cases, middle-range burglars make out with substantial amounts of property and cash. These offenders, however, lack the necessary connections of the high-level, more professional burglars. High-level burglars work in professionally organized groups of thieves and possess sophisticated breaking and entering skills and knowledge about potential targets. As a result, these offenders are able to carefully select targets and plan their crimes. High-level burglary groups carry out well-researched, highly organized, large-scale thefts involving substantial profits.

Car Thieves

Cars are stolen for a variety of reasons—for joyriding, for parts and other types of profit, or during the commission of a crime. Car thieves specialize in stealing and stripping cars for parts and profit. The most common types of parts stolen are stereo equipment and external parts such as tires, wheels, antennas, windshield wipers, luggage racks, and mirrors (Sallybanks and Thomas 2000). **Jockeys** steal cars regularly on a "steal to order basis" (Trembley et al. 1994). These professional car thieves work in groups, making up vast networks of stolen car dealers. Specific types of cars are targeted, and a great deal of planning goes into these thefts.

Professionals steal cars for parts and for profit while amateur thieves are likely to be **joyriders.** Joyriders, typically teenagers, take cars without the owners' consent as the opportunity arises, but they do not intend to keep them. Rather, the need for excitement motivates the typical joyrider. Unlocked cars and easily accessible car keys present attractive targets. Often juveniles steal cars for joyriding from someone they know (Clarke and Harris 1992; Meithe and McCorkle 1998).

Shoplifters

Shoplifters comprise a heterogeneous group of property offenders. Professionals and amateurs, the young and senior citizens, the poor and the well-to-do engage in shoplifting. Typologies of shoplifters categorize shoplifters based on motivations and demographic characteristics, prior offending, psychological factors, and measures of life purpose (Cameron 1964; Kivivuouri 1998; Klemke 1992; McShane and Noonan 1993; Moore 1984).

Mary Owen Cameron (1964) offers the most well-known typology of shoplifters. She identifies professional and novice shoplifters as boosters and snitches. **Boosters,** a small percentage of all shoplifters, are professionals who steal store items and later sell them for profit. **Snitches,** or amateur shoplifters, make up a large percentage of all shoplifters. They steal primarily for personal reasons, most often because of a lack of money or simply for excitement. Many amateur shoplifters are adolescents who engage in shoplifting for a certain amount of time and then cease shoplifting all together (Kivivuouri 1998).

Often shoplifters are able to afford the items they steal, but the thrill and excitement of shoplifting motivates their behavior. Stolen items are typically of little monetary value: They are often discarded or never used by amateur shoplifters (Katz 1988).

In a study of convicted shoplifters, Richard H. Moore (1984) identifies five types of offenders: impulsive, occasional, episodic, amateur, and semiprofessional. Impulsive shoplifters are inexperienced offenders who rarely plan their thefts. Occasional shoplifters offend more frequently than the impulsive group and usually do so for the approval of their peers. Episodic shoplifters, a small percentage of offenders, are typically beset by emotional distress. Amateur shoplifters offend on a fairly regular basis with a maximum profit and minimal risk. Semiprofessional shoplifters are highly skilled thieves who target expensive items, later to be sold to a fence—a buyer of stolen goods.

Theoretical Explanations

Various theoretical formulations are applicable to the understanding of the incidence and prevalence of property crime. Macro-level theories—social integration, social disorganization, culture, conflict, and economic inequalities—provide an explanation of the rates of various forms of property crime. Micro-level theories—social bonding, learning, rational choice, routine activities, and others—focus on an precipitants of an individual's involvement in property crime and why certain persons, places of residence, and business locations are more likely to become victims of robbery, burglary, larceny, and other types of property crimes.

Explanations of Rates of Property Crime

Robert Merton's (1968) formulation of social integration and anomie adds to the explanation of property crime rates among lower-class offenders. According to Merton, high levels of anomie and low social integration are a part of lower-class

Explanations of Rates of Property Crime

Theories and Theorists	Sociological Predictors	Hypotheses
Integration		
• Merton	Anomie	The greater the anomie, the greater the likelihood of property crimes.
Social Disorganization		
• Shaw and McKay	Social Disorganization	The greater the social disorganization, the higher the rates of property crimes.
Opportunity and Subculture		
• Miller	Focal Concerns	The greater the acceptance of the focal concerns, the greater the probability of property crimes.
• Cloward and Ohlin	Opportunity	The more a subculture advocates the commission of property crime and provides opportunities for its commission, the higher the rate of property crime.
• Cohen	Status Frustration Reaction Formation	The greater the status frustration of lower-class youth, the greater the likelihood that they will react against middle-class values. The greater the reaction of lower-class youth against middle-class values, the greater probability of involvement in property crime.
Conflict		
• Thio	Status/Power Groups	Higher-status, more powerful groups are more likely to commit lower-consensus deviance, e.g., white-collar crimes, whereas lower-status, less powerful groups are more likely to commit higher-consensus crimes, e.g., robbery, burglary, and larceny.
• Sellin	Primary Culture Conflict Secondary Culture Conflict	The higher the ratio of primary culture conflict to secondary culture conflict, the greater the rate of individual property offending, e.g., robbery, burglary, and larcency.
• Quinney	Power Groups	The more powerful groups define the behavior of the less powerful groups as criminal, the greater the perceived need to control the behavior of the powerless. The greater the perceived need by the powerful to control the behavior of the powerless, the higher the rate of property crime.

Explanations of Individual Property Crime

Theories and Theorists	Sociological Predictors	Hypotheses
Social Bonding and Control		
• Hirschi	Attachment	The weaker the attachment to conventional society, the more likely the individual will commit property crimes.
	Commitment	The weaker the commitment to conventional society, the more likely the individual will commit property crimes.
	Involvement	The greater the involvement in conventional activities, the less likely the individual will commit property crimes.
	Belief	The stronger the belief in conventional values and norms, the less likely the person will commit property crimes.
Social Learning		
• Sutherland	Differential Association	The greater the exposure to definitions favorable toward property crime, the greater the probability of engaging in property offending.
Rational Choice		
• Clarke and Cornish	Cost/benefit analysis	The greater the benefit associated with property crime, the more likely the individual will commit the offense.
Techniques of Neutralization		
• Sykes and Matza	Denial of responsibility Denial of injury Denial of a victim Condemnation of condemners Appeal to higher loyalties	Individuals are more likely to commit property crimes when they neutralize, rationalize, or provide excuses for having committed these offenses.
Routine Activities		
• Cohen and Felson	Suitable targets Motivated offenders Guardians	The presence of a suitable target, a motivated offender, and the lack of capable guardians increases the probability of committing a property crime.
Seductions of Crime		
• Jack Katz	Sneaky thrills	The greater the need for excitement or sneaky thrills, the greater the likelihood of engaging in property offending.

neighborhoods. Members of these neighborhoods internalize and accept culturally approved goals for success, but lack the means to achieve such goals. As a result, some members reject the culturally defined goals and/or means and engage in a variety of forms of property crimes throughout their lives. Rates of property crime in these areas are therefore expected to be fairly high.

In studying crime and urban growth, Shaw and McKay (1969) find that rates of crime are higher in large urban areas; rates decline with movement away from inner city areas. Crime in urban areas is correlated with a number of economic characteristics and social conditions. To Shaw and McKay social disorganization characterizes areas marked by group conflict, strain, and failure to achieve culturally defined success goals. Instabilities and social pathologies in neighborhoods and families foster conflicting moral and value systems, thus, leading to criminal life-styles that may be transmitted from one generation to another.

In a similar vein, the theorizing of Walter Miller (1958), Cloward and Ohlin (1961), and Albert Cohen (1955) support and extend the social disorganization perspective. Specifically, Miller's lower-class subculture formulation examines everyday "focal concerns" of lower-class culture. To Miller lower-class focal concerns—trouble, toughness, "street smarts," belief in fate, and the need for personal autonomy—give rise to involvement in property offending as well as other forms of criminal and deviant activity. Cohen's concepts of status frustration and reaction formation provide an understanding of lower class property crime. Frustrated by their inability to perform well in school—a middle-class oriented institution—lower-class boys react by adopting values that are diametrically opposed to those espoused by conventional society. Theft and destruction of property are common acts of revenge engaged in by frustrated lower-class adolescents. Cloward and Ohlin's opportunity structure explains how criminal subcultures recruit and train select individuals for lives of theft.

While higher-status persons do steal, most everyday theft occurs in lower-class neighborhoods and subcultures. Conflict theories of Alex Thio (1978), Richard Quinney (1970), and Thorsten Sellin (1938) are therefore applicable in the explanation of property crime rates. Thio's power theory provides the framework for these types of theories. He asserts that higher-status, more powerful groups define, apprehend, try, and punish lower-class individuals for property violations. At the same time, higher-status groups commit white-collar, corporate, and government crimes without the social stigma or punishment. Sellin reasons that everyday theft is viewed differently across social classes. While lower-class groups engage in property thefts for a variety of subcultural reasons, higher-class groups consider this behavior as deviant and in need of social control. Quinney adds that powerful groups, particularly those in capitalistic societies, cause the powerless to take on criminal roles, and then punish them for their actions in an effort to maintain power and control in business, government, and other societal organizations. Crimes of higher-status groups are aimed at increasing and maintaining power.

Explanations of Individual Property Crime

Several micro-level theories explain why offenders commit property crimes. Offenders may hold values that are favorable to committing property crime or they may rationally choose if, when, and where they will commit an offense. Other theorists propose that offenders are seduced by crime and criminal lifestyles. A few theories also explain why certain individuals become victims of robbery, burglary, and theft.

Travis Hirschi's (1969) social bond theory holds that individuals, who endorse the norms of conventional society, are less likely to engage in property offenses. Individuals often engage in robbery, burglary, and theft because of weak attachments to conventional groups. Attachment to unconventional groups that support property crimes encourages individuals to engage in these activities as well. Edwin Sutherland's (1947) differential association explains how individuals, who are exposed to behavioral definitions that favor involvement in property crime, are likely to commit these types of offenses.

Property crime offenders may rationally choose to commit robbery, burglary, or theft (Cornish and Clarke 1986). In doing so, the consequences of committing crime are weighed against the anticipated rewards gained from its commission. If the benefits associated with a particular property crime outweigh the costs or risks, an individual is more likely to carry out that crime. New avenues of research on property crime indicate that the cost/benefit analysis utilized by offenders is complicated by factors associated with self-indulged needs and wants, status, and "a party lifestyle" (Shover and Honaker 1996).

Techniques of neutralization, identified by Sykes and Matza (1957), are ways in which property offenders rationalize their decision to commit robbery, burglary, or theft. Neutralizations also give insight as to why certain victims are targets of thieves. Burglars may rationalize their crime by convincing themselves that the victim's insurance will cover the cost of the stolen items. Robbers may claim that because they do not use a weapon no one is actually injured. Offenders may also blame forces beyond their control for their actions or adhere to a "quasi-Robin Hood" mentality to steal from the rich. Thieves rationalize thefts from large corporations or wealthy individuals by denying injury or victimization or by claiming that the corporations or individuals are engaging in illegal activities as well.

Cohen and Felson's (1979) formulation of routine activities is appropriate for the explanation of how offenders decide to commit property crimes and how individuals become victims of such crimes. Routine activities theory contends that crime is more likely when three conditions are present: a suitable target, a motivated offender, and a lack of guardianship, someone capable of preventing the crime. Unless all conditions are met, crime is less likely to occur.

In *Seductions of Crime*, Jack Katz (1988) argues that property crimes—shoplifting, vandalism, youthful burglaries, and joyriding—are committed because of a desire for excitement, or a "sneaky thrill." His theory adds to the understanding why members of the upper and middle classes commit property crimes. Many times these offenders can afford the items they steal and may not actually need the pilfered goods. Only occasionally are these items used. Rather, they act as souvenirs, reminders of the thrill of committing the crime. In the case of shoplifting, Katz argues that the desire for an object does not lead to the crime, but the crime itself makes the object desirable.

Chapter Summary

- Property crimes involve the illegal taking of property, either cash or property, from individuals or places without the consent of the owner. Burglary, robbery, and larceny-theft are examples of property crimes. Robbery is also considered a crime against persons. The use of physical force or threat distinguishes robberies from larcenies and burglaries.

- Larceny is the most common type of property crime, accounting for over 75 percent of all crime. Burglary is the next most common type, and robbery accounts for a small percentage of all crime.

- Burglars, robbers, and other thieves differ in their professionalism, sophistication, and criminal decision making. Burglars usually plan their crimes while robbers and other thieves act spontaneously in response to opportunity and attractive targets.

- Professional thieves as opposed to persistent or occasional thieves make a living from crime. They often work in specialized groups whose members have technical skills and perform specific jobs.

Key Concepts

Property crimes: The illegal taking or damaging of property.

Burglary: The unlawful or forcible entry or attempted entry of a structure with the intent to commit an offense therein.

Robbery: Taking of property or cash directly from a person by force or theft of force.

Larceny-theft: Attempted theft of property or cash without using force or illegal entry.

Fraud: Theft or attempted theft of property or cash in which deception is a major component; does not involve the actual taking of property or money directly from the victim.

Vandalism: Unlawful destruction of property without the consent of the owner.

Arson: Any willful or malicious burning or attempt to burn, with or without intent to defraud the personal property of another.

Personal crimes: Robberies that involve specific individuals or occur in personal residences.

Institutional robberies: Robberies that occur in commercial settings such as banks or convenience stores.

Highway robbery: A robbery that takes place in a public place.

Strong-arm robbery: A robbery in which a weapon is not used in the commission of the crime.

Armed robbery: A robbery in which a weapon was used in the commission of the crime.

Home invasion (household robbery):   A burglary in which the offender confronts the homeowner or residents at the time of the burglary.

Professional thieves: Offenders who make a regular business of stealing, who carefully plan and possess special knowledge, technical skills, and methods.

Persistent thieves: Offenders who commit a variety of property crime offenses without specializing to any significant degree.

Occasional thieves: Offenders who commit property crimes when the opportunity arises.

Jockeys: Offenders who steal cars on a steal-to-order basis and/or sell cars or car parts for profit.

Joyriders: Offenders who take cars without the owners' consent but do not intend to keep them; theft satisfies a need for excitement.

Boosters: Professional shoplifters who steal items to later sell for profit.

Snitches: Amateur shoplifters who steal primarily for personal reasons, because of a lack of money, or for excitement.

Critical Thinking Questions

1. Which sociocultural and social psychological factors differentiate the occasional, opportunistic property offender from the career or professional property offender who depends on criminal activity for his or her livelihood?

2. Are property crimes precipitated by the general level of poverty in a given society, or the consequence of relative deprivation? Are there other explanations that account for property offending specifically?

3. How do the processes of globalization influence the incidence and rate of property offending across the world? How will globalization affect countries with historically low rates of property crime compared to those with consistently higher rates of property offending?

4. Which sociocultural and situational factors account for the incidence and prevalence of property crimes that involve the use of violence compared to those property offenses in which the offender does not confront the victim directly?

Web Extra

Check out these websites for additional information on property crime:

http://www.ojp.usdoj.gov/bjs

http://www.fbi.gov

http://www.ncjrs.org

CHAPTER 12

White-Collar and Organized Crime

PORTRAITS

of White-Collar and Organized Crime

CHECK WASHING, CARD TRAPPING, AND SKIMMING

Law enforcement agencies are investigating some of the newest forms of fraud, scams, and identity theft. *Check washing* is a process where checks are stolen from the mail and later altered using a combination of household cleansers to "wash" the written ink off of the check. Thieves then fill in fraudulent information and resign the check. Using their own driver's licenses for identification, they cash checks made out to themselves. *Card trapping* involves the theft of Automatic Teller Machine cards and Personal Identification Numbers (PIN). Thieves insert a trapping device into the machine, usually a type of glue. When a card is inserted into the card slot, it becomes stuck. Thieves wait for card owner to leave the card in the machine, then pry it out and use the card at other locations. *Skimming* is a sophisticated form of card and PIN cloning. Thieves set up computers and specialized software programs to clone card information at targeted locations. When card owners use their cards, the information encoded on the card's magnetic strip is transmitted to a connected computer. The copied information is then cloned onto a blank card and can be used to make purchases and withdraw money from accounts. (*Source:* National Check Fraud Center. *Check Washing: What is it?* Web posted at http://www.ckfraud.org/washing.htm.)

STOLEN IDENTITY

Identity theft is one of the fasted growing types of fraud. Victims of identity theft are normal individuals who find their bank accounts wiped out and overdrawn. Identity thieves obtain private information—name, checking account information, Social Security number, and birth date—that is readily available on driver's licenses and unsolicited credit card offers and use this information to duplicate checks for existing accounts. Computers, scanners, printers, and copy machines make this process fairly easy. Sophisticated and high-tech methods such as hacking into computer files are no longer necessary to steal someone's identity. In some cases identity thieves use private information to open fraudulent checking, savings, or loan accounts. Credit cards may also be issued under a fraudulent name. Other fraudulent uses include using the information to open phone or utility services or to obtain legal documents such as a driver's license, tax returns, or a Social Security card. (*Source:* J. Werrell, ed., "Identity Theft," *The Herald,* Sunday, March 3, 2002, pp. 1E, 3E.)

LEARNING OBJECTIVES

After reading this chapter you should know:

- ☐ The nature, definitions, and extent of white-collar crimes.
- ☐ The nature, historical conceptualization, and extent of organized crime.
- ☐ The theoretical explanations of rates and individual forms of white-collar and organized crime.

Introduction

White-collar and organized criminal activities are special cases of offending largely for monetary gain. To the extent that both forms of deviance are similarly motivated, they may be considered together. Both white-collar and organized crime may involve a network of offenders working in concert, or, on occasion, an offender acting alone. White-collar offenses may be committed to enhance the interests of an organization—usually a corporation or government agency—but may also be motivated by the prospect of personal gain by the offender. Typically, organized crime is primarily intended to enhance the interests of the controlling members of the crime group or network, but may directly benefit individual members of the organization. This chapter considers the various forms that white-collar crime may take within legitimate organizations, most often corporations and government agencies. The operation of illegitimate criminal organizations are reviewed in the United States and around the world.

> *"Drug trafficking in the late twentieth century will be remembered as the primary catalyst for the internationalization of organized crime."*
>
> — Albanese et al. (2003: 439)

> *"It's going to take a herculean salesmanship job to persuade a jury that the Enron executives involved in this could not appreciate the fraudulent nature of these transactions."*
>
> —Christopher J. Bebel, a former federal prosecutor and lawyer with the Securities and Exchange Commission. (Bebel, C. J. quoted in K. Eichenwald, Talk of Crime Grows Louder, Spurred by Report. Web posted at: http://www.truthout.org/docs_01/02.05A.Enron.Crime.htm).

White-Collar, Corporate, and Government Crime

The term "**white-collar crime**" originated in 1939, when Edwin Sutherland first defined it in his American Sociological Society's presidential address. According to Sutherland's (2002: 67) definition, white-collar crimes are crimes "committed by a person of respectability and high social status in the course of his occupation." Sutherland's (2002: 67) definition specifically excludes "murder, intoxication, or adultery, since these are not a part of the occupational procedures" as well as similar types of crimes committed by those who lack respectability and high social status.

Because crime was largely seen as a phenomenon of the lower classes, Sutherland's concept of white-collar crime created considerable controversy. Since this time, however, new forms of crime have prompted researchers to re-examine the nature of white-collar crime. As a result, the definition of white-collar crime has evolved and expanded to include new forms of crime and a variety of offender types (Coleman 2002).

Definitions and Forms of White-Collar Crime

Herbert Edelhertz (1970: 3), a former prosecutor with the United States Department of Justice, proposes a new definition of white-collar crime as "an illegal act or series of illegal acts committed by nonphysical means and by concealment or guile to obtain money or property, to avoid the payment of loss of money or property, or

> *SEC fined Worldcom $500 million to settle all wrong-doing. "The roughly $500 million comes to something like 1/350 of the roughly $175 billion lost by investors on the stock and bonds. The $500 million is not only a pittance, it's also a pointless penalty that takes money out of the pockets of some MCI victims and puts it in the pockets of others."*
>
> —*The Washington Post*, May 26, 2003: E01.

to obtain business or personal advantage." Edelhertz's definition does not require a white-collar offender to be of high social status; instead it focuses on the type of crime and the way in which it is carried out.

David Simon (1996) proposes another term—**elite deviance**—to further describe white-collar crime. According to Simon and others, forms of elite deviance share common characteristics. In defining elite deviance, Simon (1996: 11) offers the following common characteristics:

1. The acts are committed by persons from the highest strata of society: members of the upper and upper-middle classes.

2. Some of the acts are crimes in that they violate criminal statues and carry penalties such as fines and imprisonment. Other acts violate administrative or civil laws, which may also involve punishment. Other acts, although not illegal, are regarded by most Americans as unethical or immoral (i.e., deviant). Thus, elite deviance may be either criminal or noncriminal in nature.

3. Some of the actions are committed by elites themselves for personal gain, or they were committed by the elites or their employees for purposes of enhancing the power, profitability, or influences of the organizations involved.

4. The acts are committed with relatively little risk. When and if the elites are apprehended, the punishments inflicted were in general quite lenient, compared to those given common criminals.

5. Some of the incidents pose great danger to the public's safety, health, and financial well-being.

6. In many cases, the elites in charge of the organization are able to conceal their illegal or unethical actions for years before they become public knowledge.

Marshall Clinard and Richard Quinney (1980) suggest several other terms (referred to by others as subtypes of white-collar crime) to describe the complex nature and forms of white-collar crime. Table 12.1 presents definitions of white-collar crime and some specific examples of these offenses. **Organizational** or **business crimes** generally are "committed by an organization in the course of its regular business" (Clinard and Meier 1998: 198). A similar form of white-collar crime is referred to as corporate crime. **Corporate crime** involves any illicit activity by members of the organization to advance its interests. In short, the business rather than the individual benefits. The term **occupational crime** is applied only to crimes committed by individuals in the context of the offenders' job duties. These offenders act solely in their own personal interest and typically do not benefit their employers.

Table 12.1   White Collar Crime

	Definition	**Offenses**
Occupational	A violation of trust by an employee, usually for personal financial gain.	Employee theft Embezzlement Insider trading Fraud
Corporate	Offenses committed primarily to enhance the financial and competitive interests of the corporation.	False advertising Consumer fraud Anti-trust violations Price fixing Environmental crimes
Government	Illegal activities engaged in by agents of the government to protect or advance the political position of an administration, regime, or ruling party.	Abuse of power Bribery/corruption Concealing illegal activity

Government crimes are not unlike the types of white-collar offenses previously described. Public officials and other government employees, however, carry out these offenses. Alex Thio (1978) cites three motives for governmental criminal activity: (1) monetary gain, (2) the acquisition of power, or (3) condescending attitudes of government officials toward the public. Public officials and political candidates may accept illegal campaign contributions, embezzle government money, misuse taxpayer money, or further abuse power through criminal actions or discrimination.

Gary S. Green (1990) expands the idea of occupational crime by identifying four emergent categories. His typology of occupational offenses and offenders includes:

- **Organizational occupational crime:** Crimes committed for the benefit of an employing organization. In such instances, only the organization or the employer benefits, not individual employees.

- **State authority occupational crime:** Crimes by officials through the exercise of their state-based authority. Such crime is occupation specific and can only be committed by officials in public office or by those working for them.

- **Professional occupational crime:** Crimes by professionals in their capacity as professionals. The crimes of physicians, attorneys, psychologists, and the like are included here.

- **Individual occupational crime:** Crimes by individuals as individuals. This is a kind of catchall category that includes personal income tax evasion, the theft of goods and services by employees, the filing of false expense reports, and the like (Green 1990: 11).

Extent of White-Collar Crime

The extent of white-collar crime around the world and in the United States can only be estimated. The Federal Bureau of Investigation recently released *The Measurement of White Collar Crime* (2002b). Using the Uniform Crime Reporting Data, the FBI estimates that white collar crimes—i.e., five types of fraud, bribery, counterfeiting/forgery, embezzlement and other offenses—account for 4 percent of crime reported. Corporate, government and other types of white-collar crime are largely undetected. Furthermore, such crimes are often unknown to the public. According to James William Coleman (2002: 7), "One of the most basic difficulties in measuring white-collar crime is that the victims often do not realize they have been victimized."

Of the crimes that are known, the consequences are devastating, with financial costs in the hundreds of billion of dollars. For example, common forms of property crime result in annual losses of approximately $13 billion (FBI 2002b). The financial costs of white-collar crime are estimated to be over $200 billion (Clinard and Yeager 1980).

Several studies of victims and offenders have attempted to estimate the extent of white-collar crime. In a study of 477 United States corporations extends

---

Common Characteristics of Organized Crime Around the World

Jay S. Albanese and Dilip K. Das outline five commonalities of organized crime around the world:

1. Criminal activities are conducted in a *planned* manner for the purpose of profit.

2. There is a *continuing enterprise* or conspiracy that is based on a preexisting social, ethical, or business relationship, or around a particular illegitimate product or opportunity.

3. *Imitation, threats, and sometimes violence* are used to obtain access to the illicit opportunity and to maintain it from competing criminal groups.

4. *Corruption* (bribery and extortion) is often used to maintain a degree of immunity from government interference (law enforcement and prosecution).

5. Organized crime groups show tremendous *adaptability* in responding to changes in supply, demand, law enforcement, and competition. They sometimes move geographically, shift to another illicit product, find new partners, or take other measures to ensure profitability and degree of success in evading law enforcement.

Source: Albanese, Jay S., Dilip K. Das, and Arvind Verma. 2003. *Organized Crime: World Perspectives.* Upper Saddle River, NJ: Prentice Hall, p. 6

these findings. Marshall Clinard and Peter Yeager (2002: 88) find that "approximately three-fifths of the 477 manufacturing corporations had at least one action initiated against them," and that "200 corporations, or 42 percent of the total, had multiple cases charged against them." Clinard and Yeager (2002: 91) also find that "the oil, pharmaceutical, and motor vehicle industries were the most likely to violate the law."

The extent of white-collar crime is frequently measured by public attitudes toward large corporations and government entities. Surveys show that public confi-

---

AT A GLANCE

- Each year more than 24 million persons become victims of more than 38 million crimes of fraud or attempted fraud.
- The majority of white-collar offenders are white males in their late twenties to early thirties who have had prior contact with their victims.
- White-collar offenses account for 3.8 percent of all crimes known to the Federal Bureau of Investigation—frauds and counterfeiting/forgery account for the majority of white-collar crime.
- Except for bribery, a higher proportion of women commit white-collar offenses than other forms of property crimes.
- Drug trafficking is a $600 billion business worldwide.
- In the United States, 40 percent of organized crime profits (est. $100 billion) are the result of drug trafficking.
- The financial worth of the drug cartels in Colombia is greater than the total expenditures of the Peruvian and Colombian governments.

Sources: Mayhew, P. and J. J. M. van Dijk. 1997. *Criminal Victimization in Eleven Industrialized Countries: Key Findings from the 1996 The International Crime Victims Survey (ICVS).* The Hague: Ministry of Justice, WODC; Newman, G. (ed.) 1999. *Global Report on Crime and Justice.* New York: Oxford University Press; U.S. Department of Justice. 2000. *The National Crime Victimization Survey (NCVS)* 2000. Washington, DC: U.S. Department of Justice and Bureau of Justice Statistics; Rennsion, C. 2001. *Criminal Victimization, 2000: Changes 1999–2000 with Trends 1993-2000.* Washington, DC: U.S. Department of Justice, Bureau of Justice Statistics; Federal Bureau of Investigation, 2000. *Crime in the United States, 2002.* Washington, DC: USGPO; Office for Victims of Crime. 2000. *Victims of Fraud and Economic Crime: Results and Recommendations From an OVC Focus Group Meeting.* Web posted at http://www.ojp.usdoj.gov/ovc/publications/infores/fraud/victfraud.txt. Ryan, P. J. 2003. *Organized Crime,* Santa Barbara: ABC-CLIO. Schweitzer, H.O. "Organized Crime: An American Perspective," in Jay S. Albanese, Dilip K. Das, and Arvind Verma. 2003. *Organized Crime: World Perspectives,* Upper Saddle River, NJ: Prentice Hall; Ruiz de Olano, R. "Organized Crime: A South American Perspective," paper presented at Organized Crime Symposium, Yokohama, Japan, cited in Jay S. Albanese, Dilip K. Das, and Arvind Verma. 2003. *Organized Crime: World Perspectives.* Upper Saddle River, NJ: Prentice Hall.

dence in many elite organizations is declining with the increase in public awareness of large-scale corporate deviance. Simon (1996) notes that deviance by elites provides motivation and rationalization for non-elites to commit profit-oriented crimes. White-collar or elite criminals are rarely arrested or punished for their offenses (Coleman 2002; Sutherland 2002). The federal U.S. Sentencing Commission finds that for white-collar crimes prosecuted by federal courts, sentences tend to be extremely light; nearly half entail a fine of $5,000 or less, 80 percent are fined $25,000 or less, and even probation against executives is imposed less than one-fifth of the time. Jail and prison time tends to be almost nonexistent. As a result, the stigma that is associated with many conventional crimes does not apply to white-collar criminals; many are not considered "real" criminals (Goode 2005).

For the most part corporate elites have reaped considerable financial profit from their wrongdoing; and most have avoided criminal prosecution. In recent years, for example, the Securities and Exchange Commission referred 609 cases to U.S. attorneys for prosecution. About 31 percent were tried, but only 14 percent resulted in a jail sentence (Fortune 2002).

Rising incidence of new forms of white-collar crimes, specifically high-tech crimes, gives a grim picture of the extent of these forms of white-collar crime. Until recently, these types of offenses were rarely reported. The Federal Trade Commission's Bureau of Consumer Protection estimates that reports of identity theft may increase to 200,000 incidents annually. The misuse of Social Security numbers is closely linked to identity theft. Social Security numbers provide the basis for more than eight in ten cases of identity theft (Noack 2000; Werrell 2002).

Extent of Organized Crime

Efforts to assess the extent of **organized crime** worldwide are underway. For example, the United Nations' Global Program on Transnational Organized Crime is sponsoring a forthcoming report, *Assessing Transnational Organized Crime Groups: Dangerousness and Trends.* The report is aimed at the identification of:

Former Enron CEO Kenneth L. Lay swearing "to tell the truth, the whole truth, and nothing but the truth" during a hearing in court. In an 11-count indictment, he was charged with securities and wire fraud and making false statements. The Securities and Exchange Commission has charged him with fraud and insider trading and seeks a civil penalty and recovery of over 90 million dollars.

1. The characteristics, resources and strategies adopted by the criminal groups.

2. The social, political, and economic context in which organized crime groups act, including the response of the criminal justice system and law enforcement agencies.

3. The criminal markets in which these criminal groups operate (see http://www.uncjin.org/CICP/Folder/trans.htm).

Until such an analysis is complete, the extent of organized crime, including its group affiliations, business activities, and financial profits can only be estimated. In economic terms, annual income generated from organized crime is estimated in excess of $50 billion (Rowan 1986). This is thought to be a conservative amount, however, as other estimates approach $100 billion (Simon and Witte 1982). Drug production profits account for a large portion of illegally generated income. Afghan, South American, and Italian Mafia groups produce approximately 80 percent of the opium, cocaine, and marijuana consumed in the United States (ERRI 2001). In addition to the numerous illegal activities, organized crime groups control many legitimate commercial businesses. With regard to one crime group—the Russian Mafia—it is estimated that 362 commercial businesses in Russia are under the control of organized crime (Finckenauer and Voronin 2001).

Organized Crime Groups. Organized crime groups who operate across the globe work in concert, creating vast networks for enhanced profit and market control (Lungren 1996). Organized crime groups and international terrorists organizations collaborate on drug trafficking, money laundering, and the marketing and transportation of munitions. The Italian Mafia, the Russian Mafia, the Mexican and Colombian cartels, and Asian crime groups are among the most prominent transnational organized crime groups (Pollard).

The Italian Mafia is among the most influential of the globally organized crime groups. La Cosa Nostra is the largest and most important of the Italian Mafias. It is estimated that as many as twenty-four Italian American crime groups operate throughout the United States. New York, Chicago, Philadelphia, New Orleans, and Boston are home to some of these families: the Carlisi family, the Scarfo organization, the Stanfa organization, the Marcello gang, and the Civella mob. Organized crime families who operate in New York support memberships of 75 to 500 core members (Adinsky 1994). While the Italian Mafia is well known for gambling, racketeering, and extortion, the establishment continues to contribute to a share of the U.S. drug market, in particular cocaine and heroin.

Russian organized crime is rapidly growing around the world. Between 5,000 and 6,000 multiethnic Mafiya groups operate within Russia, with a total of approximately 100,000 members (Lindberg and Markovic 2002). These groups control an estimated 80 percent of all private business and a large portion of the nation's wealth through real estate and bank ownership (Finckenauer and Voronin 2001). Bribery of government officials ensures political influence. Russian Mafiya groups are believed to be operating in twenty-nine countries. Twelve to fifteen organized groups with approximately 4,000 core members operate in seventeen U.S. cities and fourteen states (Finckenauer and Voronin 2001). Illegal activities include many types of fraud—bank, health insurance, credit card, and telecommunications—extortion, and illegal trafficking along with various forms of larceny and violent criminal activity.

Colombian and Mexican cartels focus their activities on the drug business. Approximately thirty-five crime families in Medellin and Cali control the manufacture, marketing, and distribution of cocaine and other drugs through vast agricultural enterprises, laboratories, and production facilities. Between 50 and 70 percent of the South American cocaine and 80 percent of the marijuana is sold in the United States. South American organized crime groups also produce 20 to 30 percent of the heroin consumed in the United States (www.ojp.usdoj.nij/internationaltrafficking.html; Finckenauer et al.).

Asian crime groups, or Triads, participate in Hong Kong, Taiwan, Japan, and Mainland China. Hong Kong–based groups support over 160,000 members in fifty different organizations including the Sun Yee On, the 14K, and the Woo Group. Taiwan's major Triads include the Sung Lian, Tian Dao Man, Four Seas, and the United Bamboo. Membership ranges from several hundred to approximately 10,000 members in the United Bamboo group. Their activities revolve around legitimate businesses such as massage parlors, restaurants, and construction projects, as well as a broad range of illegal enterprises. Japanese crime groups, or yakuza, maintain strong historical crime roots in Japan. Legislation that prohibits yakuza membership, however, has resulted in decreased membership and organized criminal activities throughout Japan. It is estimated, though, that yakuza expansions in Europe and the United States generate nearly $10 billion for legitimate businesses. Chinese "tongs," or gangs, are found throughout the United States as

Explanations of Rates of Property Crime

Theories and Theorists	Sociological Predictors	Hypotheses
Opportunity		
• Cloward and Ohlin	Opportunity	The more a subculture or organization provides opportunities for the commission of organized or white-collar crime, the higher the rate of those kinds of offenses.
Conflict		
• Thio	Status/Power Groups	The higher the status, and the more power the sociopolitical group holds, the greater the likely of lower-consensus deviance, e.g., white-collar crimes.
• Sellin	Primary Culture Conflict Secondary Culture Conflict	The greater the primary culture conflict, the greater the rate of organized criminal activity.
• Quinney	Power Groups	The more the powerful segments of society attempt to control the behavior of the powerless, the higher the rate of organized criminal activity.

Explanations of Individual Property Crime

Theories and Theorists	Sociological Predictors	Hypotheses
Social Learning		
• Sutherland	Differential Association	The greater the association with persons who advocate involvement in white-collar or organized criminal activity, the greater the probability of those forms of offending.
Rational Choice		
• Clarke and Cornish	Cost/benefit analysis	The greater the benefits anticipated from white-collar or organized crime, the more likely an individual will become involved in those forms of offending.
Techniques of Neutralization		
• Sykes and Matza	Denial of responsibility Denial of injury Denial of a victim Condemnation of condemners Appeal to higher loyalties	The greater the ability of an individual to neutralize any guilt involved in the commission of a white-collar or organized crime, the greater the likelihood of engaging in those forms of offending.
Seductions of Crime		
• Jack Katz	Sneaky thrills	The greater the need for excitement or sneaky thrills, the greater the likelihood of engaging in property offending.

well and provide for much of the heroin importation from Southeast Asia (Finckenauer).

Theoretical Explanations

Explanations of white-collar and organized crime may be considered on two levels of analysis. Macro-level theories—opportunity structures, culture conflict, power relations, and economic inequalities—may explain variations in the rates of white-collar and organized crime. Micro-level theories—social learning, rational choice, techniques of neutralization, and the seduction of crime—consider why certain individuals may become involved in white-collar or organized crime.

Explanations of Rates of White-Collar and Organized Crime

Cloward and Ohlin's opportunity structure explains how criminal subcultures provide their members with the means, motivations, and support for the commission of property offenses. The criminal subcultures are largely networks of offenders who socialize recruits about criminal possibilities and assure them that the risk of apprehension is extremely low. Criminal subcultures thrive on the belief that the larger network of offenders can be trusted to act in the interests of its constituent members. A code of secrecy and honor is central to the workings of white-collar offending committed to enhance the organization as a whole, and of organized crime groups.

Power relations, economic inequality, and culture conflict are threaded through the theories of Alex Thio (1978), Richard Quinney (1970), and Thorsten Sellin (1938). Each theoretical formulation is applicable to white-collar and organized crime. Thio argues that higher-status, more powerful groups define the elements of "high-consensus" crimes, largely committed by members of lower-status, less powerful groups in society. The higher-status members then prosecute and often incarcerate the lower-status members of the commission of the high-consensus offenses. However, higher-status persons are more apt to engage in "lower-consensus" crimes—white-collar, corporate, and government crimes—often with impunity. Quinney contends that the more powerful groups in society seek to maintain their advantaged position by defining the behaviors of the less powerful as criminal and taking steps to legally control them. The disproportionate involvement of racial minorities and the poorer members of society in the criminal justice system is striking. Quinney points out those corporate and governmental criminal activities, committed largely by higher-status individuals, are intended to enhance their influence and power. Sellin contends that often the interests of a minority culture conflict with those of the dominant culture. When this clash of cultures occurs, representatives of the dominant culture may seek revenge by actively retaliating against the minority culture by criminalizing their behaviors or by making access very difficult to needed opportunities and resources—housing, jobs, medical care, and educational opportunities. Certain members of the minority culture may respond by involvement in organized criminal activity.

Explanations of an Individual's Involvement in White-Collar and Organized Crime

Edwin Sutherland's (1947) differential association combines subcultural and learning formulations to explain criminal behavior. The motivations, rationalizations, and techniques for engaging in white-collar and organized crime are learned by interacting with other persons who advocate committing either form of offending. The greater the association with others who foster criminal activity, the more likely an individual will engage in the commission of a crime. Much of white-collar and organized criminal behavior is learned directly from active offenders.

White-collar and organized criminal offenders typically rationally choose to engage in criminal activity. Cornish and Clarke (1986) argue that the benefits of committing a crime are weighed against the rewards that are anticipated. When the anticipated benefits markedly outweigh the possible risks involved, the decision to carry out the crime is typically made. White-collar and organized crimes are, for the most part, committed for a financial reward. Careful planning is essential to successfully committing a technically complicated white-collar offense or in sustaining a lucrative drug trafficking and money laundering operation. Cost and benefit analyses are commonly undertaken before engaging either in white-collar or organized criminal offending.

Sykes and Matza's (1957) Techniques of Neutralization are readily applicable to white-collar and organized criminal offenders. Both types of offenders engage in a process of neutralizing any guilt that may be associated with the violation of the law. The techniques of neutralization—denial of responsibility, denial of injury, denial of a victim, the condemnation of those who might condemn them, and appeal to higher loyalties—serve to justify a wide range of white-collar and organized criminal activities, from insider trading to marketing drugs. The decision to commit the offense may not have been theirs alone; the harm that results may be to anonymous persons who are devalued by the offender; agents of the criminal justice system—police, prosecutors, judges—are themselves corrupt and not worthy of respect; and the allegiance to one's corporation, government agency, or organized crime group or family supercedes any loyalty to society as a whole.

Jack Katz's (1988) conception of the *seduction of crime* provides intriguing possibilities for the understanding of white-collar and organized criminal offenders. The instrumental nature of white-collar and organized criminal activity suggests that the offenders are always and exclusively driven to realize some monetary gain. However, financial profit underlies both legitimate and illegitimate business practices. Trading stocks legally or illegally are intended for the same purpose—to make money. Yet, involvement in all criminal activities carries the risk of apprehension, prosecution, and possibly incarceration. The "thrill" of engaging in a high-risk venture, the surge of adrenaline that accompanies involvement in criminal activity, can become seductive. For some offenders, the prospect of a monetary rewards may be less important than the emotional payoff derived from the committing the crime.

Chapter Summary

- White-collar crimes are defined as criminal violations committed by people of high respectability and high social status in the course of their occupations. Individuals, businesses, and governments may engage in white-collar crimes.

- Advanced technology and availability of computers facilitate the increase in several forms of high-tech white-collar crimes, including identity theft and other types of fraud, forgery, and counterfeiting.

- Organized crimes are committed by formally structured criminal organizations that strive to monopolize markets and undermine the legal institutions of society. Organized crime is usually equated with ethnically homogeneous groups.

- Organized crime, like most other crimes, is becoming more global. Vast criminal networks exist in the United States, Russia, South America, Asia, Africa, and Middle Eastern countries. These groups are involved in illegal profiting from drug production, marketing, and distribution; theft; fraud; and violent crime.

Key Concepts

White-collar crime: Crimes committed by persons of respectability and high social status in the course of their occupations.

Elite deviance: Term introduced by David Simon that describes the variety of white-collar crimes.

Organizational (business) crime: Offenses committed by entire firms or industries in the course of regular business.

Corporate crime: Any criminal violation by a corporation or its executives, employees, or agents, who act on behalf or for the benefit of the corporation.

Occupational crime: Crimes committed by individuals in the context of the offender's job duties for personal gains.

Government crime: White-collar crimes committed by public officials and other government employees.

Organizational occupational crime: Crimes committed for the benefit of an employing organization.

State authority occupational crime: Crimes by officials through the exercise of their state-based authority.

Professional occupational crime: Crimes by professionals in their capacity as professionals.

Individual occupational crime: Crimes by individuals as individuals.

Organized crime: Criminal activity by an enduring structure or organization developed and devoted primarily to the pursuit of profits through illegal means.

Critical Thinking Questions

1. How are the explanations of white-collar offending similar to and different from other forms of property crime? What are the unique features of white-collar crime that distinguish it from other property offenses?

2. How are white-collar offenses committed within corporations and government agencies similar to and different from organized criminal activities? Provide examples to illustrate your answer.

3. What characteristics of an organization increase the likelihood of systematic criminal activity? How do individual members of the organization who are legally sanctioned for their involvement in white-collar crime neutralize their guilt?

4. How do the processes of globalization affect organized criminal activity within particular countries and across the world? How does globalization facilitate the forms that organized crime may take and its ability to persist through time?

Web Extra

Check out these websites for additional information on white-collar crime:

http://www.fbi.gov

http://www.nw3c.org

http://www.ojp.usdoj.gov/nij/international

CHAPTER 13

Cyberdeviance

PORTRAITS

of Cyberdeviance

- "Knowledge then . . . is utterly imminent and implicated in the forms and technologies of instrumental power, and readable only to the extent that we have the power to decode it. How we are known and what we know constitute a matrix of unjustly distributed power, except that there is no one reliable panopticon. The matrix is too complex and fragmented to offer itself to any one unifying gaze—a notion that does not seem entirely reassuring to me. . . . Hence, the attraction of the cyberspace addiction: to jack in is briefly, thrillingly, to get next to the power; not to be able to jack in is impotence. Moreover, the cyberspace addiction, the hacker mystique, posits power through anonymity. One does not log on to the system through authorized paths of entry; one sneaks in, dropping through trap doors in the security program, hiding one's tracks, immune to the audit trails that were put there to make the perceiver part of the data perceived. It is a dream of recovering power and wholeness by seeing wonders and by not being seen. But what strange and tangled dream, this power that is only gained through matching your synapses to the computer's logic, through *beating the system by being the system*." (*Source:* Moreiras, A. 1993. "The Leap and the Lapse: Hacking Private Site in Cyberspace," in V. Conley (ed.), *Rethinking Technologies.* Oxford: OH: Miami University Press, p. 198.)

- "I just do it because it makes me feel good, as in better than anything else that I've ever experienced. Computers are the only thing that have ever given me this feeling . . . the adrenaline rush I get when I'm trying to evade authority; the thrill I get from having written a program that does something that was supposed to be impossible to do, and the ability to have social relations with other hackers are all very addictive. I get depressed when I'm away from a networked computer for too long. I find conversations held in cyberspace much more meaningful and enjoyable than conversing with people in physical-reality real mode. For a long time, I was extremely shy around others, and I am able to let my thoughts run free when I am alone with my computer and a modem hooked up to it. I consider myself addicted to hacking. If I were ever in a position where I knew my computer activity was over with for the rest of my life, I would suffer withdrawal." (*Source:* Email interview cited in Paul A. Taylor. 1999. *Hackers.* London: Routledge, p. 48.)

LEARNING OBJECTIVES

After reading this chapter you should know about:

- ☐ The various forms of cyberdeviance.
- ☐ Types of cyberdeviants and cybercriminals.
- ☐ Methods of cybercrime.
- ☐ Motives for committing cybercrime.
- ☐ Ethics, values, and norms of the cyberdeviant subculture.

Introduction

Personal computers are increasingly part of everyday life. Global participation in the information age is largely a result of the expanding opportunities provided by the Internet. Access to information from sources around the world and the ability to communicate and interact directly with fellow computer users unencumbered by time, distance, or expense provide a global perspective unknown in previous times. Opportunities to engage in the process of discovery and innovation abound. The adventure of exploring the contributions of diverse cultures and interacting with others in nonphysical space intrigues many computer users. However, the opportunities for the creative use of cyberspace are not limited to legitimate pursuits. Various forms of cyberdeviance have emerged with the potential for worldwide consequences.

> *"My hacking activity actually was a quest for knowledge, the intellectual challenge, the thrill and the escape from reality."*
> —Kevin Mitnick (www.usatoday .com/cyber/tech/eth485.htm)

> *"The more things that you can do online, the more things we can do to you."*
> —Taltos, a cracker (www.wirco.com/ news/print/0,294,41625.00.html)

Cyberdeviance ranges from relatively benign invasive acts directed at particular computer systems to intentionally destructive attacks against unknown Internet users. Acts of cyberdeviance result in enormous financial losses, disrupt the operations of the military and key governmental agencies, compromise the security of corporations and businesses, and victimize untold numbers of individual computer users.

Cyberdeviance has revolutionized our concepts of crime and deviance in the twenty-first century. The sudden, clandestine acts of a lone computer programmer can wreak unprecedented havoc around the world. The sociocultural underpinnings of cyberdeviance, its scope and consequences, and theoretical understanding of cyberdeviance are considered in this chapter.

Definition

Computer crime and deviance may take various forms with targets ranging from individual victims, either known or unknown to the perpetrator, to identifiable social groups, governmental agencies, large-scale corporations, or masses of anonymous persons. Efforts to legally define each form of computer offending, and to draft legislation at the federal and state levels that is both constitutionally defensible and legally enforceable, have been a challenge. For example, in 1984, the United States Congress passed the first **Computer Fraud and Abuse Act** (CFAA 2001). This legislation was amended in 1986, 1994, 1996, and 2001, a reflection of the increasing complexity of computer-related offenses.

In addition to the federal statute, thirty-three states have passed legislation related to computer crime. Each of these state statutes prohibits unauthorized access to computers and databases, using the computer to commit fraud, and using the computer to destroy the contents of computers and their software. The successful enforcement of these statutes, however, has been difficult. Corporations and financial institutions are reluctant to admit that an intruder has breached the security of their computer systems. Consumer confidence may erode, liability claims may arise, and investors may be less willing to risk buying stock in a company that is particularly vulnerable to computer criminals (Conley and Bryan 1999).

Extent and Patterns

The extent of computer-related offending is largely a matter of speculation. What is certain is that anyone with a personal computer and access to the Internet has the opportunity to commit a computer crime. Opportunities for offending far exceed the motives and technical ability to carry out cyberdeviance.

A recent survey of Fortune 500 companies shows that all of them had been the victim of at least one "hack attack" and over half had been victimized more than thirty times (Breidenbach 1998). Other surveys indicate companies report computer crime victimization rates range from 25 to 100 percent (Charney and Alexander 1996). Targets include the Pentagon, military bases, and financial and stock institutions (Budnitz 1998; Glass 1998).

Types of Computer Crimes

David Carter (1995) has identified four types of computer crimes: computer as the target, computer as the instrument of the crime, computer as incidental to other crimes, and crimes associated with the prevalence of computers.

Computer as the Target

The computer is the target when a cyberdeviant makes use of a computer to obtain information or damage operating programs (Carter 1995). An offender may pretend that he or she is the system's manager and gain access to the system's files. Typical of such offenses are the altering, theft, or sabotage of intellectual property; theft of marketing information (e.g., consumer lists, pricing data, or marketing plans); or blackmail based on information gained from computerized files (e.g., medical information, personal history, or sexual preference). Computers containing criminal justice and other government records (e.g., arrest and criminal history data, outstanding warrants, driver's license information, passports, and tax records) are common targets of computer criminals.

Techno-vandalism and **techno-trespass** are two related forms of computer as target offenses (Carter 1995). Both of these offenses involve unlawful access to a computer. Techno-vandalism may involve malicious intent but is often motivated by the offender's need to show that the challenge of unlawful access to a computer can be met. Techno-trespass refers to an unlawful exploration of computer files simply to look at the contents, not to damage, alter, or steal any information.

Computer as the Instrumentality of the Crime

Instrumentality refers to the use of an instrument, legally in one's possession (e.g., the processes of a computer), to commit a crime. The operations of a computer may be used to reprogram another computer's analytical processes to fraudulently convert the financial assets of others to one's own purposes. Examples of such offenses include theft from bank accounts, credit card fraud, and fraudulent stock market transactions (Carter 1995).

Computer as Incidental to Other Crimes

The computer is incidental to other crimes when it is not necessary to commit the crime but does facilitate its commission. Computers may accelerate the commission of certain offenses, allowing the offender to process a great deal of information very rapidly, and make the detection of the offense and the apprehension of the offender less likely. Examples of these offenses are bookmaking, money laundering, altering crime records, and unlawful bank transactions. Offenders may encrypt incriminating evidence stored in computers that are programmed to destroy the data if the computer is not accessed properly (Carter 1995).

Computers have been used to distribute child pornography, solicit clients for prostitutes, and provide instruction on methods of criminal offending. An extreme example of the use of a computer to facilitate the commission of a crime involved the altering of a hospital patient's medication records that resulted in the administration of a fatal overdose. The offender was subsequently charged with criminal homicide (Carter 1995).

Crimes Associated with the Prevalence of Computers

The global demand for computers and related products has led to the proliferation of black markets for counterfeit equipment and software. Common offenses are the violation of copyright restrictions of commercial software and the duplication of word processing, spreadsheet, and database programs.

Computers can also be used as a tool to commit traditional forms of criminal activity (e.g., counterfeiting, fraud, larceny, embezzlement, and sexual solicitation). Ronald Standler has outlined three ways computers may be used to commit "new" forms of criminal activity: (a) unauthorized use of the computer, (b) releasing a malicious computer program, and (c) harassment and stalking in cyberspace (see www.rbs2.com/ccrime.htm).

Unauthorized Computer Use

Unauthorized use of the computer typically involves:

1. Computer voyeurism: The offender simply reads confidential documents without altering them in any way.
2. Changing data: Records and financial accounts are changed, usually to the advantage of the offender.
3. Deleting data: Entire computer files are deleted or are sabotaged.

Malicious Computer Programs

The Internet has made it possible to transmit malicious computer programs across the globe in fractions of a second. Malicious computer programs, as the name implies, are intended to destroy or wreak havoc on the computer capabilities of an unknown number of anonymous victims. These programs include viruses, worms, Trojan Horses, and logic bombs (each is discussed elsewhere in the chapter).

Harassment and Stalking

Computers also provide a means to harass or stalk a computer user. The intent of the perpetrator is to create emotional distress, malign, or compromise the victim's reputation. Threats of injury, sexual innuendo, or hate messages are common forms of harassment and stalking. Forged email sent in the name of the victim, which conveys racist or malicious messages, is used by the harasser to harm the victim socially and psychologically.

Methods of Cyberdeviance

Trap Doors

Trap doors are installed in computer software to allow programmers to make changes without going through complicated access procedures. Often these trap doors are eliminated when the program has been installed in a computer. However, when a trap door is left in place, a cybercriminal may readily gain access to system programs and files (see www.rbs2.com/ccrime.htm).

Session Hijacking

Session hijacking refers to the use of a computer by a person other than the one who has legitimately logged on. Opportunities for session hijacking arise when a computer session is not terminated properly or when telephone or telecommunication lines are reconfigured to allow for the continuance of an unauthorized computer session (see www.rbs2.com/ccrime.htm).

Timing Attacks

Timing attacks refer to the destruction or alteration of data in a computer prior to being processed. A timing attack may also occur by placing one's own name in someone else's data file before it is processed or altering the order of jobs in the computer's processing or printing queue (see www.rbs2.com/ccrime.htm).

Trojan Horses

Trojan Horses are used to infiltrate a computer system with the intention of disabling the system. A **Trojan Horse** carries instructions into a computer program that are disguised as authorized and useful. Hidden in the Trojan Horse are various destructive devices for rendering a computer system ineffective, such as viruses, worms, logic bombs, or salamis (see www.rbs2.com/ccrime.htm).

Viruses

Viruses are computer programs that have the ability to reproduce themselves. Similar to their biological counterparts, computer viruses need a host or program to continue to multiply. The virus alters a computer program by adding commands

How a Computer Virus Works

A computer virus is a program that secretly invades another computer.

- It typically gains access to a computer as an email attachment or less often by an infected disk.

- Activation of the virus occurs when the email attachment is opened or the infected disk is loaded into the computer.

- When activated, the programmed virus begins its destructive mission.

- The virus spreads to other computers by reading the user's email address book and sending itself to all persons found.

- Viruses may alter or delete files, cause damage to a computer's hardware, or render existing programs unusable.

Source: Adapted from Michael Schaefer. 2001. "Computer Viruses Take Turn for the Worst," *Foster's Daily Democrat,* December 9.

that will activate the virus (Power 2000). When the computer is activated, the virus begins to affect its operation. A computer virus may alter and destroy data or render disk space or memory unusable. Viruses may infect a computer in two ways. First, the virus may be transmitted in an email message that, when opened, permeates the victim's computer. Second, the victim may unwittingly download an infected file (Icove et al. 1995).

Worms

Unlike viruses, **worms** are computer programs that exist independently of other programs. With the ability to replicate itself, a worm is considered to be more powerful than a virus. A worm invades a computer by means of the Internet and begins to search for other computers attached to its original victim. Similar to viruses, worms may attack computer software, destroying data and operating procedures (Icove et al. 1995).

Logic Bombs

Trojan Horses may be used to plant **logic bombs** in a computer system. A logic bomb instructs the computer to execute a certain function under certain conditions, usually on a given date and time. Logic bombs may work in concert with a virus and are potentially as destructive (Icove et al. 1995).

Salamis

A **salami** attack may also be launched by means of a Trojan Horse. The salami attack focuses on the altering of financial data and works in this way. Small amounts of money are sliced from a much larger account, as a serving of salami is cut from a larger piece. The victim, who rarely misses the financial loss, is not likely to report the offense. A typical salami attack may involve the reallocation of funds that remain in an account following a rounding procedure, say, from $100.003 to an even $100. Multiplied by thousands of accounts, the fraction of a cent diverted to the offender's personal account may in time become a substantial amount (Icove et al. 1995).

Typology of Cyberdeviants

Hackers

Hackers are computer aficionados who are driven to explore the intricacies of computer programming and to extend the boundaries of their expertise. The intent of the hacker is typically not to do harm, but rather to explore uncharted computer applications. This quest may lead them to attempt to gain access to unauthorized computer systems housing confidential governmental, military, or personal information. The hacker is motivated by the challenge that inaccessible computer systems present. The thrill of accessing secured computer systems inspires the hacker to devise increasingly more intricate computer software. In a sense, computer hackers are intensely curious, creative, yet meddlesome, individuals (Raymond 1997).

Crackers

Unlike hackers, **crackers** intend to damage, manipulate, or destroy the computer operations of others. They are motivated to disrupt or destroy vital computer systems of governmental and military agencies, corporations, and financial institutions. Crackers are not simply interested in proving that they can infiltrate highly secure computer systems and networks, but they are bent on demonstrating the kinds of confusion and disorder that they can create. Planting viruses, worms, logic bombs, and salamis are routine activities of crackers (Raymond 1997).

Crackers typically band together in clandestine groups to plan and carry out their criminal missions. Similar to other relatively small-scale criminal "gangs," crackers provide themselves with ominous names—Toxic Shock Group, Computer Chaos Club, AcidMaster, or Exploiter (Taylor 1999).

Phreakers

Phreakers specialize in using telephone services without cost and preventing their calls from being traced. By devising relatively simple programs to interrupt the billing procedures of telephone companies, the phreaker can make long distance calls without considering the expense. Telephone companies around the world have responded to the activities of phreakers with increasingly sophisticated detection software of their own. This has led to the development of more innovative techniques of accessing telephone services among the phreakers. This contest between the phreakers and telephone companies is similar, in many ways, to the technological advancement in home and business security systems and innovations in methods of burglary and safecracking among professional thieves (Raymond 1997).

AT A GLANCE

- The Computer Investigations and Technology Unit of the New York City Police Department estimates that almost 40 percent of the caseload in the unit involves electronic threats and harassment.

- In a University of Cincinnati sexual victimization study, of the 696 stalking incidents, 166 (24.7 percent) involve threats by email.

- At least sixteen states have stalking statutes that explicitly cover electronic communications.

- A 2004 survey of 494 computer security practitioners in U.S. corporations, government agencies, financial institutions, medical institutions, and universities finds that:
  - 53 percent of the respondents experienced a successful attack on their computer systems.
  - One in three of the organizations suffered more than five successful attacks on its computer systems.
  - About half of the breaches of computer security originated outside the organization and half among its own employees.
  - The total amount lost as a result of breaches of computer security was $141,496,560.
  - Computer viruses accounted for the greatest financial loss—$55,053,900, followed by denial of service—$26,064,050.
  - One in five organizations reported a breach of computer security to a law enforcement agency.

Sources: A Report from the Attorney General to the Vice President. *1999 Report on Cyberstalking: A new challenge for law enforcement and industry.* Web posted at: http://www.cybercrime.gov/ cyberstalking.htm and Computer Security Institute (CSI) 2001. Financial losses due to Internet intrusions, trade secret theft and other cybercrimes soar. Web posted at http://www .gocsi.com/) Gordon, L. A., Martin P. Loeb, William Lucyshyn, and Robert Richardson. 2004. *CSI/FBI Computer Crime and Security Survey.* Computer Security Institute.

A hierarchy obviously exists among the members of the computer underground. Hackers view themselves as intellectually, technically, and ethically superior to all other members of the computer underground. Crackers' computer skills, for the most part, exceed those of the phreakers.

Marc Rogers, a Canadian behavioral scientist and cyberdetective, provides a fourfold typology of computer hackers:

1. *Old School Hackers:* Prior to the advent of the Internet, the Old School Hackers were driven to know and crack the codes of computer systems and to explore their contents. They did not intend to steal anything or to damage the operation of the computer they hacked. Old School Hackers were motivated

by personal curiosity and the desire to learn more about the workings of computer systems.

2. *Script Kiddies or Cyberpunks:* Script kiddies or cyberpunks are typically young (teenagers and young adults), white, and male. Their interest in the computer supersedes anything else. As a consequence, they often are high school dropouts who are consumed by hacking into computer systems with the intent to do harm.

3. *Professional Criminals or Crackers:* Professional criminals or crackers derive their livelihood from their illicit activities on the Internet. They may work independently or may be employed by organized criminal groups, governments, or corporations.

4. *Coders and Virus Writers:* Coders and virus writers devise codes and viruses that are then used by hackers bent on destruction of computer systems, often around the world. The network of coders and virus writers, or "Zoo," provides them with an opportunity to experiment with their destructive codes and viruses before they are released into the "Wild" or Internet (see http://www.tlc.discover.com/convergence/hackers/articles/psych.print.html).

Donn Parker (1998) has identified seven different types of cybercriminals: (1) pranksters, (2) hacksters, (3) malicious hackers, (4) personal problem solvers, (5) career criminals, (6) extreme advocates, and (7) malcontents, addicts, irrational, and incompetent people. Pranksters simply engage in playing tricks on others without intending significant harm to them. Typically, pranksters leave messages or embed jokes or strange characters into computer systems. Malicious hackers, however, intend to disrupt the work of others or to cause them significant loss. For example, they may generate computer viruses or destroy computer files and records. A common type of computer criminal is the personal problem solver. Often these offenders have experienced considerable frustration in resolving their personal problems (e.g., financial, emotional, or psychological) and have resorted to computer crime to meet their needs. Career criminals earn most of

Roenel Ramones, suspected of originating the "Love Bug" computer virus that swept the world, in the custody of Philippine National Bureau of Investigation agents. It is estimated that 45 million computer users were affected by the ILOVEYOU emailed virus and the worldwide economic costs may exceed 10 billion dollars.

Russia's Hacking Culture

Many of their peers in the Western world say Eastern Europe's computer crackers and hackers are the most skillful in the world—far superior to the so-called "script kiddies" who have gained a fair amount of notoriety.

"We call Russia the Hackzone because there are so many of us here, and we are so good at what we do," said Igor Kovalyev, a self-described cracker living in Moscow. "Here hacking is a good job, one of the few good jobs left."

Kovalyev said that stealing credit card numbers is the "best résumé" for a Russian cracker. But other popular activities are studying the ways to "get into networks of foreign businesses, plus virus writing, and password discovery," said Kovalyev, who believes that Russian websites such as *Hackzone* and "launched in Russia" *Drink or Die* are the most sophisticated of all hacking sites.

"Russian crackers do amazing things with very limited computing power. They are smart and they cover their tracks very well," said Frank Voden, a consultant with U.K. firm TechSolutions.

"And they have excellent programming skills, which many of the so-called crackers in the United States do not possess. These Russian guys aren't just downloading tools and running them without knowing what they are doing. They know exactly what they are doing."

Source: Michelle Delio, *Russia's Hacking Culture,* Web posted at: http://www.wired.com/news/culture/0,1284,42346,00.html.

their income from the illicit use of the computer. Various schemes, including fraud, the misrepresentation of goods or services for sale, and false investment opportunities, may result in considerable profit for the career computer criminal. Terrorists and political, social, or religious zealots are classified as extreme advocates. Their unwavering commitment to their cause provides them with a justification for engaging in cybercrime and deviance. Persons who are malcontent, addicted, irrational, or generally incompetent comprise the last group of cyberdeviants. Their internal discord and need to strike out against others underlie much of their deviant activity in cyberspace, where they can remain anonymous.

Cyberdeviant Subculture

Sociologist Paul Taylor (1999) provides a general outline of some key elements of the hacker subculture. These elements include technology content, secrecy and fluidity, and the generation gap and seeds of antipathy.

Technology Content

Technology content refers to the wide familiarity among the young with the computer and its various applications. Computers have been incorporated into classroom instruction beginning in the primary grades and have become vital to educational success. The Internet has provided the vehicle for the dissemination of information among cyberdeviants around the world. The sharing of advances on common computer-related problems and the recognition of individual discoveries provides the foundation for the development of a unique subculture of computer aficionados. This subculture is based on common interests and goals that are not related to typical sociological dimensions of subcultural affiliation—race or ethnicity, religious or traditional background, geographic location, and the proximity of interaction (Taylor 1999).

Secrecy and Fluidity

The cyberdeviant subculture depends in large measure on its members maintaining their own anonymity and keeping secret the activities of the subculture members. Because cyberdeviants are engaged in varying degrees of illicit activity, they must be assured that their fellow members will hold in confidence the information that is shared as well as its source.

Not only do cyberdeviants operate in secrecy, but also the structure of their subculture is characterized by a fluidity of organization that, in turn, protects them.

> There is no organized structure in the computer underworld, no mysterious chairman of the board to run things. The underground is anarchic, a confederation of phreakers/hackers and virus writers from all over the world whose common interests transcend culture or language. Most hackers have two or three handles and operate on a number of boards. They change IDs, aliases, sites, their methods, targets, and gang membership as rapidly as the authorities track them. Stamping out hacking is like trying to pin down mercury. (Clough and Mungo 1992:18)

To Paul Taylor (1999), a cyberdeviant subculture is made possible by a process of "disembodied anonymity." The organization of the cyberdeviant subculture differs in many ways from that of other common interest groups. The trappings of status and power are missing. Physical appearance, socioeconomic status, age, race, and gender do not influence the ranking of a cyberdeviant within his or her subculture. Communication among the members of the subculture is carried out in an impersonal way, largely by email, bulletin boards, and newsgroups. Without the kinds of social clues that typically accompany other forms of interpersonal communication, correspondence within the cyberdeviant subculture focuses more on the content of the message and less on the social characteristics of the sender. This method of communication serves to preserve the anonymity of the cyberdeviant and provides for a more equalitarian subcultural structure (Clough and Mungo 1992).

The Gender Gap and Antipathy

Around the world, the young dominate the cyberdeviant subculture. Hackers and other cyberdeviants tend to either age out of their nefarious pursuits as they approach the age of 30 or to be replaced by more accomplished cyberdeviants who are still teenagers. As technical sophistication increases among elementary and middle school computer users, a desire to know more and a drive to explore the potential of the computer increase. Often young computer users become more advanced than their teachers. Their frustration with the limits of the educational opportunities provided by their teachers may lead to their seeking answers on their own. Electronic bulletin boards, chat rooms, and newsgroups provide opportunities for the young to connect with the cyberdeviant subculture (Clough and Mungo 1992).

Ethics and the Cyberdeviant

A distinct ethos permeates the cyberdeviant subculture. Levy (1984) has identified five ethical standards that are commonly held by members of the computer underground:

- All information should be free.
- Mistrust authority and promote decentralization.
- Hackers should be judged by their hacking, not by bogus criteria such as degrees, age, race, or position.
- You can create art and beauty on a computer.
- Computers can change life for the better.

Adherence to these ethical principles varies within the hacking community. Elite hackers tend to hold themselves to a higher standard of behavior than more deviant members of the computer underground. The "Inner Circle" epitomizes the ethos of the hacker elites.

> No Inner Circle member will ever delete or damage information that belongs to a legitimate user of the system in any way that the member cannot easily correct himself. No member will leave another hacker's name or phone number on any computer system. He will leave his own on a system only at his own risk. All members are expected to obtain and contribute their own account information, rather than use only information given to them by other members. (Landreth 1985: 18–19)

In short, an elite hacker seeks to protect the property of others against harm or destruction. Elite hackers view themselves as "explorers, not spies, and . . . damaging computer files was not only clumsy and inelegant—it was wrong" (Landreth 1985: 25).

Motives

Often computer hackers want to demonstrate that their technical expertise far exceeds any system's capability to prevent an invasion. Their primary intention is to flaunt their computer prowess, to succeed against all odds to crack an allegedly impenetrable computer fortress. The harm that is created is secondary to their own sense of accomplishment and possible increase in status among their peers.

Other computer criminals, however, do intend harm to specific targets (e.g., military installations, corporate headquarters, or a financial institution) or non-specific targets—unknown victims of a computer virus.

To Donn Parker (1998), "intense personal problems" underlie most cyberdeviance. In his study of eighty young computer hackers in the United States and Europe, he identifies the following psychological and behavioral traits that are commonly held by cyberdeviants:

- Precociousness, curiosity, and persistence
- Habitual lying, cheating, stealing, and exaggerating
- Juvenile idealism (e.g., "power to the people," "if it feels good, do it")
- Hyperactivity
- Drug and alcohol abuse (Parker 1998)

These psychological and behavioral traits are manifest, according to Parker (1998), in one of two syndromes, either differential association or "Robin Hood." The differential association syndrome refers to the involvement of the cyberdeviant with other cyberdeviants who provide a justification for their actions. If everyone around the cyberdeviant appears to be committing some form of computer-related offense, then there is the opportunity to learn more about its commission and the rationale for doing so. Parker (1998) also notes that cyberdeviants rationalize their actions by asserting that persons themselves are not harmed, only computers.

> Cybercriminals often distinguish between the unacceptable practice of doing harm to people and the impersonal acts of doing harm to or through computers. Yet, many receive a measure of satisfaction in their crimes by personifying the computers they attack, viewing them as adversaries and deriving some enjoyment from ripping them off. (Parker 1998: 141).

The "Robin Hood" syndrome refers to the justification that cybercriminals use to steal from corporations or large-scale organizations. However, Parker (1998) points out that unlike the Robin Hood of legend, cybercriminals tend to keep what is stolen rather than give it to the poor.

Canadian behavioral scientist Marc Rogers and psychiatrist Jerrold M. Post also note that common traits distinguish hackers who engage in criminal activities from those who do not. Rogers observes that criminal hackers may minimize the consequences of their computer crimes by rationalizing that they are actually benefiting others by their actions. Computer systems, they may argue, are not human, so there really is not a "true" victim. Post agrees that criminal hackers employ an "ethical flexibility" to neutralize any feelings of guilt associated with their behavior. The hacker is just playing a game, the consequences of which they rarely take seriously (see http://www.tlc.discover.com/convergence/hackers/articles/psych_print.html).

British sociologist Paul Taylor (1999: 47) has identified six motivations for involvement in computer hacking as follows:

- Feeling of addiction
- The urge of curiosity
- Boredom with educational system
- Enjoyment of feelings of power
- Peer recognition
- Political mission

Computer hacking requires total absorption—a single-minded dedication to the task at hand. Hackers easily become obsessed with the problem of the moment. The thrill of discovery, of "cracking the code" is seductive—in many ways tantamount to an adrenaline rush that accompanies completing a dangerous physical feat or the use of certain drugs. The seductivity of hacking may be addictive. A member of the Toxic Shock Group observes:

> We are addicted to information and knowledge, and our drugs are withheld from us. We are forced to seek our precious information and knowledge elsewhere. We have to find challenge somewhere, somehow, or it tears our very souls apart. And we are, eventually, forced to enter someone's system. (Taylor 1999; 47)

Hackers are intensely curious people. They have an incessant need to expand their knowledge of the computer and its potential uses. Problems that are resolved lead to further problems that capture their attention. As Sherlock Holmes abhorred boredom and lack of mental stimulation, so, too, do computer hackers. They typically find the standard curriculum in high schools and colleges

Hacking and the Freedom of Information

One German hacker observes:

"Information freedom" is the slogan of most hackers over here (including the notorious CCC, Chaos Computer Club). We already have a situation where electronic communications are unsafe, i.e., governments may legally tap data lines and make copies of electronic mail. Plus, the suspicion of "hacking" alone (i.e., no evidence) is sufficient to get search warrants or to impound equipment. What hackers, not the kind that willfully destroy data for the fun of it, but the real hackers, are fighting for is something of a battle of principles. They want to keep the electronic media as safe or even safer than regular paper mail from intrusion by government agencies. (Taylor 1999: 61) to be stiflingly oppressive to their quest for knowledge about the only thing that matters to them—the mysteries of the computer.

Status, power, and prestige are closely linked social phenomena. Hackers rarely receive positive recognition from persons other than those in the hacking community. A hacker's status, power, and prestige are almost exclusively provided by the hacker subculture. The "outside" world is unable to understand the social milieu of the hacker.

Hackers who desire status, power, and prestige may be driven to engage in acts of cyberdeviance that have political implications. Freedom of information and rebellion against the right to own intellectual property rights are issues that propel much of the politically motivated cyberdeviance. Many hackers and other computer aficionados want to make available to all computer users all computer-related information and technology. Their political mission is to break the bureaucratic and legal shackles that limit access to useful information, software, and technology.

Theories of Cyberdeviance

While little theoretical work has been done on the various forms of cybercrime and deviance discussed in this chapter, existing theoretical formulations can help us understand these behaviors. Information about the incidence and prevalence of cybercrime and deviance is nonsystematic, incomplete, and largely anecdotal. Therefore, our discussion of the theoretical understanding of cybercrime and deviance will not attempt to distinguish between explanations and predictions of individual and rates of computer-related offending.

Seduction of Crime

Sociologist Jack Katz (1988) offers an explanation of crime and deviance that differs from traditional theoretical formulations that focus on the offender's psychological background or social environment. Rather, Katz is concerned with the experience of committing a crime, the "distinctive sensual dynamics" involved in deviant activity. To Katz (1988: 9), the central question in investigating the etiology of deviance and crime is: "What are people trying to do when they commit a crime?" In the present instance: "What does a cybercriminal hope to achieve by engaging in an illicit use of the computer?"

Katz sets forth a threefold process that provides individual offenders with the necessary conditions to engage in criminal or deviant behavior. First, there must be a *path of action*—"distinctive practical requirement for successfully committing the crime" (Katz 1988: 9). Second, the offender must engage in a *line of interpretation*—"unique ways of understanding how one is and will be seen by other" (Katz 1988: 9). And, third, there is an *emotional process*—seductions and compulsions that have special dynamics.

The process then that results in any criminal behavior, including cybercrime, involves the engagement of the offender in a plan for the illicit activity, a

Abraham Abdallah used computers in Brooklyn, New York
public libraries to target the 200
richest people identified by
Forbes magazine. His victims included: George Soros, Steven
Spielberg, Martha Stewart,
Oprah Winfrey, and Ted Turner.
He was charged with criminal
impersonation, forgery, and
fraud. Bail was set at one million dollars.

"definition of the situation" that makes sense of the crime and an anticipation of
sensual pleasure from its commission.

Underlying the process of engaging in criminal activity is a series of "moral
emotions"—humiliation, righteousness, arrogance, ridicule, cynicism, defile-
ment, and vengeance—that compel the offender to act. Cybercriminals may be
motivated to demonstrate their computer expertise in an arrogant manner. Hackers, for example, may seek to gain access to an unauthorized, highly secure, computer system simply to show that they can do it. Crackers may be driven by a
need to defile the property of others, while righteousness or vengeance may compel others to commit computer theft.

Social Learning, Differential Reinforcement, and Differential Association

Social learning, differential reinforcement, and differential association formulations are particularly relevant to the understanding of cyberdeviance (Akers and
Burgess 1966; Sutherland and Cressey 1978). In many ways, cyberdeviants are
computer virtuosos—masters of the intricacies of the Internet, software design,
and manipulation. They are driven to continually learn more about the possibilities that global computer systems offer. Largely through trial and error, cyberdeviants have the ability to learn many of the mysteries of computer technology.
However, considerable sharing of information and technique takes place within
the computer underworld—a loose confederation of cyberdeviants who exchange
news of their discoveries and claim recognition for them.

Central to differential association theory is the contention that deviant behaviors are learned from others through personal interaction. Sutherland and
Cressey (1978) further hold that differential associations vary in "frequency, duration, priority, and intensity." While cyberdeviants engage in virtual interaction
with their counterparts across the globe, they typically value these associations

Explanations of Cyberdeviance

Theories and Theorists	Sociological Predictors	Hypotheses
Integration		
• Merton	Anomie	The greater the level of anomie, the greater the possibility that an individual is to engage in cyberdeviance.
Social Bonding and Control		
• Hirschi	Attachment	The weaker the attachment to conventional society, the more likely the individual is to engage in cyberdeviance.
	Commitment	The weaker the commitment to conventional society, the more likely the individual is to engage in cyberdeviance.
	Involvement	The greater the involvement in conventional activities, the less likely the individual is to engage in cyberdeviance.
	Belief	The stronger the belief in conventional values and norms, the less likely the individual is to engage in cyberdeviance.
Social Learning		
• Sutherland	Differential Association	Individuals who are exposed to definitions favorable toward cyberdeviance are more likely to engage in cyberdeviance.
• Akers	Differential Reinforcement	The greater the punishment for cyberdeviance, the less likely an individual is to engage in cyberdeviance.
Seductions of Crime		
• Katz	Sneaky Thrills	The greater the thrill of the experience, the more likely an individual is to engage in cyberdeviance.
Neutralization Theory		
• Sykes and Matza	Denial of Responsibility	If an individual fails to accept responsibility for his or her own actions, then he or she is more likely to engage in cyberdeviance.
	Denial of Injury	If an individual maintains that no one is hurt by his or her behavior, then he or she is more likely to engage in cyberdeviance.
	Denial of a Victim	If an individual feels that his or her victim deserves to be victimized, then he or she is more likely to engage in cyberdeviance.
	Condemnation of Condemners	If an individual views others as hypocrites or hidden deviants, then he or she is more likely to engage in cyberdeviance.
	Appeal to Higher Loyalties	If an individual feels that the demands of his or her group affiliation take precedence over societal values and rules, then he or she is more likely to engage in cyberdeviance.
Rational Choice		
• Cornish and Clarke	Cost/Benefit Analysis	The greater the benefit associated with cyberdeviance, the more likely an individual is to engage in cyberdeviance.

more so than most of the personal contacts they have with others. By differentially associating with members of the computer underworld, would-be cyberdeviants learn the "motives, drives, rationalization, and attitudes" necessary to engage in computer-related illicit activity. They also learn the techniques that may be used to commit various computer-related offenses.

Related to Sutherland and Cressey's differential association is Akers and Burgess' concept of differential reinforcement. When a cyberdeviant is sufficiently socialized into the computer underworld, acts of illicit computer ingenuity become widely known and admired. The cyberdeviant is granted considerable recognition and respect within the cyberdeviant subculture. Acts of computer mayhem may well be "differentially reinforced"—and as a result, motivate the offender to engage in increasingly more daring computer-related deviance.

Rational Choice

To Derek Cornish and Ronald Clarke (1985), rational choice theory holds that the decision to commit a deviant or criminal act is primarily influenced by the need to maximize pleasure while minimizing pain. The decision to engage in computer-related criminal activity tends to involve a deliberate, rational process. The offender must first acquire the highly sophisticated computer expertise to access secured computer property. They decide that their expertise can be markedly improved by invading the computer space of others. Cyberdeviants weigh the pleasure and possible recognition that may attend the commission of a computer crime against the costs involved in being apprehended for such an offense. Cyberdeviants engage in a process of rationally deciding to carry out a computer-related crime. The anticipation of the thrill of discovery or of personally conquering a seemingly insurmountable obstacle—e.g., breaking into the computer system of the Pentagon—may override any perceived risk involved in their criminal activity. In short, cyberdeviants make a "rational choice" to commit a computer-related offense.

Techniques of Neutralization

Cyberdeviance may well lend itself to techniques that have been used to neutralize guilt associated with the commission of deviant or criminal acts. Nondestructive computer hackers, or cyberdeviants who access the intellectual property or software of others or pirate long-distance phone service, may employ one or several of Greshman Sykes and David Matza's (1957) techniques of neutralization. Sykes and Matza identify five techniques of neutralization that may be invoked by persons who engage in deviant acts. The techniques of neutralization are: *denial of responsibility, denial of injury, denial of the victim, condemnation of the condemners,* and *appeal to higher loyalties.* Cyberdeviants who engage in what they view to be innocuous cyber exploration may well deny that an injury has occurred or that there is a real victim involved in their foray into cyberspace. Even when there is intentional theft, say, of software or computer games, the cyber-deviant may contend that their loyalties to their fellow computer users super-cede any concern they may have for the losses that may be incurred by the owners of the pirated software. The cyberdeviant may argue that if computer technology or software can potentially benefit the world at large, then no one per-son or corporate entity can have exclusive rights to it (see the section on com-puter ethics in this chapter).

Social Control

Central to Travis Hirschi's (1969) bonding theory of social control is the con-tention that individuals who are integrated into conventional society are less apt to engage in acts of crime or deviance. The bonds to conventional society include attachment, commitment, involvement, and belief. Cyberdeviants tend to be less interested in the everyday activities of conventional life and more absorbed in the intricacies of cyberspace. As a group, they are less attached to the norms of con-ventional society and less interested in observing the social customs and mores that are important to others. While they may not deliberately choose to violate rules of social conduct, they simply are disinterested in them. They commit little time or energy to everyday affairs—having lunch with friends, recreation and leisure activities, or community projects. Their lack of involvement in everyday life signals their rejection of a common set of beliefs and values that may guide their behavior.

Anomie

Robert Merton's (1968) specification of Emile Durkheim's (1951) original concep-tualization of anomie further helps to explain involvement in cyberdeviance. To Merton, anomie occurs when there is a disjunction between the institutionalized means and culturally approved goals in society. Individuals experience anomie as stress, strain, or tension that must be adapted to in their everyday lives. Mer-ton identifies five adaptations to the stressful consequences of anomie: confor-mity, innovation, ritualism, retreat, and rebellion. Two of these adaptations are particularly applicable to cyberdeviance: innovation and retreatism. Innovation refers to the acceptance of culturally approved goals, while rejecting the institu-tionalized means to those goals. Cyberdeviants may aspire to status and recogni-tion, financial gain and power, or autonomy and self-determination. Rather than engaging in conventional means to these ends, the cyberdeviant uses innovative strategies to gain illicit access to computer systems or cyber-related intellectual property.

Cyberdeviants may also use their computer expertise to devise intricate un-derground networks of fellow computer aficionados. These underground net-works provide the opportunity to retreat into cult-like areas of cyberspace. In cyberworld, a cyberdeviant, in Merton's terms, can reject both institutionalized means and culturally approved goals found in conventional society.

Chapter Summary

- Cyberdeviance encompasses a wide spectrum of computer-related offenses. The federal government and individual states have only recently passed legislation that legally defines forms of computer-related offending. The successful enforcement of the legislation is difficult, and numerous amendments to such legislation are necessary to keep up with the evolving and complex nature of computer crime.

- The extent of computer related offending is largely unknown. However, most U.S. corporations surveyed report being victims of cybercrime.

- Many cyberdeviants do not intend harm to specific or even nonspecific targets. Rather, the primary objective is to flaunt their computer prowess. Hackers describe such acts of cyberdeviance as having seductive and addictive qualities.

- Computers are used as a tool by cyberdeviants to commit traditional types of crimes as well as new types of criminal activity. Sandler identifies three types of computer activity that are now considered crimes:
  - Unauthorized use of the computer
  - Releasing a malicious computer program
  - Harassment and stalking in cyberspace

- Carter identifies four types of computer-related offenses:
  - Computer as the target
  - Computer as the instrumentality of the crime
  - Computer as incidental
  - Crimes associated with the prevalence of computers

- Techno-vandalism and techno-trespass are two forms of computer crime where the computer is the target. Each involves unlawful access to a computer.

- Parker identifies seven types of cybercriminals:
  - Pranksters
  - Hacksters
  - Malicious hackers
  - Personal problem solvers
  - Career criminals
  - Extreme advocates
  - Malcontents, addicts, irrational, and incompetent people

- Rogers' typology of computer hackers includes:
  - Old School Hackers
  - Script Kiddies, or Cyberpunks
  - Professional Criminal or Crackers
  - Coders and Virus Writers

- Cyberdeviants utilize a variety of cyberdeviant methods including:
  - Trap doors

- o Session hijacking
- o Timing attacks
- o Trojan Horses
- o Viruses
- o Worms
- o Logic bombs
- o Salamis

- Cyberdeviants, especially hackers, are a part of a subculture of cyberdeviance who hold common beliefs, share knowledge, and abide by ethical standards, norms, and values.

- Parker identifies two syndromes that characterize cyberdeviants: differential association and Robin Hood. Differential association refers to the involvement of the cyberdeviant with other cyberdeviants and the learning process by which cyberdeviants rationalize and justify their computer related offenses. The Robin Hood syndrome is one justification cyberdeviants use to steal from corporations or large-scale organizations.

- Taylor provides three key elements of the hacker subculture:
  - o Technology content
  - o Secrecy and fluidity
  - o Generation gap and antipathy

- Theoretical explanations of cyberdeviance have yet to be formulated; however, traditional sociological theories can be applied.

Key Concepts

Cyberdeviance: The use of the computer or Internet to victimize computer systems; ranges from relatively benign invasive acts directed at particular computer systems to intentionally destructive attacks against unknown Internet users.

Computer Fraud and Abuse Act (CFAA): Legislation passed by Congress to address various forms of computer offending.

Techno-vandalism: A form of computer crime where unlawful access to a computer is gained; the offender may have malicious intent but most often tries to meet the challenge of the unlawful entry.

Techno-trespass: A form of computer crime where unlawful access to a computer is gained; refers to an unlawful exploration of computer files simply to look at the contents, not to damage, alter, or steal information.

Trap doors: Device installed in computer software that allows programmers to make changes without going through complicated access protocols.

Session hijacking: Use of a computer by a person other than the one who is legitimately logged on.

Timing attacks: Destruction or alteration of data in a computer prior to being processed; placing one's own name on someone else's data file before it is processed; or altering the order of jobs in the computer's processing or printing queue.

Trojan Horse: Device that carries instructions into a computer program that are disguised as authorized and useful, but has hidden within it viruses, worms, or logic bombs used to disable a system.

Viruses: Programs that are sent through email or downloaded from the Internet that have the ability to reproduce themselves, alter computer programs, alter and destroy data, or render disk space or memory unusable.

Worms: Computer programs that invade a computer by means of the Internet and attack computer software, destroying data and operating procedures; they exist independently of other programs and possess the ability to replicate themselves and attack other computers attached to the original victim.

Logic bombs: Computer programs that work in concert with a virus to instruct the computer to execute a certain function under certain conditions, usually on a given date and time.

Salami: Computer attack that alters financial data by slicing small amounts of money from a much larger account; the victim rarely misses the financial loss.

Hackers: Cyberdeviants who are driven to explore the intricacies of computer programming and uncharted computer applications and to extend the boundaries of their expertise; typically their intent is not to do harm.

Crackers: Cyberdeviants who intend to damage, manipulate, or destroy the computer operations or computer systems of others.

Phreakers: Cyberdeviants who interrupt the billing procedures of telephone companies, specializing in using telephone services without cost and preventing their calls from being traced.

Critical Thinking Questions

1. What sociocultural characteristics distinguish cyberdeviants from other forms of deviant actors? What social psychological factors may account for the motives for and continued involvement in cyberdeviance?

2. What factors may distinguish between occasional or episodic involvement in cyberdeviance and long-term involvement in cyberdeviance?

3. How are cyberdeviant subcultures formed and sustained through time? How are members recruited, selected, and socialized by a cybercrime subculture?

4. What are the differences between cyberdeviants who do not intend harm to other computer users or their computer systems and those who intend malicious damage and theft?

Web Extra

Check out this website for additional information on cybercrime:

http://www.cybercrime.gov

CHAPTER 14

Positive Deviance

P O R T R A I T S

of Positive Deviance

- At age 13, Bill Gates began programming computers. During his college years at Harvard, he developed the programming language BASIC for the first microcomputer. Gates dropped out of Harvard in his junior year to focus on Microsoft, a computer software company he designed to bring personal computers to every office desktop and every home. Today, Gates and Microsoft Corporation are the leading software providers for the personal computer. According to the most recent *Guinness Book of Records*, Gates is considered the richest private individual in the world, with a net worth of $36.4 billion.
- Skip Wrightson and Justin Carven recently drove their Volkswagen van cross-country. They developed a way to use grease rather than gasoline to fuel their van. When it was time to fill up the tank, Wrightson and Carven stopped at various restaurants to collect grease that would otherwise be thrown away. (*Source:* http://www.greasecar.com.)

LEARNING OBJECTIVES

After reading this chapter you should know:

- ☐ The nature, definition, and types of positive deviance.
- ☐ The functions of positive deviance.
- ☐ The process of discovery.
- ☐ The resources essential for creative activity.
- ☐ The basic values held by scientists and scholars.
- ☐ The characteristics of the scientific elite.
- ☐ Social conditions that produce innovation and creativity.

Introduction

Behaviors usually considered deviant—criminal involvement, substance abuse, and mental disorder and self-destruction—have negative consequences for us as well as for others. Innovations, creative achievement, and altruism, however, are exceptional or deviant behaviors that often result in a common good. Appreciation for innovative, creative, or altruistic works is not always immediate; it is often delayed beyond the life of the positive deviant. Breakthroughs in medical science (e.g., Salk's discovery of the polio vaccine or advances in treatment of remedies for heart attack and stroke victims), have an immediate impact on people's lives and are seen as positive. Innovations in entertainment and personal adornment (e.g., video games, unrestricted access to the Internet, body piercing and tattooing among the young), however, may not be universally viewed as positive.

Positive Deviance

Most of what we know about deviant behavior is derived from analyses of its negative forms. We know much about harmful behaviors to others and to ourselves, about mental aberrations and atypical sexual practices. Positive deviance, however, receives scant attention. Yet, positive deviance in the form of innovation, creativity, and acts of extreme altruism energize the social and cultural environment. To thrive, societies must foster creative problem solving or risk decline and possible extinction.

> *"Problems cannot be solved at the same level of awareness that created them."*
>
> —Albert Einstein (posted at www.therightside.demon.co.uk/quotes/einstein/ae5.htm)

> *"We can do no great things; only small things with great love."*
>
> —Mother Teresa (posted at http://home.comcast.net/~motherteresasite/quotes.html)

Definition

Typically, when we think about deviant behavior, visions of negative behaviors (e.g., crime and destruction, harm and disorder, aberrations and pathologies) come to mind. The deviant behavior of others evokes fear, disgust, avoidance, but rarely admiration and the desire to emulate it. We do not consciously try to socialize our children to harm others, to be mentally ill or self-destructive, to be addicted or to be sexually perverse. Nor do we intentionally encourage others to engage in deviant behaviors. Not only is deviance problematic in others, it is in us as well. The consequences of our deviant acts harm us as well as those around us. All in all, there seems little to recommend involvement in behaviors that are violations of commonly held social norms or judged by others to be unacceptable, particularly those with whom we interact on an everyday basis.

Can deviant behavior be positive? Positive deviance is often viewed as an oxymoron, a contradiction in terms that detracts attention from the explanation and prediction of negative forms of deviance, or a concept that contributes nothing to our understanding of deviant behavior (Best and Luckenbill 1991; Goode 1991; Sagarin 1985). Yet other sociologists contend that consideration of positive deviance clarifies theorizing on the nature and consequences of deviant behavior (Ben-Yehuda 1990). **Positive deviance** embodies many definitions: behaviors that exceed normative standards in a positive way—that is, innovative, virtuous, or altruistic behaviors (Winslow 1970).

Positive deviance may also be considered from a labeling or social reaction perspective. Behaviors that are judged to contribute significantly to a highly prized cultural value (e.g., patriotism, entrepreneurism, athletic prowess in the extreme) may be deviant (Norland et al. 1976; Scarpitti and McFarlance 1975). Single highly regarded acts can also be viewed as constituting positive deviance. The discovery of the North Pole, the climbing of a previously unscaled mountain, or the sailing across the Atlantic in an open boat are all positive acts of daring and accomplishment that may inspire others.

Five types of positive deviance are proposed: **altruism, charisma, innovation, supra-conformity,** and **innate characteristics** (Heckert 2000). Altruism refers to acts of self-sacrifice that are intended to benefit others without the expectation of extrinsic reward. Charisma is a characteristic of persons with extraordinary ability to inspire others to follow their lead. Charismatic leadership is premised on the intention of the leader to draw others to his or her teachings and example (e.g., Gandhi and Jesus Christ) and the desire of others to place their faith and trust in the charismatic leader. Charismatic leadership need not be positive, of course, as in the case of Adolph Hitler or David Koresh of the Branch Davidian compound near Waco, Texas; Jim Jones, leader of the Jonestown mass suicide; or Marshall Applewhite, the leader of the Heaven's Gate mass suicide in California.

Highly innovative persons may also be positive deviants. Persons who are able to put existing things or ideas together in new and imaginative ways that have the potential to benefit others are rare in society. Scientific discoverers, literary and artistic masters, and inventors are examples of persons whose innovative abilities set them apart from the mainstream in a positive way. Supra-conformity constitutes a form of positive deviance that results from the adherence to certain societal norms to the extreme. Norms may function on two levels: the ideal—while perhaps preferred, is exceedingly difficult to accomplish, and the real—well within the ability of the majority of people to achieve. The behavior of the supra-conforming positive deviant complies in an ideal way with the requirements of particular social norms. For example, ideally we should be honest in our dealings with others and should tell the truth. However, to always be honest and truthful may be harmful to others, as in the case when a person is asked his or her opinion about someone's new clothes or choice of boyfriend or girlfriend. A more realistic interpretation of the norm of honesty may be less deviant than its strict adherence.

Finally, persons with innate characteristics that are culturally valued, such as exceptional good looks, intelligence, athletic or musical ability, may be viewed as positive deviants. Certainly there are subcultural variations as to what consti-

Sho Yano, age 12, is currently a student at the University of Chicago in the combined M.D./Ph.D. program. He started college at age 9 and graduated in three years (Summa Cum Laude) from Loyola University in Chicago.

tutes beauty or intelligence or useful talents. It may be that physical prowess or seductiveness, being streetwise, and having the ability to make a living from a variety of criminal enterprises are more positively valued by members of an oppositional subculture.

Functions

Beyond its obvious contributions, positive deviance serves important social functions. First, the many forms of positive deviance provide for cultural change. Unless societies actively seek solutions to the problems posed by their physical and cultural environment, they will soon regress and face extinction. Second, positive deviance ensures that cultural change proceeds in a beneficial way. Cultural change may be either adaptive or maladaptive. That is, it may generate solutions to societal problems or it may exacerbate those problems. By providing innovative and creative solutions to urgent as well as everyday problems, positive deviance enhances social well-being. Third, widely recognized positive deviance provides a basis for defining other behaviors as less positive or negatively deviant. It is only when we define exceptionally positive behavior that we can define behaviors that are not in the interest of society, those that threaten the functioning of the society as a whole and the well-being of its individual members. Fourth, the acclaim that society provides for its exemplary members encourages others to engage in positive deviance, which in turn increases the problem-solving ability of that society. In short, positive deviance serves the function of perpetuating itself. (See Heckert 2000; Norland et al. 1976; Scarpitti and MacFarlane 1975.)

Creative Process

Robert Sternberg and Todd Lubart (1995) argue that creativity is not innate but can be developed. They propose a process by which individuals can enhance their creativity:

1. *Redefine problems. Don't accept what you've been told about how to think or act.* This step involves the questioning of basic assumptions about the nature of a problem or the possibilities for its solution.

2. *Look for what others don't see.* Put things together in ways that others don't and think about how past experiences, even ones that may initially seem irrelevant, can play a part in your creative endeavors. To be creative it is necessary to interpret environmental clues in ways that others have not. Creative people are not only able to see what others see, but to perceive what could be there.

3. *Learn to distinguish your good from your poor ideas and pay attention to their potential contribution.* The ability to separate ideas that have a potential for making a meaningful scientific or artistic contribution from those that are trivial or marginally important significantly relates to the creative process. Time and energy is not wasted going down paths that lead nowhere.

4. *Don't feel that you have to know everything about the domain in which you work before you are able to make a creative contribution.* Often innovative ideas come

from persons who are not "the" expert in a given field but from a younger member of a research team or someone from another discipline who has recently changed a field of study.

5. *Cultivate a legislative, global style.* Creativity depends, in part, on the desire to explore alternatives to the ways things are traditionally done. The creative process is also enhanced by the ability to think on a global level, beyond the mundane problems faced locally.

6. *Persevere in the face of obstacles, take sensible risks, and be willing to grow.* Obstacles to the creative enterprise are inevitable, so too is failure. Creative persons are able to pursue their goal despite the obstacles that come along.

7. *Discover and tap into your intrinsic motivations.* Creative persons are far more apt to be driven by internal rather than external rewards. That is, involvement in the creative process is its own reward. The possible benefits granted by others are of less concern to a creative person.

8. *Find or create environments that reward you for what you like to do.* The working conditions of a creative person may either enhance or impede the creative process. When imaginative thinking is discouraged or penalized, innovation and creativity are most unusual.

9. *Resources needed for creativity are interactive, not additive.* Individual resources (e.g., intelligence, internal motivation, persistence and so on) must be present for the creative process to be successful. In addition, an environment that is conducive to creativity is an important element in the process.

10. *Make a decision about a way of life that fosters creativity.* The willingness to redefine a problem or discard assumptions about its solvability is essential to creativity. Creativity involves a conscious decision to look at ideas and things differently.

The Processes of Discovery

Robert Root-Bernstein (1999: 559) defines **discovery** as "the finding of something unexpected. . . . discoveries change not only the extent of what is known but also how we think about it. Discoveries, in short, cause us to rethink and restructure knowledge and the actions we derive from it." To Robert Root-Bernstein (1999: 560) discovery is not the consequence of a single act of inspiration but the result of a process—a series of interlinked steps. This series of interlinked steps include: (1) the recognition of a problem, (2) the collection of relevant information, (3) the formulation of hypotheses to explain and predict outcomes, (4) the testing of hypotheses, and (5) the verification of the findings. Most often the findings either do not support the hypotheses as stated or provide little or no support. Therefore, the hypotheses must be reformulated and the process begun again. In the event that the findings support the hypotheses, the next step is to convince the scientific community and larger society of the merits of the findings that in fact the findings are to be trusted and acted upon.

Robert Root-Bernstein (1999) provides analyses of six key issues about the processes of discovery: who discovers, what is discovered, when discoveries are made, where discoveries are made, why discoveries are made, and how discoveries are made.

Who Discovers. Discoveries tend to be made by single persons rather than groups of researchers, "think-tanks," or corporations. The distinguishing characteristics of persons who make significant discoveries are: (1) mentoring by an accomplished scientist or scholar (e.g., Nobel Prize winner or highly innovative researcher), (2) intense involvement in creative hobbies or leisure pursuits (e.g., poetry, painting, music, sculpture), (3) age—younger persons are more apt to make significant discoveries than are older researchers or scholars. The peak age for mathematicians is 25; for physicists, 30; for chemists, 35; and for biologists in the early forties. Notable discoveries are made by two groups of researchers: those that make a single discovery only (e.g., Jonas Salk, the polio vaccine and James Crick and Francis Watson, the structure of DNA [deoxyribonucleic acid]), and those who are extremely productive throughout their lifetimes (e.g., Thomas Edison was granted 1,093 patents, and Linus Pauling, who contributed significantly to our understanding of chemical bonding, protein structure, and the effects of Vitamin C). Amateur scientists (e.g., Charles Darwin, Jane Goodall) also provide discoveries far greater than their academically trained peers.

What Is Discovered. We tend to think that what is discovered is a solution to a problem. Certainly James Watson and Francis Crick worked on an existing problem—the structure of DNA—that stumped their fellow scientists. Their discovery was, in large part, made possible by the efforts of other geneticists and technicians who provided the groundwork and analytical equipment necessary to solve the problem. However, much of discovery involves the finding of a new problem or a redefinition of an existing one. Not posing the "right" question can never result in a significant discovery.

Mother Teresa of Calcutta—winner of the Nobel Peace Prize.

Albert Einstein

"With just a pen and paper, he peeked further behind Nature's curtain than any one had since Newton—then spent the rest of his years living it down. Now when we think of genius we see his face."

"Everything's relative. Speed, mass, space, and time are all subjective. Nor are age, motion, or the wanderings of the planets measures that humans can agree on any more; they can be judged only by the whim of the observer. Light has weight. Space has curves. And coiled within a pound of matter, any matter, is the explosive power of 14 tons of TNT. We know all this . . . because of Albert Einstein."

In 1905, Einstein, a 26-year-old Swiss patent clerk, submitted three papers to *Annalen der Physik,* a leading journal in physics. His three papers on theoretical physics, published in the same issue of the journal, immediately revolutionized the way physicists viewed the world—everything became relative. He refined his ideas over the next eleven years and in 1916 proposed his general theory of relativity, verified some three years later. To Einstein: "Light had mass, and space and time were simply space-time." The profundity of his thought is sometimes lost in the simplicity of its expression. $E = mc^2$ is widely known, but few understand the depth of the mystery it unravels.

Einstein won the 1922 Nobel Prize in Physics and by 1935 he joined the faculty at Princeton University. His requirements were simply: "A desk, some pads and a pencil, and a large wastebasket—to hold all of my mistakes." Einstein was to live out his life on the campus thinking the theories of quantum physics, helping children with their homework, and more than occasionally forgetting his address. (*Source:* www.time.com/time/time100/scientist/profile/einstein02.htlm.)

Discoverers then are able to perceive dimensions of an existing problem that others do not and thereby recast the research question that will lead to a previously unanticipated solution. Or, discoverers may pose a previously unrecognized question resulting in an equally surprising solution.

When Discoveries Are Made. Significant discoveries are usually made within the first five to ten years of a scientist's career. For the most part, an individual will make a single discovery, but will be unable to make a second discovery without changing scientific fields. For most discoverers the creative process must begin again for any one person to arrive at a recognized "breakthrough" in science. Changing one's field of inquiry is one way to rejuvenate creative energy.

Curiously enough only about a third of discoveries are the result of the dogged determination of the scientist. The image of the "mad scientist" working day and night until the problem is solved does not accurately reflect the process of discovery employed by most acclaimed scientists. Rather, about a third of the time the scientific breakthroughs occur when the discoverer has stopped working on the problem and has focused attention on other questions. And, the final third

Francis Crick (left) and James Watson (right) won the
Nobel Prize for their collective discovery of the structure
of deoxyribonucleic acid (DNA).

of the discoveries are made when the scientist is not working at all but relaxing, playing, or even sleeping.

The prevailing social and cultural climate also influences the creative processes and prevalence of discoveries. Discoveries are more common during times of economic prosperity and the confluence of cultural and intellectual resources. Growing economies provide the assets and time necessary to engage in scientific inquiry. The coming together of culturally diverse perspectives and intellectual traditions extends the boundaries of scientific inquiry. By looking at problems from unfamiliar vantage points, the creative person is energized, the creative process is reshaped, and the chance of making a discovery is enhanced.

Where Discoveries Are Made.   To Thomas Kuhn (cited in Root-Bernstein 1999), science may be divided into normal and revolutionary. Normal science is conducted within the parameters of carefully constructed theoretical formulations, well-defined conceptualized problems, and standard methods of empirical analysis. Normal science constitutes much of the work that is conducted in our major research universities and laboratories. Revolutionary science, however, seeks to redefine the problems that science is intended to address, questions the theoretical paradigms that guide "normal" scientific inquiry, and proposes alternative strategies for analysis. An additional form of science—"new science"—has been added to Kuhn's typology. New science refers to the development of entirely new fields of study. For example, radiology, immunology, and genetic engineering emerged in the latter part of the twentieth century.

Scientific discoveries tend to emanate from the nontraditional centers of research. Ironically, creativity is enhanced in settings that do not carry out large mainstream research projects that are typically dependent on federal funding.

AT A GLANCE

- The United States has won 231 Nobel Prizes, outright or shared, including the most for Physiology or Medicine (74), Physics (62), Chemistry (43), Peace (18), and Economics (23). France has won the most for Literature, with 12.
- There are over six million patents in the United States alone and tens of millions in other countries. Almost three million U.S. patents have been issued since 1975.
- The Library of Congress is the largest library in the world, with nearly 119 million items on approximately 530 miles of bookshelves. The collections include some 18 million books, 2 million recordings, 12 million photographs, 4 million maps, and 53 million manuscripts. The Library receives some 22,000 items each working day and adds approximately 10,000 items to the collections daily. The majority of the collections are received through the copyright registration process, as the Library is home to the U.S. Copyright Office.

Sources: Guiness Book of Records, 1998. http://www.britannica.com/eb/article?eu=60174. Library of Congress http://www.loc.gov/about.

Rather, many important breakthroughs are made in less prestigious institutions where more innovative researchers are free to carry out "revolutionary" science. New science also emerges in institutional settings at the periphery of the mainstream scientific community.

Why Discoveries Are Made. Robert Root-Bernstein (1999: 567) notes that discoverers are motivated by "control, curiosity, necessity, serendipity, or aesthetics." Creative people, for the most part, want to be in control of their lives, free to exercise their curiosity and pursue their own goals. Dreaded diseases, for example, polio or smallpox, have motivated scientists to discover vaccines to eradicate them. Serendipity—making a discovery when looking for something else—accounts for about half of all scientific breakthroughs. Surprising discoveries, while not rare in science, are nonetheless a consequence of a process of orderly inquiry. Finally, discoverers are often driven to search for the aesthetic in science or in the arts and literature.

How Discoveries Are Made. While simple "how to" recommendations for making a discovery are not realistic, certain strategies tend to increase its possibility. First, focus on fundamental questions within a field of inquiry. Incongruities between theories and observations, gaps in our basic knowledge about a given scientific field, or inconsistencies in research findings may point to the kinds of basic issues that lead to important discoveries.

The discoverers' attention to basic issues within a field of inquiry is related to their willingness to repeatedly fail. Discovery often comes unexpectedly after a series of failures, mistakes in judgement and focus, and simply asking the wrong questions. Building on the errors of others and extrapolating from discoveries in related areas are also important strategies for making a significant discovery. An awareness and understanding of failures as well as the successes of others greatly enhance the creative process.

Characteristics of Positive Deviants

Robert Sternberg and Todd Lubart (1995) note six individual resources that are essential for creative activity: intelligence, knowledge, thinking styles, personality, motivation, and environmental context. Related to intelligence is the ability to be synthetic, analytic, and practical. Synthetic refers to the ability to view the problem or recast it in a wholly different way. This synthesis of information allows the person to view problems and challenges from a unique perspective. Analytic ability is key in making information understandable and in assessing the relative merits of the findings. Practical intelligence is the ability to present the idea or innovation to others in an understandable and appealing manner.

Knowledge refers to the awareness of the state of one's field of endeavor—what are the assumptions, the generally accepted information, and parameters for the advancement of the field? With this base of knowledge the creative person can begin to improvise alternative strategies for assessing key problems and their solutions. Thinking styles refers to the ways in which individuals use their intelligence and knowledge. Unconventional thinking styles—questioning the prevailing order and understandings—are characteristic of creative persons. Typically, the total personality of the person is involved in the creative process. Much of the self is invested in the attempt to innovate or discover something new. "Durus epidermis"—a thick skin—is extremely helpful for creative persons to be able to withstand attempts to discredit them and the fruits of their innovative work. Motivation is intrinsic, highly charged, and persistent. Creative people are undaunted in their pursuit of their goal, undeterred by obstacles and personal affronts. Environmental context may foster the creative process or impede it. The expression of ideas and the desire to engage in exploratory projects may be either encouraged or condemned. Creativity in stifling environments is most unusual (Sternberg and Lubart 1995).

In Kenneth Hardy's (1974) study of the social origins of U.S. scientists and scholars, he isolates seven basic values espoused by highly productive scientists and scholars that distinguish them from their unproductive peers. These values are: (1) naturalism; (2) intrinsic valuation of learning, knowledge; (3) dignity of man; (4) personal dedication; (5) egalitarianism; (6) antitraditional orientation; and (7) being centered on near future. Table 14.1 provides a comparison of the basic values of productive and unproductive scientists and scholars.

As Table 14.1 shows, the worldview of highly productive scholars differs markedly from that of their less accomplished colleagues. Highly productive

Table 14.1 Cultural Values Associated with High or Low Production
of Scholars and Scientists

High Productivity	Low Productivity
Naturalism. Belief in a world of order, law, pattern, meaning	*World is unknowable, incomprehensible.* Events are capricious, mysterious, whimsical.
Intrinsic valuation of learning, knowledge. To be learned, wise, is highly valued. Broad conception of valued learning.	*Suspicion of learning, education.* Constricted view of valued learning. Anti-intellectual.
Dignity of man. Optimism concerning man's ability to discover truth, accomplish things, change the world	*Disparagement of man.* Man is powerless, at the mercy of fate, destiny, luck, chance. He is evil, incompetent.
Personal dedication. Seriousness of purpose, sense of mission, positive mysticism. Long-range striving. Responsibility beyond family.	*Sense of indirection.* Must take, enjoy what is available now. Loyalty to family, kin.
Egalitarianism. Active promotion of causes to improve status of disadvantaged. High status for women, children. Pacifism.	*Authoritarianism.* Reliance on authority. Power relations important. Patriarchal order; male dominance. Aggressiveness, militarism.
Anti-traditional orientation. Not satisfied with established ways of doing things. Restless, inquiring spirit.	*Traditional.* Past is respected, romanticized. Filial piety valued.
Being centered on near future. Concerned with this world. Orientation toward the foreseeable future.	*Centered on present and distant future.* Hope for a better break in the distant future, the next life.

Source: Reprinted with permission from Hardy, K.R., *Science* 185: 497–506 (1974). Copyright 1974 AAAS.

scholars tend to believe in naturalism—the view that the world is orderly and that empirical events form discernible patterns. This belief leads to an *intrinsic valuation of learning and knowledge.* Learning what is known and engaging in the discovery of what is not known stands among the most honorable of human pursuits. The value attached to learning and discovery is closely aligned with the belief in the *dignity of man.* The intrinsic worth of human beings prompts the desire to change things in the world that diminish the human condition. Highly productive scholars are driven by *personal dedication* to accomplish as much as possible in their lifetimes. Typically, other goals—leisure, material, power—are set aside to pursue their life's passion. It is by advancing our understanding of the world and the ways in which things work that a more just society can be realized. *Egalitarianism*—the value of providing all persons with the advantages gained by scientific advances—is highly valued among accomplished scholars. The willingness to disrupt the status quo, or *antitraditionalism,* is also commonly valued among elite scholars. They want to change the world in which they live. *Being centered on the near future* rather than distancing themselves from their social environment ensures that the results of their labors will benefit their world. Taken together these values focus the attention of scientists and scholars on the natural order of the world, the intrinsic worth of human beings, and the significance of creativity in the pursuit of knowledge that will benefit others in the here and now (Hardy 1974).

Social Characteristics of Discoverers and Creative Persons

Certain social characteristics set persons who make significant scientific discoveries or who are recognized for their creativity apart from others. Harriet Zuckerman's (1997) in-depth investigation of 93 Nobel laureates in science shows that much of the success experienced by the Nobel laureates is the result of the "accumulation of the advantage in science." Advantage in science "accumulates when certain individuals or groups repeatedly receive resources and rewards that enrich the recipients at an accelerating rate and conversely impoverish (relatively) the nonrecipients" (Zuckerman 1997: 59–60). There are certain prerequisites for acquiring an "advantage in science." Zuckerman notes that the socioeconomic status of the person's family of origin, religious background, and prestige colleges and universities attended combine to provide social advantages that facilitate entrance into the community of scientific elites.

With regard to the Nobel laureates' families of origin, Zuckerman finds that 82 percent of their fathers are professionals, managers, or proprietors, compared to 11 percent in the U.S. population; persons from a Jewish background are disproportionately found among Nobel laureates. This is true for prizewinners from the United States and the world at large. That is, while Jews constitute about 3 percent of the U.S. population, they account for 27 percent of the U.S. Nobel prizewinners. This compares with 72 percent of U.S. Nobel laureates who come from 66 percent of the overall population with Protestant backgrounds, and 1 percent of the prizewinners are drawn from 25 percent of the Catholic families across the United States. Worldwide, 19 percent of the 286 Nobel laureates in Zuckerman's study are awarded to Jews—a distinctly disproportionate number compared to their percentage of the general population across the globe. In other words, Jews are vastly overrepresented and Catholics greatly underrepresented. In addition, Zuckerman observes that one in four Nobel laureates graduated from one of five Ivy League institutions: Columbia, Harvard, Yale, Cornell, and Dartmouth. Berkeley, MIT, Cal Tech, the University of Chicago, and the University of Illinois, account for an additional 24 percent of the Nobel Prize winners. That is, Zuckerman finds that ten U.S. colleges and universities produce about half of the Nobel laureates in science in the United States (Zuckerman 1997).

The advantages of social origin set in motion two processes—self-selection and social selection—that facilitate the "accumulation of the advantage in science." Self-selection refers to a process by which a student decides to seek admission to an elite university or college to study with a particularly eminent professor (preferably a Nobel laureate) in his or her chosen field. The desire to participate in the research of a Nobel prizewinner must be coupled with the willingness of the laureate to mentor the student. If the master–apprentice relation-

Renown theoretical physicist Stephen Hawking is the Lucasian Professor of Mathematics at Cambridge University, a chair formerly held by Issac Newton. Professor Hawking suffers from Amyotrophic Lateral Sclerosis, a life threatening degenerative illness and can only speak with the aid of a portable computer and a voice synthesizer. He is now working out in his mind a theory that unifies General Relativity with Quantum Mechanics—a theory that "explains everything" about the origins and workings of the universe.

ship is established, then the process of accumulating the advantages in science begins. Older Nobel laureates mentor over half of Nobel laureates in science from the United States. This mentoring relationship is even more common in Nobel laureates in Europe. This intense working relationship with an eminent scientist provides access to resources and the opportunity to become involved in an important and typically highly funded research project (Zuckerman 1997).

But equally important, the student is socialized into the scientifically elite community. The Nobel prizewinners in Zuckerman's study consistently report that the process of socialization into the scientific community is more important than the substantive information that their mentors pass on to them. The confidence they gain in their own abilities to creatively assess problems in science and to devise alternative approaches to their solution far surpass any technical knowledge gained from their mentors. Being effectively socialized into the scientific culture, being able to understand and accept the value of scientific inquiry with its uncompromising standards, and being able to immerse themselves in the scientific enterprise flow from being socialized by a member of the scientific elite (Zuckerman 1997).

The advantage of being mentored by an eminent scientist significantly affects the student's initial job placement. Almost all (93 percent) of the Nobel laureates in Zuckerman's study are university faculty members, and seven in ten begin their careers in an elite university, compared to 41 percent of their peers who are not mentored by as prominent scientists (Zuckerman 1997).

Explanations of Positive Deviance

Opportunity Theory

A disproportionate number of elite scientists and highly creative persons acquire considerable advantages from the status of their families and the opportunity to be educated in elite institutions. Families that socialize their children to value

James Watson and Francis Crick

"On February 28, 1953, Francis Crick walked into the Eagle Pub in Cambridge, England, and, as James Watson later recalled, announced that 'we had found the secret of life.' Actually, they had. That morning, Watson and Crick had figured out the structure of deoxyribonucleic acid, DNA. And that structure—'a double helix' can 'unzip' to make copies of itself—confirming suspicions that DNA carries life's hereditary information."

This profound discovery was the result of Watson and Crick's unwillingness to accept many of the prevailing ideas of the scientific community. To the American Watson, "A goodly number of scientists are not only narrow-minded and dull but also just stupid." The precocious Watson graduated from the University of Chicago at the age of 19 and earned a doctorate three years later. While twelve years older than Watson, Francis Crick, an Englishman, was less academically accomplished and far less driven to compete with his fellow scientists. Nonetheless, their harmonious working relationship allowed them to exchange ideas freely with one another and to maximize their unique strengths.

Other scientists, notably Rosalind Franklin and her colleague Maurice Wilkins, were also trying to discover the structure of DNA. However, friction between Franklin and Wilkins led to Wilkins' providing Watson and Crick with Franklin's best X-ray diffraction pictures of DNA. This information was key to Watson and Crick's ability to "crack the code" of DNA. While the work of Franklin was instrumental to Watson and Crick's discovery, she received little public recognition. Four years following the death of Rosalind Franklin, the Nobel Prize was awarded to Watson, Crick, and Wilkins.

Writing about Watson and Crick's monumental scientific breakthrough, psychologist Robert Wright notes: ". . . one truth seems likely to endure, universal and immutable. It emerges with equal clarity whether you examine the DNA molecule or the way in which it was revealed. The secret of life is complementarity." *Source:* www.time.com/time/time100/scientist/profile/watsoncrick.htlm

learning and encourage creativity and critical thinking immeasurably increase their potential for excellence.

Richard Cloward and Lloyd Ohlin's (1960) delinquent opportunity structure theory of negative deviance may be applied to innovative and creative forms of positive deviance. Opportunity structures (e.g., familial, educational and associational) facilitate innovation and creativity. Opportunity structures include a selection and recruitment process, socialization strategies for instilling essential values and norms of conduct, and an organizational structure that provides for increased access to resources and opportunities.

As mentioned earlier, being educated in elite colleges and universities by eminent scientists and scholars significantly enhances the students' opportunities to excel later in life. While it is possible to be innovative and creative apart from exceptional educational and socialization advantages, it is far less common. Many artists and writers, however, do develop their talents through personal experience, self-education, and dogged determination. They take advantage of informal opportunity structures, i.e., association with other artists and writers, that provide a testing ground for ideas and a source of encouragement and reward.

Both formal and informal opportunity structures enhance individual innovation and creativity. In a sense these opportunity structures serve to maximize the potential of individuals to deviate positively from their peers in science, literature or the arts. Just as the opportunity to become a car thief does not guarantee a successful career, positive opportunity structures can only provide the conditions that are more apt to lead to high achievement.

Social Integration

Innovation, creativity, and exceptional altruism are unusual under conditions of high social integration. When individuals are tightly bound into conventional society, when they accept without question the cultural scripts for living—what is important, what to do, and how to do it—there is little need or motivation to innovate, create, or deviate from what is considered "right." Change is viewed as threatening to the social order; the individual who advocates change is either punished or ostracized.

However, under conditions of low integration—when values are less commonly held or individuals challenge the existing social and cultural order—innovation, creativity, and unconventional positive behaviors are more likely. Positive deviance is also more probable when anomic conditions are prevalent. When societies are undergoing rapid change, when the social order is threatened by economic turmoil or cultural upheaval, innovative and creative solutions to problems are more necessary and become more highly valued. When the stock market plummets or soars to unprecedented heights, when urban rioting and racial strife abound, when standards for sexual conduct or drug use are questioned, social creativity and innovation are more common.

To Robert Merton (1968), individuals resort to innovation when institutionalized means for achieving culturally approved goals are not available or are unworkable for them. When institutionalized means typically do not lead to culturally approved goals, when graduating from college does not result in a job with considerable opportunity for advancement, society is said to be in a state of anomie. Considerable stress and tension is experienced as members of society struggle to realize those goals particularly valued in their culture. Alternative strategies for achieving the goals of money, material goods, status, or power are sought. Innovative means are developed, tested, refined, and put into practice. As innovative strategies become more effective and are socially accepted, they may become institutionalized, a new conventional order is created.

Similarly, Robert Agnew (1992) argues that when an individual's social interactions do not benefit him or her, or when others block that person's attempts to gain certain goals, negative emotions, anger, rage, self-deprecation, and loss of self-esteem may follow. These negative emotions create considerable strain for the individual that must be alleviated. Often attempts to lessen strain—"to blow off stream"—involve negative behaviors, verbal or physical aggression, or self-inflicted harm. However, strain may also trigger more creative ways to resolve the problem. The person is forced to alter the existing conflictual situation by developing new ways to deal with it or by exploring alternative ways to achieve desired goals.

High social integration tends to lessen creative and innovative thinking. Conventional ways of conducting everyday life are widely accepted and stringently defended. Travis Hirschi (1969) contends that when the bonds that tie an individual to society are very strong, that person is less likely to engage in negatively defined deviance. The greater the involvement in conventional society and acceptance of the prevailing value structure, the less the desire to deviate from deeply held norms and beliefs. Similarly, individuals who are tightly bound into conventional society are considerably less prone to engage in positive deviance, less likely to find the need for innovation and creativity. Why disrupt things that seem to be working just fine for them? There is little room for social or cultural change. Under conditions of tightly meshed values and behavior, innovation and creativity are deemed unnecessary, more often threatening to the social order, and subject to control and eradication. When positive forms of deviance are widely condemned, social stagnation ensues.

Conflict

Conflict at both the micro and macro levels of sociological analysis is recognized as a source of cultural and interpersonal change. Where there is widespread discontent and violence, when urban areas erupt in riots, when citizens take to the streets to protest governmental policy or threatening social conditions, a signal for change is made publicly manifest. Likewise, when relations between two or more persons become so contentious that they are no longer able to resolve their conflicts peacefully, when communication deteriorates into verbal abuse and accusation, when physical violence is either threatened or actually carried out, change is necessary to avoid irreversible destruction. Rolf Dahrendorf (1959) and Lewis Coser (1967) argue that social conflict does function to bring about cultural change. Conflict between social groups and between large segments of society and national and local governments generates strain on the existing social order. Similarly, at the individual level, interpersonal relations marked by chronic conflict are stressful for all parties involved—wives and husbands, their children, and friends—and often threaten the health of the combatants and others near them, their relations with others outside the conflictual relationship (e.g., co-workers, neighbors, and so on), and their social and legal status in the community. Unless conflict leads to change either at the societal or individual level that positively resolves the dispute, negative outcomes may well follow. Violence and destruction are common. Strife becomes institutionalized and is transmitted from one generation to the next as in the case of Protestants and Catholics in Northern

Explanations of Positive Deviance

Theories and Theorists	Sociological Predictors	Hypotheses
Social Integration and Control		
• **Durkheim**	Social Integration	The greater the social integration, the less the involvement in positive forms of deviance (e.g., innovation and creativity).
• **Merton**	Anomie	The more anomic social life becomes, the greater the involvement in positive forms of deviance (e.g., innovation and creativity).
• **Hirschi**	Attachment	The weaker the attachment to conventional society, the more likely positive forms of deviance (e.g., innovation and creativity) will occur.
	Commitment	The weaker the commitment to conventional society, the more likely positive forms of deviance (e.g., innovation and creativity) will occur.
	Involvement	The greater the involvement in conventional activities, the less likely positive forms of deviance (e.g., innovation and creativity) will occur.
	Belief	The stronger the belief in conventional values and norms, the less likely positive forms of deviance (e.g., innovation and creativity) will occur.
• **Agnew**	Strain	The more strained social relationships become, the more likely positive forms of deviance (e.g., innovation and creativity) will occur.
Societal Reaction		
• **Becker**	Societal Reaction	The more affirmative the societal reaction to positive forms of deviance, the more likely those forms of behavior will continue.
Social Conflict		
• **Coser**	Conflict	The greater the conflict in society, the greater the need for social change. The greater the need for social change, the greater the likelihood of positive deviance (e.g., innovation and creativity).
Opportunity and Cultural Supports		
• **Cloward and Ohlin**	Opportunity	The greater the access to opportunities for positive forms of deviance, the more likely will innovation and creativity occur.

Ireland or the legendary Hatfields and McCoys. This cultural transmission of fundamental conflict between nations or social and cultural groups is acquired through the socialization process of children as they learn about their heritage and what is right and wrong, good and bad, prized and condemned and is mindlessly played out in everyday life.

Responses to conflict may be negative or positive. That is, conflict at the societal, group, or individual level may generate violent or other destructive outcomes, or it may spark innovation or creativity. Innovative ways of resolving complex sociopolitical conflicts may be devised. Technological or medical advances may result from the demand to protect oneself from harm at the hand of an enemy or outbreak of disease or other threats to physical or mental health. Such innovations may find widespread support and encouragement.

Alex Thio's (1978) power theory, while intended to account for negative deviance, may be applied to positive deviance as well. Thio argues that the powerless, those with few economic or political advantages, do not have access to professional organizations, governmental agencies or representatives, or other influential groups. As a consequence, outlets for their innovative or creative ideas are limited. Departure from normative behavior, positive as well as negative, by the powerless tends to be discouraged. Deviations from acceptable modes for conduct may be viewed by the powerful as threatening and, therefore, negatively defined. To Thio, then, the powerless are more apt to engage in high consensus deviant behavior. Innovations and creativity among the powerless tend to be ignored or deliberately blocked from public expression.

However, the powerful tend to be economically, politically, and socially in a position to have their creative or innovative ideas and products recognized positively. The powerful have the educational and professional opportunities to develop their potential for creativity. As we have seen, prominent scientific, literary, and artistic persons typically have access to social institutions (e.g., universities, "think tanks," and professional organizations) that provide the facilities and financial resources necessary to carry out creative and innovative work. Perhaps more of the creative capital of the powerful concerns their contribution to economic gain. Product development and innovation, marketing and advertising, investment and management of financial resources are paramount concerns of corporations and smaller scale business enterprises. To survive in an expanding free market economy, businesses must continually be ahead of their competition. Innovation and creativity is highly valued, rewarded, and compensated, particularly in the United States.

Societal Reaction

A central tenet of societal reaction or labeling formulations of deviant behavior is: an individual's behavior will tend to be consistent with the reaction of others or the "label" that is attached to it. Becker (1963) notes that the deviant is one to whom the label has been successfully applied. By successful application, he means that the person has accepted the label that he or she has defined himself or herself in the same way that others do.

The dynamics of societal reaction or labeling are the same whether they are applied to negative or positive behaviors. For example, if a child is defined by a schoolteacher as bright and creative, then that child is more likely to be inquisitive, to want to explore new things, to be confident in expressing ideas and perceptions. Societal reaction or labeling plays a large part in socializing persons to be innovative and creative. Montessori schools are intentionally designed to encourage discovery and creative expression in children. The rigid curricula of traditional schools are replaced by a flexible method of instruction that maximizes the student's control over the educational process.

However, institutional arrangements for the socialization of children (e.g., familial, daycare, afterschool programs) tend to value conforming behavior. The more compliant children are, the easier it is for their guardians to care for them, their teachers to teach them, and their neighbors to accept them. In time they fit well into organized work settings and carry out functions in an orderly and predictable manner. Their contribution is not to deviate, either negatively or positively, but to ritualistically perform those tasks that have been assigned to them. In a sense they hold society together, but they do not advance it. The innovators, whose ideas and actions deviate from mainstream thought, are permitted to engage in unconventional activities early in life, defined positively for doing so, and consistently rewarded for their efforts.

Chapter Summary

- Positive deviance includes those behaviors that exceed normative standards in a positive way. These behaviors include:
    - Innovation—the ability to put existing things or ideas together in a new or imaginative way that has the potential to benefit society.
    - Altruism—acts of self-sacrifice.
    - Charisma—extraordinary leadership.
    - Supra-conformity—adherence to certain societal norms to the extreme.
    - Innate characteristics—culturally valued characteristics of beauty, intelligence, or talent.

- Positive deviance serves important social functions:
    - Provides for cultural change.
    - Ensures that cultural change proceeds in a beneficial way.

- Positive deviance (i.e., creativity and innovation) is not innate, but can be developed.

- The process of discovery involves six key issues: who discovers, what is discovered, when discoveries are made, where discoveries are made, why discoveries are made, and how discoveries are made. For example:
    - Discoveries tend to be made by single persons rather than groups of people.
    - Discovery involves the finding of a new problem or a redefinition of an existing one.
    - Discoveries are usually made when a researcher has stopped working on the problem.

- ○ Discoveries tend to emanate from nontraditional centers of research.
- ○ Discovers are motivated by control, curiosity, necessity, serendipity, and aesthetics.
- ○ Discovery often comes unexpectedly after a series of failures, mistakes in judgement and focus, and simply asking the wrong questions.
- Intelligence, knowledge, thinking styles, personality, motivation, and environmental context are six individual resources essential for creative activity.
- In addition, naturalism, intrinsic valuation of learning and knowledge, dignity of man, personal dedication, egalitarianism, anti-traditional orientation, and centeredness on the near future are seven basic values held by highly productive scientists and scholars.
- According to one study, socioeconomic status, family of origin, religious background, and attending a prestigious college or university combine to provide the social advantages that facilitate entrance into the community of scientific elites. For example:
  - ○ Jews are overrepresented and Catholics are underrepresented among the scientific elite.
  - ○ One in four future Nobel laureates graduates from one of five Ivy League institutions.
  - ○ Over half of the Nobel laureates in the United States are mentored by an older Nobel laureate.

Key Concepts

Positive deviance: Behaviors that exceed normative standards in a positive way; behaviors that are judged to contribute significantly to a highly prized cultural value.

Altruism: Acts of self-sacrifice that are intended to benefit others without the expectation of extrinsic reward.

Charisma: A characteristic of persons with an extraordinary ability to inspire others to follow their lead.

Innovation: The ability to put existing things or ideas together in new and imaginative ways that have the potential to benefit others.

Supra-conformity: Adherence to certain societal norms to the extreme.

Innate characteristics: Acquired characteristics such as exceptional good looks, intelligence, athletic, or musical ability.

Discovery: The finding of something unexpected.

Critical Thinking Questions

1. Imagine that you want to socialize a child to become a positive deviant. You may want her or him to become a remarkably altruistic or to be a renowned writer, artist, or scientist. What would you consciously need to do to maxi-

mize the chances of your child's becoming a truly positive deviant? What would you do to minimize the likelihood of her or his becoming a positive deviant?

2. What sociocultural conditions must be present to ensure that a sufficient number of positive deviants—altruistic and creative persons—are generated to serve the interests of the larger society?

3. Can involvement in positive deviance be scientifically predicted? If so, what are the key macro- and micro-level variables that increase the likelihood of positively deviant behavior?

4. Consider a society in which positive deviance is not present. Altruism is unknown, innovation and creativity are shunned. How would you describe the everyday lives of members of this society, their emotional and psychological well-being, and the ways that they commonly interact with one another?

Web Extra

Check out this website for additional information on positive deviance:

http://www.positivedeviance.org

CHAPTER 15

Extreme Forms of Everyday Behaviors: Exercising, Working, and Web Surfing

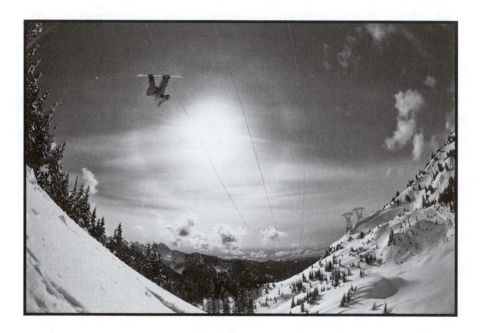

P O R T R A I T S

of Extreme Forms of Behavior

WORKAHOLISM

- "I was wildly successful in my career, a very effective worker, and my employers loved me. But outside of work . . . well, there is no outside of work. I never thought I had a problem until I tried to get into a close relationship, for something like the fifth time. That was my wake-up call, and it probably helped that my partner was in his own 12-step recovery for another addiction at the time. . . . He was getting better and I realized I had my own addiction—to adrenaline." (*Sources:* WebMD Feature, "Workaholism: The 'Respectable' Addiction," posted at: http://aolsvc.health.wemd.aol.com/content/Article/36/1728_57274.htm?printing=true)

COMPUTER ADDICTION

- Luci spent ten or more hours every day on the Web. She enjoyed playing games, chatting, gambling, and having fantasy sex. Most of all, the computer and Internet allowed her to escape the demands of her two small children, her housework, and her divorce. Her addiction to the computer led to the neglect of her children. Due to her excessive computer use, Luci lost custody of her children.

EXTREME SPORTS

- "Five . . . four . . . three . . . two . . . one . . . see ya! And Chance McGuire, 25, is airborne off a 650-ft. concrete dam in Northern California. In one second he falls 16 ft., in two sec- onds 63 ft., and after three seconds and 137 ft., he is flying at 65 mph. He prays that his parachute will open facing away from the dam, that his canopy won't collapse, that his toggles will be handy, and that no ill wind will slam him back into the cold concrete. The chute snaps open, the sound ricocheting through the gorge like a gunshot, and McGuire is soaring, carving S turns into the air, swooping over a winding creek. When he lands, he is a speck on a path along the creek. He hurriedly packs his chute and then, clearly audible above the rushing water, lets out a war whoop that rises past those mor- tals still perched on the dam, past the com- muters puttering by on the roadway, past even the hawks who circle the ravine. It is a cry of defiance, thanks and victory; he has survived another BASE jump."

- MARK WELLMAN, 39, MOUNTAINEER. "I don't remember much about the night I spent alone at Seven Gables in the John Muir Wilderness after falling 100 ft. I was hungry and cold. And I had no feeling in my legs. Since then I have been in this wheelchair, for seventeen years. At first I lay in the hospital for seven months, feeling sorry for myself. I couldn't see anything positive. Then I began climbing again with customized gear. I'm the first disabled person to climb the 3,000-ft. face of Yosemite's El Capitan and the first paraplegic to ski across the Sierra Nevada." (*Source: Time,* 154 (10), p. 28 September 6, 1999.)

LEARNING OBJECTIVES

After reading this chapter you should know:

☐ The nature, characteristics, and consequences of workaholism, computer addiction, and extreme sports.

☐ Gender differences in workaholism, computer addiction, and extreme sports participation.

☐ Explanations of workaholism, computer addiction, and extreme sports participation.

Introduction

Everyday behaviors—working, exercising, surfing the net—are not typically viewed as deviant. They are things we do routinely; we seldom take particular notice of them. While we are rarely conscious of the social norms that shape our everyday behaviors, they nonetheless guide even our routine actions. When we work incessantly, exercise or engage in extreme forms of athletic competition, or hack away on the computer day and night, our everyday behaviors take on deviant forms. In some instances these everyday behaviors practiced in the extreme may be viewed as positive. Persons who work far beyond what is required of them are often considered an asset to an organization; others who engage in extreme forms of competitive games or contests may be viewed as heroic, providing evidence of extraordinary human endurance and potential; and computer hackers may be perceived as able to develop innovative computer strategies that benefit others. Conversely, these same behaviors may have negative consequences not only for the actors but also for those closest to them and the society at large.

> *"Workaholism masquerades as a positive trait in the cultural lore of our nation"*
> (Fassel 1992).

> *"I have been a computer addict since I was 11. . . . I'm afraid that I will run away if my parents take my computer away. . . . it is almost like the computer owns me."*
> —14-year-old boy's email (Orzack, cited in Cronie 1999)

> *"People may think we are mad. We think they are insane to endure such humdrum lives."*
> —David Kirke, world's first bungee jumper (cited in Soden 2003:1)

In this chapter we will consider three extreme forms of everyday behavior: workaholism, computer addiction or webaholism, and ultra-competitions. While these behaviors are not typically considered in deviant behavior textbooks, it is important to understand how everyday behaviors are guided by social norms and supported by cultural values. Social norms provide a framework, albeit subtly, for our everyday behaviors. Cultural values reinforce social norms by defining the accepted meaning of our actions. When these boundaries are breached, our everyday behaviors take on a form of deviance that lies outside the realms of law, medicine, or religion. They are not crimes, illnesses, or sins, yet as extreme forms of everyday behavior they are of concern to us here.

The Nature of Overwork

In our increasingly fast-paced society, time is measured in nanoseconds, "**time deepening**"—doing multiple things simultaneously (e.g., walking on a treadmill, eating, watching TV, and talking on the telephone)—is commonly practiced (Robinson 1996). The Internet allows us to communicate instantly day and night anywhere across the globe, and 24/7 has become the prevailing way to describe the working lives of a significant segment of U.S. society. Yet working to excess is a relatively recent phenomenon. Workers in the United States now spend more hours on the job than any other advanced industrial nation (Lardner 1999). Judith Schor, the Harvard economist, in her book *The Overworked American* (1991), provides considerable evidence that Americans have added a month of work a year in the latter part of the twentieth century. In comparative terms, Americans on the average work two months a year longer than the average Western European. For example, in Norway and Sweden workers typically receive four to six weeks of vacation each year and as much as one year parental leave from their jobs (Lardner 1999). In France, it is illegal to work more than 35 hours in any given week (United Press International 1999).

Definition

Americans pride themselves on working hard. Hard work, thrift, and self-reliance are core values of U.S. culture, derived in large part from the Protestant work ethic. Yet, in the latter third of the twentieth century, Americans have increasingly compressed more work into less time, worked more hours or taken on second jobs, ironically to pay for leisure time activities. The virtue of work is being raised to an unprecedented level. A recent study by the International Labor Organization of work in 240 countries finds that Americans work the equivalent of more than two weeks longer now than twenty years ago. By contrast, the Japanese show a decline in hours worked. Work, particularly among white-collar employees and professionals, has taken on an almost cultlike quality, an emotional attachment to the ethos of work (Joyner 1999). **Workaholism** has become commonplace in the workplace.

The term *workaholism* was introduced in 1971 by Wayne Oates, a Protestant clergyman, who described it as an addiction, a compulsive need to work as long and as often as possible (Oates 1971). To Oates, the workaholic is one who is overcommitted, inflexible, and driven relentlessly to achieve. Psychologist Bryan Robinson concurs that workaholism is synonymous with work addiction, which he defines as an "obsessive-compulsive disorder that manifests itself through self-imposed demands, an inability to regulate work habits, and an overindulgence in work to the exclusion of most other life activities" (Robinson 1998: 7). In a recent Gallup Poll, 44 percent of Americans report that they are "workaholics" (U.S. News and World Report Editors 2000).

Marilyn Machlowitz's (1980: 33-35) in-depth investigation of the behavior of workaholics provides the basis for a fourfold typology. The four types of workaholics that emerge are: *Dedicated* workaholics—single-minded and one-dimensional—are so involved in their work that any other activity is viewed as an intrusion and is consciously avoided. *Integrated* workaholics occupy jobs that require nonworking activities. Product representatives must travel to call on their potential customers, for example, and corporate executives must entertain politicians and community leaders. Travel and entertainment are viewed as essential to the performance of their jobs. *Diffused* workaholics are typically involved in several projects at the same time. They are able to juggle unrelenting demands on their time, retain the details of their various job-related commitments, and appear to be in control of their daily lives. *Intense* workaholics pursue leisure with the same passion, purposefulness, and pace as work. If told to relax, to rest, then they will do so with dogged intensity and on schedule. Leisure activities, golf, or tennis, for example, are pursued with vengeance.

Common among workaholics, then, is their sense of "time urgency"—that is, the desire to accomplish something every minute of every day. They often attempt to do several things at the same time (time deepening) in order to maximize their time and effort. Time spent away from the job is viewed as wasted. Eating, sleeping, and nonwork-related family activities are seen as unfortunate necessities, impingements on their harried schedule, and should be kept to a minimum.

Three behavioral patterns of workaholics are compulsive-dependent, perfectionist, and achievement-oriented. The compulsive-dependent workaholics are driven to work; they are unable to control their need to work incessantly. While they may understand that their work habits are excessive, threats to their health and social well-being, and unnecessary, they are unable to stop themselves from continuing to work longer and longer hours. Not to work would be anxiety producing; working serves to reduce their symptoms of withdrawal and emotional upheaval. Perfectionist workaholics are characterized by their need to be in control of their work situation, as well as all other aspects of their lives. To maintain

Time-Deepening: The Acceleration of Life

Robinson and Godbey outline four ways that time-deepening may occur:

1. *Attempting to speed up a given activity.* Eating only microwavable food, using an electric toothbrush.

2. *Substituting a leisure activity that can be done more quickly for one that takes longer.* Playing computer golf rather than actually going to the golf course, walking on a treadmill rather than in the park.

3. *Doing more than one activity at once.* Eating while talking on the phone, watching TV, and doing Tai Chi.

4. *Undertaking a leisure activity with more precise regard to time.* Scheduling work and leisure activities with little time in between.

Source: Robinson, J. and Godbey, G. 1997. *Time for Life: The Surprising Ways Americans Use Their Time.* University Park: The Pennsylvania State University Press (p. 39).

control over their work environment, the perfectionist workaholic tends to be inflexible and rigid, focusing on details, rules, and lists. They often resort to aggressive and domineering tactics to control the work of their colleagues. Achievement-oriented workaholics have a strong desire for upward occupational mobility. They are strongly committed to their careers, are highly competitive, and are driven by the need to be a success. They devote far more time to work than is required. Even when not on the job, the achievement-oriented workaholics are thinking about solutions to work-related problems. They strive for excellence and recognition as leaders in their fields (Scott, Moore, and Miceli 1997).

Characteristics of Workaholics

Machlowitz (1980: 26–32) characterizes workaholics in the following way: *Workaholics are intense, energetic, competitive, and driven.* Workaholics literally take the 24/7 view of work. They pursue their work goals in a relentless, untiringly way. They pride themselves on their capacity for work—seven days a week, 52 weeks a year. Their passion is to work, to constantly achieve new goals, and to set increasingly higher standards for themselves. Life is a zero-sum game, they either win or lose; there is no middle ground.

Workaholics have strong self-doubts. Ironically, workaholics who appear to be the epitome of self-confidence, to always be in control of the situation, are often gripped by a fear that they are not up to the task they have set for themselves. Machlowitz (1980: 28) notes, "Working hard can be a way of concealing or compensating for such suspected shortcomings."

Workaholics prefer labor to leisure. Workaholics derive their greatest pleasure from the work they do. All other activities—family activities, recreation, socializing—diminish their sense of well-being. Days off, typically Sundays and holidays, are stressful, depressing, or otherwise emotionally disconcerting to the workaholic. Withdrawal from their addiction to work is painful and to be avoided.

Workaholics can—and do—work anytime and anywhere. The addiction to work must be satisfied at all times. Workaholics are very creative about finding times to indulge themselves in work. Weekends, late at night, very early in the morning are times they are not distracted by phone calls or co-workers who want to socialize on the job. During these off-times the workaholic is able to concentrate more fully on the task at hand. The psychic rewards are great.

Workaholics make the most of their time. Time is to be treasured, hoarded, and protected from the constant threat of theft. There is a need to maximize every moment; time is not to be wasted—something must be accomplished. Workaholics are vigilant about their use of time, always striving to devise time-saving strategies and ways to do more things simultaneously.

Workaholics blur the distinctions between business and pleasure. Business is pleasure: there is no distinction. Workaholics typically derive their greatest, if not their only, pleasure from work. Misery is experienced away from the job, pleasure is found while working. Machlowitz quotes a workaholic as saying, "I don't think of work as any different from play. I mean I do enjoy it—I'd rather do that than anything else. I don't know why one has to draw the distinction" (Machlowitz 1980: 32).

Workaholism: When More Is Less

Atlantan Carey Sipp was so consumed with work at one time that each time she was in the delivery room in labor with her two children she was on the phone with clients. At the time, she was working 16-hour days, six days a week, and earning a six-figure salary creating fund-raising packages for non-profit groups.

I still read bedtime stories to my children and I breast-fed my children and they were in the house with me. But my big rush was to get downstairs and come up with a headline that worked and nail a deadline."

To Carey Sipp, working incessantly: ". . . beat the heck out of dealing with the financial and emotional side of my marriage." Work addiction, she argues, "like food addiction and alcoholism, is about escaping reality. But in our society, work addiction is the one addiction that is truly applauded."

Following her divorce and bouts with ill health, she decided to forego her workaholic lifestyle, move into a much smaller home, and devote herself to raising her two children.

Source: Joyner, T. "All Work is American Way of Life." *Atlanta Journal Constitution.* (November 14, 1999), p. R1.

Sex-Role Differences.   Workaholics are drawn to professions and occupations that do not have rigid working schedules, e.g., corporate executives and entrepreneurs, scientists and academics, writers and artists, and that reward creativity and innovation (Machlowitz 1980). Until the advent of the women's movement, men dominated these positions. In the later third of the twentieth century women made significant gains in their participation in the workforce. Women now exceed men among undergraduate students and constitute a significant proportion of the enrollments in medical and law schools across the United States. Women constitute an unprecedentedly high proportion of university and college presidents, elected political leaders, corporate executives and managers, and public and nonprofit administrators. For example, in recent years the percentage of women college administrators doubled from 9.5 to 19.3 percent ("More Women Serve" 2000). Women now hold a quarter of the top executive positions in the Fortune 500 firms (Oldman 2000). It may be expected, therefore, that the gender disparity in workaholism may also be lessening.

Ellen Cantarow (1979) argues that the women's movement, not only provided women with professional and managerial opportunities, but also markedly increases the risk of becoming a workaholic. Positions of high responsibility typically demand an extraordinary time commitment. Yet women, far more so than men, continue to be responsible for the daily welfare of their families. The resultant role conflict between the demands of work and familial responsibilities may well shape the forms that workaholism may take among women. Any guilt that women may feel over their inability to meet the less predictable familial and other social demands may, in part, be resolved by focusing on seemingly more controllable work-related problems, the resolution of which may be more immediately rewarding.

Ronald J. Burke's (1999) analysis of workaholism in organizations shows both similarities and differences between men and women. No significant gender differences are found in their work involvement, perfectionism, and nondelegation. However, women workaholics are significantly more prone to job stress, but spend significantly less time on the job as measured by hours per week and overtime hours. A study of academic social workers reveals that compared to men, women faculty members are significantly more likely to feel driven to work, to experience job stress, to be more involved in their jobs, and to commit more time to them (Spence and Robbins 1992).

Socialization and Psychological Factors in Overwork

Machlowitz (1980) notes that workaholics tend to be socialized by parents who encourage and reward profit making activities, e.g., selling lemonade or magazines, shoveling snow, or raking leaves. Children who are involved in several extracurricular projects learn to manage their time to accomplish as much as possible. The more they do, the more their caretakers approve of them. However, the more children accomplish, the more they are expected to accomplish. They soon become trapped in a no-win situation. This endless cycle of increasing accomplishment and progressive expectations, Machlowitz argues, generates self-doubt in workaholics.

Self-doubt leads to a need to control all aspects of their lives, to maximize their own time as well as their associates'. Machlowitz (1980: 45) observes that "control—or the illusion thereof—is vitally important to workaholics." Accompanying this obsession with control is the haunting fear that things are spinning out of control, a fear that precipitates increasing self-doubt.

Consequences of Overwork

On the Job. Workaholism is either viewed as a positive or a negative form of addiction. Some organizational theorists consider the passion for work that the workaholic exudes is an asset to be encouraged among employees (Korn, Pratt, and Lambrou 1987; Sprankle and Ebel 1987). It is in the organization's interest to encourage its workers to dedicate themselves wholly to the task at hand and to expect the same from their co-workers. Other researchers consider workaholism to be extremely dangerous to its victims and disruptive to their working associates (Naughton 1987; Porter 1996, 2001). Being driven by their need to work and their expectation that others keep pace, workaholics may well create conflicts and dissension within an organization. Anthony Brody (1979) finds that the behavior of workaholics is counterproductive—workaholics are inefficient, disruptive to their fellow workers, and the cause of high rates of absenteeism and loss of employees. In addition, the self-doubt and low self-esteem of the workaholic—the need for approval from others coupled with the relentless need to control the work environment—combine to undermine organizational functioning.

AT A GLANCE

Exercising

- Extreme sports and competitive tests of endurance are now institutionalized forms of athletic events, which rival traditional professional sports (e.g., baseball, basketball, and football) for media attention.

Working

- A Gallup Poll found that 44 percent of Americans call themselves "workaholics."
- The average American works the equivalent of an astonishing eight weeks a year longer than the average Western European. In Norway and Sweden, ordinary workers get four to six weeks of vacation and up to a year of paid parental leave.
- According to the International Labor Organization (ILO), "the Japanese work longer hours than most other industrial nations."
- The average Japanese businessperson takes only half his or her paid holidays.

Computer Addiction

- Some researchers say 5 to 10 percent of Internet users have the potential for an addiction problem.
- Over half of regular computer users may qualify as compulsive surfers.
- Between 6 and 10 percent of college students are computer-addicted.

Sources: Raymond, J. "Going to Extremes." *American Demographics,* June 1, 2002 http:// www.netaddiction.com; Greene, R. 1998. "Internet Addiction." *Computer World,* September 21; *U.S. News and World Report* Editors. June 26, 2000. "No Time to slow down: Can we keep working harder and harder indefinitely?"

However unproductive they become, workaholics continue to work with increasing tenacity. Work may not result in any tangible rewards—recognition, economic gain, and self-worth—yet it is not abandoned. Only when working does the workaholic feel emotionally stable. Work is a necessity, its own reward (Machlowitz 1980).

Family.   As would be expected, the demands of family life—time spent with a spouse and children—are often seen by the workaholic as an interference with his or her primary concern in life, to work. Workaholics are "role-bound" individuals. Activities other than work are disdained; every effort is made to keep them to a minimum.

As a consequence, the workaholic's relationship with a spouse, children, or other family members tends to be forced, stressful, and emotionally draining for both the workaholic and his or her relatives and friends. Workaholics reluctantly schedule time with their family members. Often these "appointments" to attend a child's music recital or athletic event are arranged by the parent's secretary. Known euphemistically as "quality time," there is very little time and possibly less quality involved in these arranged meetings with children and spouses (Machlowitz 1980).

Divorce is common among workaholics. Spouses who choose not to divorce their workaholic partner may focus their attention on their children, creative outlets or community activities. They may alternately engage in forms of addictive behaviors—alcohol, drugs or sex—or become anxious, depressed or develop other emotional or physical disorders (Coles 1977).

Health. Workaholism is termed a "progressively fatal disease" (Fassel 1992: 13). The compulsion of workaholics to work well beyond their physical and mental capacity jeopardizes their health and emotional well-being. Cardiologists Friedman and Roseman contend that Type A behavior patterns significantly increase the risk of a heart attack. Type A behavior patterns include conducting routine activities—walking, eating, talking—in a rapid manner, impatience with others who do things at a slower pace, "polyphasic thought or action"—trying to think about or do more than one thing at a time, persistent time urgency—the sense that time will run out before everything gets done (Friedman and Roseman 1974). Workaholics, then, fit well the profile of the Type A individual, placing them at greater risk for heart disease.

It has long been recognized that chronic stress may have deadly consequences (Rabin 1999). Job-related stress is endemic and increasing in postindustrial societies. A recent U.S. survey shows that 40 percent of workers consider their jobs to be very or extremely stressful (www.cdc.gov/nisoh/stress99.html). The Second European Survey on Working Conditions (www.cdc.gov/nisoh/stress99.html) indicates that 28 percent of workers report experiencing stress on the job. Job-related stress is even more pronounced in Japan where 63 percent of workers suffer from anxiety or worry about their job performance or conditions of employment. The Japanese also work significantly more hours than do their counterparts in Europe and the United States. The Management and Coordination Agency in Japan reports that full-time male workers between the ages of 25 and 49 work more than 2,500 hours a year, more than four months longer than their peers in France and Germany (Kato 1995).

The consequences of excessive overworking in Japan are often fatal. **Karoshi** is the recently coined Japanese word for *death from overwork*. It is estimated that *Karoshi* accounts for 10 percent of all deaths of men in the Japanese work force (Yates 1988). A survey conducted by the Yomiuri Shimbun newspaper posed the question, "Are you concerned that *Karoshi* might hit you or a family member?" Forty-eight percent of the Japanese public surveyed answered "yes." Survivors of *Karoshi* victims are now appealing to the courts in Japan for the loss of their family members. These petitions have taken two forms: death as the direct result of overwork and suicide precipitated by overwork. *Karoshi* victims commonly experience exhaustion, insomnia, and fear of disappointing their em-

Death by Overwork

In Japan, it's called *karoshi*—"death by overwork"—and it's estimated to cause 1,000 deaths per year, nearly 5 percent of that country's stroke and heart attack deaths in employees under the age of 60.

In the Netherlands, it's resulted in a new condition known as "leisure illness," estimated to affect 3 percent of its entire population, according to one study. Workers actually get physically sick on weekends and vacations as they stop working and try, in vain, to relax.

. . . in the United States, workaholism remains what it's always been: the so-called "respectable addiction" that's as dangerous as any other and could affect millions of Americans—regardless of whether they hold jobs.

Sources: WebMD Feature, "Workaholism: The 'Respectable' Addiction" posted at: http://aolsvc.health.wemd.aol.com/content/Article/36/1728_57274.htm?printing=true

ployers and co-workers. The impact of chronic work-related stress may be so debilitating that sudden death ensues. Alternatively, chronic stress may lead to clinical depression, a sense of hopeless entrapment in an unrelenting work schedule that permits little time away from the job. The Japanese National Police Agency reports that "work-related problems" are the central etiological factor in suicides of persons 50 to 59 years of age (Robinson 1996). Because suicide as a consequence of overwork is so common in Japan, a special term, *karo-jisatsu*, has emerged to distinguish it from other suicides. Recently, the Nagano District Court ruled that the suicide of a Japanese man was the direct result of his routinely working 80-hour weeks. His survivors were awarded $17,000 a year compensation for his death. In a similar case, the court awarded 168 million yen ($1.6 million) to the family of a 24-year-old advertising employee who worked for 17 months prior to his suicide without a day off, averaging between 30 minutes and 2 hours sleep a night (Kageyama 1999). Overall, *Karoshi* victims appear to be getting younger. The father of a 24-year-old was awarded 126 million yen ($1.1 million) by the court when his son simply worked himself to death in an attempt to placate his employer.

Computer Addiction

Considerable controversy surrounds the recently emerging phenomenon of protracted use of the computer. Alternately known as computer addicts, Internet addicts, net addicts, or webaholics, persons who use their computers to excess have come to the attention of clinical psychologists, psychiatrists, academic researchers, and the media. The term "**internet addiction disorder**" was first recognized in 1995, and then only half seriously, by psychiatrist Ivan Goldberg (Yang 2000).

Since that time various definitions of computer addiction have been offered. Peter Mitchell, writing in *The Lancet*, defines Internet addiction as the "compulsive use of the Internet with disturbed and irritated behavior when access is denied, including withdrawal symptoms and the loss of emotional control" (Mitchell 2000: 632). To Harvard clinical psychologist Meressa Hecht Orzack (Cromie 1999), computer addiction is "an emerging disorder suffered by people who find the virtual reality on computer screens more attractive than everyday reality." While Orzack (cited in Cromie 1999) contends that normal and pathological computer use is difficult to define, there are symptoms of computer addiction:

- Using the computer for pleasure, gratification, or relief from stress.
- Feeling irritable and out of control or depressed when not using it.
- Spending increased amounts of time and money on hardware, software, magazines, and computer-related activities.
- Neglecting work, school, or family obligations.
- Lying about the amount of time spent on computer activities.
- Risking loss of career goals, educational objectives, and personal relationships.
- Failing at repeated efforts to control computer use.

Based on the American Psychiatric Association's *Diagnostic and Statistical Manual of Mental Disorders'* (1994) definition of pathological gambling, Kimberly Young developed an eight-item Diagnostic Questionnaire to determine addictive Internet use. Table 15.1 presents the DSM-IV questions that are used to determine Internet addiction.

Table 15.1   Diagnostic Criteria for Internet Addiction Disorder

Individuals are Internet dependent if they answer "yes" to four or more of following questions:

1. Do you feel preoccupied with the Internet (think about previous online activity or anticipate the next online session)?

2. Do you feel a need to use the Internet with increasing amounts of time to achieve satisfaction?

3. Have you repeatedly made unsuccessful efforts to control, cut back, or stop Internet use?

4. Do you feel restless, moody, depressed, or irritable when attempting to cut down or stop Internet use?

5. Do you stay online longer than originally intended?

6. Do you use the Internet as a way of escaping problems or relieving a dysphoric mood (e.g., feelings of helplessness, guilt, anxiety or depression)?

7. Have you lied to family members, therapists, or others to conceal the extent of involvement with the Internet?

8. Have you jeopardized or risked the loss of a significant relationship, job, or educational or career opportunity because of the Internet?

Source: Dr. Kimberly S. Young, Executive Director of the Center for Online Addiction. Web posted at www
.netaddiction.com/articles/symptoms.htm

Types of Internet Addiction

The Center for On-Line Addiction (www.netaddiction.com) has identified five specific types of Internet addiction.

1. **Cybersexual Addiction:** The preoccupation with online pornography and involvement in the playing out of sexual fantasies in chat rooms.
2. **Cyber-Relational Addiction:** The establishment of virtual relationships in chat rooms or through email. These relationships typically involve males and females who may engage in forms of virtual adultery.
3. **Net Gaming:** Involves gambling, gaming, shopping, or stock trading. Examples include virtual casinos, interactive games, e-auction houses, and e-brokerage houses.
4. **Information Overload:** The fascination with the availability of increasing amounts of information and data from around the world may result in excessive online activity.
5. **Computer Addiction:** The obsessive playing of games that are built into the computer itself and do not require an online connection, e.g., Solitaire and Minesweeper.

Consequences of Computer Addiction

Psychologist Robert Kraut and his colleagues (1998) arranged to have computers with free Internet service installed in 73 homes without computer access. Software installed in their household computer monitored the computer use of the 169 residents over a one- to two-year period. Participants in the study were interviewed about their interaction with other family members and friends, symptoms of depression, and loneliness. The findings show that even when the participants used the computer between one and four hours per week, their social interaction and emotional well-being suffered. The researchers conclude that: Excessive Internet use is linked to increased depression and loneliness (Kraut et al. 1998: 1567). It appears that virtual interaction provided by email and chat rooms does not compensate for the benefits of face-to-face interaction with family and friends.

Adverse consequences are documented for persons who use the computer to excess. Twenty persons who spend more than 30 nonworking hours using the computer each week over the past three years report that they would forego sleep, shrug family responsibilities, and go to work late to find time to "surf the net" or participate in chat rooms. Marital problems, school failures, job loss, and financial problems are commonly experienced by excessive computer users (Holliday 2000). A recent study of employees of 1,500 companies across the United States shows that workers who are fired for excessive computer use are engaged in online pornography, shopping, or gambling (Yang 2000). Perhaps less serious than losing a job are the physical consequences of prolonged computer use— repetitive stress injuries, backaches, and dry eyes (Gawel 1999).

Prevalence of Computer Addiction

Few studies are available on the prevalence of computer addiction or dependency. Yet, current research shows remarkably consistent findings. In a survey of 810 Northeastern University students, Linda Welsh finds that almost 8 percent met the criteria of "Internet dependent" (Cromie 1999). It has been estimated that between 5 and 10 percent of Americans using the Internet have the potential to be addicted to it (Greene 1998). In the largest single study of computer addiction, ABC News' survey of more than 17,000 Americans shows that 6 percent or 6 million Internet users could be addicted (Yang 2000). For more than 30 percent of those in the survey, the Internet provided an escape from negative emotions and fostered feelings of time distortion, intimacy, and inhibition (http://www.netaddiction.com).

As access to personal computers expands and ease and attractiveness of their use becomes increasingly recognized by more diverse segments of the population, extreme computer use, addiction, and dependency are likely to escalate.

Gender Differences. Recent research on gender differences in the use of the computer shows that the varying interests of women and men are played out in their use of the Internet. Kimberly Young (http://www.netaddiction.com), a psychologist who specializes in Internet addiction, reports that men are attracted to online competitive games where power and dominance are at stake. Games that involve the establishment of status in the group based on the player's ability to destroy other participants and thereby to gain recognition and respect are particularly intriguing to men. Cybersex is another male-dominated online activity. Cybersex is carried out in chat rooms in which men and women converse in sexually explicit, uninhibited ways. This free exchange of sexual desires and fantasies allows the participants to engage in behaviors in a virtual way that they could not experience in real time and space. Cyberporn also provides men with vicarious sexual encounters unavailable to them in their everyday lives.

Women are drawn to chat rooms but for far different reasons. For the most part, women use the Internet to establish warm, supportive relationships. Online friendships are sought to share common problems and explore various ways of handling their "real-life" relationships. Help-seeking interactions are facilitated by the relative anonymity provided by email and chat rooms.

Women also enjoy anonymous interaction with men with whom a relationship may develop. Personal appearance and social background are masked by online communication. The lack of physical attractiveness does not impede the process of developing a personal relationship. The advantages of not being judged on superficial visual characteristics attract and sustain women's interest in cyber-communication (http://www.netaddiction.com).

What Makes the Internet Addictive?

Kimberly Young also explores the issue of what makes computer-mediated communication addictive. She finds that the use of the Internet to gather information is far less addictive than virtual interaction provided in chat rooms and multi-user dungeons. Both chat rooms and multi-user dungeons allow simultaneous communication to occur among as many as 1,000 persons. Chat rooms typically involve multiple conversations among persons who are interested in a common topic or who have common characteristics that draw them together. Multi-user dungeons differ from chat rooms in that they involve the establishment of a game in which the players take on various character roles. For example, the game may involve a medieval battle with dragons and maidens, knights in armor, and villains hiding in the woods. By assuming a role in the drama, Internet players are provided opportunities for recognition and power typically not available to them in their everyday lives. Because the user's anonymity is ensured, they are able to experiment with new identities, personality characteristics, and social backgrounds. In addition, changes in gender—a male may become female, or vice versa—may greatly enhance identity transformation.

Anonymity also facilitates the process of seeking social support and involvement in sexually explicit online interactions. Users who otherwise may not be able to ask for help with an embarrassing or potentially socially stigmatizing problem may well seek counsel and support as an anonymous Internet patron. Similarly, persons who are interested in deviant sexual practices and who would not pursue them in everyday life may take advantage of their virtual availability on the Internet.

Extreme Sports

In the 1990s, **extreme sports** and athletic events gained considerable popularity. These forms of competitive and recreational activities range from high-risk, potentially life-threatening events—e.g., BASE jumping, rock climbing, street-luge racing, and sky surfing—to sports that test the endurance of the participants—e.g., ultraman marathons and the Ironman Triathlon events, Race Across America (bicycle race), and the Eco-challenge. BASE is an acronym for building, antenna, span (bridge), and earth (cliffs) jumping. The time between the start of the jump and the landing is so limited that a second chance to open the parachute is impossible. BASE jumping is described as "a human leaving safety behind to leap into the void" (Greenfield et al. 1999: 9). In the first eighteen years, BASE-jumping claimed the lives of 46 of its participants, making it the sport with the highest fatality rate in the world.

Ultraman marathons and Ironman Triathlon events involve testing the limits of human endurance. Since 1983, ultramarathons have been organized around the world, with participants from England, Japan, Germany, France, Poland, Brazil, Argentina, Canada, Austria, Australia, Latvia, Mexico, Slovenia, Puerto Rico, New Zealand, and the United States. An ultramarathon is a three-day event that includes a 6.2-mile open ocean swim followed by a 90-mile bike ride the first day, a 171.4-mile bike ride on day two, and a 52.4-mile ride on the final day. Far more common are Ironman Triathlon events that require the participants to swim 2.4 miles, cycle 112 miles, and complete a marathon (26 miles, 385 yards) on the same day (Greenfield 1999).

The Eco-challenge involves four-person teams (men and women combined) who race for 24 hours a day for seven days over 300 miles of very hazardous, re-

Eco-challenge competitor defying death by crossing an ice crevice on ropes.

mote terrain. Each team, equipped with only a map and compass, must finish the race together. Only nonmotorized means of transportation—canoes, kayaks, mountain bikes, whitewater rafts, horses, and climbing ropes—are permitted. If any member of the team is injured, becomes ill, or cannot complete the course, the team is disqualified. A recent challenge "began with a marathon-length horse-back segment, in which team members took turns riding and running alongside for 26 miles. The teams then slogged through narrow, water-filled canyons, some-times swimming with backpacks through 50-degree water; hiked more than 100 miles across stretches of waterless desert; negotiated 1,200-foot cliff faces on

Australian team Foxtel members planning their 300 mile Eco-Challenge race across the mountains of British Columbia.

ropes; rafted class IV (advanced) rapids on the Colorado River; and capped it off with a 12-hour, 50-mile canoe paddle across Lake Powell" (Hamilton 1995: 78).

The Race Across America (RAAM) is the longest nonstop bicycle race in the world, from the west to east coasts of the United States. The 2001 RAAM began in Portland, Oregon and ended in Gulf Breeze, Florida, a distance of 2,980 miles. Rob Kish, a 37-year-old land surveyor, set a record time for the RAAM of eight days, three hours, and eleven minutes (Pavelka 1992). Kish openly admits that RAAM is his life: "it is all I do." When he arrived in New York City, he "climbed off his bike looking like a man from a lifeboat after a month adrift: burned, peeling skin; thick, crusty lips; ratty beard and hair; a streak of dried blood in his nose" (Pavelka 1992: 57).

Extreme sports and athletic events, while involving varying degrees of risk, are all sensation-seeking activities. Psychologist Marvin Zuckerman (1994: 27) defines sensation as the "*seeking* of varied, novel, complex and *intense* sensations and experiences, and the willingness to take physical, social, and *legal*, and *financial* risks for the sake of such experience." Zuckerman's Sensation Seeking Scale Form V (SSSV) is widely used to assess the willingness to participate in nonconventional or high-risk behaviors, including substance use, experimenting

Extreme Sports: In Search of Myself

"Our society is so surgically sterile. It is almost like our socialization desensitizes us. Every time I'm out doing this I'm searching my soul. It's the Lewis and Clark gene, to venture out, to find what your limitations are." (Greenfield 1999: 10)

Journalist Rob Schultheis, an inexperienced rock climber, recounts his attempt to scale a Colorado peak without ropes or hardware. On his descent he lost his grip on an overhang and landed on a ledge, very near a sheer drop of 200 feet. Seriously injured, he writes of his quest for survival:

Something happened on that descent, something I have tried to figure out ever since, so inexplicable and powerful it was. I found myself very simply doing impossible things: dozens, scores of them, as I down-climbed Neva's lethal slopes. Shattered, in shock, I climbed with the impossible sureness of a snow leopard, a mountain goat. I crossed disintegrating chutes of rock holds vanishing from under my hands and feet as I moved, a dance in which a single missed beat would have been fatal. I used bits of rime clinging to the granite as fingerholds. They rattled away into space but I was already gone, away. . . . *What I am doing is absolutely impossible*, I thought. *I can't be doing this. But I have the grace, the radiant mojo, and here I am!* . . . Looking back on it, I really cannot explain or describe properly that strange person I found inhabiting my body that afternoon. . . . The person I became on Neva was the best version of myself, the person I should have been throughout my life.

Source: Schultheis, R. 1996. *Bone Games: Extreme Sports, Shamanism, Zen, and the Search for Transcendence.* New York: Breakaway Books, pp. 10–12.

with alcohol and other drugs, sexual behaviors, smoking, speeding, and risky sports. The SSSV includes four subscales: Thrill and Adventure Seeking (TAS), Experience Seeking (ES), Disinhibition (DIS), and Boredom Susceptibility. The Thrill and Adventure Seeking subscale measures the individual's propensity to act in risky, impulsive, and adventurous activities (Malkin and Rabinowitz 1998). Overall, persons who engage in high-risk sports and athletic events typically score very high on Zuckerman's Sensation Seeking Scale, and in particular on the Thrill and Adventure Seeking subscale (Wagner and Houlihan 1994). Mountain climbers are found to have higher total SSSV scores as well as higher Experience-Seeking and Thrill and Adventure Seeking subscale scores (Cronin 1991). Persons who participate in high-risk sports are also likely to be high sensation seekers. Mountain athletes (free climbers, ski jumpers, and speleogists) score high on the total SSSV and each of its subscales except Boredom Susceptibility (Rossi and Cereatti 1993). A study of elite mountain climbers—all members of the Norwegian Everest expedition—shows that they score higher overall and on all subscales of the SSSV, except Disinhibition (Breivik 1996). This provides further evidence that risk-taking and sensation seeking may be linked. The rush of adrenalin and the sense of accomplishment against all odds motivates persons to seek out extreme, sometimes life-threatening challenges.

Theoretical Understanding of Extreme Forms of Everyday Behavior

Specific theoretical formulations have not been set forth to account for extreme forms of everyday behavior. However, it is possible to draw on theories of negative deviant behaviors to better understand the workaholic, computer addict, and the extreme sports competitor.

Social Integration

As with positive forms of deviance, the extent of social integration—or the sharing of common values—affects involvement in extreme forms of everyday behavior (see Durkheim, 1951). Persons who are highly integrated into conventional society, who structure their lives in a balanced and predictable ways, tend not to be bothered by their daily routine behavior. Nine to five jobs, two weeks vacation, and a balance between family life, job, and civic responsibility are not seen as burdens but as a preferred way to live. In Robert Merton's (1968) terms, the conformists and ritualists—persons who accept the conventional goals of society and the means for achieving them—are not likely to engage in extreme forms of behavior. To both conformists and ritualists, culturally approved goals and the institutionalized means for attaining them are linked. Excessive working, computer obsession, or involvement in dangerous or extreme sports or games holds no interest for them. Persons who adopt an innovative strategy for achieving culturally approved goals, however, may work to excess, develop an addiction to the Internet, or seek out virtual alternatives to achieve their personal rewards and social acceptance unavailable to them in everyday life.

Reciprocity

Widespread thrill-seeking and risk-taking behaviors seem to depend on the societal conditions marked by economic prosperity and lack of external or internal conflict. Ironically, the general sense of economic well-being and minimal conflict or the sense that society is becoming a safer, healthier, more humane place may well precipitate the feeling of suffocating reciprocity in everyday life. Excessive reciprocity occurs when the playing out of our social roles—employee, student, spouse, parent, and friend—becomes too easy. That is, our actual role behavior—the ways in which we carry out our roles—and the expectations that we have for our performance for these roles closely match. Motivation is reduced and we go about daily lives in a disengaged, dispassionate way. As a consequence, involvement in risky, highly challenging sports and athletic events is on the rise.

Stuart Palmer (1970) sets forth a status-role reciprocity formulation of deviant and conforming behavior. Role reciprocity refers to "the extent to which performances of the status-roles mutually and simultaneously expedite one another" (Palmer 1970: 42). The greater the status-role reciprocity, the less the tension both within social situations and the individuals involved. Conversely, the less the role reciprocity, the greater the tension both within social situations and the person involved. Palmer argues that extremes of tension, either too high or too low, lead to aberrant behavior. Too little tension may well result in an effort by the individual to increase it; too much tension signals a need for its reduction.

When excessive status-role reciprocity is obtained, persons are able to function quite well with a limited degree of effort. Those around them facilitate the playing out of their status-roles. Employers, friends, wives, children and so on are supportive and appreciative of the ways in which the person enacts complementary status-roles. Under conditions of excessive status-role reciprocity, tension falls to dangerously low levels. To reintroduce a degree of tension into their lives, persons who are experiencing excessive status-role reciprocity may engage in high-risk or extreme forms of behavior. The rush of adrenaline or conquering an extraordinary physical and mental challenge provides the level of tension necessary to sustain an otherwise monotonous everyday life. Virtual life made possible by the Internet and devotion to working far beyond expectations are additional ways to ease a deadening routine.

Strain

Robert Agnew's (1992) strain theory may also be brought to bear on extreme forms of everyday behavior. Strain is a consequence of the variation between individuals' actual goal attainment and what they would like to achieve. When relations with others are so contentious that role performance is greatly impeded, negative emotions may ensue. Alternative forms of social relations may be sought. Chat room and virtual relationships may be found to be far less stressful, more emotionally gratifying, and beneficial to other goal attainment. Excessive working may also provide a respite from negative social relation-

Explanations of Extreme Forms of Everyday Behavior

Theories and Theorists	Sociological Predictors	Hypotheses
Social Integration and Control		
• Durkheim	Social integration	The greater the social integration, the less the involvement in extreme forms of everyday behavior.
• Merton	Anomie	The more anomic social life is, the greater the involvement in extreme forms of everyday behavior.
• Agnew	Strain	The more strained social relationships become, the more likely that extreme forms of everyday behavior will occur.
Societal Reaction		
• Becker	Societal Reaction	The more positive the societal reaction to extreme forms of everyday behavior, the more likely those forms of behavior will continue.
Social Conflict		
• Coser	Conflict	The greater the conflict between the personal rewards of everyday behavior and the anticipated rewards of alternative behaviors, the greater the likelihood of extreme forms of everyday behavior.
• Palmer	Role Reciprocity	The greater the degree of role reciprocity, the greater the likelihood of extreme forms of everyday behavior.
Differential Association and Social Learning		
• Sutherland	Differential Association	The greater the interaction with others who advocate involvement in extreme forms of everyday behavior, the greater the likelihood that an individual will engage in those behaviors.
• Akers	Social Learning	The greater the personal rewards for engaging in extreme forms of everyday behavior, the more likely those behaviors will continue.
Rational Choice		
• Clarke and Cornish	Rational Choice	The more anticipated pleasure exceeds expected pain from extreme forms of everyday behavior, the more likely an individual will choose to engage in those behaviors.

ships—with spouse, children, or other family members or friends. Becoming immersed in work-related activities may provide the kinds of emotional benefits and status rewards not available in an individual's other spheres of life. Strain may also lead to involvement in extreme sports or unusually demanding physical contests.

Differential Association and Learning Theory

Differential association theory combines concepts found in social learning and subcultural conceptualizations. A central hypothesis of differential association theory is: the more interaction with others who advocate certain behaviors, the greater the likelihood that the motives, rationalizations, and techniques for engaging in those behaviors will be learned. In formulation differential association theory, Edwin Sutherland (1978) is primarily interested in explaining delinquent and criminal behavior. However, the principles of differential association theory may be applied to extreme forms of everyday behavior as well. Workaholics, computer and Internet addicts, and participants in extreme sports and games who interact with others of similar interests are more likely to continue their excessive behavior.

Ronald Akers (1998) extends differential association theory by introducing the concept of differential reinforcement. Differential reinforcement refers to the process by which individuals receive rewards and benefits for some of the behaviors but not others. Those behaviors that are rewarded tend to be repeated; those that do not benefit the individual are in time discarded. Extreme forms of everyday behavior tend to result in personal rewards, less so in social recognition. However, increasing media attention given to extreme sports has generated athletic identities and increasing economic benefit for those who excel.

Rational Choice

Rational Choice theory—based on the hedonistic principle of human behavior—posits that the decision to act is governed by the desire to maximize anticipated pleasure and minimize expected pain. From this perspective, actor involvement in extreme forms of everyday behavior may be a rational expression of free will, an anticipation that pleasure will flow from atypical involvement in work, computer use, and athletic events and competitions. From the perspective of outsiders, persons who engage in extreme forms of everyday behavior may be irrational, disordered psychologically and emotionally, and destructive to themselves and to those close to them (Clarke and Cornish 1985b).

Societal Reaction

Manifestations of excessive behavior are met with mixed reactions (see Becker 1968). Workaholics may be viewed positively within certain organizations, while they are seen as disruptive in others. Junior members of large law firms, for example, are expected to work to excess to generate "billable hours" to demonstrate their organizational worth. Medical students and interns are expedited to be available in the hospital and its laboratories sometimes around the clock to take advantage of unexpected opportunities to advance their medical education. In other organizational settings, however, overly zealous work habits are less expected and accepted by fellow workers.

Computer aficionados are valued members of many complex organizations. Their willingness to provide computer "troubleshooting" for their co-workers is most welcome. Those who are addicted to computer games or Internet interactions, however, devote an inordinate amount of their working day to the pursuit of their own interests. Organizational conflicts may arise that may threaten the continued employment of the computer addict.

Media attention has recently focused on extreme sports and games. Major television and cable networks have televised a wide variety of extreme athletic competitions and Eco-challenges from around the globe. Accomplished extreme sport athletes are becoming widely known, more daring feats of physical agility and strength are being attempted, and corporate sponsors are increasingly becoming involved. New products—sporting equipment, nutritional and strength-enhancing aids, and apparel—are being introduced. Outstanding competitors in a variety of extreme sports and games are being recognized not only as exceptional athletes but also as media personalities and corporate representatives. As children and adolescents identify and attempt to emulate the abilities of extreme athletes, the recruitment into these forms of competition will increase. Traditional sports—e.g. baseball, football, and basketball, may be seen as passé—reserved for the less adventurous.

Chapter Summary

- When we work incessantly, exercise or engage in extreme forms of athletic competition, or hack away on the computer day and night, our everyday behaviors may take on deviant forms.
- Workaholism—being highly committed to work, spending a disproportionate amount of time working, but showing little enjoyment in doing it—is common in the workplace.
- Workers in the United States now spend more hours on the job than any other advanced industrial nation.
- These workers possess the following characteristics:
  - Intense, energetic, competitive, and driven
  - Strong self-doubts
  - Prefer labor to leisure
  - Can—and do—work anytime and anywhere
  - Make the most of their time
  - Blur the distinctions between business and pleasure
- Until recently, the majority of workaholics were men. However, as women increasingly enter professions that reward workaholic behaviors, the gender disparity in workaholism will lessen.
- Workaholics tend to be socialized by parents who encourage and reward profit-making activities.
- Workaholism has been viewed as a positive and negative form of addiction. Some of the consequences of overwork include:
  - Disruption of family life
  - Decline in physical and mental health
  - Chronic stress
- *Karoshi* is the recently coined Japanese word for death from overwork.

- Persons who use their computers incessantly—playing games, emailing, involved in chat rooms, or lost in cyberspace—are known as computer addicts, Internet addicts, or webaholics.
- Five types of Internet addiction have been identified:
  - Cybersexual addiction
  - Cyber-relational addiction
  - Net gaming
  - Information overload
  - Computer addiction
- The co-morbidity of excessive computer use with more traditional psychiatric disorders (e.g., depression, social phobia, impulse control disorder, and attention deficit disorder) is now recognized.
- Adverse consequences are documented for persons who use the computer to excess. These include:
  - Marital problems
  - School failures
  - Job loss
  - Financial problems
  - Health problems
- Varying interests of women and men are played out in their use of the Internet.
- Researchers find that those who use the Internet to gather information are far less likely to become addicted than those who use the Internet for virtual interaction in chat rooms and multi-user dungeons.
- High-risk and potentially life-threatening athletic events are institutionalized forms of athletic competition.

Key Concepts

Time-deepening: Doing several things at the same time in order to maximize time and effort.

Workaholism: An addiction to work, the compulsion or the uncontrollable need to work incessantly.

Karoshi: Death from overwork.

Internet addiction disorder: Compulsive use of the Internet with disturbed and irritated behavior when access is denied, including withdrawal symptoms and the loss of emotional control; an emerging disorder suffered by people who find the virtual reality on computer screens more attractive than everyday reality.

Cybersexual addiction: The preoccupation with online pornography and involvement in the playing out of sexual fantasies in chat rooms.

Cyber-relational addiction: The establishment of virtual relationships in chat rooms or through email.

Net gaming: Gambling, gaming, shopping, or stock trading on the Internet.

Information overload: The fascination with the availability of increasing amounts of information and data from around the world resulting in excessive online activity.

Computer addiction: The obsessive playing of games that are built into the computer itself and do not require an online connection.

Extreme sports: Forms of competitive and recreational activities that range from high-risk, potentially life-threatening events to sports that test the endurance of the participants.

Critical Thinking Questions

1. What are the key sociocultural conditions that give rise to workaholism? Why do these sociocultural conditions motivate some individuals to engage in workaholism and not others? Are workaholics socialized from childhood to work to the extreme, or do life experiences later in life precipitate overworking?

2. Do similar sociocultural conditions generate a wide range of extreme form of everyday behaviors? For example, are workaholics, computer addicts, and participants in extreme sports affected by similar sociocultural conditions? If so, what might account for the behavioral differences that result from these conditions?

3. Can involvement in extreme forms of everyday behavior be predicted or are they forms of idiosyncratic behavior that fall outside the scope of scientific prediction?

4. Is it possible to engage in a form of extreme everyday behavior but otherwise have a conformist lifestyle? How is it possible for the sociocultural conditions that give rise to extreme behaviors to selectively affect individual behavior?

Web Extra

Check out these websites for additional information on extreme forms of deviant behavior:

http://www.netaddiction.com

http://www.computeraddiction.com

http://www.basejumper.org

CHAPTER 16

Terrorism

P O R T R A I T S

of Terrorism

SUICIDE BOMBER'S LETTER

Excepts from a translation of a handwritten Arabic letter of instruction to the 9–11 hijackers found by FBI agents.

The Last Night

- Pledge of allegiance for death and renewal of intent.
- To be perfect with the plan very well of all its aspects and expecting the reaction or resistence from the enemy.
- Reading and understanding well . . . what Allah has prepared for the believers or the permanent bliss for the martyrs.
- Reminding one's self of listening well and obeying that night for you are going to face critical situations, which require strict abiding and obeying.
- Pray for your soul, the bag, the clothes, the knife, the stuff, whatever that stuff is, your ID, your passport, and all your papers.
- Check your weapons, before departure and before you leave . . . sharpen his knife.
- Tighten up your clothes and this is the medal of the righteous predecessors may God be content with them all.

The Second Stage

- When the taxi takes you to the airport . . . remember God much in the car (supplication of riding—supplication of the town—supplication of place . . .)
- When you arrive and get off the taxi then say the supplication of the place and every place you go say in it the supplication of the place and smile and be comforted for God is with

the believers and the angels guard you and you do not feel them.
- And also do not let perplexing and confusion and nervous tension appear upon you. Be cheerful, happy, serene, and comforted because you are doing a job which God loves and accepts hence it will be day with God's permission you will spend it with the most beautiful women in paradise.
- Smile in the face of death, oh young man! For you are on your way to the everlasting paradise!
- Any place you go or any action you do you should supplicate and God is with his slaves the believers with support and guard with facilitation and success and conquest and victory and everything.

The Third Stage

- In combat hit firmly and strongly as the heroes do who do not wish to come back to the worldly life and say aloud God is Great for saying that (causes) horror and terror to enter the hearts of the disbelievers.
- Then apply the tradition of captivity and capture among them and kill them as God the Almighty said, "No Prophet must have prisoners of war until he weakens (the enemy) on the land. Do you want to have the best of the worldly life and God wants the hereafter and God is the most Mighty and the Most Wise."
- The zero hour came open up your jacket and open up your chest welcoming death for the way of God and. . . . and end with praying if it is possible start it before the target in a few seconds or the last of your speech is – There is no God except Allah and Muhammad is His Messenger.

Source: Paz, Reuven. 2001. *Programmed Terrorists: An Analysis of the Letter Left Behind by the September 11 Hijackers.* International Policy Institute for Counter Terrorism, December. Web posted at http://www.ict.org.il/articles/articledet.cfm?articleid=419.

LEARNING OBJECTIVES

After reading this chapter you should know:

☐ Definitions of terrorism.

☐ Types of terrorism—international and domestic.

☐ Extent and patterns of terrorism and hate crime.

☐ Terrorist organization, dynamics, and recruitment for suicide and other terrorist attacks.

☐ Definition and extent of cyberterrorism.

☐ Explanations for terrorism.

Introduction

The events of September 11, 2001 shocked the world and traumatized the U.S. social order. The unimaginable had occurred: Four American airliners were hijacked by nineteen al-Qaida terrorists on the same day with the intention of flying them into the twin towers of the World Trade Center, the Pentagon, and possibly the White House—each a symbol of U.S. economic, military, and political dominance.

The U.S. State Department (2002: 1) summarizes the events of 9-11 as follows:

> *"While nothing is easier than to denounce the evil doer, nothing is more difficult than to understand him."*
>
> —Fyodor Mikhailovich Dostoevsky (Hudson 1999: 16)

> *"I am very happy and proud of what my son did and, frankly I am a bit jealous. I wish I had done (the bombing). My son has fulfilled the Prophet's (Mohammed's) wishes. He has become a hero! Tell me, what more could a father ask."*
>
> —Father of 22-year-old Jordanian suicide bomber Saeed Hotari (www.usatoday.com/news/world/june01/2001-06-26-suicide-usat.htm).

- Five terrorists hijacked American Airlines flight 11, which departed Boston for Los Angeles at 7:45 A.M. An hour later it was deliberately piloted into the North Tower of the World Trade Center in New York City.

- Five terrorists hijacked United Airlines Flight 175, which departed Boston for Los Angeles at 7:58 A.M. At 9:05 the plane crashed into the South Tower of the World Trade Center. Both towers collapsed shortly thereafter, killing approximately 3,000 persons, including hundreds of firefighters and rescue personnel who were helping to evacuate the buildings.

- Four terrorists hijacked United Airlines flight 93, which departed Newark for San Francisco at 8:01 A.M. At 10:10 the plane crashed in Stony Creek Township, Pennsylvania, killing all 45 persons on board. The intended target of this hijacked plane is not known, but it is believed that passengers overpowered the terrorists, thus preventing the aircraft from being used as a missile.

- Five terrorists hijacked American Airlines flight 77, which departed Washington Dulles Airport for Los Angeles at 8:10 A.M. At 9:39 the plane was flown directly into the Pentagon in Arlington, Virginia, near Washington, DC. A total of 189 persons were killed, including all who were on board the plane.

The events of 9-11 mark the worst instance of international terrorism in history. Imagine that these events had not actually occurred, but were the basis for a proposed movie script. It is very likely that the movie concept would be rejected on the grounds that it fell into the realm of fantasy, without the advantage of the element of magic. It was simply a dreadful tale—surrealistic perhaps but not likely to capture the attention of the movie going public.

Rather than becoming another rejected movie script, the events of September 11, 2001, altered the course of history in the twenty-first century. The threat of an unexpected and horrific terrorist attack marked daily life in the United States. Law enforcement and other government agencies scrambled to devise a first response to the possibility of another attack. A massive reordering of governmental priorities ensued. Congress established a Department of Homeland Security that combined twenty-two federal agencies that employed approximately 180,000 persons. Billions of dollars were appropriated to support counterterrorism strategies. Congress also enacted the USA PATRIOT Act that significantly extended the powers of law enforcement agencies to investigate and detain persons suspected of terrorist activities or those who may have information about such activities (U.S. Department of Homeland Security 2004; USA PATRIOT Act 2001).

Despite the previous attack on the World Trade Center and isolated instances of international terrorism specifically directed at U.S. citizens around the world, the possibility of terrorist activities within the United States seemed to be remote. The terrorist attacks on 9-11 redefined the U.S. view of the world and its relation to the United States. In turn, the U.S. way of life—in particular, its foreign policies and global economic interests—were critically assessed by nations around the world. Issues related to terrorism and homeland security are continually debated in the media, on university and college campuses, and among thoughtful persons around the world (The Pew Research Center 2002).

This chapter considers key issues related to international terrorism that continually define life in the twenty-first century. Throughout the chapter, attention is focused on the terrorist activities of Islamic extremist organization—currently the most prevalent form of international terrorism. The chapter is structured in the following way: First, various official definitions of terrorism are assessed. Second, the characteristics of three broad forms of terrorism—international, domestic, and hate crimes—are discussed. Third, a detailed typology of terrorism is presented. Two forms of terrorism are highlighted: suicide bombing and cyberterrorism. Fourth, the motivations that drive individuals to commit acts of terrorism and the processes of recruiting, selecting, and training potential members of terrorist organizations are reviewed. The structure and the clandestine nature of their organization, methods of communication, and decision-making processes are also discussed. Last, sociological and social psychological theories of deviant behavior that help us to understand the commission of terrorist acts are presented.

What Is Terrorism?

From the Reign of Terror in France (1793-1794) to the present, attempts to instill terror in the minds of one's adversaries have taken many forms. Alex P. Schmidt and Albert I. Jongman's (1988) survey of terrorist scholars revealed 109 different definitions of terrorism. The following elements were most commonly found in this array of definitions: violence, force (83.5 percent), political motivation (65 percent), intent to instilling fear or terror (51 percent), prior threats (47 percent), anticipated psychological effects (41.5 percent), the victims were distinguished from the targets (37.5 percent), intentional, planned action (32 percent). Schmidt (1984) considers three elements central to an understanding of terrorism: (1) the use of victims as symbolic target, (2) instilling fear as a result of an exceptional use of violence, and (3) the creation of an audience beyond the victims of the terrorist attack. Walter Laqueur (1987) opts for a simple definition of terrorism—the illegitimate use of force to achieve a political objective by targeting innocent people.

To Paul Pillar (2004), former deputy chief of the Central Intelligence Agency's Counterterrorism Center, terrorism is marked by four basic elements:

1. Premeditation—planned in advance, rather than an impulsive act of rage.
2. Political motivation—not criminal, like the violence that groups such as the mafia use to get money, but designed to change the existing political order.
3. Directed at civilian populations—not at military targets or combat-ready troops.
4. Carried out by subnational groups, rather than by a county's regular army.

Harvard professor and terrorism expert Jessica Stern (1999: 11) defines terrorism as an "act or threat of violence against noncombatants with the objective of exacting revenge, intimidating, or otherwise influencing an audience." To Stern, terrorism differs from war in that non-combatants are victims, and from crime by eliciting dread and creating fear in the larger society. Certainly the events of September 11, 2001, the bombing of the federal building in Oklahoma, and the burning of black churches in the South, and the killing of ten persons by an unknown sniper in and around the nation's capital are acts committed against noncombatants, driven by revenge, with the intention of creating fear and dread among persons in the larger population.

More recently, Donald Black (2002) argues that terrorism in its purest form must be viewed as a form of self-help. Black (2002) defines pure terrorism as "unilateral self-help by organized civilians who covertly inflict mass violence on other civilians." Black (1983, 1998) identifies nine characteristics of pure terrorism: (1) a form of self-help, that is, it is a way to address grievances by means of aggression; (2) highly violent; (3) a punitive response to a moral wrong—a form of private capital punishment; (4) identifies a collective liability—persons located in social space characterized by nationality, race, religion, ethnicity, or political party; (5) recurrent, that is, a series of attacks that occur over time; (6) involves unilateral mass violence—terrorists are typically the aggressors, rather than the victims; (7) well-organized, covert activity; (8) a form of quasi-warfare, directed toward an outside ethnic group, or nation; and (9) typically terrorists work in small groups whose missions may well involve their own destruction.

Terrorism and Crime

Donald Black (2002) notes that criminal behavior often is a form of social control. Crime is committed to exert a form of control over persons whom the offender(s) views as immoral or threatening. While unlike crime activity in many ways, terrorism is also a form of social control, a way to redress perceived wrongs committed against one's nationality, race, religion, ethnicity, or political party.

D. Douglas Bodrero (2000) draws distinctions between criminals and terrorists. He notes that politically disinterested persons often commit crimes for personal reasons. Crimes are committed as opportunities arise, and the perpetrator makes considerable effort to avoid detection and apprehension. Acts of terrorism, however, are typically ideologically or religiously motivated and involve a specific political purpose. The collective interests of terrorists supercede the self-interests of any member of a terrorist organization.

Official Definitions of Terrorism

Various official definitions of **terrorism** and **terrorists** have been formulated to guide the actions of national representatives or governmental agencies. The United Nations defines terrorism as "the act of destroying or injuring civilian lives or the act of destroying or injuring civilian property without the expressly chartered permission of a specific government, thus, by individuals or groups acting independently or governments on their own accord and belief, in the attempt to affect some political goal." And a terrorist is defined as "any person who, acting independently of the specific recognition of a country, or as a single person, or as a part of a group not recognized as an official part or division of a nation, acts to destroy or injure civilians or destroy or damage property belonging to civilians or governments in order to effect some political goal." (www.un .org/terrorism)

The U.S. State Department (2004) defines terrorism as "premeditated, politically motivated violence, perpetrated against noncombatant targets by subnational groups or clandestine agents, usually intended to influence an audience." International terrorism involves terrorist acts between "citizens or the territory of more than one country." And "terrorist group" refers to "any group practicing or that has significant subgroups that practice, international terrorism."

The U.S. Department of Defense defines terrorism as "the unlawful use or threatened use of force or violence against individuals or property to coerce or intimidate governments or societies, often to achieve political, religious, or ideological objectives (*Code of Federal Regulation:* 28 CFR Section 0.85)."

The Federal Bureau of Investigation (1999b) defines terrorism as "the unlawful use of force or violence against persons or property to intimidate or coerce a government, the civilian population, or any segment thereof, in furtherance of political or social objectives (FBI 1999b)."

Depending on the *origin, base,* and *objectives* of the terrorist organization, terrorism is considered either domestic or international (FBI 1999b).

- **International Terrorism:** Terrorism involving citizens or the territory of more than one country; terrorism committed by a group or individual who has some connection to a foreign power or whose activities transcend national boundaries.

- **Domestic Terrorism:** The commission of acts of terrorism by U.S. citizens— either groups or individuals—who are based and operate entirely within the United States without foreign direction or influence, and whose acts are directed at elements of the U.S. government or population.

- **Hate Crime or Bias Crime:** A criminal act or attempted act against a person, institution, or property that is motivated in whole or in part by the offender's bias against a race, color, religion, gender, ethnic/national origin group, disability status, or sexual orientation group (FBI 2002a).

The FBI further distinguishes between types of terrorism and hate crimes. Characteristics of the offenders, victims, and the offense itself are considered in the classification of crimes of terrorism or hate. Table 16.1 summarizes the FBI's classification schema.

International Terrorism

Small bands of persons of common ancestry and common purpose find homes in various countries, integrate themselves into the daily life of the community, and become known simply as friendly, law-abiding, and hardworking. Their success depends in part on their anonymity, their ability to simply blend into the fabric of a foreign culture. These small groups of immigrants, also known as cells, are part of a larger network whose sole purpose is to engage in acts of international terrorism. Each cell stands ready to carry out a specific terrorist mission, usually against the citizens of their adopted country, when called on to do so.

Domestic Terrorism

Anti-government activists also typically form into small groups to carry out their mission—to disrupt significantly the operation of the political order. By attacking agencies of the federal government, for example, domestic terrorists hope to focus attention on acts of political injustice and elicit public sympathy for their acts of retaliation.

The 1995 bombing of the Alfred P. Murrah Federal Building in Oklahoma City was carried out by two anti-government activists—Timothy McVeigh and Terry Nichols. On April 19th around 9:00 in the morning, as children were being escorted into the daycare center in the federal building, a bomb made from fertilizer and fuel oil was delivered in a rented truck. The explosion that ensued caused the deaths of 169 persons. The bombing of the federal building was in

Table 16.1 Classification of Terrorist Acts and Hate Crimes

	International Terror	**Domestic Terror**	**Hate Crime**
Offender			
Who/Origin	Citizens, states, or territories of more than one country or person or group with connection to a foreign power	U.S. citizens—either groups or individuals—who are based and operate entirely within the United States without foreign direction or influence	Individuals or groups (e.g., hate groups)
Motive	Intimidate or coerce in furtherance of political and/or social objectives	Intimidate or coerce in furtherance of political and/or social objectives	In whole or in part by bias against a person's race, religion, sexual orientation, disability, or national origin
Victims/ Targets	Government, the civilian population or any segment thereof—persons or property	Elements of the U.S. government or population	Person, group, institution, or property
Offense			
Where	Transcends national boundaries	U.S.	Any location
Examples	Suicide bombers; Weapons of mass destruction	Pipe bombs; Abortion clinic bombings; Animal rights activists; Skinheads	Church arsons; Cross burnings; Dragging

Sources: Federal Bureau of Investigation, 1996b; 2002a)

response to the Federal Bureau of Investigation's assault on the Branch Davidian compound in Mount Carmel, Texas, on the same date two years before. The Branch Davidians, a religious sect, were suspected of storing a large number of weapons in their compound. An initial attempt by the Bureau of Alcohol, Tobacco, and Firearms to seize the weapons in a surprise attack resulted in the deaths of four agents and six Branch Davidian members. Following a 51-day siege, the Federal Bureau of Investigation launched an all-out assault that resulted in the burning of several buildings in the compound and the deaths of eighty Branch Davidian members, including men, women, and children (PBS 1995).

Hate Crimes

Extreme acts of violence tend to be committed by small groups, or individuals motivated by an intense hatred of a particular sociocultural group. Neither political or ideological issues nor the prospect of material gain are involved in the

---

AT A GLANCE

- In 2003, there were 208 international terrorists attacks, a slight increase from the 199 incidents recorded in 2002, but substantially fewer than the 355 attacks in 2001 and 426 in 2000.

- 625 persons were killed and 3,646 were wounded in acts of international terrorism in 2003.

- More than 3,000 victims of terrorism were reported as causalities in the September 11, 2001, attacks in New York, Washington, DC, and Pennsylvania. An even higher number were wounded.

- The U.S. Secretary of State designates seven governments as state sponsors of international terrorism: Iran, Iraq, Syria, Libya, Cuba, North Korea, and Sudan.

- The U.S. Department of State designates 38 groups as Foreign Terrorist Organizations.

- The highest number of anti-U.S. terrorist attacks in 2002 occurred in Latin America.

- U.S. businesses abroad were the most likely targets of international terrorism during 2003.

- Bombings have accounted for 2 of every 3 international terrorist attacks during 2003.

Sources: U.S. Department of State. 2004. *Patterns of Global Terrorism 2003.* Washington, DC: U.S. Department of State. Web posted at www.state.gov; Leader, Stefan H. 1997. *The Rise of Terrorism.* Web posted at www.securitymanagement.com/library/000339.html.

---

commission of the typical hate crime. Rather, the primary motive is to seriously injure or cause the death of persons of a hated racial, ethnic, or religious group.

Consider, for example, the circumstances that surrounded the death of James Byrd in the small East Texas town of Jasper. On June 7, 1998, James Byrd, a 49-year-old black man, was kidnapped by three white supremacists—John William King, 24, Lawrence Brewer, 32, and Shawn Berry, 24. They beat James Byrd senseless, pulled down his pants, chained his ankles to the bumper of their pick-up truck and dragged him more than three miles over a rough dirt road. His head and one shoulder were torn from his body. The remains of James Byrd were dumped at the entrance of a black cemetery for former slaves.

John William King and Lawrence Brewer were members of the Confederate Knights of America—a racist group formed by inmates at Beto prison unit in Texas. When King and Brewer were released from prison, they tried to start a chapter of the Confederate Knights of America in Jasper. They befriended Shawn Berry with the hope of recruiting him into their newly formed racist organization. As part of the Shawn Berry's initiation into the Confederate Knights of America, he was expected to participate in the kidnapping and murder of James Byrd (CNN 1999a).

Typology of Terrorism

Various typologies of terrorism have been proposed. However, it is generally conceded that six forms of terrorism are most commonly practiced: nationalist, religious, state-sponsored, left-wing, right-wing, and anarchist (Hudson 1999: 21). The aim of **nationalist terrorism** is to create a self-governing nation that exists apart from its current political domination. Examples include the Irish Republican Army, the Palestinian Liberation Organization, the Basque Fatherland and Liberty, and the Kurdistan Workers' Party. Each of these organizations uses terrorist tactics to call attention to oppressive social conditions and to garner widespread support for its intention to establish an independent nation-state.

Religious terrorism is carried out to defend religious doctrines or sacred lands from assaults by nonbelievers. Bruce Hoffman (1995, 1999), a noted terrorism expert at RAND, notes that religious terrorist comprise about half of the 56 active international terrorist groups. Unlike nationalist terrorists, religious terrorists are not limited by considerations of nationalism or ideologies. Rather, as Bruce Hoffman (1995, 1999) points out, religious terrorists may victimize any member of a religious group that is not their own and engage in "almost limitless violence against a virtually open-ended category of targets: that is, anyone who is not a member of the terrorists' religion or religious sect." Extreme religious terrorists include the al-Qaeda—Osama bin Laden's international network of terrorists, Hamas—the Palestinian Sunni Muslin organization, the Hezbollah—the radical Israeli group, and Aum Shinrikyo—the fatalistic Japanese extremists.

State-sponsored terrorism refers to contracting the services of mercenary terrorists to carry out acts of destruction that serve the interests of the state or nation. While the state provides financial support for acts of terrorism, it does not overtly engage in them. In 2004, the U.S. State Department identified seven countries as sponsors of terrorist activities: Iran, Sudan, Libya, Syria, North Korea, Cuba, and Iraq.

At opposite ends of a political continuum are left- and right-wing terrorism. On the one hand, **left-wing terrorists** seek to overthrow capitalism and create a

James Byrd, Jr., the victim of one of the most brutal hate crimes in history, was abducted by three white men near Jasper, Texas, chained to a pick-up truck, and dragged down a country road until he was decapitated and his body dismembered. He was then dumped at the entrance to a black cemetery.

communistic or socialistic form of economic system. The German Baader-Meinhof group, the Japanese Red Army, and the Italian Red Brigades all sought to remedy what they considered the exploitation of capitalism. In addition, the Workers' World Party, Reclaim the Streets, and Carnival Capitalism operate on an international scale to disrupt the spread of the capitalistic economic system. On the other hand, the objective of **right-wing terrorists** is to replace liberal democratic governments with neo-Nazi or fascist states that establish Aryan supremacy. Examples of right-wing terrorists are the Skinheads in Europe and World Church of the Creator and the Aryan Nations in the United States—anti-government organizations marked by distinct racial hatred. Last, **Anarchism** simply wants to destroy any form of government and be able to live unencumbered by the restrictions of political control. Groups that protest the creation of a world bank, the emergence of economic globalization, and the resultant blending of cultures around the world are examples of terrorists in pursuit of anarchy (U.S. Department of State 2004).

Terrorist Organizational Structure

James Fraser and Ian Fulton (1984) contend that the hierarchical structure of a terrorist organization resembles a pyramid. There are four hierarchical levels: command, active cadre, active supporters, and passive supporters. At the top of the pyramid is the command, the smallest unit in the structure, responsible for setting policy and devising a strategic plan for the terrorist organization. Because secrecy is vital the survival of the terrorist group, the commanders do not freely communicate with the other members of the organization. The active cadre is entrusted with carrying out specific acts of terrorism. Active supporters provide the assistance necessary for the active cadre to carry out its missions. Intelligence gathering, establishing means of communication, and providing places to hide from oppositional forces are responsibilities of the active supporters. The passive supporters, the largest segment of the terrorist organization, create conditions that are generally favorable to terrorist activities by fostering public acceptance and goodwill.

Terrorist organizations are composed of cells, each with a unique task. Each cell, typically made up of four to six persons, is responsible for carrying out a specific function—intelligence, technical assistance, training, supplies, and so on. Cells may be actively engaged in planning and carrying out a particular mission, or they may be "sleeper" cells whose members stand ready to respond to a call to participate in a terrorist activity at some future, but unspecified time. Central to the success of a terrorist organization is its ability to operate in complete secrecy. To ensure the secrecy of its activities, terrorist organizations must carefully control the flow of information within and between cells. Often members of the organizations do not know what others are doing. The planning of missions is reserved for few terrorist leaders and divulged to the members only when the mission is to be carried out. The necessity to maintain utmost secrecy is also enhanced by a decentralized form of organization (White 2002). Jonathan White (2002: 38) also notes that "the larger the (terrorist) group, the greater the degree of decentralization." Decentralized organizations enhance security—cell members, largely unknown to one another, can operate independently without fear of detection. Organizations' leaders coordinate the efforts of the various cells by demanding strict adherence to their directives. Jonathan White (2002: 36–37) notes: "In essence, what the commanders continually threaten to do is to terrorize the terrorist organization. Factionalism and autonomy are controlled through fear of retribution."

Terrorist Organizational Dynamics

Many of the recruits into terrorist organizations are marginal persons—young, uneducated, and powerless—with few prospects for a meaningful life. Acceptance into a terrorist organization offers a sense of belonging, self-worth, and purpose in life. To Eric Shaw (1986) the membership in terrorist organization solves many life problems.

> The terrorist identity offers the individual a role in society, albeit a negative one, which is commensurate with his or her prior expectations and sufficient to compensate for past losses. Group membership provides a sense of potency, an intense and close interpersonal environment, social status, potential access to wealth and a share in what may be a grandiose but noble social design. The powerful psychological forces of conversion in the group are sufficient to offset traditional social sanctions against violence . . . To the terrorists their acts may have the moral status of religious warfare or political liberation. (Shaw 1986: 38–39)

The identity of the "new recruit" is fused with that of the terrorist organization. In exchange for a meaningful identity, the "new recruit" abandons individual freedom of thought or action. The terrorist organization frames its mission, determines the extent of involvement of its individual members, and provides a justification for engagement in lethal violence (Post 1986). Albert Bandura (1990: 161–91) outlines four strategies for moral disengagement that may be used by terrorist organizations. First, terrorism is viewed as necessary to combat an "evil" force and therefore morally justified. Second, individual members of the terrorist organization are simply carrying out the directives of their leaders and cannot be held responsible for their individual actions. Third, terrorists reject the notion that the pain and suffering of their victims is any greater than their own. In this way they insulate themselves from any guilt that may ensue from their acts of violence. And, fourth, victims of terrorists' attacks tend to be depersonalized and dehumanized—a faceless, oppressive enemy that deserves to be destroyed. Bonnie Cordes (1987: 43) notes that "renaming themselves, their actions, their victims and their enemies accords the terrorist respectability."

Suicide Bombers

Yoran Schweitzer (2001) defines a **suicide attack** as "a violent, politically motivated attack, carried out in a deliberate state of awareness by a person who blows himself up together with his chosen target. The pre-meditated certain death of the perpetrator is the pre-condition for the success of the attack."

Who Are the Suicide Bombers

- 47 percent of the suicide bombers have an academic education and an additional 29 percent have at least a high school education

- 83 percent of the suicide bombers are single

- 64 percent of the suicide bombers are between the ages of 18–24; most of the rest are under 30

- 68 percent of the suicide bombers have come from the Gaza Strip (Shuman 2001)

Suicide Attackers in the United States

The nineteen terrorists responsible for the hijacking of four planes on September 11, 2001 did not fit the profile of previous suicide attackers.

- Many of the men were older than the typical suicide bomber, who is usually in his early twenties. Mohamed Atta, age 33, is suspected of planning and carrying out the 9–11 attack on the World Trade Center.

- Rather than poor, alienated youths who fanatically engage in acts of terrorism, the 9–11 terrorists were well-educated, technologically sophisticated,

Women Suicide Bombers

The al-Aqsa Martyrs Brigades, a militant group allied with Yasser Arafat's Fatah movement, claims responsibility for many of the suicide bombings in the Middle East. The militia reportedly has set up a special suicide bomber unit for women. One of the few women bombers participating in this militia was Ayat Akhras, an 18-year-old Palestinian high school senior. She detonated explosives strapped to her body one afternoon outside of a Jewish SuperSol supermarket during shopping hours. Three people were killed, including the bomber, and as many as twenty others were injured. A security guard and a 17-year-old Israeli girl were the other casualties. As reports of the bombing spread, many Palestinians cheered and celebrated, handing out candy and firing guns into the air. Ayat was held up as a hero. Her friends described it as "a courageous act," and many wished to be in her shoes. Like many of her friends, Ayat heaped scorn on Arab leaders and in her farewell video stated, "I am going to fight instead of the sleeping Arab armies who are watching Palestinian girls fighting alone, it is an intefada until victory."

Source: AP, Jerusalem, "Female Suicide Bomber Kills Two in Jerusalem," *USA Today,* www.USATODAY.com; Hazboun, I. Associated Press. "Suicide Bomber Popular Schoolgirl," www.sltrib.com; ABCnews.com, "Tale of Two Teens," www.abcnews.com; Barr, C. "Why a Palestinian Girl Now Wants to be a Suicide Bomber," *Christian Science Monitor.* Web posted at www.csmonitor.com/2002/0401/p07s01-wome.htm.

and capable of engineering a long-term, complicated terrorist plan involving several persons.

- They blended well into mainstream U.S. culture, spoke English exceedingly well, and did not draw attention to themselves in any way (Parker, Copeland, and Sharp 2001).

Noted terrorism expert Jerrold Post (2001), who has interviewed thirty-five failed suicide bombers imprisoned in Israel, reports: "I find it chilling that in contrast to the immature youths shaped and brainwashed by their leaders, these people were carrying out their sense of mission within them as they were leading this middle-class life."

Recruitment

Potential terrorists, particularly suicide bombers, are often identified in places of public prayer and religious teaching. The British Broadcasting Company reports that suicide bombers "are likely to be motivated by religious fervor" and typically are "picked out from mosques, schools and religious institutions" (Shuman 2001). Al-Qassam, the military arm of Hamas, and the Palestinian Islamic Jihad both recruit suicide bombers. Members of these highly integrated terrorist cells frequently visit schools and mosques in the West Bank and Gaza Strip. Typically, they will talk with students, usually between the ages of 12 and 17, about the prospect of dying for Allah. Those who express interest in the possibility of religious martyrdom are identified as having "special merit." With rare exception, the students who qualify for "special merit" are closely tied to a person who has been imprisoned, killed, or seriously hurt by the Israelis. Their personal suffering and sense of humiliation prepare them for the socialization process necessary to form a successful suicide bomber (Hudson 1999: 117–118).

Hamas, the radical Islamic group, reports that an intense period of indoctrination is provided to potential suicide bombers.

> The bombers believe that they are sent on their missions from God, and by the time that they're ready to be strapped with explosives . . . they have reached a hypnotic state. Their rationale: that by blowing themselves up in a crowd of Israelis, they are forging their own gateway to heaven (Shuman 2001).

Intensive instruction in the Koran and the Hadith, the teachings of Prophet Mohammed, are provided the potential suicide bomber. The extreme honor of dying for Allah, the promises of an afterlife with unimaginable sensuous pleasures, and the opportunity to strike a blow directly at the Israelis who, they argue, are responsible for stealing the homeland of the Muslims are key elements of the process of indoctrination. In addition, Hamas provides the poverty-ridden families of the suicide bomber with a monthly stipend of about $1,000, food and household supplies, resettlement funds for families who are targets of Israeli retaliation, and scholarships for the remaining children (Hudson 1999).

During the final days prior to the suicide attack, the recruit prepares himself by repeating scriptural verses that ensure his immediate entrance into heaven and neutralize any guilt that he may have for taking the lives of persons unknown to him. Among the more common verses is: "Think not of those who are slain in Allah's way as dead. No, they live on and find their sustenance in the presence of their Lord" (Hudson 1999: 118). Comforted by this belief, the suicide bomber is able to mingle among his victims in a relaxed and causal manner. An additional safeguard against the detection of the mission and the recruit's last-minute change of heart is the practice of reserving instruction in the use of explosives for the end of his training, just before the mission is to be carried out (Hudson 1999: 118–119).

The New Suicide Bomber

A new suicide bomber is emerging, working along side those traditionally re-cruited by Hamas and Islamic Jihad. Young Palestinians driven by the desire to avenge the ravages of perceived political oppression volunteer to become suicide bombers. They do not receive the kinds of intense indoctrination that is typically provided young recruits whose public demonstrations of devotion set them apart from their peers and whose view of their chances of a worthwhile life are particu-larly bleak. Rather, young, secular, college-educated Palestinians are offering to serve as suicide bombers. Often less than a week elapses before they are provided with an explosive device, directed toward a suitable target, and given instruc-tions as to how to carry out the suicide attack. A transformation in Palestinian culture is occurring, which according to Dr. Iyad Sarraj (cited in Bennet 2002), a Palestinian psychiatrist, shapes the meanings that children attach to life and death. In a culture marked by powerlessness and humiliation, where suicidal at-tacks are commonplace, personal power is achieved only in a death that involves the killing of the enemy. Martyrdom is an expression of righteous rage. *New York Times* reporter James Bennet (2002: 1) observes, "But as much as any manipulative militant leader, it appears to be the very culture of a ravaged and disoriented Palestinian society that now feeds the recruitment of suicide bombers."

A young Palestinian woman poses with her child just before becoming a suicide bomber.

Terrorism: Psychopathology versus Rational Behavior

On the surface it may appear that acts of terrorism—the killing of innocent civilians unknown to the assailants—provide evidence of insanity. Viewed from the outside, suicide bombers are easily understood as individuals driven by a psychotic rage. Yet, considered within a sociopolitical and cultural context, terrorist behaviors may be interpreted as the reactions of psychologically normal individuals to extraordinary circumstances and processes.

Psychologist Clark R. McCauley (2001) notes that terrorists' behavior is shaped by their single-minded dedication to a cause and their intense involvement with a terrorist group. Potential members of a terrorist organization are identified and recruited based on their demonstration of an inordinate public commitment to a cause. Once they have been accepted into a terrorist group, they are effectively isolated from the influence competing values from the outside. The process of separation and isolation are commonly practiced by a wide range of groups interested in molding the mentality and behaviors of its members. The merging of the individual's identity and sense of purpose with that of the terrorist group results in the creation of a person capable of carrying out self-sacrificing acts of terrorism.

To Brookings Institute Fellow Shibley Telhami (2002: 23), the "most pervasive psychology in the Arab world today is collective rage and feelings of helplessness." Governments are no longer able to resolve international conflicts. Individual action is needed to counter the humiliation of the chronic political ineptness. Shibley Telhami (2002: 23) argues that "suicide bombings thrive in anarchy." They "take root because they free the desperate from the need to rely on governments altogether." Suicide bombers are not limited, Telhami (2002) observes, to radical Islamic groups such as Hamas, but are also found among secular Palestinians who find it an effective political strategy. Mouin Rabbani, director of the Palestinian American Research Center in Ramallah, also contends that intractable political oppression creates the willingness to engage in suicide bombing attacks.

> Without exception, the suicide bombers have lived their lives on the receiving end of a system designed to trample their rights and crush every hope of a brighter future. . . . Confronted by a seemingly endless combination of death, destruction, restriction, harassment and humiliation, they conclude that ending life as a bomb—rather than having it end by a bullet—endows them, even if only in their final moments, with a semblance of purpose and control previously considered out of reach. (Telhami 2002: 23)

Motivations

The motivations for involvement in terrorist activities may be classified into three categories: rational motivation, psychological motivation, and cultural motivation (see http://www.terrorism.com).

Rational Motivation

A rational decision-making process may well precede the commission of a terrorist act. Terrorist organizations set goals and objectives to advance their causes. The costs and benefits of engaging in a specific terrorist act are weighed. A critical question is: Can the proposed terrorist act achieve its goals without causing a reaction that will jeopardize the cause?

Psychological Motivation

Dissatisfaction with life and a dismal view of one's future tend to characterize persons engaged in terrorist activities. Potential terrorists are often described as "true believers" who perceive the world in dichotomous terms—their cause is sacred and righteous, those who oppose them are evil and inhuman. There is a strong need to belong to a group that will advance their beliefs and provide them with a sense of purpose in life.

Cultural Motivation

Terrorist behaviors must be understood within a sociocultural framework. The view that the life of every individual must be protected and preserved is commonly held in Europe and North America. Other societies, particularly in the Middle East and Asia, consider identification with a group—nation, family, or tribe—to take precedence over individual life. Threats to the survival of a culture—its ethnic identity, religion, language, or territory—often result in uncompromising retaliatory acts of violence. Terrorism in the defense of religious belief is, arguably, carried out with the most intense fervor. The sacrifice of one's life for the good of cultural preservation is uniformly valued and highly rewarded.

Doctrine of Necessity

H.H.A. Cooper (1977) contends that terrorists justify the commission of violent acts against innocent persons, including women, children, and the elderly by concluding that peaceful means for conflict resolution are not viable and must be rejected. The use of violence is viewed as the most reasonable way to achieve their goals. Cooper (1977: 8-18) argues that terrorists adopt a "doctrine of necessity" to justify their acts of destruction. Violence becomes a moral imperative.

For example, Al-Qaeda and other Islamic extremists seek to preserve their Islamic cultural heritage, including their interpretation of *Sharia* or Islamic law. To do so they must engage in a *Jihad* or holy war against the enemies of Islam. The United States and Israel are among the principal opponents of Islam as, they believe, Allah intended it to be practiced.

Cyberterrorism

In a report commissioned by the National Academy of Sciences, the potential destructive force of **cyberterrorism** is highlighted. The report begins:

> We are at risk. America depends on computers. They control delivery, communications, aviation, and financial services. They are used to store vital information, from medical records to business plans to criminal records. Although we trust them, they

Ohio Truck Driver Lyuman Faris who was working as an al-Qaida agent to commit terrorist attacks in the United States.

are vulnerable—to the effects of poor design and insufficient quality control, to accident and perhaps most alarmingly, to deliberate attack. The modern thief can steal more with a computer than with a gun. Tomorrow's terrorist may be able to do more damage with a keyboard than with a bomb. (National Research Council 1991)

Definition

To Mark M. Pollitt cyberterrorism involves two elements: cyberspace and terrorism (see http://www.cs.georgetown.edu/~denning/infosec/pollitt.html). Cyberspace refers to the "virtual world"—the "symbolic—true, false, binary, metaphoric representations of information—that place in which computer programs function and data moves" (Collins 1996). Pollitt adopts the U.S. State Department definition of terrorism—the "premeditated, politically motivated violence perpetrated against noncombatant targets by subnational groups or clandestine agents." Combining the two definitions, Pollitt defines cyberterrorism as "the premeditated, politically motivated attack against information, computer systems, computer programs, and data which results in violence against noncombatant targets by subnational groups or clandestine agents."

Computers may be used in the furtherance of terrorist activities. Increasing global dependence on computer technology has resulted in an unprecedented vulnerability to attack.

Rod Stark (1999) defines cyberterrorism as:

the purposeful or threatened use of politically, socially, economically or religiously motivated cyber warfare or cyber-targeted violence, conducted by a non-state or state-sponsored group for the purposes of creating fear, anxiety, and panic in the targeted population, and the disruption of military and civilian assets.

The development of the Internet has led to acceleration of the "information age," the global economy, and the increasing possibilities of cyberterrorism.

Warfare is also becoming transformed. The dependence of civilian populations on the flow of information to conduct their everyday lives makes them particularly attractive targets for cyberterrorist attacks. Cyberterrorism may involve the destruction, alteration, and/or the acquisition and retransmission of information. Disruptions in the flow of information have the potential to confuse and demoralize civilian populations across the world simultaneously. Confidence in the viability economic transactions, in the safety of public transportation, in the ability to rely on the validity of medical records may well be undermined (Collins 1996; Shahar 1997).

Explanations of Terrorism

Sociological or social psychological theorizing about the precipitants of terrorism, its organization, and its perpetuation is relatively uncommon compared to other forms of violent behavior. However, it is possible to apply extant theories of violence to issue related to terrorist activities. While they provide an incomplete understanding, the theoretical formulations considered here help us to think about the intricacies of terrorism and its social context.

Rational Choice

Derek B. Cornish and Ronald V. Clarke's (1986) rational choice formulation of criminal behavior is useful in understanding acts of terrorism. They argue that prior to the committing a crime, the offender rationally and deliberately assesses the cost and benefits involved in its commission. If the potential benefits substantially outweigh the possible costs that may be incurred, then the offender may well carry out the crime. Terrorists tend to be driven by an overwhelming desire to advance an extremely highly valued cause—one that is inextricably tied to personal identity and provides an elemental meaning to life. Involvement in acts of terrorism provides an opportunity to contribute to the larger social good—to redress political oppression and humiliation at the hand of the enemy. The cost of the terrorist life is considered minimal compared to the immediate and everlasting rewards of martyrdom.

Social Integration

To Emile Durkheim (1951) the degree of social integration—or the adherence to a set of strongly held common values—provides an explanation for deviant behaviors. His seminal study of rates of suicide links the extent of social integration of a society with three distinct types of suicide. Under conditions of low integration, marked by the absence of commonly held values, egoistic suicide tends to occur. Societies marked by high integration, where important social values are held in common, altruistic suicide is more usual. And, in societies undergoing rapid and unpredictable social change, normlessness more typically characterizes everyday life. Under these conditions, anomic suicide is more likely to occur. Terrorism is more common when social integration is high and individuals are willing to sacrifice themselves for the good of a recognized social entity. Suicide bombers and other forms of self-destructive terrorist acts are typically carried out to advance well-defined political or religious objectives.

Routine Activities

Lawrence Cohen and Marcus Felson (1979) advance a routine activities explanation of criminal behavior. Their theoretical formulation includes three components: a motivated offender, suitable target, and the absence of an effective guardian. The commitment of terrorists to the success of their mission is essential. Ambivalence on the part of a would-be terrorist may well result in failure of the mission and compromise the security of the organization. Further, terrorists take into account the attractiveness of their intended target, assessing the potential for instilling widespread and lasting "terror" in the minds of the members of the larger public. The likelihood that a guardian of the target will thwart the terrorist's mission is also carefully considered. In brief, the routine activities theory identifies the three criteria for a successful terrorist attack.

Culture Conflict

Thorsten Sellin (1938) argues that clash of conduct norms may give rise to the occurrence of various forms of deviant behavior. Conflict in norms may occur when distinct sociocultural groups are close proximity with one another, when the laws of a dominant sociocultural group are imposed on a less powerful group, or when one sociocultural group moves into the lands occupied by another group. Recent terrorist activities, particularly emanating from the Israeli-Palestinian conflict, are consistent with Sellin's cultural conflict formulation. Disputes arising from the right to occupy the certain lands, most notably the West Bank and the Gaza Strip, and the resultant sense of cultural degradation have led to the proliferation of suicide bombings of Israeli targets by young Palestinians.

Frustration-Aggression

John Dollard and his colleagues (1939) contend that frustration, usually thought to involve the blockage of important needs and goals, will inevitably lead to some form of aggression. The more critical are the personal needs and the more vital are the cultural goals that are blocked, the more intense the experience of frustration and the more violent the resultant aggression.

Aggression may either be directed outwardly—a violent act committed against external target—or directly inwardly toward the self. Frustration may also result in an individual acting in such a way as to harm or destroy an external target as well as him or herself. The experience of long-term frustration—e.g., over self-governance—at the hands of a dominant political force—e.g., the conflict between the Irish Republican Army and the British Government, or the clash between the Palestinians and the Israelis—has led to repeated acts of terrorism over several years.

Strain

Closely related to the frustration-aggression hypothesis is Robert Agnew's (1992) strain theory of deviant behavior. Agnew argues that negative social interaction, typically involving blockage of important needs and goals, is particularly stressful for an individual. Sustained negative social interaction results in the chronic

Explanations for the Incidence of Terrorism

Theories and Theorists	Sociological Predictors	Hypotheses
Social Integration/Anomie		
• Durkheim	Social Integration	The greater the social integration, the greater the possibility of altruistic suicide.
		The greater the possibility of altruistic suicide, the greater the possibility of terrorism.
Routine Activities		
• Cohen and Felson	Motivated Offender Suitable Target Lack of a Guardian	The convergence of an offender who is motivated to engage in terrorism with a suitable target, and the lack of an adequate guardian for the target, the greater the probability that an act of terrorism will be carried out.
Social Learning		
• Sutherland	Differential Association	The greater the exposure to definitions favorable toward terrorism, the greater the probability of engaging in terrorist activities.
• Akers	Differential Association Definitions Differential Reinforcement Imitation	The greater the interaction with members of terrorist organizations, the greater the value assigned to acts of terrorism, the greater the actual or anticipated rewards for engagement in terrorism, and the more terrorist are viewed as models for one's behavior, the greater the likelihood of involvement in terrorist behaviors.
Subcultural		
• Cloward and Ohlin	Opportunity	The more a subculture advocates the commission of terrorism and provides opportunities for its commission, the higher the incidence of terrorism.
• Wolfgang and Ferracuti	Subculture of Violence	The greater the integration into a subculture of violence, the greater the probability of involvement in acts of terrorism.
Cultural Conflict		
• Sellin	Culture Conflict	The more intense the primary culture conflict, the greater the likelihood that act of terrorism will occur.
Frustration Aggression/Strain		
• Dollard et al.	Blocked Goals	The greater important needs and goals are perceived to be blocked by others, the greater the experience of frustration.

The greater the experience of frustration caused by others, the greater the probability of outwardly directed aggression.

The greater the likelihood of outwardly directed aggression, the greater the probability of engagement in terrorist behaviors.

• Agnew	Negative Social Interaction	The greater the experience of negative social relations, the greater the experience of negative emotions.
		The greater the experience of negative emotions, the greater the probability of engagement in terrorist behaviors.

Rational Choice

• Cornish	Cost/Benefit Analysis	The greater the benefit associated with terrorism, the more likely the individual will commit terrorist activities.

Techniques of Neutralization

• Sykes and Matza	Denial of Responsibility	The greater the use of the techniques of neutralization, the less the guilty associated with acts of terrorism.
	Denial of Injury	
	Denial of the Victim	The less the guilt associated with acts of terrorism, the greater the probability of involvement in terrorist behaviors.
	Condemnation of the Condemners	
	Appeal to Higher Loyalities	

experience of negative emotions such as anger, rage, depression, and anxiety. An unalleviated negative emotional state often drives an individual to seek immediate and permanent relief. Terrorists often consider the experience of long-term humiliation at the hand of a dominant political foe to cause them to resort to extreme acts of terrorism, often resulting in their own death.

Social Learning

Edwin Sutherland (1939) and Ronald Akers (1998) argue that deviant behavior is, for the most part, learned in the process of interacting with others who serve as role models. Both Sutherland's theory of differential association and Akers' social structure and social learning formulation articulated the processes involved in becoming a deviant. To Sutherland, the more an individual interacts directly with others who advocate the violation of the law, the more likely that individual will learn the motives, drives, rationalization, and techniques that are essential in the commission of deviant acts. Potential terrorists are carefully selected, rigorously trained to carry out terrorist missions, and indoctrinated by terrorist organizers. Intense and exclusive interaction with members of terrorist cells over an extended period of time results in the molding of a reliable and unwavering member of a terrorist organization.

Ronald Akers's social structure and social learning formulation provides a context for understanding the learning process involved in becoming a terrorist. To Akers there are four social structural conditions that facilitate learning to engage in deviant acts. The first condition is *differential social organization*—the conditions of the community that give rise to criminal acts, e.g., social inequality, economic deprivation, and illicit opportunities. The second condition is the individual's *differential location in the social structure,* or the sociodemographic characteristics that position them in the larger socioeconomic structure of society. The third condition is the presence within the community of *theoretically defined structural variables,* or a critical mass of known precipitants of criminal involvement, e.g., strain, deprivation, exclusion and degradation. The fourth condition, *differential social location,* refers to the placement in the larger social structure of an individual most important membership groups, family, social organizations, and religious affiliations.

Persons who engage in acts of terrorism are often drawn from communities that are marginal to the mainstream of society. Their opportunities for economic success are limited, as are their chances for other forms of positive social recognition. They are members of devalued ethnic and religious groups who have suffered long-standing humiliations and political disenfranchisement. Their social structural positioning has rendered them personally powerless to combat the forces of oppression. As a consequence, they become highly motivated to seek revenge through acts of terrorism.

Techniques of Neutralization

Gresham Sykes and David Matza (1957) consider the issue of guilt that may attend the commission of a deviant or criminal act. Given that intense guilt may impede engagement in acts of terrorism, it must be "neutralized" to ensure the success of a terrorist mission. Sykes and Matza identify five techniques that may effectively neutralize any guilt associated with terrorist activities. These techniques are: *denial of responsibility, denial of injury, denial of the victim, condemnation of the condemners,* and *appeal to higher loyalties.* Terrorists often invoke a *denial of responsibility,* arguing that they were forced to engage in extreme forms of violence because of their demeaning living conditions and the humiliations that they suffered at the hands of their oppressors. While *denial of injury* is less usual, some Islamic terrorists believe that God will provide well for their victims in the afterlife. More often, terrorist engage in a process of *denial of the victim*—the belief that the victim is really the offender and acts of terrorism are necessary to remedy a protracted state of domination and humiliation. *Condemnation of the condemner* is a common practice among members of terrorist organizations. Those who condemn the acts of terrorism are themselves often considered morally corrupt, demonized, and unworthy to render judgment. Finally, a related strategy used by terrorist to neutralize guilt is an *appeal to higher loyalties.* Terrorist missions are viewed mandated by the will of God—divinely inspired, and justified. The terrorist is acting as an instrument of the God they envision. No secular government or sociocultural group of "non-believers" can legitimately question their actions, however violent or self-destructive they may be.

Chapter Summary

- Terrorism has emerged as a specific and extreme form of deviant behavior with global implications.
- Most definitions of terrorism include the unlawful use of force against civilians/noncombatant targets by subnational groups/clandestine agents in furtherance of a political or social objective. Depending on the origin, base, and objectives of the terrorist organization, terrorism is considered either domestic or international.
    - Domestic terrorism includes acts of terrorism by U.S. citizens without foreign influence and directed at elements of the U.S. government or population.
    - International terrorism involves citizens of more than one country and transcends national boundaries.
- The U.S. State Department has designated 35 groups as foreign terrorist organizations.
- The most commonly practiced forms of terrorism included:
    - Nationalist terrorism
    - Religious terrorism
    - State-sponsored terrorism
    - Left-wing terrorism
    - Right-wing terrorism
    - Anarchist terrorism
- Terrorists motivations may be understood from three perspectives: rational, psychological, and cultural.
- Hate crimes or bias crimes are motivated by the offender's bias against a race, color, religion, gender, ethnic/national origin group, disability status, or sexual orientation group.
- Cyberterrorism refers to any terrorist attack against information, computer systems, computer programs or data which may result in violence or disruption and create fear, anxiety, or panic in the target population.

Key Concepts

Terrorism: The act of destroying or injuring civilian lives or property without governmental permission in the attempt to affect some political goal.

Terrorist: Any person acting without governmental permission to destroy or injure civilian or government property in order to bring about some political goal.

Domestic terrorism: The commission of acts of terrorism by U.S. citizens, either groups or individuals, who are based and operate entirely within the United States without foreign direction or influence and whose acts are directed at elements of the U.S. government or population.

International terrorism: Terrorism involving citizens or the territory of more than one country; terrorism committed by a group or individual who has some connection to a foreign power or whose activities transcend national boundaries.

Hate crime (bias crime):   A criminal act or attempted act against a person, institution, or property that is motivated in whole or in part by the offender's bias against a race, color, religion, gender, ethic/national origin group, disability status, or sexual orientation.

Nationalist terrorism: Terrorism aimed at the creation of a self-governing nation that exists apart from its current political domination; a response to oppressive social conditions.

Religious terrorism: Terrorism carried out to defend religious doctrines or sacred lands from assaults by nonbelievers.

State-sponsored terrorism: Terrorism contracted out to mercenary terrorists groups in order to serve the interests of the state or nation.

Left-wing terrorism: Terrorism aimed at overthrowing capitalism in order to create a communistic or socialistic form of economic system.

Right-wing terrorism: Terrorism aimed at replacing liberal democratic governments with neo-Nazi or fascist states that establish Aryan supremacy.

Anarchist terrorism: Terrorism aimed at destroying any form of government in order to end political control and restrictions.

Suicide attack (bombing):   A violent, politically motivated attack carried out by a person who blows himself/herself up with the chosen target.

Cyberterrorism: Any terrorist attack against information, computer systems, computer programs, or data that may result in violence or disruption and create fear, anxiety, or panic in the target population.

Critical Thinking Questions

1. What distinguishes acts of terrorism from other forms of violent behavior? Are there unique sociocultural conditions that generate terrorist behavior? Or, are the underlying causes of terrorism and violence similar?

2. Do the processes of globalization—e.g., worldwide communication, transnational commerce and trade, and borderless political and cultural exchange—precipitate terrorist activities? If so, how do the processes of globalization give rise to transnational terrorism and/or domestic terrorism?

3. In what ways are suicide bombers and "homicide followed by suicide offenders" similar to and different from each other? Compare the societal and individual dynamics that lead to each form of violent behavior.

4. Compare cyberterrorism to more traditional forms of terrorism. Consider the similarities and difference in the processes of recruitment, socialization, and organization of each form of terrorism. Other than sophisticated technological skills, what distinguishes cyberterrorists from terrorists who commit more direct acts of violence?

Web Extra

Check out these websites for additional information on terrorism:

http://www.state.gov

http://www.dhs.gov

http://www.defenselink.mil

http://www.fbi.gov

http://www.ict.org/il

http://www.terrorism.com

http://www.ojp.usdoj.gov/nij/international

References

Abadinsky, H. 1989. *Drug Abuse: An Introduction.* Chicago: Nelson-Hall.

Abbott, J., et al. 1995. "Domestic Violence Against Women: Incidence and Prevalence of Emergency Department Populations." *Journal of the American Medical Association* 273: 1763–67.

Acharya, K. 2001. "Poverty and Mental Health in the Developing World." *Contemporary Review* 279: 136–137.

Adinsky, H. 1994. *Organized Crime,* 4th ed. Chicago, IL: Nelson-Hall.

Agnew, R. 1992. "Foundation for a General Strain Theory of Crime and Delinquency." *Criminology* 30: 47–88.

Akers, R. 1985. *Deviant Behavior: A Social Learning Approach,* 3rd ed. Belmont, CA: Wadsworth Publishing Company.

Akers, R. 1991. "Addiction: The Troublesome Concept." *Journal of Drug Issues* 21: 777–93.

Akers, R. L. 1992. *Drugs, Alcohol, and Society: Social Structure, Process and Policy.* Belmont, CA: Wadsworth.

Akers, R. 1994. *Criminological Theories: Introduction and Evaluation.* Los Angeles: Roxbury.

Akers, R. 1998. *Social Learning and Social Structure.* Boston: Northeastern University Press.

Akers, R., and R. Burgess. 1966. "A Differential Association-Reinforcement Theory of Criminal Behavior." *Social Problems* 14: 128–47.

Albanese, J. S., D. K. Das, and A. Verma. 2003. *Organized Crime: World Perspectives.* Upper Saddle River, NJ: Prentice Hall.

Alcoholics Anonymous. 1930. New York: Works.

Alexander, L., and J. LaRosa. 1994. *New Dimensions in Women's Health.* Boston: Jones and Bartlett Publishers.

Amanpour, C. 1997. "South Africa Copes with Skyrocketing Rape, Abuse Rates." CNN, February 23. Web posted at http://www.cnn.com/WORLD/9702/23/safrica.rapes/.

American Medical Association. 1992. *American Medical News* posted at www.amednews.com

American Psychiatric Association. 1994. *Diagnostic and Statistical Manual of Mental Disorders (DSM-IV),* 4th ed. Washington, DC: Author.

Anderson, E. 1999. *Code of the Street: Decency, Violence, and the Moral Life of the Inner City.* New York: W.W. Norton.

Arena, K. 2001. "Child Sex Abuse Study Debunks Myths." CNN, September 10. Web posted at http://www.cnn.com/2001/LAW/09/10/arena.child.abuse.otsc/index.html.

Association of British Insurers. 1999. *News Release: Most Property Crime Pre-Meditated According to New Research,* October 11. Web posted at http://www.abi.org.uk/hottopic/nr270.asp.

Atkinson, R., et al. 1996. *Hilgard's Introduction to Psychology.* Fort Worth: Harcourt Brace College Publishers.

Bachman, R. 1991. "An Analysis of American Indian Homicide: A Test of Social Disorganization and Economic Deprivation at the Reservation County Level." *Journal of Research in Crime and Delinquency* 28: 456–471.

Bachman, R. 1992. *Death and Violence on the Reservation—Homicide, Family Violence, and Suicide in American Indian Populations.* Westport, CT: Auburn House.

Bachman, R., and L. Saltzman. 1995. *Violence Against Women: Estimates from the Redesigned Survey.* Washington, DC: U.S. Department of Justice, Office of Justice Programs, and Bureau of Justice Statistics.

Bales, R. A. 1946. "Cultural Differences in Rates of Alcoholism." *Quarterly Journal of Studies on Alcohol* 6: 480–500.

Bandura, A. 1990. "Mechanisms of Moral Disengagement," Pp. 161–91 in *Origins of Terrorism: Psychologies, Ideologies, Theologies, States of Mind,* edited by W. Reich. Cambridge, UK: Cambridge University Press.

Barnett, C. 2004. *The Measurement of White-Collar Crime Using Uniform Crime Reporting (UCR) Data.* Washington, DC: U.S. Department of Justice, Federal Bureau of Investigation, Criminal Justice Information Services (CJIS) Division.

Barron, L., and M. Straus. 1989. *Four Theories of Rape in American Society: A State-Level Analysis.* New Haven, CT: Yale University Press.

Beals, J., et al. 1997. "Psychiatric Disorder among American Indian Adolescents: Prevalence in Northern Plains Youth." *Journal of the American Academy of Child and Adolescent Psychiatry* 36: 1252–59.

Beccaria, C. 1963. *On Crimes and Punishment.* Indianapolis: Bobbs-Merrill.

Becker, H. S. 1953. "Becoming a Marijuana User." *American Journal of Sociology* 66: 235–242.

Becker, H. 1963. *Outsiders: Studies in the Sociology of Deviance.* New York: Free Press.

Bennet, J. 2002. "Mideast Turmoil: The Bombers; Rash of New Suicide Bombers Exhibit No Patterns or Ties." *The New York Times,* June 21, Section A, Column 1, p. 1.

Benore, A. 1999. "Laws Look to Fight Internet Sex Crimes." *The State News,* February 18. Web posted at www.statenews.com.

Bentham, Jeremy. 1948. *The Principles of Morals and Legislation.* New York: Hefner.

Ben-Yehuda, N. 1990. "Positive and Negative Deviance: More Fuel for a Controversy." *Deviant Behavior* 11: 221–43.

Berg, B., and B. Glassner. 1980. "How to Avoid Alcohol Problems." *American Sociological Review* 45: 647–64.

Berlin, N. I. 1987. "Suicide Among American Indian Adolescents: An Overview." *Suicide and Life-Threatening Behavior* 17: 218–32.

Bernard, J. 1982. *The Future of Marriage,* 2nd ed. New York: Bantam.

Bertone, A. 2000. "Sexual Trafficking Women: International Political Economy and the Politics of Sex." *Gender Issues* 18: 4.

Best, J., and Luckenbill, D. 1982. *Organizing Deviance.* Englewood Cliffs, NJ: Prentice-Hall.

Black, D. 1976. *The Behavior of Law.* New York: Academic Press.

Black, D. 1983. "Crime as Social Control." *American Sociological Review* 48: 34–45.

Black, D. 1998. *The Social Structure of Right and Wrong.* San Diego: Academic Press.

Black, D. 2002. "Terrorism as Social Control." *American Sociological Association's Crime Law and Deviance Newsletter,* Spring.

Blum, R. H., and E. M. Blum. 1969. "A Cultural Case Study." Pp. 188–227 in *Drugs I: Society and Drugs,* edited by R. H. Blum, et al. San Francisco: Jossey-Bass.

Bodrero, D. 2000. *State Roles, Community Assessment, and Personality Profiles.* Tallahassee, FL: Institute for Intergovernment Research.

Braithwaite, John. 1989. *Crime, Shame, and Reintegration.* New York: Cambridge University Press.

Bray, M. 2001. "Call for crackdown on child sex laws." CNN, November 22. Web posted at http://www.cnn.com/2001/WORLD/asiapcf/southeast/11/22/asia.childsex/index.html.

Breidenbach, S. 1998. "Outlaws on the Loose: Making It Easy for Cybercriminals to Elude the Cops." *Network World,* February 16, p. 1.

Breivik, G. 1996. "Personality, Sensation Seeking and Risk Taking among Everest Climbers." *International Journal of Sport Psychology* 27: 308–20.

Brent, D. A., et al. 1994. "Personality Disorder, Personality Traits, Impulsive Violence, and Completed Suicide in Adolescents." *Journal of American Academy of Child and Adolescence Psychiatry* 33: 1080–86.

Brezina, T. 1999. "Teenage Violence Toward Parents as an Adaptation to Family Strain: Evidence from a National Survey of Male Adolescents." *Youth and Society* 30: 416–44.

Brody, A. 1979. "The Work-Obsessed." *The New York Times,* December 19, Section 3.

Brown, M. "Transnational Organized Crime and Terrorism." Terrorism Research Center. Web posted at http://www.terroism.com/terroism/sept97a.shtml.

Browne, A. 1987. *When Battered Women Kill.* New York: Macmillan Free Press.

Browne, A., and D. Finkelhor. 1986. "Impact of Sexual Abuse: A Review of the Research." *Psychological Bulletin* 99: 66–77.

Brownmiller, S. 1975. *Against Our Will: Men, Women, and Rape.* New York: Simon and Schuster.

Budnitz, M. E. 1998. "Privacy Protection for Consumer Transactions in Electronic Commerce: Why Self-Regulation Is Inadequate." *South Carolina Law Review* 49: 847–886.

Bureau of Justice Statistics (BJS). 1994. *Violence Between Intimates.* Washington, DC: US Department of Justice, Office of Justice Programs, Bureau of Justice Statistics.

Burke, R. 1999. "Workaholism in Organizations: Gender Differences." *Sex Roles: A Journal of Research* 41: 333–45.

Califano, J. A., Jr. (2002). *Teen Tipplers: America's Underage Drinking Epidemic.* New York: The National Center on Addiction and Substance Abuse at Columbia University.

Cameron, M. 1964. *The Booster and the Snitch: Department Store Shoplifting.* New York: Free Press.

Canetto, S., and I. Sakinofsky. 1998. "The Gender Paradox in Suicide." *Suicide and Life-Threatening Behavior* 28: 1–23.

Cantarow, E. 1979. "Women Workaholics." *Mother Jones.*

CAPTA, Child Abuse Prevention and Treatment Act. 2003. 42 USC 510g Sec. 111. Washington, DC: U.S. Department of Health and Human Services.

Carter, D. L. 1995. "Computer Crime Categories." *FBI Law Enforcement Bulletin* 64: 21.

Carter, C. J. 1998. "U.S. Leads Richest Nations in Gun Deaths." Associated Press, April 17. Web posted at http://www.guncite.com/CNNgunde.html.

Carter, J. 1977. Web posted at www.Taima.org/jp/quotes.htm#carter.

Castells, M. 1996. *The Rise of the Network Society (The Information Age: Economy, Society, and Culture, vol. I).* Oxford: Blackwell.

Castells, M. 1997. *The Power of Identity (The Information Age: Economy, Society, and Culture, vol. II).* Oxford: Blackwell.

Cavan, S. 1970. "B-Girls and Prostitutes." Pp. 55–63 in *Observations of Deviance,* edited by J. Douglas. New York: Random House.

CDC unpublished mortality data from the National Center for Health Statistics (NCHS) Mortality Data Tapes posted at www.cdc.gov.

Centers for Disease Control and Prevention (CDC). 1988. "Current Trends Operational Criteria for Determining Suicide." *Morbidity and Mortality Weekly Report* 37: 773–74, 779–80.

Centers for Disease Control and Prevention (CDC). 1996. "Suicide Among Older Persons, United States, 1980–1992."*Morbidity and Mortality Weekly Report* 45: 3–6.

Centers for Disease Control and Prevention (CDC). 1998. "Suicide Among Black Youths, United States, 1980–1995." *Morbidity and Mortality Weekly Report* 47: 193–196.

Charney, S., and K. Alexander. 1996. "Computer Crime." *Emory Law Journal* 45: 931–957.

Clarke, R. V., and Cornish, D.B. 1985b. "Modeling Offenders' Decisions: A Framework for Research and Policy." Pp. 147–185 in *Crime and Justice,* edited by M. Tonry and N. Morris. Chicago, IL: University of Chicago Press.

Clarke, R., and D. Cornish (eds.). 1985a. *Crime Control in Britain: A Review of Police and Research.* Albany: State University of New York Press.

Clarke, R. and P. Harris. 1992. "Auto Theft and Its Prevention." in *Crime and Justice: A Review of Research,* edited by M. Tonry. Chicago, IL: University of Chicago Press.

Clifford, W. 1976. *Crime Control in Japan.* Lexington, MA: D.C. Heath.

Clifton, K., and D. Lee. 1995. "Gender Socialization and Women's Suicidal Behaviors." in *Women and Suicidal Behavior,* edited by S. S. Canetto and D. Lester. New York: Springer, (1995).

Clinard, M., and R. Meier. 1998. *Sociology of Deviant Behavior,* 10th ed. Fort Worth, TX: Harcourt Brace Publishers.

Clinard, M., and R. Quinney. 1980. *Criminal Behavior Systems.* New York: Free Press.

Clinard, M., and P. Yeager. 1980. *Corporate Crime.* New York: Free Press.

Clinard, M., and P. Yeager. 2002. "Corporate Crime: Clarifying the Concept and Extending the Data." Pp. 82–94 in *Corporate and Governmental Deviance: Problems of Organizational Behavior in Contemporary Society,* 6th ed., edited by M. Ermann and R. Lundman. New York: Oxford University Press.

Clough, B., and P. Mungo. 1992. *Approaching Zero: Data Crime and the Computer Underworld.* London: Faber and Faber.

Cloward, R., and L. Ohlin. 1961. *Delinquency and Opportunity.* Glencoe, IL: Free Press.

CNN. 1997. "Internet Sting Identifies 1,500 Suspected Child Pornographers." CNN, September 30. Web posted at http://www.cnn.com/US/9709/30.old/cybersting/index.html.

CNN. 1998. "FBI to Parents: Internet Pedophiles a Serious Threat." CNN, March 11. Web posted at http://www.cnn.com/TECH/computing/9803/11/cyber.stalking/index.html.

CNN. 1999a. "Racism to Be Key Issue in Third Dragging-Death Trial: Accused to Blame Co-Defendents." CNN, October 26. Web posted at http://www.cnn.com/US/9910/26/dragging.death.01/.

CNN. 1999b. "UNESCO Launches Campaign to Fight Internet Pedophilia." CNN, June 15. Web posted at http://www.cnn.com/WORLD/americas/9906/15/un.pedophiliaindex.html.

CNN. 2001. "Sex Offenders Put Online in S. Korea." CNN, August 28. Web posted at http://www.cnn.com/2001/WORLD/asiapcf/east/08/28/korea.sexoffenders.index.html.

CNN. 2002. "Dozens Arrested in Child Porn Probe: 50 More Arrests Expected by Week's End." CNN, March 19. Web posted at http://www.cnn.com2002/US/03/18/fbi.child.porn/index.html.

Cohen, A. 1955. *Delinquent Boys.* New York: Free Press.

Cohen, M. L. et al. 1975. "The Psychology of Rapists." Pp. 113–140 in *Violence and Victims,* edited by S. A. Pasternack. New York: Spectrum Publications.

Cohen, L., and M. Felson. 1979. "Social Change and Crime Rate Trends: A Routine Activity Approach." *American Sociological Review* 44: 588–608.

Coleman, J. 2002. *The Criminal Elite, Understanding White-Collar Crime,* 5th ed. New York: Worth Publishers.

Coles, R. 1977. *The Privileged Ones,* Vol. 5 of Children of Crisis. Boston: Little, Brown.

Collins, B. 1996. *The Future of Cyberterrorism: Where the Physical and Virtual Worlds Converge.* Paper presented at the 11th annual International Symposium on Criminal Justice Issues, The University of Illinois at Chicago.

"Computer Addiction: Is It Real or Virtual?" 1999. *Harvard Medical Health Letter,* January 17.

Conklin, J. 1992. *Criminology,* 4th ed. New York: Macmillan Publishing Company.

Conley, J. M., and R. M. Bryan. 1999. "A Survey of Computer Crime Legislation in the United States." *Information and Techology Law* 8: 35–57.

Cooley, C. 1902. *Human Nature and the Social Order.* New York: Scribner.

Cooper, H. H. A. 1977. "What Is a Terrorist? A Psychological Perspective." *Legal Medical Quarterly* 1: 8–18.

Cordes, B. 1987. *When Terrorists Do the Talking: Reflections on Terrorist Literature.* Santa Monica, CA: Rand.

Cornelius, J. R., et al. 1995. "Disproportionate suicidality in patients with comorbid major depression and alcoholism." *American Journal of Psychiatry* 152: 358–364.

Cornish, D., and R. Clarke (eds.). 1986. *The Reasoning Criminal.* New York: Springer-Verlag.

Cornish, D., and R. Clarke. 1987. "Understanding Crime Displacement: An Application of Rational Choice Theory." *Criminology* 25: 933–47.

Coser, L. 1967. *Continuities in the Study of Social Conflict,* New York: Macmillan.

Cromie, W. 1999. "Computer Addiction Is Coming On-Line." *The Harvard University Gazette,* January 21. Web posted at www.hno.harvard.edu/gazette/1999.01 .21/computer.html.

Cromwell, P. 2004. "Burglary: The Offender's Perspective." Pp. 297–302 in A. Thio and T. C. Calhoun, *Reading in Deviant Behavior.* Boston: Pearson Education.

Cronin, C. 1991. "Sensation Seeking among Mountain Climbers." *Journal of Personality and Individual Differences* 12: 653–54.

Cross National Collaborative Group. 1992. "The Changing Rate of Major Depression: Cross-National Comparisons." *The Journal of the American Medical Association* 268: 3098–3105.

Dahrendorf, R. 1959. *Class and Class Conflict in Industrial Society.* Stanford, CA: Stanford University Press.

Daly, K., and M. Chesney-Lind. 1988. "Feminism and Criminology." *Justice Quarterly* 5: 497–538.

Danner, M. 1989. "Socialist Feminism: A Brief Introduction." *Critical Criminologist* 1: 1–2.

Daro, D., A. Cohn. 2000. *Child Abuse and Prevention: Accomplishments and Challenges.* Paper presented at the meeting of the Collaborative Violence Prevention Initiative, San Francisco, CA.

Davis, K. 1976. "Sexual Behavior." Pp. 245–252 in *Contemporary Social Problems,* edited by R. Merton and R. Nisbet. New York: Harcourt Brace Jovanovich.

Dobash, R., and R. Dobash. 1988. "Research as Social Action: The Struggle for Batter Women." *Feminist Perspectives on Wife Abuse,* edited by Kersti Yllö and Michele Bograd. Newbury Park, CA: Sage.

Dohrenwend, B., and B. Dohrenwend. 1975. "Sociocultural and Socio-Psychological Factors in the Genesis of Mental Disorders." *Journal of Health and Social Behavior* 16: 365–392.

Dohrenwend, B., et al. 1992. "Socioeconomic Status and Psychiatric Disorders: The Causation-Selection Issue." *Science* 255: 946–52.

Dollard, J. et al. 1939. *Frustration and Aggression.* New Haven, CT: Yale University Press.

Douglas, J. 1967. *The Social Meanings of Suicide.* Princeton, NJ: Princeton University Press.

Doyle, A. C. 1984. "The Adventure of the Cooper Beeches." Pp. 157–181 in *The Sherlock Holmes Mysteries.* New York: Penguin Books.

Durkheim, E. 1938. *The Rules of the Sociological Method.* New York: Free Press.

Durkheim, E. 1951. *Suicide: A Study in Sociology.* Glencoe, NY: Free Press.

Dutch Study on Physician Assisted Suicide, NEJM (Feb. 24, 2000). Cited in D. B. Yeaw "Physician-Assisted Suicide." Web posted at http://www.seniorliving.about.com/people/seniorliving/library/weekly/aa022500a.htm.

Dutton, M. 1993. "Understanding Women's Responses to Domestic Violence: A Redefinition of Battered Women Syndrome." *Hofstra Law Review* 21: 1191–1242.

Dworkin, A. 1981. *Pornography: Men Possessing Women.* New York: Plenum.

EchoHawk, M. 1997. "Suicide: The Scourge of Native American People." *Suicide and Life-Threatening Behavior* 27: 60.

Edelhertz, H. 1970. *The Nature, Impact, and Prosecution of White Collar Crime.* Washington, DC: U.S. Government Printing Office.

Egbert, A. M. 1993. "The Older Alcoholic: Recognizing the Subtle Clinical Clues." *Geriatrics* 48: 63–69.

Erickson, K. 2005. *Wayward Puritans.* Boston: Allyn and Bacon Classics.

ERRI Counter-Terrorism Archive Page. 2001. *World-wide/CIA Assessment: DCI Tenet Says Usama Bin Laden Biggest Threat to U.S.* Web posted at http:///www

.emergency.com/cntrterr00lhtm. (Full report: web posted at http://www.cia .gov/public_affairs/speeches/UNCLASWWT_02072001.html.).

Farber, M. 1968. *Theory of Suicide.* New York: Funk and Wagnalls.

Farberow, N., and E. Schniedman (eds.). 1961. *The Cry for Help.* New York: McGraw-Hill.

Farrington, David. 1986. "Age and Crime." Pp. 189–250 in *Crime and Justice: An Annual Review of Research,* edited by M. Tonry and N. Morris. Chicago: University of Chicago Press.

Fassel, D. 1992. *Working Ourselves to Death.* San Francisco, CA: Harper Collins.

Federal Bureau of Investigation (FBI). 1991. *Uniform Crime Reports.* Washington, DC: USGPO.

Federal Bureau of Investigation (FBI). 1999a. *Crime in the United States, 1999.* Washington, DC: USGPO.

Federal Bureau of Investigation (FBI). 1999b. *Terrorism in the United States 1999.* Washington, DC: USGPO. Web posted at http://www.fbi.gov/publications/ terror/terror99.pdf.

Federal Bureau of Investigation (FBI). 2000. *Crime in the United States, 2000.* Washington, DC: USGPO.

Federal Bureau of Investigation (FBI). 2002a. *Crime in the United States, 2002.* Washington, DC: USGPO. Web posted at http://www.fbi.gov/ucr/ucr.htm.

Federal Bureau of Investigation (FBI). 2002b. *The Measurement of White Collar Crime.* Washington, DC: USGPO.

Feeney, F. 1986. "Robbers as Decision Makers." Pp. 53–71 in *The Reasoning Criminal,* edited by D. Cornish and R. Clarke. New York: Springer-Verlag.

Feeney, F., and A. Weir (eds.). 1974. *The Prevention and Control of Robbery.* Davis: Center on Administration of Criminal Justice, University of California at Davis.

Feld, S., and M. Straus. 1990. "Escalation and Desistance from Wife Assualt in Marriage." Pp. 489–505 in *Physical Violence in American Families: Risk Factors and Adaptations to Violence in 8,145 Families,* edited by M. Straus and R. Gelles. New Brunswick, NJ: Transaction Publishers.

Felson, M. 1998. *Crime and Everyday Life,* 2nd ed. Thousand Oaks, CA: Pine Forge Press.

Felson, R. et al. 2000. "Acquaintance robbery." *Journal of Research in Crime and Delinquency* 37: 284–305.

Finckenauer, J. O. et al. *Mexico and the United States: Neighbors Confronting Drug Trafficking.* Web posted at http://www.ojp.usdoj.gov/nij/international/trafficking .html.

Finckenauer, J. O. *Chinese Transnational Organized Crime: The Fuk Ching.* Web posted at http://www.ojp.usdoj.gov/nij/international/chinese.html.

Finckenauer, J. O., and U. Voronin. 2001. *The Threat of Russian Organized Crime.* Washington, DC: National Institute of Justice. Web posted at http://www.ncjrs .org/txtfiles1/nij/187085.txt.

Finkelhor, D. 1997. "The Homicides of Children and Youth: A Developmental Perspective. Pp. 17–34 in *Out of Darkness: Contemporary Perspectives on Family Violence*, edited by G. Kaufman Kantor and J. Jasinski. Thousand Oaks, CA: Sage.

Finkelhor, D., K. Mitchell, and J. Wolak. 2001. *Online Victimization: A Report on the Nation's Youth*. Arlington, VA: National Center for Missing and Exploited Children.

Finkelhor, D., and R. Ormrod. 2000a. *Juvenile Victims of Property Crimes*. Washington, DC: U.S. Department of Justice and Office of Juvenile Justice and Delinquency Prevention. (NCJ# 184740).

Finkelhor, D., and R. Ormrod. 2000b. Characteristics of Crimes Against Juveniles. Washington, DC: U.S. Department of Justice and Office of Juvenile Justice and Delinquency Prevention. (NCJ# 179034).

Finkelhor, D., and R. Ormrod. 2001a. *Homicides of Youth and Children*. Washington, DC: U.S. Department of Justice, Office of Justice Programs, and Office of Juvenile Justice and Delinquency Prevention. (NCJ# 187239).

Finkelhor, D., and R. Ormrod. 2001b. *Child Abuse Reported to the Police*. Washington, DC: U.S. Department of Justice and Office of Juvenile Justice and Delinquency Prevention.

Finkelhor, D., and K. Yllö. 1985. *License to Rape: Sexual Assault of Wives*. New York: Holt, Rinehart, and Winston.

Fisher, B., et al. 2002. "Being Pursued: Stalking Victimization in a National Study of College Women." *Criminology and Public Policy* 1: 257–308.

Flavin, D. K., and R. M. Morse. 1991. "What Is Alcoholism," *Alcohol Health and Research World*, 15: 266–71.

Foo, L., and G. Margolin. 1995. "A Multivariate Investigation of Dating Aggression." *Journal of Family Violence* 10: 351–77.

Fortune, "The Odds Against Doing Time." March 18, 2002. Web posted at http://www.fortune.com/fortune/subs/article/0,15114,371596,00html.

Fox, J., and J. Levin. 2001. *The Will to Kill: Making Sense of Senseless Murder*. Boston: Allyn and Bacon.

Fox, J., and M. Zawitz. 2004. *Homicide Trends in the United States*. Washington, DC: U.S. Department of Justice, Office of Justice Programs, and Bureau of Justice Statistics. Web posted at http://www.ojp.usdoj.gov/bjs/pub/pdf/ntius.pdf.

Fraser, J., and I. Fulton. 1984. *Terrorism Counteraction*. Fort Leavenworth, KS: U.S. Army Command and General Staff College.

Friedman, M., and R. H. Roseman. 1974. *Type A Behavior and Your Heart*. New York: Knopf.

Friedman, M. and R. Friedman. 1984. *Tyranny of the Status Quo*. San Diego: Harcourt Brace Javonovich.

Gawel, R. 1999. "Web Addiction." *Electronic Design*, August 9, p. 32D.

Gelles, R. 1994. "An Exchange/Social Control Theory." Pp. 268–284 in *Theories of Deviance,* 4th ed, edited by S. H. Tranb and C. B. Little. Itasca, Ill: F. E. Peacock Publishers.

Gelles, R. 1987. *Family Violence.* Newbury Park, CA: Sage.

Gelles, R., and J. Harrop. 1989. "Violence, Battering, and Psychological Distress Among Women." *Journal of Interpersonal Violence* 4: 400–20.

Gelles, R., and M. Straus. 1979. "Determinants of Violence in the Family: Towards a Theoretical Integration." Chapter 21 in *Contemporary Theories About the Family,* edited by W. Burr et al. New York: Free Press.

Gibbons, D. 1968. *Changing the Lawbreaker.* Englewood Cliffs, NJ: Prentice-Hall.

Gibbs, J. 1968. *Suicide.* New York: Harper and Row.

Gibbs, J. 1989. *Norms, Deviance, and Social Control.* New York: Elsevier.

Gibbs, J., and W. Martin. 1964. *Status Integration and Suicide.* Eugene: University of Oregon Press.

Giddens, A. 2000. *Runaway World: How Globalization Is Reshaping Our Lives.* New York: Routledge.

Giles-Sims, J. 1998. "The Aftermath of Partner Violence." Pp. 44–72 in *Partner Violence: A Comprehensive Review of 20 Years of Research,* edited by J. Jasinski and L. Williams. Thousand Oaks, CA: Sage.

Glaser, D. 1956. "Criminality Theories and Behavioral Images." *American Journal of Sociology* 61: 433–44.

Glaser, D. 1960. "Differential Association and Criminological Prediction." *Social Problems* 8: 6–14.

Glass, A. J. 1998. "U.S. Military Face Potential Cyberattack." *Atlanta Journal Constitution,* February 26, p. A8.

Gledhill-Hoyt, J., L. Hang, J. Strote, and H. Wechsler. 2000. "Increased Use of Marijuana and Other Illicit Drugs at U.S. Colleges in the 1990s: Results of Three National Surveys." *Addiction* 95: 1655–67.

Goffman, E. 1961. *Asylums.* Garden City, N.Y.: Doubleday-Anchor.

Goldstein, P. 1979. *Prostitution and Drugs.* Lexington, MA: Lexington Books.

Gomberg, E. S. 1995. "Older Women and Alcohol Use and Abuse." Pp. 61–79 in *Development in Alcoholism, vol. 12,* edited by M. Galanter. New York: Plenum Press.

Goode, E. 1991. "Positive Deviance: A viable concept." *Deviant Behavior* 12: 289–308.

Goode, E. 1993. *Drugs in American Society,* 4th ed. New York: McGraw-Hill.

Goode, E. 2005. *Deviant Behavior,* 7th ed. Upper Saddle River, NJ: Prentice-Hall.

Goode, W. J., and P. K. Hatt. 1952. *Methods in Social Research.* New York: McGraw Hill.

Gossop, M., et al. 1994. "Sexual Behavior and Its Relationship to Drug-Taking among Prostitutes in South London." *Addiction* 89: 961–70.

Gottfredson, M., and T. Hirschi. 1983. "Age and the Explanation of Crime." *American Journal of Sociology* 89: 552–84.

Gottfredson, M., and T. Hirschi. 1990. *A General Theory of Crime.* Palo Alto, CA: Stanford University Press.

Gove, W., et al. 1972. "Does Marriage Have Positive Effects on the Psychological Well-being of the Individual?" *Journal of Health and Social Behavior* 24: 122–31.

Granfield, R., and W. Cloud. 1996. "The Elephant That No One Sees: Natural Recovery among Middle-Class Addicts." *Journal of Drug Issues* 26: 45–61.

Green, G. 1990. *Occupational Crime.* Chicago, IL: Nelson-Hall.

Greene, R. 1998. "Internet Addiction." *Computer World,* September 21, p. 78.

Greenfeld, L. 1997. *Sex Offenses and Offenders: An Analysis of Data on Rape and Sexual Assault.* Washington, DC: US Department of Justice, Office of Justice Programs and Bureau of Justice Statistics (NCJ #163392). Web posted at http://www.ojp.usdoj.gov/bjs/pub/pdf/soo.pdf.

Greenfeld, L., and S. Smith. 1999. *American Indians and Crime.* Washington, DC: US Department of Justice, Office of Justice Programs, and Bureau of Justice Statistics. (NCJ 173386)

Greenfeld, L., et al. 1998. *Violence by Intimates: Analysis of Data on Crimes by Current or Former Spouses, Boyfriends, and Girlfriends.* Washington, DC: US Department of Justice, Office of Programs, and Bureau of Justice Statistics.

Greenfield, K., et al. 1999. "Life on the Edge." *Time,* September 6, p. 9.

Groth, N. 1983. "Rape: Behavioral Aspect." In *Encyclopedia of Crime and Justice,* vol. 4, edited by S. Kadish. New York: Free Press.

Gunroe, M., and C. Mariner. 1997. "Toward a Developmental-Contextual Model of the Effects of Parental Spanking on Children's Aggression." *Archives of Pediatric and Adolescent Medicine* 151: 768–75.

Gupta, K. 1993. "Alcoholism in the Elderly: Uncovering a Hidden Problem." *Postgraduate Medicine* 93: 203–6.

Haddock, D. 2001. *Granny D: Walking Across America in My 90th Year.* New York: Villard Books.

Hagan, J. 1989a. *Structural Criminology.* New Brunswick, NJ: Rutgers University Press.

Hagan, J. 1989b. "Micro and Macro-structures of Delinquency Causation and a Power-Control Theory of Gender and Delinquency." Pp. 213–27 in *Theoretical Integration in the Study of Deviance and Crime: Problems and Prospects,* edited by S. F. Messner, M. D. Krohn, and A. E. Liska. Albany: State University of New York Press.

Hamilton, K. 1995. "Outer Limits." *Newsweek,* June 19, pp. 78(4).

Hanson, G., and P. Venturelli. 2001. *Drugs and Society.* Sudbury, MA: Jones and Bartlett Publishers.

Hardy, K. R. 1974. "Social Origins of American Scientists and Scholars." *Science* 185: 497–506.

Harris, C., and J. Barraclough. 1997. "Suicide as an Outcome for Mental Disorders: A Meta-Analysis." *British Journal of Psychiatry* 170: 205–28.

Hazelwood, R., and A. Burgess, (eds.). 1995. *Practical Aspects of Race Investigation: A Multidisciplinary Approach.* New York: CRC Press.

Heath, D. B. 1982. "Sociocultural Variants in Alcoholism." Pp. 426–40 in *Encyclopedic Handbook of Alcoholism,* edited by E. M. Pattison and E. Kaufman. New York: Gardner Press.

Heath, D. B. ed. 1995. *International Handbook on Alcohol and Culture.* Westport, CT: Greenwood Press.

Heckert, D. M. 2000. "Positive Deviance" Pp. 30–42 in *Constructions of Deviance: Social Power, Context, Interaction,* edited by P. Adler and P. Adler. Belmont, CA: Wadsworth.

Hendricks, S., et al. 1999. "A Matched Case-Control Study of Convenience Store Robbery Risk Factors." *Journal of Occupational and Environmental Medicine* 41: 995–1004.

Henriksson, M., et al. 1993. "Mental Disorders and Comorbidity in Suicide." *American Journal of Psychiatry* 150: 935–940.

Henry, A. F., and J. F. Short, Jr. 1954. *Suicide and Homicide.* New York: Free Press.

Hepburn, J. 1984. "Occasional Property Crime." In *Major Forms of Crime,* edited by R. Meier. Beverly Hills, CA: Sage.

Hindelang, M. 1976. *Criminal Victimization of Eight American Cities: A Descriptive Analysis of Common Theft and Assault.* Cambridge, MA: Ballinger.

Hirschi, Travis. 1969. *Causes of Delinquency.* Berkeley: University of California.

Hoffman, B. 1995. "Holy Terror: The Implications of Terrorism Motivated by Religious Imperative." *Studies in Conflict and Terrorism* 18: 271–84.

Hoffman, B. 1999. *Inside Terrorism.* New York: Columbia University Press.

Holliday, H. 2000. "Hooked on the Net." *Psychology Today* 33: 10.

Hollingshead, A., and F. Redlich. 1958. *Social Class and Mental Illness.* New York: Wiley.

Holmes, M. D., and J. A. Antell. 2001. "The Social Construction of American Indian Drinking: Perceptions of American Indian and White Officials." *The Sociological Quarterly* 42: 151–74.

Hotaling, G., and D. Sugarman. 1990. "A Risk Marker Analysis of Assaulted Wives," *Journal of Family Violence* 5: 1–13.

Hudson, R. A. 1999. *The Sociology and Psychology of Terrorism: Who Becomes a Terrorist and Why?* Washington, DC: Library of Congress.

Huff, C. R. 1978. "Historical Explanations of Crime: From Demons to Politics." Pp. 208–220 in *Crime and the Criminal Justice Process,* edited by J. Inciardi and K. Hass. Dubuque, Iowa: Kendall Hunt Publishing.

Hutson, H. R., et al. 1998. "Suicide by Cop." *Annals of Emergency Medicine* 32: 665–9.

Icove, D. J., K. A. Seger, and W. R. VonStorch. 1995. *Computer Crime: A Crime-fighter's Handbook.* Cambridge, MA: O'Reilly & Associates.

"Increasing Signs of Stress (Japan)." 1983. *Time,* August 1, pp. 67.

International Crime Victimization Survey. Web posted at http://ruljis.Ledenuniv.nl/group/jfcr/www.icvs/index/htm.

Ishii, K. 1991. "Measuring Mutual Causation: Effects of Suicide News on Suicides in Japan." *Social Science Research* 20: 188–95.

Jacobs, J. 1967. "A Phenomenological Study of Suicide Notes." *Social Problems* 15: 60–73.

Jaffe, P. et al. 1990. *Children of Battered Women.* Newbury Park, CA: Sage.

Jamison, K. 1999. *Nights Falls Fast: Understanding Suicide.* New York: Alfred A. Knopf.

Janus, S. S and C. L. Janus. 1993. *The Janus Report on Sexual Behavior.* New York: John Wiley and Sons.

Jasinski, J., and L. Williams (eds.). 1998. *Partner Violence: A Comprehensive Review of 20 Years of Research.* Thousand Oaks, CA: Sage.

Jellinek, E. M. 1960. *The Disease Concept of Alcoholism.* New Haven, CT: College and University Press.

Jessor, R., et al. 1968. *Society, Personality and Deviant Behavior: A Study of a Tri-Ethnic Community.* New York: Holt, Rinehart, and Winston.

Jonas, K. 1992. "Modeling and Suicide: A Test of the Werther Effect." *British Journal of Social Psychology* 31: 295–306.

Jones, L., and D. Finklehor. 2001. *The Decline in Child Sexual Abuse Cases.* Washington, DC: U.S. Department of Justice and Office of Juvenile Justice and Delinquency Prevention. (NCJ # 184741).

Jones, S. E., et al. 2001. "Binge Drinking among Undergraduate College Students in the United States: Implications for Other Substance Abuse." *Journal of American College Health* 50: 33–38.

Joyner, T. 1999. "Job Addict." *Atlanta Journal Constitution,* November 14. Web posted at www.accessatlanta.com/partners/ajc/read/workholics/.

Kageyama, Y. 1999. "Court Orders Japanese Government to Pay for Suicide from Overwork." *The Detroit News,* March 13. Web posted at www.detnews.com/1999/biz/9903/12/03130055.htm.

Kaplan, H. B. 1980. *Deviant Behavior in Defense of Self.* New York: Academic Press.

Kaplan, H. B. 1995. "Drugs, Crime and Other Deviant Adaptations." In *Drugs, Crime and Other Deviant Adaptations: Longitudinal Studies,* edited by H. B. Kaplan. New York: Plenum.

Kato, T. 1995. "Workaholism: It's Not in the Blood." *Look Japan,* February 1995, p. 1. Web posted at www.member.nifty.neljp/kotote/WORKAHOLSIM.html.

Katz, J. 1988. *Seductions of Crime: Moral and Sensual Attractions in Doing Evil.* New York: Basic Books.

Keller, M., and J. Doria. 1991. "On Defining Alcoholism." *Alcohol Health and Research World* 15: 253–59.

Kessler, R., and P. Cleary. 1980. "Social Class and Psychological Distress," *American Sociological Review* 45: 463–78.

King, M., and E. Woollett. 1997. "Sexually Assaulted Males: 115 men consulting a counseling service." *Archives of Sexual Behavior* 26: 579–88.

Kivivuouri, J. 1998. "The Case of Temporally Intensified Shoplifting." *British Journal of Criminology* 38: 663.

Klaus, P. 2000. *Crimes Against Persons Age 65 or Older, 1992–97.* Washington, DC: U.S. Department of Justice, Office of Justice Programs, and Bureau of Justice Statistics. (NCJ 176352)

Klemke, L. 1992. *The Sociology of Shoplifting: Boosters and Snitches Today.* Westport, CT: Praeger.

Knickerbocker, B. 1998. "Sanctioned Euthanasia: Lessons from Abroad." *Christian Science Monitor,* Dec. 3, 1998. Web posted at http://www.csmonitor.com/cgi-bin/durableredirect.pl?/durable/1998/12/03/pls2=csm.shtml.

Korn, E., Pratt, G., and Lambrou. P. 1987. *Hyper-performance: The AIM Strategy for Releasing Your Business Potential.* New York: John Wiley & Sons.

Koss, M., et al. 1987. "The Scope of Rape: Incidence and Prevalence of Sexual Aggression and Victimization in a National Sample of Higher Education Students." *Journal of Consulting and Clinical Psychology* 55: 162–70.

Koss, M. P., and H. H. Cleveland. 1997. "Stepping Stones: Social Roots of Date Rape Lead to Intractability and Politicalization." Pp. 4–21 in *Researching Sexual Violence Against Women: Methodological and Personal Perspective,* edited by M. D. Schwartz. Thousand Oaks, CA: Sage.

Kraut, R. et al. 1998. Internet Paradox: A Social Technology That Reduces Social Involvement and Psychological Well-Being? *American Psychologist* 53: 1017–1031.

Krug, E. G. et al. 1998. "Firearm-Related Deaths in the United States and 35 Other High- and Upper-Middle-Income Countries." *International Journal of Epidemiology,* 27:214–221.

Landau, S. 1975. "Pathologies among Homicide Offenders: Some Cultural Profiles." *British Journal of Criminology* 15: 157–68.

Landreth, B. 1985. *Out of the Inner Circle.* Washington, DC: Microsoft Press.

Langan, P., and D. Farrington. 1998. *Crime and Justice in the United States and England and Wales, 1981–96.* Washinton, DC: U. S. Department of Justice, Office of Justice Programs, and the Bureau of Justice Statistics. (NCJ # 169284). Web posted at http://www.ojp.usdoj.gov/bjs/pub/pdf/cjusew96.pdf.

Laqueur, W. 1987. *The Age of Terrorism.* Boston: Little, Brown.

Lardner, J. 1999. "World-Class Workaholics: Are Crazy Hours and Takeout Dinners the Elixir of America's Success?" *U.S. News and World Report Cover Story,* December 20. Web posted at http://www.usnews.com/usnews/issue/991220/overwork.htm.

Lash, L., and J. Urry. 1994. *Economies of Signs and Space.* London: Sage.

Leenarrs, A. (ed.). 1999. *Lives and Deaths: Selections from the Works of Edwin S. Schneidman.* Philadelphia: Brunner/Mazel.

Lemelson, R., and J. Winters. 2001. "Strange Maladies." *Psychology Today,* December 2001, pp. 60–64.

Lemert, E. 1967. *Human Deviance, Social Problems, and Social Control.* Englewood Cliffs, NJ: Prentice Hall.

Leonard, K., and M. Senchak. 1993. "Alcohol and Premarital Aggression Among Newlywed Couples." *Journal of Studies on Alcohol* 54: 96–108.

Let's Talk Facts about: Mental Health of the Elderly. 1997. Washington, DC: American Psychiatric Association. Web posted at http://www.psych.org/public_info/ELDERL~1.HTM.

Leuchtag, A. 1995. "Merchants of Flesh." *The Humanist* 55: 11–16.

Levy, S. 1984. *Hackers: Heroes of the Computer Revolution.* New York: Bantam, Doubleday, Dell.

Lidz, T., et al. 1965. *Schizophrenia and the Family.* New York: International Universities Press.

Lindberg, R. and Markovic, V. 2002. "Organized Crime Outlook in the New Russia." Web posted at http://www.search-international.com/Articles/crime/russiacrime.htm.

Lindesmith, A. R. 1947. *Opiate Addiction.* Bloomington, IN: Principia Press.

Lindesmith, A. R. 1968. *Addiction and Opiates.* Chicago: Aldine.

Linton, R. 1955. *The Tree of Culture.* New York: Knopf.

Loftus, E. 1997. "Creating False Memories." Pp. 12–17 in *Perspectives: Social Psychology,* edited by M. Acker. Boulder, CO: Coursewise Publishing.

Luckenbill, D. 1977. "Homicide as a Situated Transaction." *Social Problems,* 25: 176–86.

Lungren, D. 1996. *California Attorney General, Russian Organized Crime.* Sacramento: California Department of Justice. Web posted at http://members.tripod.com/~orgcrime/ruscali.htm.

Machlowitz, M. 1980. *Workaholics: Living with Them, Working with Them.* Reading, MA: Addison-Wesley.

MacKinnon, C. 1989. *Toward a Feminist Theory of the State.* Cambridge, MA: Harvard University Press.

Maguire, M. 1982. *Burglary in a Dwelling.* London: Heinemann.

Malkin, M., and Rabinowtiz, E. 1998. "Sensation Seeking and High-Risk Recreation." *Parks & Recreation* 33: 6.

Maris, R. 1981. *Pathways to Suicide—A Survey of Self-Destructive Behaviors.* Baltimore: The Johns Hopkins University Press.

Marx, K. 1956. *Selected Writings in Sociology and Social Philosophy.* New York: McGraw Hill.

Mastekaasa, A.1994. "Marital Status, Distress, and Well-being: An International Comparison." *Journal of Comparative Family Studies* 23: 183–305.

Matsumoto, D. 1997. *Culture and Modern Life.* Pacific Grove, CA: Brooks/Cole Publishing Company.

May, P. A. 1996. "Overview of Alcohol Abuse Epidemiology for American Indian Populations." Pp. 235–61 in *Changing Numbers, Changing Needs: American Indian Demography and Public Health,* edited by G. Sandefur, R. Rindfuss, and B. Cohen. Washington, DC: National Academy Press.

Mayor, S. 2001. "Alcohol and Drug Misuse Sweeping the World, Says WHO." *British Medical Journal* 322: 7284.

McAuliffe, W. E., and R. A. Gordon. 1974. "A Test of Lindesmith's Theory of Addiction: The Frequency of Euphoria Among Long-Term Addicts." *American Journal of Sociology* 79: 795–840.

McCaghy, C. H., J. K. Skipper, and M. Lefton (eds.). 1968. *In Their Own Behalf: Voices from the Margin.* New York: Appleton-Century Crofts.

McCauley, C. R. 2001. *The Psychology of Terrorism.* New York: The Social Science Research Council. Web posted at http://www.ssrc.org/sept11/essays/mccauley.htm.

McGrew, A. 1992. "A Global Society?" in *Modernity and Its Futures,* edited by S. Hall, D. Held, and A. McGrew. Cambridge: Polity Press.

McIntosh, J. L. 1980–1981. "Suicide Among Native American: A Compilation of Finding." *Omega* 11: 303–16.

McLeer, S., and R. Anwar. 1989. "A Study of Battered Women Presenting in an Emergency Department." *American Journal of Public Health* 79: 65–66.

McShane, F., and B. Noonan. 1993. "Classification of Shoplifters by Cluster Analysis." *International Journal of Offender Therapy and Comparative Criminology* 37: 29–40.

Mead, G. H. 1934. *Mind, Self, and Society.* Chicago: University of Chicago Press.

Mechanic, D. 1968. *Medical Sociology.* New York: Free Press.

Meier, R., and G. Geis. 1997. *Victimless Crime: Prostitution, Drugs, Homosexuality, and Abortion.* Los Angeles, CA: Roxbury.

Meithe, T., and R. McCorkle. 1998. *Crime Profiles: The Anatomy of Dangerous Persons, Places, and Situations.* Los Angeles, CA: Roxbury.

Merton, Robert K. 1957. *Social Theory and Social Structure.* Glencoe, IL: Free Press.

Merton, Robert K. 1968. *Social Theory and Social Structure.* New York: Free Press (Enlarged CD.).

Messner, S. M. Krohn, and A. Liska. 1989. Theoretical Integration in the Study of Deviance and Crime: Problems and Perspectives. Albany: State University of New York.

Meuer, Tess, Anne Seymour, and Harvey Wallace. 2002. "Domestic Violence," Chapter 9 in *National Victim Assistance Academy Textbook,* edited by A. Seymour et al. Washington DC: Office for Victims of Crime.

Miech, R., et al. 1999. "Low Socioeconomic Status and Mental Disorders: A Longitudinal Study of Selection and Causation during Young Adulthood." *The American Journal of Sociology* 104: 1096.

Miller, W. 1958. "Lower Class Culture as a Generating Milieu of Gang Delinquency." *Journal of Social Issues* 14(3): 5–19.

Mitchell, K., et al. 2001. "Risk Factors for and Impact of Online Sexual Solicitation of Youth." *Journal of the American Medical Association* 285: 3011–14.

Mitchell, P. 2000. "Internet Addiction: Genuine Diagnosis or Not?" *The Lancet,* February 19, p. 632.

Mohandie, K., and J. R. Meloy. 2000. "Clinical and Forensic Indicators of Suicide by Cop." *Journal of Forensic Science* 45: 384–89.

Moore, C. 1790. *A Full Inquiry Into the Subject of Suicide, Vol.1.* London: Rivington.

Moore, R. 1984. "Shoplifting in Middle America: Patterns and Motivational Correlates." *International Journal of Offender Therapy and Comparative Criminology* 23: 55–64.

Moran, P. A., and J. R. Moran. 1995. "Prevention of Alcohol Misuse: A Review of Health Promotion among American Indians." *American Journal of Health Promotion* 9: 288–99.

"More Women Serve as College Presidents, ACE Survey Shows." 2000. *Higher Education and National Affairs American Council on Education,* September 11.

Mosiciki, E. 1996. "Epidemiology of Suicidal Behavior." *Suicide and Life-Threatening Behavior* 25: 22–35.

Mulford, H. A., and J. L. Fitzgerald. 1992. "Elderly versus Younger Drinker Profiles: Do They Indicate a Need for Special Programs for the Elderly?" *Journal of Studies on Alcohol* 53: 601–10.

Mullen, P. 1991. "The Consequences of Child Sexual Abuse: Psychosocial Disorders Are Common in Adults Abused as Children." *British Medical Journal* 303: 144–45.

Mumford, E. 1983. *Medical Sociology: Patients, Providers, and Policies.* New York: Random House.

Murphy, J. M. 1976. "Psychiatric Labeling in Cross-Cultural Perspective." *Science* 191: 1019–28.

Murray, C., et al. 1996. *Summary: The Global Burden of Disease: A Comprehensive Assessment of Mortality and Disability from Diseases, Injuries, and Risk Factors in 1990 and Projected to 2020.* Cambridge, MA: Harvard School of Public Health on behalf of the World Health Organization and the World Bank, Harvard University Press. Web posted at http://www.who.int/msa/mnh/ems/dalys/intro.htm.

Murray, J. 2000. "Psychological Profile of Pedophiles and Child Molesters." *The Journal of Psychology* 134: 211–24.

Nadon, S., et al. 1998. "Antecedents to Prostitution: Childhood Victimization." *Journal of Interpersonal Violence* 13: 206–21.

The National Center on Addiction and Substance Abuse at Columbia University. 2001. *So Help Me God: Substance Abuse, Religion and Spirituality.* New York: Author.

The National Elder Abuse Study. 1996. Web posted at http://www.aoa.dhhs .gov/eldfam/Elder_Rights/Elder_Abuse/AbuseReport_Full.pdf.

National Institute of Mental Health (NIMH). 1999a. *Chapter 7: Sociocultural and Environmental Processes.* Bethesda, MD: National Institute of Mental Health and National Institutes of Health.

National Institute of Mental Health (NIMH). 1999b. *Brief Notes on the Mental Health of Children and Adolescents.* Bethesda, MD: National Institute of Mental Health and National Institutes of Health.

National Institute of Mental Health (NIMH). 2001a. *The Numbers Count: Mental Disorders in America.* Bethesda, MD: National Institute of Mental Health and National Institutes of Health. Web posted at http://www.nimh.nih.gov/publicat/ burden.cfm.

National Institute of Mental Health (NIMH). 2001b. *The Impact of Mental Illness on Society.* Bethesda, MD: National Institute of Mental Health and National Institutes of Health. Web posted at http://www.nimh.nih.gov/publicat/childnotes.cfm.

National Institute of Mental Health (NIMH). 2001c. *Women Hold Up Half the Sky: Women and Mental Health Research: A Brief Overview of Research into Mental Illness in Women.* Bethesda, MD: National Institute of Mental Health and National Institutes of Health. Web posted at http://www.nimh.nih.gov/publicat/womensoms.cfm.

National Institute of Mental Health (NIMH). 2003. *In Harm's Way: Suicide in America.* Bethesda, MD: National Institute of Mental Health and National Institutes of Health. Web posted at http://www.nimh.nih.gov/publicat/NIMHharmsway.pdf.

National Institute of Occupational Safety and Health. 1996. *Violence in the Workplace: Risk Factors and Prevention Strategies.* Current Intelligence Bulletin 57. Washington, DC: Author.

National Research Council. 1991. *Computers at Risk.* National Academy Press.

National Sexual Violence Resource Center. 2000. *Sexual Assault in Indian Country: Confronting Sexual Violence.* Enola, PA: Author. Web posted at http://www.nsvrc .org/publications/booklets/indian.htm.

Naughton, T. 1987. "A conceptual view of workaholism and implications for career counseling and research." *The Career Development Quarterly* 35: 180–87.

Nephew, T. M., et al. 1999. *Apparent Per Capita Alcohol Consumption: National, State, and Regional Trends, 1977–97.* Bethesda, MD: National Institute on Alcohol Abuse and Alcoholism.

Neuman, G. (ed.) 1999. Global Report on Crime and Justice. New York: Oxford University Press.

Noack, D. 2000. "Identity Theft Thrives in Cyberspace." *APBNews,* March 8.

Nordenmark, M., and M. Strandh. 1999. "Towards a Sociological Understanding of Mental Well-being among the Unemployed: The Role of Economic and Psychosocial Factors." *Sociology* 33: 577.

Norland, S. et al. 1976. "The Effects of Labeling and Consistent Differentiation in the Construction of Positive Deviance." *Sociology, Soc Res* 61: 83–95.

Oates, W. 1971. *Confessions of a workaholic: The facts about work addiction.* New York: World Publishing.

Office for Victims of Crime. 2001. *Internet Crimes Against Children.* Washington, DC: U.S. Department of Justice, Office of Justice Programs and Office for Victims of Crime. December 2001). Web posted at http://www.ojp.usdoj.gov/ovc/publications/bulletins/internet22001/NCJ184931.txt.

Oldman, C. 2000. "Women Have More Top Jobs at Fortune 500 Firms." *Greensboro News and Record,* November 26, p. F2.

O'Leary, K., et al. 1989. "Prevalence and Stability of Physical Aggression." *Journal of Consulting and Clinical Psychology* 57: 263–68.

Orava, T. 1996. "Perceptions of Control, Depressive Symptomatology, and Self-esteem of Women in Transition from Abusive Relationships." *Journal of Family Violence* 11: 167–86.

Palmer, S. 1970. *Deviance and Conformity.* New Haven: College and University Press.

Palmer, S. and J. A. Humphrey. 1990. *Deviant Behavior: Patterns, Sources and Control.* New York: Plenum Press.

Palmer, S. 1972. *The Violent Society.* New Haven, CT: College and University Press.

Park, R., E. Burgess, and R. McKenzie (eds.). 1928. *The City.* Chicago: The University of Chicago Press.

Parker, D. 1998. *Fighting Computer Crime: A New Framework for Protecting Information.* John Wiley & Sons.

Parker, L., L. Copeland, and D. Sharp. 2001. "Profiles of Attackers Shatter Assumptions." *USA Today,* September 21. Web posted at http://www.usatoday.com/news/nation/2001/09/21/profiles.htm.

Pavelka, E. 1992. "RAAM Slam: Kish Dethrones Forney in Record Time to Win the Closest-Ever Race Across America." *Bicycling,* October, pp. 57(3).

Paykel, E. S. 1974. "Life Stress and Pychiatric Disorder: Applications of the Clinical Approach." Pp. 135–149 in *Stressful Life Events: Their Nature and Effects,* edited by B. Dohrenwend and B. Dohrenwend. New York: John Wiley & Sons.

PBS. 1995. "Waco: The Inside Story." Web posted at http://www.pbs.org/wbgh/pages/frontline/waco.

Pearson, J. L. et al. 1997. "Elderly Suicide: A Multinational View." *Aging and Mental Health.* 1(2): 107–111.

Peck, D. 1984. "Lethality of Method of Suicide among a Youthful Sample of Committers: An Examination of the Intent Hypothesis." *Psychological Reports* 55: 861–62.

Peck, D. 1985–1986. "Complete Suicides: Correlates of Choice of Method." *Omega* 16: 309–23.

The Pew Research Center (For the People and for the Press). 2002. *What the World Thinks in 2002: How Global Publics View: Their Lives, Their Countries, The World,*

America. Washington, DC: Author. Web posted at http://people-press.org/reports/pdf/165.pdf.

Phillips, D. 1974. "The Influence of Suggestion on Suicide: Substantive and Theoretical Implications of the Werther Effect." *American Sociological Review* 39: 340–54.

Pillar, Paul. 2004. "Terrorism: An Introduction." Council on Foreign Relations.

Pino, N., and R. Meier. 1999. "Gender Differences in Rape Reporting." *Sex Roles: A Journal of Research* 40: 979.

Pollard, N. "Terrorism and Transnational Organized Crime: Implications of Convergence." *Terrorism Research Center.* Web posted at http://www.terrorism.com/terrorism/crime.shtml.

Pollitt, M. *Cyberterrorism—Fact or Fancy?* Web posted at http://www.cs.georgetown.edu/~denning/infosec/pollitt.html.

Porter, G. 2001. "Workaholic Tendencies and the High Potential for Stress among Co-workers." *International Journal of Stress Management.*" 8: 147–164.

Porter, G. 1996. "The Organizational Impact of Workaholism: Suggestions for Researching the Negative Outcomes of Excessive Work." *Journal of Occupational Health Psychology,* 1: 70–84.

Post, J. M. 1986. "Hostilité, Conformité, Fraternité: The Group Dynamics of Terrorist Behavior." *International Journal of Group Psychology* 36: 211–24.

Post, J. M. 2001. *Killing in the Name of God: Osama Bin Laden and Radical Islam.* Web posted at http://theapm.org/cont/posttext.html.

Potterat, J., et al. 1998. "Pathways to Prostitution: The Chronology of Sexual and Drug Abuse Milestones." *The Journal of Sex Research* 35: 333.

Power, R. 2000. *Tangled Web.* Indianapolis: Que.

Pynoos, R., and K. Nader. 1988. "Children Who Witness the Sexual Assaults of Mothers." *Journal of the American Academy of Child and Adolescent Psychiatry.*

Quinney, R. 1970. *The Social Reality of Crime.* Boston: Little Brown.

Quinney, R. 1977. *Class, State, Crime.* New York: Longman.

Rabin, B. 1999. *Stress, Immune Function, and Health: The Connection.* New York: Wiley-Liss.

Rada, T. 1978. *Clinical Aspects of the Rapist.* New York: Grune and Stratton.

Radomsky, E., et al. 1999. "Suicidal Behavior in Patients with Schizophrenia and Other Psychotic Disorders." *American Journal of Psychiatry* 156: 1590–95.

Radzinowicz, L. 1948. *A History of English Criminal Law and Its Administration from 1750.* New York: Macmillan.

Rand, M. 1997. *Violence-related Injuries Treated in Hospital Emergency Departments.* Washington, DC: US Department of Justice, Office of Justice Programs, and Bureau of Justice Statistics. (NCJ-156921). Web posted at http://www.ojp.usdoj.gov/bjs/pub/pdf/vrithed.pdf.

Randall, T. 1990. "Domestic Violence Intervention Calls for More than Treatment Injuries." *Journal of the American Medical Association* 262: 939–40.

Raymond, E. S. 1997. *The Hacker's Dictionary*, 3rd ed. Cambridge, MA: MIT Press.

Rennison, C. 2001. *Criminal Victimization, 2000 with Trends 1993–2000*. Washington, DC: U.S. Department of Justice, Office of Justice Programs, and Bureau of Justice Statistics. (NCJ# 187007). Web posted at http://www.ojp.usdoj.gov/bjs/pub/pdf/cv00.pdf.

Rennison, C.M., and S. Welchans. 2000. *Intimate Partner Violence*. Washington, DC: US Department of Justice, Office of Justice Programs, and Bureau of Justice Statistics. (NCJ# 178247).

Reppetto, T. 1974. *Residential Crime*. Cambridge, MA: Ballinger.

Reuters. 2000. "Genetic Test Might Spot Suicidal Tendencies." *USA Today*, January 31.

Reuters. 2000b. "Japanese Man Charged for Child Porn in Cambodia." June 20. Web posted at www.lycosnew.com.

Riggs, D., and K. O'Leary. 1989. "A Theoretical Model of Courtship Aggression." Pp. 53–71 in *Violence in Dating Relationships: Emerging Social Issues*, edited by A. A. Pirog-Good and J. E. Stets. New York: Praeger.

Righthand, S., and C. Welch. 2001. *Juveniles Who Have Sexually Offended: A Review of the Professional Literature*. Washington, DC: US Department of Justice, Office of Justice Programs, and Office of Juvenile Justice and Delinquency Prevention. (NCJ # 184739).

Rigler, S. K. 2000. "Alcoholism in the Elderly." *American Family Physician* 61: 1710–16.

Robins, L., and D. Reiger (eds.). 1991. *Psychiatric Disorders in America: The Epidemiologic Catchment Area Study*. New York: The Free Press.

Robinson, B. E. 1998. *Chained to the Desk: A Guidebook for Workaholics, Their Partners and Children, and the Clinicians Who Treat Them*. New York: New York University Press.

Robinson, G. 1996. "Death-by-Overwork Suits on the Rise in Japan." *Institute for Global Communications*, November 27. Web posted at www.hartford-hwp.com/archives/55a/021.html.

Robinson, J., and Godbey, G. 1997. *Time for Life: The Surprising Ways Americans Use Their Time*. University Park: The Pennsylvania State University Press.

Root-Bernstein, R. 1995. "Discovery" In *Encyclopedia of Creativity*, edited by Mark A. Runco and Steben R. Pritzker. San Diego, CA: Academic Press.

Rosenbaum, M. 1990. "The Role of Depression in Couples Involved in Murder-Suicide and Homicide." *American Journal of Psychiatry* 147: 1036–39.

Rosenhan, D. 1973. "On Being Sane in Insane Places." *Science* 179: 250–58.

Rossi, B., and Cereatti, L. 1993. "The Sensation Seeking in Mountain Athletes as Assessed by Zuckerman's Sensation Seeking Scale." *International Journal of Sport Psychology* 24: 417–43.

Rowan, R. 1986. "The Biggest Mafia Bosses." *Fortune*, November 10, pp. 24–38.

Roy, M. 1988. *Children in the Crossfire: Violence in the Home—How Does It Affect Our Children?* Deerfield Beach, FL: Health Communications.

Ruiz de Olano, R. 2003. "Organized Crime: A South American Perspective." Paper presented at Organized Crime Symposium, Yokohama, Japan. Cited in J. S. Albanese, D. K. Das and Arvind Verma, *Organized Crime: World Perspectives.* Upper Saddle River, NJ: Prentice Hall.

Ryan, G., et al. 1996. "Trends in a National Sample of Sexually Abusive Youths." *Journal of the American Academy of Child and Adolescent Psychiatry* 35: 17–25.

Ryan, P. J. 1995. *Organized Crime.* Santa Barbara: ABC-CLIO.

Sagarin, E. 1985. "Positive Deviance: An Oxymoron." *Deviant Behavior* 6: 169–81.

Sallybanks, J., and N. Thomas. 2000. "Thefts of External Vehicle Parts: An Emerging Problem." *Crime Prevention and Community Safety: An International Journal* 2: 17–22.

Sampson, R., and J. Laub. 1993. *Crime in the Making: Pathways and Turning Points Through Life.* Cambridge, MA: Harvard University Press.

Sampson, R., and W. Wilson. 1995. "Toward a Theory of Race, Crime and Urban Inequality." Pp. 37–54 in *Crime and Inequality,* edited by J. Hagan and R. Peterson. Stanford, CT: Stanford University Press.

Sampson, R., and J. Wooldredge. 1997. "Linking the Micro- and Macro-Level Dimensions of Lifestyle—Routine Activity and Opportunity Models of Predatory Victimization." *Journal of Quantitative Criminology* 3: 371–93.

Sarason, I., and B. Sarason. 1996. *Abnormal Psychology: The Problem of Maladaptive Behavior,* 8th ed. Upper Saddle River, NJ: Prentice Hall.

Scarce, M. 1997. "Same-Sex Rape of Male College Students." *Journal of American College Health* 45: 171.

Scarpitti, F. R. and P. T. McFarlance. 1975. *Deviance: Action, Reaction, Interaction.* Reading, MA: Addison-Wesley.

Schaer, M. 1996. The EXIT Program, *The Practice of Assisted Suicide in Switzerland.* Web posted at http://www.finalexit.org/swissframe.html.

Scheff, T. J. 1966. *Being Mentally Ill: A Sociological Theory.* Chicago: Aldine.

Scheff T. J. 1984. *Being Mentally Ill: A Sociological Theory* (rev. ed). New York: Aldine de Gruyter.

Schmalleger, F. 2002. *Criminal Law Today: An Introduction with Capstone Cases.* Upper Saddle River, NJ: Prentice Hall.

Schmidt, A. P. 1984. *Political Terrorism: A Research Guide to Concepts, Theories, Data Bases, and Literature.* New Brunswick, NJ: Transaction.

Schmidt, A. P., and A. I. Jongman. 1988. *Political Terrorism.* SWIDOC: Amsterdam and Transaction Books.

Shniedman, E. 1996. *The Suicidal Mind.* New York: Oxford University Press.

Shniedman, E., et al. 1994. *Psychology of Suicide.* Lanham, MD: Jason Aronson.

Schnittker, J., et al. 2000. "Nature, Nurture, Neither, Nor: Black-White Beliefs about the Causes and Appropriate Treatment of Mental Illness." *Social Forces* 78: 1101–30.

Schor, J. 1991. *The Overworked American.* New York: Basic Books.

Schur, E. M. 1971. *Labeling Deviant Behavior: Its Sociological Implications.* New York: Harper & Row.

Schweitzer, H. O. 2003. "Organized Crime: An American Perspective." In J. S. Albanese, D. K. Das, and A. Verma, *Organized Crime: World Perspectives,* Upper Saddle River, NJ: Prentice Hall.

Schweitzer, Y. 2000. *Suicide Terrorism: Development and Characteristics.* International Policy Institute for Counter Terrorism, August 21. Web posted at http://www.ict.org.il.

Scott, K., Moore, K. and Miceli, M. 1997. "An Exploration of the Meaning and Consequences of Workaholism." *Human Relations* 50: 287(28).

Scully, D. 1990. *Understanding Sexual Violence: A Study of Convicted Rapists.* New York: Routledge.

Scully, D., and J. Marolla. 1996. "Convicted Rapists' Vocabulary of Motive: Excuses and Justificaitons." Pp. 103–116 in *Deviant Behavior,* 5th ed., edited by D. Kelly. New York: St. Martin's Press.

Sellin, Thorsten. 1938. *Culture, Conflict, and Crime.* New York: Social Science Research Council.

Settertobulte, W., B. B. Jensen, and K. Hurrelmann. 2001. *Drinking among Young Europeans.* World Health Organization: Regional Office for Europe.

Shaffer, D., et al. 1996. "The NIMH Diagnostic Interview Schedule for Children Version 2.3 (DISC-2.3): Description, Acceptability, Prevalence Rates, and Performance in the MECA Study. Methods for the Epidemiology of Child and Adolescent Mental Disorders Study." *Journal of the American Academy of Child and Adolescent Psychiatry* 35: 865–77.

Shaffer, H. J., Hall, M. N., and Bilt, J. V. 2000. "Computer Addiction." *American Journal of Orthopsychiatry* 70: 162(7).

Shahar, Y. 1997. *Information Warfare: The Perfect Terrorist Weapon.* International Policy Institute for Counter Terrorism, February 26. Web posted at http://www.ict.org/il/articles/infowar.htm.

Shaw, C., and H. McKay. 1969. *Juvenile Delinquency and Urban Areas.* Chicago: The University of Chicago Press.

Shaw, E. D. 1986. "Political Terrorists: Dangers of Diagnosis and an Alternative to the Psychopathology Model." *International Journal of Law and Psychiatry* 8: 359–68.

Shover, N. 1996. *Great Pretenders: Pursuits and Careers of Persistent Thieves.* Boulder, CO: Westview Press.

Shover, N., and D. Honaker. 1996. "The Socially Bounded Decision Making of Persistent Property Offenders." Pp. 181–99 in *Deviant Behaivor: A Text Reader in the Sociology of Deviance,* 5th ed., edited by D. Kelly. New York: St. Martin's Press.

Shuman, E. 2001. "What Makes Suicide Bombers Tick?" *Israel Insider,* June 4. Web posted at http://israelinsider.com/channels/security/articles/sec_0049.thm.

Silbert, M., et al. 1982. "Substance Abuse and Prostitution." *Journal of Psychoactive Drugs* 14: 193–97.

Silverman, R., and S. K. Mukherjee. 1987. "Intimate Homicide: An Analysis of Violent Social Relations." *Behavioral Science and the Law* 5: 37–47.

Simon, C., and A. Witte. 1982. *Beating the System: The Underground Economy.* Boston: Auburn House.

Simon, D. 1996. *Elite Deviance.* Boston: Allyn and Bacon.

Simons, R., et al. 1998. "Socialization in the Family of Origin and Male Dating Violence: A Prospective Study." *Journal of Marriage and the Family* 60: 467–78.

Snyder, H. 2000. *Sexual Assault of Young Children as Reported to Law Enforcement: Victim, Incident, and Offender Characteristics.* Washington, DC: U.S. Department of Justice, Office of Justice Programs, and Bureau of Justice Statistics. (NCJ# 182990)

Snyder, H., and M. Sickmund. 1999. *Juvenile Offenders and Victims.* Washington, DC: U.S. Department of Justice, Office of Justice Programs, and Office of Juvenile Justice and Delinquency Prevention. (NCJ # 178257)

Soden, G. 2003. *Falling.* New York: W.W. Norton and Company.

Spence, J. T., and Robbins, A. S. 1992. "Workaholism: Definition, Measurement, and Preliminary Results." *Journal of Personality Assessment* 58: 160–78.

Sprankle, J., and Ebel, H. 1987. *The Workaholic Syndrome.* New York: Walker Publishing.

Srole, L., and A. Fischer (eds.). 1978. *Mental Health in the Metropolis: The Midtown Manhattan Study.* New York: New York University Press.

Stack, S. 1996. "The Effect of the Media on Suicide: Evidence from Japan 1955–1985." *Suicide and Life-Threatening Behavior* 26: 132–42.

Stack, S. 1997. "Homicide Followed by Suicide." *Criminology* 35: 436–54.

Stares, P. 1996. *Global Habit: The Drug Problem in a Borderless World.* Washington, DC: The Brookings Institution.

Stark, E., A. Flitcraft, and W. Frazier. 1979. "Medicine and Patriarchal Violence: The Social Construct of a Private Event." *International Journal of Health Services* 9: 461–98.

Stark, R. 1999. *Cyber Terrorism: Rethinking New Technology.* Washington, DC: Department of Defense and Strategic Studies.

Stephens, J. 1987. "Cheap Thrills and Humble Pie: The Adolescence of Female Suicide Attempters." *Suicide and Life-Threatening Behavior* 17: 107–18.

Stephens, R. C. 1987. *Mind-Altering Drugs: Use, Abuse, and Treatment.* Beverly Hills, CA: Sage.

Stern, J. 1999. *The Ultimate Terrorist.* Cambridge, MA: Harvard University Press.

Sternberg, R., and Lubart, L. 1995. *Defying the Crowd.* New York: Free Press.

Stets, J., and M. Straus. 1990. "Gender Differences in Reporting of Marital Violence and its Medical and Psychological Consequences." In *Physical Violence in*

American Families: Risk Factors and Adaptations to Violence in 8,145 Families, edited by M. Straus and R. Gelles. New Brunswick: Transaction Publishers.

Stevens, D. 1999. *Inside the Mind of a Serial Rapist.* San Francisco, CA: Austin and Winfield.

Stout, K. 2001. "Law Catching up with Online Sex Crimes." CNN, April 23. Web posted at http://www.cnn.com/2001/BUSINESS/asia/04/20/hongkong .cyberstalking/index.html.

Straus, M. A. 1980. *Behind Closed Doors: Violence in the American Family.* Garden City, NJ: Anchor.

Straus, M. A. 1983. "Ordinary Violence, Child Abuse, and Wife-Beating: What Do They Have in Common?" In *The Dark Side of Families,* edited by D. Finkelhor, et al. Beverly Hills, CA: Sage.

Straus, M. A. 1992. *Children as Witnesses to Marital Violence: A Risk Factor for Lifelong Problems Among a Nationally Representative Sample of American Men and Women.* Paper presented at the Twenty-third Ross Roundtable on Critical Approaches to Common Pediatric Problems.

Straus, M. A. and D. Donnelly. 2001. *Beating the Devil Out of Them: Corporal Punishment by American Families and Its Effects on Children,* 2nd ed. New Brunswick, NJ: Transaction Publications.

Straus, M. A. and D. Donnelly. 2001. "The Benefits of Never Spanking: New and More Definitive Evidence and a Possible Backlash." Chapter 12 in *Beating the Devil Out of Them: Corporal Punishment by American Families and Its Effects on Children,* 2nd ed., New Brunswick, NJ: Transaction Publications.

Straus, M. A., and R. Gelles. 1995. *Physical Violence in American Families: Risk Factors and Adaptations to Violence in 8,145 Families.* New Brunswick, NJ: Transaction Publishers.

Straus, M. A., and G. Kantor. 1994. "Corporal Punishment of Adolescents by Parents: A Risk Factor in the Epidemiology of Depression, Suicide, Alcohol Abuse, Child Abuse, and Wife Beating." *Adolescence* 29: 543–62.

Straus, M. A., and M. Paschall. 1998. *Corporal Punishment by Mothers and Child's Cognitive Development: A Longitudinal Study.* Paper presented at the 14th World Congress of Sociology, Montreal, Quebec, Canada. Durham, NH: Family Research Laboratory, University of New Hampshire.

Straus, M. A. et al. 1997. "Spanking by Parents and Subsequent Antisocial Behavior of Children." *Archive of Pediatric and Adolescent Medicine,* 151: 761–67.

Substance Abuse and Mental Health Services Administration (SAMHSA). 2004. *Overview of Findings from the 2003 National Survey on Drug Use and Health.* Rockville, MD: U.S. Department of Health and Human Services.

Substance Abuse and Mental Health Services Administration (SAMHSA). 2001. *Summary of Findings from the 2000 National Household Survey on Drug Abuse.* Rockville, MD: U.S. Department of Health and Human Services.

Sugarman, D., and G. Hotaling. 1989. "Dating Violence: Prevalence, Context, and Risk Markers." Pp. 3–31 in *Violence in Dating Relationships: Emerging Social Issues,* edited by A. A. Pirog-Good and J. E. Stets. New York: Praeger.

Sumner, W. 1906. *Folkways.* Boston: Ginn.

Sutherland, E. 1939. *Principles of Criminology,* 3rd ed. Philadelphia: Lippincott.

Sutherland, E. 1940. "White-Collar Criminality." *American Sociological Review* 5: 2–10.

Sutherland, E. 1947. *Criminology.* Philadephia: Lippincott.

Sutherland, E. 1956. *The Professional Thief.* Chicago, IL: University of Chicago Press.

Sutherland, E. 2002. "White Collar Crime: Formulating the Concept and Providing Corporate Crime Baseline Data." Pp. 67–81 in *Corporate and Governmental Deviance: Problems of Organizational Behavior in Contemporary Society,* 6th ed., edited by M. Ermann and R. Lundman. New York: Oxford University Press.

Sutherland, E., and D. Cressey. 1978. *Criminology,* 10th ed. Philadelphia: Lippincott.

Sykes, G., and D. Matza. 1957. "Techniques of Neutralization: A Theory of Delinquency." *American Sociological Review* 22: 664–70.

Szasz, T. S. 1974. *The Myth of Mental Illness.* rev. ed. New York: Harper and Row.

Talaga, T. 1999. "Suicides Among Elderly Men Epidemic: MDs. Doctors Say Society Ignoring Treatable Problem." *Toronto Star* August 20.

Tannenbaum, Frank. 1938. *Crime and the Community.* Boston: Ginn.

Tansella, M. 1998. "Gender Differences in Mental Health." *World Health* 51: 26.

Taylor, P. A. 1999. *Hackers,* London: Routledge.

Telhami, S. 2002. "Why Suicide Terrorism Takes Root." *The New York Times,* April 4, p. A23.

Thio, A. 1978. *Deviant Behavior.* Boston: Houghton Mifflin.

Thio, A. 1983. *Deviant Behavior.* Boston: Houghton Mifflin.

Thomas, W. and F. Znaniecki. 1918. *The Polish Peasant in Europe and America.* Chicago: The University of Chicago Press.

Thornhill, R., and C. Palmer. 2000. "Why Men Rape." *The Sciences* 40: 30.

Timrots, A., and M. Rand. 1987. *Violent Crime by Strangers and Nonstrangers.* Washington, DC: U.S. Department of Justice. (NCJ # 130702).

Tittle, C. 1995. *Control Balance: Toward a General Theory of Deviance.* Boulder, CO: Westview Press.

Tittle, C. R., and R. Paternoster. 1993. *Social Deviance and Crime.* Los Angeles: Roxbury Publishing Co.

Tjaden, P., and N. Thoennes. 1998. *Stalking in America: Findings from the National Violence against Women Survey.* Washington, DC: National Institute of Justice.

Tjaden, P., and N. Thoennes. 2000. *Full Report on the Prevalence, Incidence, and Consequences of Violence Against Women.*

"To the Extreme." 2000. *Business Journal* (Phoenix), January 28, p. 31.

Tolan, P. 2000. *Youth Violence Prevention.* Paper presented at the meeting of the Collaborative Violence Prevention Initiative, San Francisco, CA.

Tomlinson, J. 1999. *Globalization and Culture.* Chicago: The University of Chicago Press.

Tondonato, P., and B. Crew. 1992. "Dating Violence, Social Learning Theory, and Gender: A Multivariate Analysis." *Violence and Victims* 7: 3–14.

Trembley, P., et al. 1994. "Jockeys and Joyriders: Changing Patterns in Car Theft Opportunity Structures." *British Journal of Criminology* 34: 314.

Tsushima, M. 1996. "Economic Structure and Crime: The Case of Japan." *The Journal of Socio-Economics* 25: 497–515.

Tullis, L. 1991. *Handbook of Research on Illicit Drug Traffic: Socioeconomic and Political Consequences.* Westport, CT: Greenwood Press.

Turk, A. 1969. *Criminality and Legal Order.* Chicago: Rand-McNally.

United Nations. 2005. Office on Drugs and Crime, *2005 World Drug Report.* Vienna, Austria, 2005.

United Nations. 2005. Demographic Yearbook 2001.

United Nations. *Assessing Transnational Organized Crime Groups: Dangerousness and Trends.* Web posted at http://www.uncjin.org/CICP/Folder/trans.htm.

United Press International. 1999. *French Workaholics Told to Stop.* United Press International, January 15.

USA PATRIOT Act. 2001. *Uniting and Strengthening American by Providing Appropriate Tools Required to Intercept and Obstruct Terrorism, HR 3162.* Web posted at http://www.epic.org/privacy/terrorism/hr3162.pdf.

U.S. Advisory Board on Child Abuse and Neglect. 1995. *A Nation's Shame: Fatal Child Abuse and Neglect in the United States, Fifth Report.* Washington, DC: U.S. Department of Health and Human Services.

U.S. Bureau of the Census. 2004. "Population Clock." Web posted at http://www.census.gov.

U.S. Department of Health and Human Services. 1999a. *Mental Health: A Report of the Surgeon General.* Rockville, MD: U.S. Department of Health and Human Services, Substance Abuse and Mental Health Services Administration, Center for Mental Health Services, National Institutes of Health, National Institute of Mental Health. Web posted at http://www.surgeongeneral.gov/Library/MentalHealth/html.

U.S. Department of Health and Human Services. 1999b. *Mental Health: Culture, Race, and Ethnicity.* Rockville, MD: U.S. Department of Health and Human Services, Substance Abuse and Mental Health Services Administration, Center for Mental Health Services, National Institutes of Health, National Institute of Mental Health. Web posted at http://www.surgeongeneral.gov/Library/MentalHealth/html.

U.S. Department of Health and Human Services. 2000. *Child Maltreatment 1998: Reports from the States to the National Child Abuse and Neglect Data System.* Washington, DC: Author. Web posted at http://www.ccf.hhs.gov/programs/cb/publications/cm02/cm02.pdf.

U.S. Department of Homeland Security. 2004. *Securing our Homeland: U.S. Department of Homeland Security Strategic Plan.* Washington, DC: Author. Web posted at http://www.dhs.gov/interweb/assetlibrary/DHS_StratPlan_FINAL_spread.pdf.

U.S. Department of Justice (USDOJ). 1998. *Violence by Intimates: Analysis of Data on Crimes by Current or Former Spouses, Boyfriends, and Girlfriends.* Washington, DC: U.S. Department of Justice and Bureau of Justice Statistics.

U.S. Department of Justice (USDOJ). 2000. *National Crime Victimization Survey, 2000.* Washington, DC: U.S. Department of Justice and Bureau of Justice Statistics.

U.S. Department of Justice (USDOJ). 2001. *Criminal Victimization in the United States, 1999 Statistical Tables.* Washington, DC: U.S. Department of Justice, Office of Justice Programs, and Bureau of Justice Statistics. (NCJ# 184938). Web posted at http://www.ojp.usdoj.gov/bjs/abstract/cvusst.htm.

U.S. News and World Report Editors. 2000. "No Time to Slow Down: Can We Keep Working Harder and Harder Indefinitely?" *U.S. News and World Report Outlook,* June 26. Web posted at www.usnews.com/usnews/issue/000626/26atlarge.htm.

U.S. State Department. 2002. *Patterns of Global Terrorism 2001.* Washington, DC: Author. Web posted at http://www.state.gov/documents/organization/10319.pdf.

U.S. State Department. 2004. *Patterns of Global Terrorism 2003.* Washington, DC: Author.

van Dijk, J. 1994. "Understanding Crime Rates: On the Interactions between the Rational Choices of Victims and Offenders." *British Journal of Criminology* 34: 105–21.

van Koppen, P., and R. Jansen. 1999. "The Time to Rob: Variations in Time of Number of Commercial Robberies." *Journal of Research in Crime and Delinquency* 36: 7.

Vatz, R., and L. Weinberg. 1993. "Is Mental Illness a Myth?" *USA Today,* July 1993, pp. 62–63.

Violence Against Women Grants Office. 1998. *Stalking and Domestic Violence: The Third Annual Report to Congress under the Violence against Women Act.* Washington, DC: Violence against Women Grants Office. (NCJ# 172204). Web posted at http://www.ojp.usdoj.gov/vawo/grants/stalk98.pdf.

Wagner, A., and Houlihan, D. 1994. "Sensation Seeking Trait Anxiety in Hang-Glider Pilots and Golfers." *Journal of Personality and Individual Differences* 16: 975–77.

Walker, L. 1979. *The Battered Woman.* New York: Harper Row.

Walker, L. 2000. *The Battered Woman Syndrome.* New York: Springer.

Wallace, L. et al. 1996. *Homicide and Suicide Among Native Americans, 1979–1992.* Centers for Disease Control and Prevention, National Center for Injury Prevention and Control. Web posted at http://www.cdc.gov/ncipc/whatsnew/natam.htm.

Warchol, G. 1999. *Bureau of Justice Statistics Special Report: Workplace Violence, 1992–96.* Washington, DC: U.S. Department of Justice, Office of Justice Programs, and Bureau of Justice Statistics. (NCJ 168634)

Wasserman, I. 1984. "Imitation and Suicide: A Reexamination of the Werther Effect." *American Sociological Review* 49: 427–36.

Wechsler, H., 1995. "Correlates of College Binge Drinking." *American Journal of Public Health* 85: 921–26.

Wechsler, H., J. E. Lee, M. Meichum, and H. Lee. 2000. "College Binge Drinking in the 1990s: A Continuing Problem." *Journal of American College Health* 48: 199–210.

Weich, S., and G. Lewis. 1998. "Poverty, Unemployment, and Common Mental Disorders: Population Based Cohort Study." *British Medical Journal* 317: 115(5).

Weiner, N. 1970. "The Teen-age Shoplifter: A Microcosmic View of Middle-Class Delinquency." Pp. 213–217 in *Observations of Deviance*, edited by J. Douglas. New York: Random House.

Weisman, M., et al. 1993. "The Epidemiology of Personality Disorders: A 1990 Update." *Journal of Personality Disorders* Spring: 44–62.

Weitzer, R. (ed.). 2002. *Deviance and Social Control: A Reader.* New York: McGraw Hill.

Werrell, J. 2002. "Identity Theft." *The Herald,* March 3, pp. 1E, 3E. Rock Hill, SC.

West, D. 1966. *Homicide Followed by Suicide.* Cambridge, MA: Harvard University Press.

West, D. J., and D. Farrington. 1977. *The Delinquent Way of Life, Third Report of the Cambridge Study of Delinquent Development.* London: Heinmann Educational Books Ltd.

Wheaton, B. 1980. "The Sociogenesis of Psychological Disorder: An Attributional Theory." *Journal of Health and Social Behavior* 21: 100–24.

White, J. R. 2002. *Terrorism: An Introduction,* 3rd ed. Belmont, CA: Wadsworth Group.

Widom, C. 1992. *The Cycle of Violence.* Washington, DC: National Institute of Justice.

Widom, C. 1995. *Victims of Childhood Sexual Abuse—Later Criminal Consequences.* Washington, DC: U.S. Department of Justice, Office of Justice Programs, and National Institute of Justice (NCJ# 151525).

Wilson, M., and K. Daly. 1993. "Spousal Homicide Risk and Estrangement." *Violence and Victims* 8: 3–16.

Wilson, W. 1987. *The Truly Disadvantaged: The Inner City, the Underclass, and Public Policy.* Chicago, IL: University of Chicago Press.

Winslow, R. W. 1970. *Society in Transition: A Social Approach to Deviance.* New York: Free Press.

Wolak, J., and D. Finkelhor. 1998. "Children Exposed to Partner Violence." Pp. 73–111 in *Partner Violence: A Comprehensive Review of 20 Years of Research,* edited by J. Janinski and L. Williams. Thousand Oaks, CA: Sage.

Wolfe, D., et al. 1995. "Strategies to Address Violence in the Lives of High Risk Youth." In *Ending the Cycle of Violence: Community Responses to Children of Battered Women,* edited by P. Jaffe and J. Edelson. New York: Sage.

Wolfgang, M. 1958. "An Analysis of Homicide-Suicide." *Journal of Clinical and Experimental Psychopathology and Quarterly Review of Psychiatry and Neurology* 19: 208–21.

Wolfgang, M., and F. Ferracuti. 1967. *The Subculture of Violence.* London: Tavistock.

Wolfgang, M., R. Figlio, and T. Sellin. 1972. *Delinquency in a Birth Cohort.* Chicago: University of Chicago Press.

Wolfgang, M., T. Thornberry, and R. Figlio. 1987. *From Boy to Man, From Delinquency to Crime.* Chicago: University of Chicago Press.

World Health Organization (WHO). 1973. *Report of the International Pilot Study of Schizophrenia,* vol. 1. Geneva: WHO.

World Health Organization (WHO). 1991. *World Health Statistics Quarterly.* Geneva: WHO.

World Health Organization (WHO). 1995. *World Health Statistics.* Switzerland: WHO.

World Health Organization (WHO) Annual Reports posted at www.who.int/whr/previous/en/

World Health Organization (WHO). *World Health Statistics Annual 1993 and 1994, 1994 and 1995* posted at www.who.int/whr/previous/en/

Wright, R., and S. Decker. 1994. *Burglars on the Job: Streetlife and Residential Break-ins.* Boston: Northeastern University Press.

Wright, R., and S. Decker. 1997. *Armed Robbers in Action: Stickups and Street Culture.* Boston: Northeastern University Press.

Yamey, G. 1999. "Survey Finds That 1 in 10 Children Has a Mental Disorder." *British Medical Journal* 319: 1456.

Yang, D. 2000. "Craving Your Next Web Fix." *U.S. News and World Report,* January 15, p. 41.

Yates, R. 1988. "Japanese Live and Die for Their Work." *Chicago Tribune,* November 13, p. 531.

Yllö, K. 1984. "The Status of Women, Marital Equality, and Violence Against Wives." *Journal of Family Issues* 5: 307–20.

Yllö, K., and M. Bograd (eds.). 1988. *Feminist Perspectives on Wife Abuse.* Newbury Park, CA: Sage.

Zinberg, N. E. 1981. "Alcohol Addiction: Toward a More Comprehensive Definition." Pp. 97–227 in *Dynamic Approaches to the Understanding and Treatment of Alcoholism,* edited by M. H. Bean and N. E. Zinberg. New York: Free Press.

Zuckerman, H. 1994. *Expressions and Biosocial Bases of Sensation Seeking.* New York: Cambridge University Press.

Zuckerman, H. 1997. *Scientific Elite.* New York: Free Press.

Zuckerman, M. 1983. "Sensation Seeking and Sports." *Journal of Personality and Individual Differences* 4: 285–93.

Photo Credits

Chapter 1: 2, Bob Daemmrich/The Image Works; 8 (top), PhotoEdit; (bottom), Richard Lord/The Image Works; 10, PhotoEdit; 11, Reuters/Corbis/Bettmann.

Chapter 2: 22, Gideon Mendel/Corbis/Bettmann; 27, Archivo Iconografico, S.A./Corbis/Bettmann; 28, Getty Images, Inc.; 31, Reuters/Corbis/Bettmann; 32, ARPL/The Image Works.

Chapter 3: 38, PhotoEdit; 50, PhotoEdit; 52, Ashley Gilbertson/Aurora Photos; 54, Museum of Modern Art/Film Stills/Photofest.

Chapter 4: 60, Monika Graff/The Image Works; 66, Gideon Mendel/Corbis/Bettmann; 67, PhotoEdit.

Chapter 5: 88, Bob Daemmrich/The Image Works; 100, PhotoEdit; 104, Getty Images, Inc.

Chapter 6: 118, © Reuters/Corbis/Bettmann; 125, PhotoEdit; 134, AP Wide World Photos.

Chapter 7: 144, Henry Barrios/Corbis/Sygma; 150, Peter Turnley/Corbis/Bettmann; 154, Peter Turnley/Corbis/Bettmann.

Chapter 8: 166, Helen King/ Corbis/Bettmann; 176, AP Wide World Photos.

Chapter 9: 186, Russell Underwood/ Corbis/Bettmann; 195, Knut Mueller/Das Fotoarchiv/Peter Arnold, Inc.; 197 (top), Daniel Laine; (bottom), Joel Gordon Photography; 198, (top), Bob Daemmrich/The Image Works; (bottom), Getty Images, Inc.

Chapter 10: 206, Loretta Rae/Corbis/Bettmann; 213, Way Gary/Corbis/Bettmann; 223, (top), Adam Scull/Rangefinders/Globe Photos, Inc.; (bottom), Image 100/Corbis Royalty Free; 224, Getty Images, Inc.

Chapter 11: 236: John Nordell/The Image Works; 246, Jutta Klee/Corbis/Bettmann; 248, Esbin-Anderson/The Image Works.

Chapter 12: 258, AP Wide World Photos; 265, Paul Hosefros/New York Times Agency.

Chapter 13: 272, Kim Kulish/Corbis/Bettmann; 281, Reuters/Corbis/Bettmann; 288, Reuters/Corbis/Bettmann.

Chapter 14: 296, Syracuse Newspapers/Peter Chen/The Image Works; 299, AP Wide World Photos; 302, Susan Greenwood/Getty Images, Inc.—Liaison; 304, Perrin Pierre/Corbis/Sygma; 309, The Scotsman/Corbis/Sygma.

Chapter 15: 318, Chase Jarvis/Corbis/Bettmann; 332 (top), Kevin T. Gilbert/Corbis/Bettmann; (bottom), Kevin T. Gilbert/Corbis/Bettmann.

Chapter 16: 342, Corbis/Sygma; 351, Getty Images, Inc.—Liaison; 356, © Reuters/Corbis/Bettmann; 359, Handout/Reuters/Corbis/Bettmann.

Index